NAVAL DISASTERS IN RHODE ISLAND

300 YEARS OF MILITARY MISFORTUNE

NAVAL DISASTERS IN RHODE ISLAND

300 YEARS OF MILITARY MISFORTUNE

James F. Jenney

NAVAL DISASTERS IN RHODE ISLAND

300 YEARS OF MILITARY MISFORTUNE

CreateSpace
7290 B. Investment Drive
Charlestown, SC 29418
U.S.A.

Printed in U.S.A.

ISBN-13: 978-1480178328
ISBN-10: 1480178322

Cover design by Varoujan Karentz
Image by Pierre Ozanne

Contents

Introduction

In 2007 the Beavertail Lighthouse Museum Association (BLMA) prepared a storyboard exhibit of Narragansett Bay shipwrecks displayed in its museum building at Beavertail Light Station on Conanicut Island. One of the sources used was the work of Jim Jenney, a Newport Rhode Island native, diver and marine author residing in Florida who still retains his passion for Rhode Island's historical shipwrecks and marine events.

An affiliation between the BLMA and Jenney developed to continue his research expanding into an unusual ambitious project to identify and record every maritime disastrous event in Rhode Island waters. The BLMA would archive the results for retrieval and use by the museum's visitors, historians and researchers. Jenney enthusiastically rose to undertake this challenge and in October of 2008 became the Association's Marine Historian.

Jim's interest in shipwrecks started as a young boy who took instruction in SCUBA with a dream of finding buried treasure. Reading old news articles at the Newport Historical Society brought him back to reality and fueled his new interest in identifying shipwrecks and their historical content. He went on to write eight books, numerous related articles and lectured using data sources worldwide. His personal database of thousands of records is overwhelming in itself.

During the present documentation project estimated to be 2500 events, it became evident military naval and paramilitary incidents themselves represent a historical segment of Rhode Island's maritime records deserving significance and consolidation under a single cover. In mid 2011 Jenney redirected his work and concentrated on completing this sector, hence this accumulation of mor than one hundred documented events. The events took place during the colonial 1700s to present day and involve naval vessels of the Unites States, Great Britain, France and Germany plus dubious privateers providing quasi service to their military counterparts.

Within each of these described events an interweaving of stories unfold coupled with actual references supporting the facts as they happened. It is these reports which add much credibility to the accounts Jenney has gathered between these covers.

The format of each described event (his Wreck Data Sheet ...WDS) provides information parameters often omitted or neglected to be noted in typical condensed reports. Jenney has devised a configuration, and layout both unique and useful as is evident in the following pages, providing readers an uncanny synopsis of Rhode Island's military maritime experiences in Narragansett Bay, Rhode Island and Block Island Sounds.

Varoujan Karentz
Beavertail Lighthouse Museum Association

Preface

The subject of the maritime history of Rhode Island covers a period of more than 350 years, from the days that Roger Williams first entered the region and forged a bond with the local Indian tribes to modern times when the tribes have all but disappeared. One of those tribes, the Narragansett's, gave its name to the impressive natural bay which forms the centerpiece of the state. In the discussion of our state and maritime events, the waters of Narragansett Bay are a focal point since it is one of the most important bodies of water on the eastern seaboard of North America, both commercially and militarily. This book is presented as a historical study of marine disasters in Rhode Island and, more specifically, a study of disasters involving naval vessels throughout the history of the state. The subject matter includes vessels of military ownership and those involved with military or paramilitary operations (such as privateers, government aids to navigation, and other vessels in service to the military while not actually owned by them). Also included because of their direct relationship to military vessels are those vessels which have been the victim of military action, though civilian in ownership. The study deals with naval vessels that have been stationed in, visited, or passed through state waters.

As to the geographical scope of the work, all state waters are included (a breakdown of Rhode Island into specific study areas with a list of distressed vessels that have taken place in each area is included in Appendix A) which covers all from Rhode Island's border with Massachusetts to the border with Connecticut and from the headwaters of the Providence River to the north, to the offshore waters south of Rhode Island Sound and Block Island. In terms of chronological boundaries, the material includes incidents from the colonial era through modern times. There is no intention to state or imply that all events within this group are included. The information presented herein is the result, so far, of this ongoing all-inclusive study of the subject of maritime disasters within state waters throughout its history.

Narragansett Bay has been, from the earliest times, recognized as one of the best on the entire eastern seaboard of North America so it comes as no surprise that military as well as civilian interests were drawn to this safe haven. Situated midway between the ports of New York and Boston, the bay's strategic location was another important factor. Within the confines of the bay are 147 square miles of water, which includes more than two dozen islands. A number of coastal cities and towns can be found but two are of most significance to this study - Providence, the capital city, to the northern end of the state and Newport, the "City by the Sea", at the southern end of the bay and located at its most popular entrance, the East Passage.

From the earliest years of its settlement, when states were merely colonial outposts for an ever expanding United Kingdom, the potential for Rhode Island was clear and it soon became obvious that Rhode Island was going to live up to that potential. From the perspective of marine disasters in general, the areas of greatest concern to mariners were along the coast at the entrance to the bay, at the entrance to the Sakonnet River (to the east), the East Passage (central and main access to the bay), and the West Passage (to the west). Watch Hill Point, Point Judith, Beavertail Point, Brenton Point, Sachuest Point and Sakonnet Point are the most obvious mainland sites of concern and are the areas where the greatest number of wrecked vessel remains can be found. That said, the pattern for maritime disaster with regard to non-military vessels and their military counterparts is not a match due to the very specific location of naval stations and related operations. Thus we see a much larger number of incidents to military vessels within the confines of Narragansett Bay than in the open ocean waters beyond the entrance to the bay.

After many years of studying shipwrecks in the state of Rhode Island the idea of putting together a compilation of the information seemed appropriate. At the time this meant a collection of stories of vessels lost in storms, collisions and other equally exciting means with the result that the remains of the vessel would be left scattered on the bottom for an enterprising SCUBA diver to find. For a long time the focus of such a shipwreck study was limited to that type of incident. Then, through good luck or accident, the researcher was introduced to the idea that there could be many, equally interesting, events which did not result in the loss of a vessel. Thus, the seed for a much larger project was begun. To date, there have been more than 2,500 unique events discovered which will be recorded and shared for the sake of future historians and others interested in the rich history of the "Ocean State". As that project continued, a group of incidents unique to this area became evident as being of particular interest—the military and paramilitary vessels which have spent time in Narragansett Bay and its surrounding waters. It is believed that these vessels and incidents are of sufficient interest to warrant a separate work.

Before diving into a more detailed explanation of the study, it seems appropriate to present a short background of the presence of various military forces here. Understand that I am by no means an expert on the subject of the military stations and operations in Rhode Island; my area of expertise lies in the incidents of maritime disaster. With that said, I believe it is important for those who may not be intimate with the details of naval involvement in Rhode Island to present a brief overview of that history, as much as is known to the researcher at this time. Please allow for possible errors in this very general overview.

A Military Presence in Narragansett Bay

When Roger Williams relocated from Massachusetts to Rhode Island and first established a settlement at Providence there was no need, nor even a thought of a need, for a military presence in Narragansett Bay. The colonists who followed were simply in search of a place where they could be left alone and live in peace. Security for the new colonists was almost a non-issue for were there any serious issues, the King would certainly send vessels so that his subjects would be stress-free in order to maximize their time in the pursuit of activities that would best suit his majesty's needs. And, of course, Great Britain also had other issues to deal with such as off-and-on wars with the Dutch, French and the Spanish. A military presence by the British in the New World was continual for a century and a half until the American Revolutionary War brought that to an end. In the earliest years of their presence in America the British spent most of their time in the Caribbean although their influence extended as far north as Nova Scotia. New York City, though a good location for the headquarters of the British forces in the region, was not the best suited for a naval force. With their attention centered on activities in the Caribbean, where trade routes and enemy vessels loaded with treasure were a common site, any thoughts of establishing a more permanent naval base in America were, for the moment, not worthy of action. As America grew some port cities gained particular prominence in commercial circles. Newport was one of those cities and by the middle of the 18th century the British had begun to consider the establishment of a naval base there. In 1764, in a letter from Robert Melville, who had been engaged in surveying the bay with a base in mind said, *"I have been constantly engaged in obtaining the surveys and drafts of this* [Newport] *harbor and Narragansett Bay ... and the positions for docks, shipyards, hospitals, etc. The whole bay is an excellent man-of-war harbor ... affording good anchorage, sheltered in every direction, and capacious enough for the whole of His Majesty's navy ... the vicinity of the ocean is such that in one hour a fleet may be from their anchorage to sea; or from the sea to safe anchorage, in one of the best natural harbors the world affords."* It was clear that the British saw value here. After numerous specific events of rebellion, the onset of war became inevitable and in late 1776 the British invaded (from an American perspective) or occupied (from a British perspective) the city of Newport and for almost three years that city served in the capacity of an established base of operations. As French support for the Americans brought increased pressure to bear, the British were compelled to leave Newport in 1779; with the end of the war in 1781, Rhode Island, in general, and Newport, in particular, spent years trying to restore itself to its former level of commercial leadership.

Near the end of the 18th century the thought of establishing an American navy base in Newport was visited once again. In 1798 and 1799 Congress began a feasibility study into locating a dockyard on the southern New England coast. Several citizens from Newport drew up a memorandum describing the advantages that Newport would offer but their argument was not successful and no naval presence in Rhode Island resulted at that time. The next sixty years, in terms of naval interests in America were limited and there was no formal naval presence in Rhode Island though vessels would come into the bay from time to time. During the Civil War, the United States Naval Academy was temporarily relocated to Newport which brought Rhode Island to the attention of federal authorities once more but interest in a permanent naval station there was still not found necessary. The key to a more permanent naval presence in Rhode Island came in 1869 when the Secretary of War established the experimental torpedo station on Goat Island in Newport. The intent of the torpedo station was to develop torpedoes, torpedo equipment, explosives and electrical equipment. The timing of the opening perfectly coincided with the talent available and the location to produce results well beyond the initial concept. With the establishment of the Newport facility the torpedo was transformed from an immobile explosive mine of the Civil War period to become an efficient, self-propelled weapon that would alter the shape of naval warfare for years to come.

One major result of this was an ever increasing number of naval vessels that traveled to and from the bay for replenishment and training on the latest weapons systems. Boosted by the needs of the navy during the Spanish-American War in 1898, and the First World War, in the first quarter of the 20th century, navy influence and presence in Narragansett Bay continued to grow. A large parcel of land at Coddington's Point was ceded to the navy and construction of the infrastructure necessary to support a fleet of vessels was begun. In 1919, what had been the Second Naval District (the Naval Training Station) was combined with the First Naval District and its headquarters placed at Newport. After the end of the First World War, a decrease in naval presence occurred but a few forward-thinking leaders within the Navy Department continued to see and promote the value of the existing naval facilities and allowed them to continue in operation. With the approach of the Second World War, the Newport Naval Base was well positioned for the upcoming needs of the country. Paramount within the varied naval interests here was the Torpedo Station which continued to make important advances in its specialized field. During the Second World War it was not unusual for 100 torpedoes per day to be test fired. Since that last World War, the navy presence has continued though to a lesser degree. The Naval War College remains and today, what started out as the Naval Torpedo Station exists as the Naval Undersea Warfare Center or NUWC.

Military or Paramilitary Maritime Incidents in Rhode Island

The history of the establishment of naval forces in Narragansett Bay details the amount and growth of this activity over a period of more than two hundred years. With that growth and an increasing number of vessels in our waters, maritime incidents were inevitable. The purpose of this work is to document those events. It would be untrue to say that all of them are presented here for as any study of this type is by no means complete as new sources of information continue to be discovered. However, represented in this volume is the most comprehensive collection of data concerning and related to these vessels and personnel that has been researched as of this time and it is hoped that the information will be found to be valuable and insightful. No single period is emphasized over any other and events deal with vessels of various sizes and uses and the stories are presented as interesting historical events of Rhode Island and Narragansett Bay.

Organization of the Study

Much thought has gone into the organization of this material to make the presentation of greatest value to the reader. The decision was made to organize the material in a strictly chronological order with an alphabetical listing where more than one incident has taken place on the same date. An Appendix is provided to give a brief description of each of the unique areas within the state where the disasters took place followed by a listing of the incidents in that area which includes a page reference for quick access to each data sheet. Before getting to the data sheets, an overview of the material is provided that will provide insight into the collection as a whole. The following aspects of this study are worthy of specific note and some discussion. These include the nationality of the vessel, the type of disaster, cause of the event, and the final fate of the vessel. Each of these will be discussed briefly with the goal of showing in a wider view of the history.

Vessel Nationality

It might seem obvious that in dealing with military vessels and military incidents in the waters of the state of Rhode Island those would all be American vessels. For those of you familiar with the history of our state, it will come as no surprise that this is not the case. In the earliest years, as mentioned above, Rhode Island was a colony for more than one hundred and forty years from its founding in 1635 until the war of the American Revolution. During those years, though civilian shipping was made up of a mixture of American vessels and those of other European countries, most of the military vessels found here were principally from Great Britain. This leads to an interesting mix of vessels and maritime disasters to vessels that were of various styles, rigging, and other elements of design.

In terms of the number of incidents in this study, there are seventy-seven of one hundred and thirty-one, just 59%, that involved American vessels. The second largest group, thirty-nine incidents, or 30%, directly involved British vessels. The final three incidents, 11% of the total, involved French and German vessels. Logic would dictate correctly that most of the British vessel incidents took place during the years before Rhode Island became a state. In fact, all of the incidents involving British vessels took place in the years prior to 1778. There has not been another incident of note with a British military or paramilitary vessel in Rhode Island waters since that time. Likewise, the two incidents involving French vessels also took place in the earliest years of our state, one during the attack on Newport by Count D'Estaing in 1778 and the other when the French returned under Lafayette in 1781. The single incident to a German vessel came much later, at the end of World War II, when a U-boat torpedoed and sank a coal collier in the waters southeast of Point Judith and within hours was itself located and destroyed east of Block Island.

Disaster Type

A study of the various types of disaster that a vessel can encounter indicates diversity for the military and paramilitary vessel that is as great as for non-military vessels. In the group of vessels in this study the greatest numbers of vessels in trouble were "sunk". Forty vessels in this study involve vessels that were sunk. Most of these sinkings were related to acts of war but the exact cause of the sinking is another subject to be discussed. Also to be discussed later is the final fate of those vessels that had the misfortune to go to the bottom - some were raised and others not. Also of interest in this regard is the severity of the sinking, deep water versus shallow, with accompanied loss of life or with all hands saved. There are several different types of sunken vessels as you will see. Two or three of the sinkings will be specifically mentioned here as they were out of the ordinary in terms of their story. One incident actually involved two vessels at the same time. That is the story of the German submarine U-853 and the coal collier BLACK POINT. One other sinking of interest is much less well known and, once again, involves a submarine. In this case the event took place in peacetime and was accidental in nature, a collision between the American submarine S-51 and a 3,000-ton freighter CITY OF ROME. Collision at sea is the third most common cause of this type of disaster.

The second most common type of maritime disaster to the military and paramilitary vessels was "stranding" or grounding, not an uncommon type of marine mishap in Rhode Island waters at all.

Thirty-six vessels suffered from this type of incident and although most of the incidents of stranding have come about as a result of natural causes like storms and hurricanes, some came about due to intentional acts of war and many vessels were "chased ashore" in an effort to capture them and take vessel and cargo as a prize. A subset of those considered "chased ashore" is those which were intentionally put ashore to prevent their capture as a prize.

The third most common type of disaster in this collection involves vessels which went "ashore and burned". With the exception of one in this category, a dozen took place within a six-year period between 1772 and 1778. One small group of vessels lost in this manner remain to this day with a question of whether they were intentionally put ashore and burned under orders from their fleet commander or were put ashore by the individual vessel's commander whose actions could be considered prudent lest the enemy capture them. To this day, that question remains unanswered, at least for this group of British vessels. All of these vessels were lost due to acts of war in an era when the value of a captured vessel - intact - was significant. In another war, the War of 1812, an American ship was forced ashore and burned, but in that case the burning was done with the intention of her cargo not being captured to be of use to the enemy.

There were fourteen vessels that were simply reported as "damaged". This was generally the result of minor collision with other vessels and repairs the ultimate corrective action. Of particular note was a collision of a more serious but non-fatal nature and one that seems incredibly unlikely to occur. This involved the collision of a moving vessel with an anchored light vessel. Those who say that it is a big ocean and the lightship is a small target would be as correct as would those who say that there is nothing like accuracy when sailing your course. Collisions resulting in the sinking of a lightship were actually not that unusual an event overall.

Seven vessels in this study were reported as "burned and sunk". This type of disaster could be due to accident or intentional action. Those, to which the term accident is most descriptive, usually had issue with an onboard fire whereas those intentionally burned and sunk were usually due to an act of war.

Seven vessels appear only with "destroyed" as the type of disaster. These appear with the cause of war or intentional in every case and that is because the details of the destruction are often not known. Of greatest interest in this category are the vessels (or boats from vessels) that were destroyed in protest to acts of the British prior to the American Revolutionary War.

Three vessels in the study are listed as "attacked" as the type of disaster. All are, obviously, war related incidents and in each case the vessel under attack survived or escaped from the attacking vessel to continue in the service of their respective service or owner.

Two vessels are listed as "ashore and sunk" which is a somewhat difficult concept to understand. A normal stranding leaves the vessel on the shore or on a rock or reef but usually relatively unharmed. The same incident, where a vessel is destroyed is usually considered a wreck. But the in-between category is where a vessel runs aground on an offshore rock or reef and receives sufficient damage to result in its sinking immediately adjacent to (or sometimes at a distance from) the obstruction struck.

Two vessels in the study are noted to have "burned". There are two implications to this category of disaster. The first is that the vessel did not sink. The second, that the vessel may have not been under way at the time (perhaps moored to a dock or at anchor).

Two vessels of the group fall into that most bizarre category of having "disappeared". Almost always that is a situation that happens to a vessel in the earliest period, when the number of vessels at sea at any given time was small. Another possibility of this occurring is when a vessel has been sent to a distant port and is out of sight of land for some time. In the case of these vessels, both disappeared at the same time and, presumably, to the same cause. Their story is both interesting and intriguing.

One vessel is reported as "adrift" which is normally a condition of severe weather or some malady to the crew. The result of this type of disaster is either that the vessel finally becomes a wreck somewhere or is picked up by a passing vessel.

One vessel in the study is reported as having been "capsized", which is usually a cause rather than a type of disaster but when there is a stated cause for the capsizing, the incident itself is best described as a capsizing.

A single vessel in the study is termed "captured" as the type of disaster, but greatly implying that the vessel's final fate was condemnation (if war related or abandoned when captured), sold (if the capture was by a paramilitary vessel) or reassigned to another service or for some other use by the captor.

One vessel in the study fits the category of "threatened" which indicates enough significance to warrant its own story but insufficient damage of any kind to warrant placement in that group.

The final single vessel disaster type was mentioned above (briefly) and is "wrecked". The event was documented well enough to indicate that the vessel was wrecked but not well enough to indicate what type of disaster actually took place. Usually, the implication for this is that the vessel went ashore or struck some other object and became a wreck.

Causes of Disaster

The cause of a disaster is another interesting aspect of this study with results that were somewhat surprising. Anyone familiar with New England waters from a mariner's perspective would guess that the weather, specifically fog, would play a major role, but that would not be correct. One might also suspect that acts of war would represent only a small percentage of the total number of incidents in this study. Once again, that would be wrong, for "war" is the most common reason for maritime disasters to military and paramilitary vessels in Rhode Island waters. Forty-two of the vessels in this study group met with disaster due to war. One might wonder why this is so as our more recent history has not been marked by the presence of enemy vessels or other craft to threaten or destroy ships in the area. The single case of modern-day maritime disaster directly attributable to war was the sinking of the coal collier BLACK POINT and the resulting destruction of the German U-853 off Block Island. To look at the incidents where war was the primary cause involves a look back, as mentioned earlier, to those times before Rhode Island was even a state, to a time when the British controlled and directed the actions of Americans. It is during this period, the mid to late 18th century, when the vast majority of the forty-two incidents in this group will be found. Forty of the forty-two incidents directly attributable to acts of war took place between 1772 and 1813. Notable are the incidents to the British vessels of occupation during the Battle of Rhode Island and other events leading up to the War of the American Revolution. Two-thirds of the total involved British vessels which were stationed in Narragansett Bay or patrolled our waters in search of rebels and smugglers who were intent on stealing from the king. Of the remaining one-third, many were victims of the British during those years and that service.

The second most common cause of maritime disaster to military vessels in Rhode Island waters is weather, usually specified only as "storm". There are twenty-one incidents where storms are the cause of the disaster. Though Rhode Island has been the target of several major hurricanes over the years, those extreme storms have not had a particularly significant influence on this group. In fact, only five vessels in this study are noted as being in distress due to hurricanes.

Thirteen vessels found themselves in hard times due to "collision" which is the third main cause of maritime disaster in this study. Of those, only three included a reference to fog. Within this category are vessels which have collided with other vessels or with non-moving structures. Also, with the exception of two notable collisions, these events have occurred during daytime hours.

Ten incidents of maritime disaster were caused by "pilot error". Pilot error is an infrequently used cause of disaster (unless all else cannot possibly be found to be plausible) and was found in some cases as early as the incident where a British Ship ran aground on the inside of Poppasquash Point in October, 1775 while the British were engaged in a *"foraging expedition"* to the upper part of Narragansett Bay. Though she suffered no more damage than the indignity of running ashore in front of others in her small fleet, the incident nonetheless is worthy of inclusion in this study. Another incident where this was clearly the cause involved an American vessel whose misfortune may have been attributable to the desire of her master to find a short cut inside Watch Hill Reef while enroute from Newport to New London, CT in 1811.

The fifth most frequent cause for disaster is reported as "intentional". An intentional maritime disaster cannot, in fairness, be considered a disaster as the event has been planned. However, there are those which happened at the spur of the moment and others which took place in a natural process of removing an unwanted vessel from the roster or because the vessel was put to good use as a target.

Seven vessels were affected by what I consider the most interesting cause of a maritime disaster in Rhode Island, that being that they were "torpedoed". Usually the thought of a vessel being torpedoed brings an image of war or battle to mind. In this case, however, that thought would be incorrect as just one of the seven vessels torpedoed in Rhode Island waters over the years was due to an intentional act of war. The remaining vessels affected in this way were victims of accidental torpedo attacks. The story of each is unique and should be interesting for those who were not aware of the extent of torpedo testing here.

As in any study of this kind, information will often be incomplete or missing. For this reason, the seventh most common cause of disaster to military vessels in Rhode Island is "unknown". The majority of these seven incidents involved the vessel running ashore but it seems that the reporters were loath to assign pilot error as a cause or the accident could simply not be explained.

Research shows that there have been three vessels for which the cause of disaster was clearly "fog". Given the propensity of fog during certain periods of the year in our waters, the small number of vessels affected indicates that our military vessel operating crews were either very lucky or very skilled or both.

Another three vessel incidents identified "explosion" as the direct cause. Although you might expect this to be associated with powered vessels only, there is at least one incident where the explosion took place on a sailing vessel. In at least two of these cases it is known that the vessel survived. In the third, the final fate of the vessel is not known.

Two incidents in the study involve what is simply called "accident" which is hardly a clearly defined cause. It is worthy of note that both instances where this is the named cause involved the same vessel (at different times) and in both cases, that vessel was repaired and returned to service.

Two other incidents are noted as being caused by "attack". It could be suggested that there is little difference in this cause and war. In one of the two instances that suggestion could be deemed accurate but in the other, there was no state of war at the time and the incident, although ultimately contributing to the decision to declare war, was not the result of war.

Another two incidents list the cause of disaster as "fire". Perhaps the greatest fear of mariners universally is the threat of fire while at sea. In this study, one of the two vessels mentioned was reported as lost due to the fire while the other was reported as damaged and was rebuilt.

In this study, two vessels reported the cause of disaster as being a "leak". Usually a vessel in distress due to a leak is an older vessel whose watertight integrity has been compromised by years of use. One of those reporting this cause fits that formula but the other does not and in both situations the cause of the leak is given as unknown or mysterious.

Another less common cause of disaster involved two vessels researched. Reported simply as "mechanical failure" neither of the affected vessels was lost. In one case the vessel was merely threatened with loss due to this cause while in the other instance the vessel ended up ashore but was later rescued.

Of the remaining stated causes, each involved a single incident. Without a doubt, the most bizarre maritime disaster to or caused by military action was the near sinking of a fishing vessel by "practice artillery" from a shore installation. One can only imagine the surprised crew when an unexpected artillery shell descended from the sky to wreak havoc on their craft. Although all survived to tell and retell the story for years to come, the near miss could surely have been fatal if the uninvited shell had been anything but a practice shell or if it had struck the vessel in a more vulnerable spot.

One incident in the study gave the cause of the disaster as "capsizing". It could be said that weather was the cause of this incident which resulted in the loss of several lives but history indicates that the sea condition was only a contributing factor to this deadly event, hence the label of capsizing for the cause of the disaster.

I am not sure what the difference would be between a disaster caused by "engine room error" versus one labeled as an "engineer error" but most likely it was a question of whether or not the engineer was popular or not (although it could also indicate whether or not the engineer was present in the engine room when the disaster occurred). In the case of the incident where there was an error by the engineer, the result was that the vessel sank (at least temporarily). In the case where there was an engine room error, a much larger vessel ran ashore.

Last but not least, although there have been several devastating hurricanes in Rhode Island waters during the last three centuries, and numerous vessels have been destroyed as a result, there is only one case that I have found where a "hurricane" has resulted in the loss of a military vessel. And, interestingly enough, that vessel, as is the case with a few others in this study, was involved in more than one documented maritime incident in this area.

The Final Fate of the Vessels

In this study there are forty-seven incidents (36%) that clearly ended in the total loss of the vessel. Of the remaining 64%, most survived their incident and some, but not all, were returned to service. This makes "total loss" the single most common fate of the distressed vessels in the study.

At the other end of the spectrum are the twenty-one vessels reported as "got off" (clearly action taken following a stranding or grounding situation). If you recall, there were thirty-six reported cases of vessels stranding so it appears that the odds of being rescued from that condition were favorable.

The third most common final fate relates to vessels which were sunk and nineteen of these were reported as "raised" (with another eleven reported as probably raised). Based on a statistic of forty vessels sunk, it seems that the odds of being sunk and totally lost were about 50-50. Clearly, the depth of the water is a factor here though there are a couple of well documented instances where a vessel sunk in water over one hundred feet in depth were raised.

Fifteen of the cases of maritime disaster in this study were "repaired". The majority of those so reported were the result of collisions, but other disaster types which were able to be addressed with repairs include attacks, explosions and fires. The status of repair indicates that the damage inflicted during the incident would not be classified as major or critical. In the latter case, it would often require a rebuilding of the vessel to restore her to a condition where she could be returned to service.

The next most common final fate was "towed in" which applies only to vessels which were for whatever reason disabled at sea. Nine vessels in this study resulted in being towed in. In the situation where that is the stated final fate there is insufficient information to clarify whether these vessels were repaired or not. This was a determination that could only be made after a survey of the damage.

The final fate of three of the vessels researched is "unknown". Oddly the incidents in which they were involved took place in the 20th century when you would expect that their final fate would be relatively easy to determine. Two of these incidents took place under storm conditions and that could answer the lack of detailed information as reporting sources are often overwhelmed with information during events of that nature. The third involves a small vessel for which further information was simply not provided.

Two vessels in this study were attacked and "escaped" capture or destruction by the enemy. Both involved vessels during the colonial period. One was a British ship and the other an American brig.

Of the remaining stated final fates, each involved a single incident. At least one vessel discovered during this study was "rebuilt". This one was of Revolutionary War vintage and was rebuilt after an explosion and fire caused by an enemy attack. One vessel, a 4,000-ton steamship that had been accidentally torpedoed off Jamestown, had the good fortune to be "rescued". The fate of at least one captured vessel during the Revolutionary War had a final fate of being condemned and "sold" for the benefit of the privateers who captured her. And there was a single vessel incident in which the stated final fate was that she "went to pieces".

Summary

The statistical information provided in this brief overview of the project is offered in an attempt to present a broader view of the data. Understanding the background of the project in terms of whose navy was here at what time and for what purpose is important. Understanding through definition of the disaster type, cause and final fate of the vessels studied is helpful, I believe, in viewing the history of the group of vessels included. As I mentioned earlier, this compilation is by no means complete but will hopefully help the student of maritime history as relates to a greater appreciation of the effect that these events had on the history of the state of Rhode Island. Each wreck data sheet (WDS) is a stand-alone snapshot detailing the known information regarding the event. All research sources are included for those who may wish to delve further into one or more of these events. There are some instances where a multiple-wreck data sheet (MWDS) is provided for clarity of an event where more than one vessel is involved.

Acknowledgments

To bring a project such as this to fruition requires a number of things – the stamina of a marathon runner, the agility of a speed reader, the ability to learn the language of our predecessors, but, perhaps most of all the ability to understand how to use "multipliers" and learn from others who are usually more knowledgeable in their areas of expertise than you are. First and foremost there must be a spark, and for this author it was a passion to know all about lost vessels on the bottom of the sea. But one man, Varoujan Karentz gave me the insight to look beyond shortsightedness. Without his recommendation that I should look into the stories of vessels which met with maritime disaster but were not lost, this project would never have continued for as long as it has. Others were invaluable in providing assistance in many different ways. First, for their support in this effort, I would like to recognize Mr. Richard Sullivan and Mr. Guy Archambault, past presidents, and Mr. George Warner, current president, of the Beavertail Lighthouse Museum Association for their enthusiastic support. Also, Sue Maden and Rosemary Enright, both from the Jamestown Historical Society have been gracious in allowing me access to their materials and have provided long distance legwork for me. Karen Eberhart from the Rhode Island Historical Society in Providence and Lisa Long from the Redwood Library in Newport have also provided invaluable assistance. Bob Cembrola, Curator of Maritime History at the Naval War College and a long-time friend has been helpful in providing information and in directing to other sources of information. On that note the following individuals from government sources have participated in the data gathering process: Albert E. "Skip" Theberge, Jr., of the NOAA Central Library, William H. Thiesen, Atlantic Area Historian for the US Coast Guard and Christopher J. Martin, Archival Technician for the Naval History & Heritage Command. Other specialists from private institutions that have offered information freely include: Norene Rickson, Librarian/Archivist and John Palmieri, Curator, both from the Herreshoff Marine Museum, and Alyce N. Guthrie, from the WWII PT Boats Museum and Archives. Finally, there are a couple that I have worked with over the years who have provided moral support and assistance in data gathering, Dr. Kathy Abbass, of the Rhode Island Marine Archaeology Project and, a private researcher, Joan Charles, whose trips to the Mariners Museum in Newport News have been most valuable. Last but certainly not least, I want to thank Deneb Karentz for her invaluable assistance in the preparation of the manuscript.

Section I - Colonial Era

During the colonial period, military maritime disasters were almost always the result of war or precursors of war. And it should come as no surprise that most of the vessels affected during this time were not American vessels. There was no American naval force during most of this period and when there was it was greatly outnumbered by His Majesty's vessels. In the years leading up to the actual declaration of war with Great Britain, Narragansett Bay was the sight of events that ranked with the famous Boston Tea Party in terms of intensity as American "rebels" sought to throw off the yoke of oppression which we would call "taxation without representation". Events like the burning of a ship's boat from the MAIDSTONE and the destruction of the LIBERTY were both harbingers of things to come and these acts took place well before the first shot was fired at Lexington. Perhaps more well known than those two incidents was the burning of His Majesty's revenue schooner GASPEE near the mouth of the Providence River. This single act and the "cover-up" by local officials of those involved in the incident are well remembered to this day as one of the final examples that the American colonists did not want to be ruled by the throne any longer. But these events aside, the single most disaster-prone period of this era were the war years, between 1775 and 1783. During one ten-day period, between July 30th and August 8th of 1778, there were more disasters to military vessels in Narragansett Bay than during any other period in our history. The infamous Battle of Rhode Island brought about the destruction of no fewer than 21 vessels. Some were transport and other support vessels sunk as block ships to prevent the French from entering the harbor at Newport while others were military vessels that were either forced or were intentionally run ashore by the British to prevent capture by the vessels of the French fleet. Most of the data sheets included in this section involve individual events, but there are several which show multiple vessels which were affected in events which took place at a specific time.

THE 1745 MYSTERY

Vessels Involved

The mystery of 1745 not only involves strange circumstances about which little is known but also involves two vessels about which little is known. The event involved a Rhode Island merchant, Godfrey Malbone, whose career was both exciting and clandestine. It was also very prosperous. To make his fortune, the well known and talented merchant was reputed to deal in everything from smuggling and the slave trade to privateering. In 1744, a good opportunity for the later activity presented itself in what was called "The French War". It is uncertain whether it was on his own or with other merchants but Malbone decided to build a pair of what were described as large ships that would be suitable to seek out and capture vessels for profit. The ships were new when they sailed on the day before Christmas, 1745.

Narrative

In 1882, an address was presented to the members of the Rhode Island Historical Society by William P. Sheffield. The subject of this paper was privateersmen of Newport. Sheffield presented the following overview of the incident. *In 1745 Godfrey Malbone built two large privateer ships and fitted them for sea, one under the command of Captain Cranston, and the other under Captain Brewer. They were destined to sail in company and cruise on the Spanish-Main. According to the custom of the time their horoscope was cast, and the figures had disclosed that they should sail on Friday, the 24th of December, 1745. It was then a violent snow storm. They sailed fully manned by 400 men, but they were never afterwards heard from. It was said that in the disaster perished the heads of 200 families in Newport.*

That this incident has earned a place in Rhode Island's maritime history is certain. What is not clear are the details and location of the incident. Did the vessels lose sight of one another and come together in such a violent manner as to cause them both to sink? Were they attacked by some other vessel or vessels and sank due to that action? Or were they simply overcome by the intensity of this snowstorm and sunk? In modern times the loss of a single vessel, let alone two large ships, is marked by floating wreckage as there are countless objects on a vessel that will drift on the surface of the sea for long periods of time. In the early 18th century, this was even more the case as the vessels were wooden from their keel to their top-mast. That said, in the latter days of December in New England in 1745, there were few vessels to spot the remains of a distressed ship unless the incident took place very near shore. It is anyone's guess as to the location and type of disaster which over took these privateers and their loss remains a mystery to this day.

THE 1745 MYSTERY

Godfrey Malbone

In 1881, Wilfred Munro wrote a book called "Picturesque Rhode Island" which offers the following information about Godfrey Malbone: ... *Another famous merchant of that early time was Godfrey Malbone. When a mere lad he ran away to sea, and was not heard from for many a year. About the beginning of the last century he settled in Newport, and soon became the most noted of all its merchant princes. Dark and full of mystery are some of the tales that are told concerning him. His adventures upon the sea seem to have been unusually lawless, even for that lawless age, and the fair fame of the city in which he dwelt suffered in consequence. During the French War, which began in 1744, Newport sent forth more than a score of privateers. The Frenchmen called the town a "nursery of corsairs", and planned its capture. "Perhaps we had better burn it as a pernicious hole, from the number of privateers that fitted out, as dangerous in peace as in war," wrote one officer to his superior in rank. Smuggling, Malbone of course indulged in. It was hardly deemed discreditable to any one – not at all to be censured if he who engaged in it happened to be a man of wealth. Persons now living have seen upon the estate Malbone once owned, the entrance to an underground passage which afforded easy communication with the beach, and thus enabled him to elude the vigilance of the custom-house officers. It is said that his "corsairs" preyed upon both Spanish and Frenchmen with an impartial disregard for treaties; and it is a well established fact that large sums of money were recovered from him in England, by legal process, for the spoilations he systematically practiced upon the Dutch. In 1745 two of his privateers, large and beautiful vessels, fresh from the stocks, sailed out of the harbor on the day before Christmas, bound for the Spanish-Main. A violent snowstorm came up, and the gale soon changed to a hurricane. Newport had two hundred widows in consequence, for the ships were never heard of afterward.*

Research Sources

1. Address of William P. Sheffield to the Rhode Island Historical Society in 1882
2. "Picturesque Rhode Island" by Wilfred H. Munro (1881)

UNIDENTIFIED

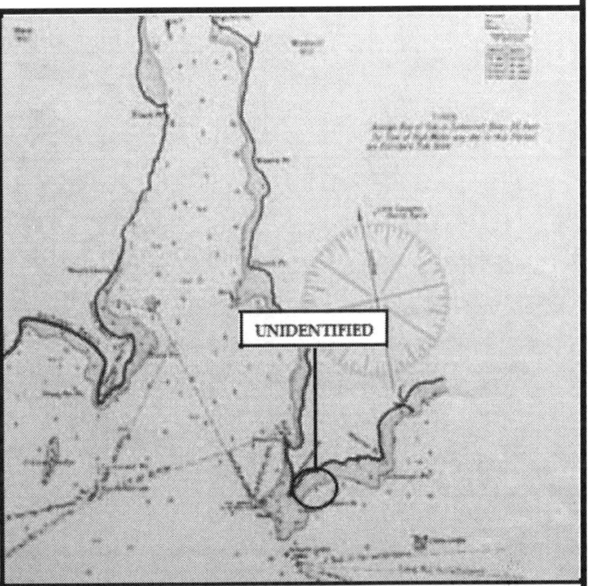

The Vessel

Type: Ship
Construction: Wood
Use: Privateer
Nationality: American
Home Port: Newport, RI
Port of Destination: Newport, RI

Final Voyage

Date of Loss: December, 1748
Disaster Type: Stranding
Cause: Storm
Final Status: Total loss
Location: On rocks on the east side of Seaconnet Point

Narrative

In 1748 communication in the colonies was, at best, challenging. With a small population spread throughout Rhode Island, the news of an important event in a remote area was long in coming and often by the time it arrived was not of sufficient importance to be included in the few newspapers of the day. Such was likely the case of the stranding and destruction of an unidentified privateer which had the misfortune to run on the rocks on the east side of Sakonnet Point. In this instance, news of the disaster came to light in a biographical sketch of one Captain Potter, a privateer. In an address delivered by William P. Sheffield at the Rhode Island Historical Society in February of 1882, the following information was found, "*... Captain Potter's vessel, after he left her, was still in the service, until one cold stormy December night in 1748, amid hardships and suffering among her crew, while she was seeking her home port, she struck on the rock on the east side of Seaconnet Point and was wrecked. Happily the officers and crew, with the exception of one negro and perhaps one other man, were saved, and among her officers was Mark Anthony DeWolf. ...*"

Research Sources

1. "An Address Delivered By William P. Sheffield Before The Rhode Island Historical Society In Providence, February 7, A.D., 1882"

ST. JOHN

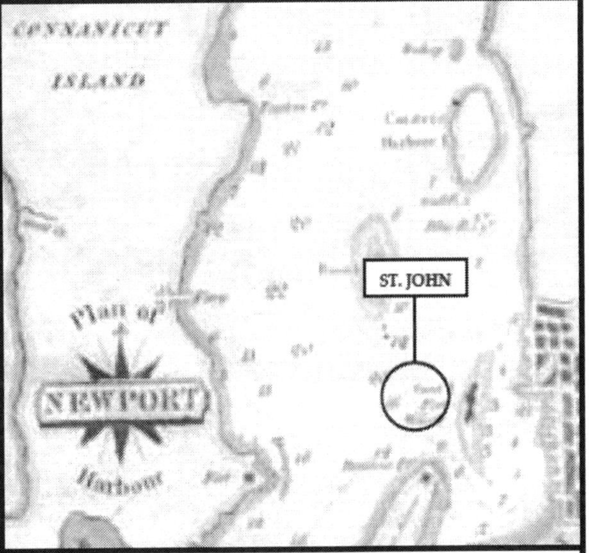

The Vessel

Type: Schooner
Construction: Wood
Use: Warship
Dimensions: 48′ x 18′ x 8′
Tonnage: ~ 90
Launched: Boston, MA in 1764
Owner: British Navy
Nationality: British
Home Port: Newport, RI

The Event

Port of Departure: N/A
Port of Destination: N/A
Master: Lt. Thomas Hill
Cargo: N/A
Date of Incident: July 9, 1764
Disaster Type: Damaged
Cause: Cannon fire
Status: Repaired
Location: Off Fort George, Goat Island

Prelude to the Revolutionary War

During the years leading up to the occupation of Newport, the British influence in America was felt in every colony. Colonists became increasingly dissatisfied with the efforts of the British to control and tax them for the purpose of the enrichment of Great Britain. This dissatisfaction became clear in incidents such as the burning of a boat from the frigate MAIDSTONE, the destruction of the armed sloop LIBERTY and, of course, the burning of the GASPEE. But prior to all of these there was a lesser known incident involving the British schooner **ST JOHN**.

Newport Mercury - July 16, 1764 P3

The following affair, which at the beginning seemed to indicate a tragical issue, happened here last Monday, viz., some men belonging to his majesty's schooner ***ST. JOHN****, then in this harbor, commanded by Captain Hill, had been guilty, several days before, of some irregularities in town, of which information was given by one concerned in the same, who had made his escape, and being observed to be on a wharf nearly opposite to her, a boat with some men armed, came in quest of him, or, as is said, to impress men to work on board a vessel. But whatever were their motives for their coming ashore in that manner, this is certain, that a smart skirmish was the consequence by which, it is said, the schooner's men were considerably bruised, and very expeditiously went off, leaving their commanding officer behind, who was immediately taken into custody. The defensive party, it is also said, received some slight wounds. This transaction, with the men, who had been guilty of the disorders, being detained on board the schooner, after*

ST. JOHN

they had been demanded by authority, greatly incensed the people of the town. But it may be proper to observe that B. Smith, Esq., commander of his majesty's ship SQUIRREL, (who since his residence here, by a conduct becoming a spirit of a gentleman of honor and generosity, has justly merited the esteem of the inhabitants) and the captain of the schooner were absent, otherwise the affair might probably have been amicably adjusted. But it being apprehended that the delinquents might make their escape, orders were sent over to Fort George to stop the schooner, in case she should attempt going out of the harbor Towards evening she got under sail, intending to come to under the SQUIRREL's stern, who lay without the fort, and was endeavouring to beat out (the wind being a-head) when she was hailed from that fort, which she disregarded. Soon after the gunner, pursuant to his orders, fired a shot, which, being ineffectual, was repeated, to the number of 8 or 10, none of which had any effect, and the schooner got safely moored under the SQUIRREL's stern. Captain Smith has since ordered the man, who was the cause of the above disorder, to be delivered up, to be dealt with agreeable to law.

The newspaper account is not really clear about the cause of the issue although clear about the firing upon the vessel. From a pamphlet on the history of Goat Island comes the following: *In 1764, resistance climaxed in the case of the British schooner **ST. JOHN**, commanded by an overzealous young officer. The **ST. JOHN**'s arrival in Newport brought the town's molasses trade to a sudden halt. The friction between the **ST. JOHN** and the Newporters grew quickly, heightened by the supercilious behavior of the ship's officer and by the theft of some pigs and chickens by crew members. Finally, it was agreed to instruct Daniel Vaughn, the master gunner at Fort George on Goat Island, to fire his 18-pounder cannon at the **ST. JOHN**. Officially Vaughn's shots were in response to the **ST. JOHN**'s refusal to surrender the hog thieves. Sheriff Benton rowed out to Goat Island to instruct Vaughn. About 100 townspeople rowed after him, either to take part or to watch. Firing began just before sunset, the first shot falling short. The **ST. JOHN** hurriedly raised anchor and sails but not quickly enough. The third shot from Goat Island was a direct hit, and subsequent shots pierced the mainsail and foresail and cut the flag lanyards. Vaughn fired a total of thirteen shots before the **ST. JOHN** escaped up the bay to the protection of a British frigate, and the townspeople seemed pleased with the evening's entertainment. To the British demand for an explanation of the firing, Deputy Governor Walton replied, "The gunner at Fort George was acting by proper authority, and will answer for it when we think it necessary."*

Another source attributes the cause of the incident to be the illegal capture of a cargo of sugar which had been landed near Howland's Ferry:
*... From the lieutenant's narrative it appeared that while the **ST. JOHN** was lying at anchor in Newport Harbor on June 30, news was received that a brig was unloading in a creek near Howland's Ferry. The vessel had unloaded her cargo and sailed before Lt. Hill reached Howland's Ferry. The cargo consisted of ninety-three hogsheads of sugar. Lt. Hill sent an armed boat in pursuit of the brig, which was captured and proved to be the BASTO of New York, Wingate, master, from Monti Christo.*

The cargo was reloaded on the brig which was sent to Newport where it set off the commotion leading to the firing on the British schooner one week later. Regardless of what the reason for the action was, the firing from the American fort took place, just another incident leading to war.

Research Sources

1. Newport Mercury, July 16, 1764 P3
2. "History of Newport County, Rhode Island 1638-1887" by Richard M. Bayles (1888)
3. "Three Centuries of Democracy" by Charles Carroll (1932)
4. A History of Goat Island (pamphlet)

MAIDSTONE

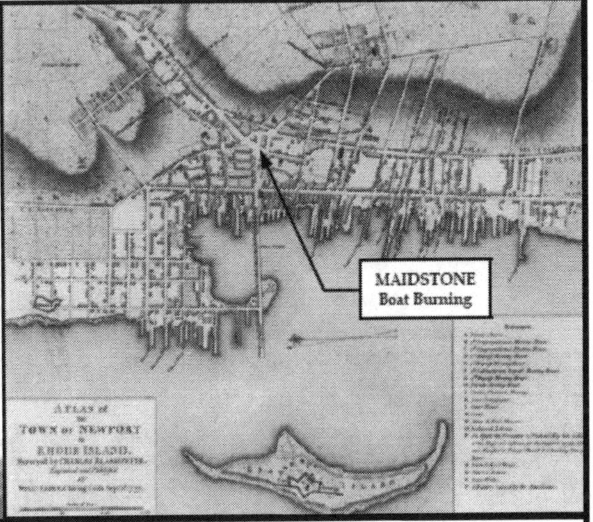

The Vessel

Type: 6th rate frigate
Construction: Wood
Use: Warship
Dimensions: 120′ x 33′ x 14′
Tonnage: 558
Launched: 1758
Owner: British Navy
Nationality: British

The Event

Master: Alan Gardner
Date of Incident: June 4, 1765
Disaster Type: One of her boats was burned
Cause: Intentional as a protest by locals
Status: Total loss
Location: The boat had been at a wharf and was dragged ashore and up to the common in front of the courthouse and burned

Narrative

The incident to the **MAIDSTONE** or, more correctly, to one of her boats, was one in a string of events which demonstrated the growing dissatisfaction of Rhode Island colonists with British control in the years leading up to the Revolutionary War. The following account details the exact cause of this incident and the events that transpired. Sometime in 1764, the British frigate **MAIDSTONE** arrived in Newport. Whether under direct orders or by Captain Antrobus's interpretation of his orders, the frigate spent a number of months actively engaged in the impressment of seamen from many vessels trading with merchants of Newport and other Rhode Island ports to serve in the British Navy. As the months wore on, this practice became more prevalent and even local seamen were being illegally taken. On more than one occasion the colonial governor demanded that this activity be stopped and the impressed men be freed, but these demands apparently fell on deaf ears. This action was particularly troublesome to Rhode Islanders as their ports became known far and wide as destinations to avoid with the result that Newport, in particular, was essentially cut off from normal communication with the outside world. But communication was slow and some vessels continued to arrive in Newport with various cargoes. On June 11, 1765 a brig arrived from Africa and the commander of the **MAIDSTONE** decided that a definitive example should be made and he proceeded to impress the entire crew. This was the final straw as far as the Newporters were concerned and in an act that many considered to be a riot, a group of some 500 men gathered and went to a local wharf where one of the boats from the **MAIDSTONE** was tied up. The boat was taken and run ashore

MAIDSTONE

and then dragged through the streets to the common where she was set fire and destroyed to the cheers of the crowd. The master of the frigate was not pleased with this protest and made a formal complaint to the Chief Justice of the county but was not successful in determining who the perpetrators were. No one was ever brought to trial. On July 12th, a month after the incident, Governor Ward sent to following letter to Captain Antrobus of the **MAIDSTONE** which summarized the situation, *"The men whose discharge I requested were detained several weeks; many others, in the meantime, impressed; the very fishing boats which daily supplied the town were fired at and interrupted so much in their fishing that some of them dared not go out of the harbor; and the town, if these measures continued, would soon have greatly suffered; nay, to such an extravagant height of imprudence and insolence had your people arrived as to enter on board a wood boat having only two men in her, and to take one of them out, and even to follow the vessel to the wharf. This encouraged the populace, and was the immediate occasion of the riot, which ended in burning the* ***MAIDSTONE*** *boat. These things gave a general uneasiness to the inhabitants, who not only saw the great disadvantage they must suffer in their trade and commerce, but were also apprehensive that the supplies which came to the town by water (without which they cannot subsist) would be so much obstructed as greatly to enhance the price of the necessities of life. And here sir, I must observe, that the impressing of Englishmen is, in my opinion, an arbitrary action, contrary to law, inconsistent with liberty, and to be justified only by urgent necessity. You assert that while your ship is afloat the civil authority of this colony does not extend to and cannot operate within her. But I must be of opinion, sir, that while she lies in the body of a county, as she then did and still does, within the body of the county of Newport, all her officers and men are within the jurisdiction of this colony, and ought to conform themselves to the laws thereof; and while I have the honor to be in the administration, I shall endeavor to assert and maintain the liberties and privileges of his majesty's subjects; and the honor, dignity and jurisdiction of the colony. As the men, whose discharge I was anxious to, have been dismissed, and no further complaints have been made me on that head, I am content to drop the dispute, and hope for the future there may be no occasion for renewing it."*

The actions of the British continued to stir resentment and anger in the minds and hearts of the colonists but it would be more than a decade before the actual outbreak of war. Between this event and war at least two more incidents of some importance would take place: the destruction of the British armed sloop LIBERTY in 1769 and the burning of the schooner GASPEE in 1772. The stories of both of these significant events will be found elsewhere in this collection of events that make up the maritime history of the state of Rhode Island.

Research Sources

1. "A History of the Destruction of His Britannic Majesty's Schooner Gaspee" (1861)
2. "Historical Address of the City of Newport" (7/4/1876)
3. "A History of American Privateers" by Edgar Stanton Maclay (1899)
4. "Three Centuries of Democracy" by Charles Carroll (1932)

LIBERTY

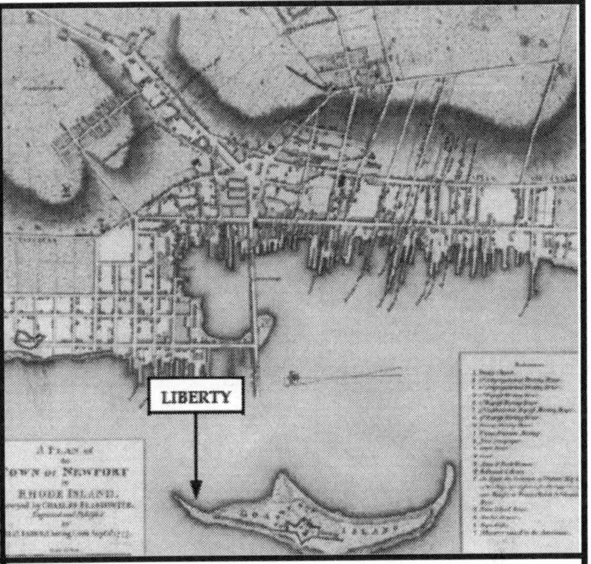

The Vessel

Type: Sloop
Construction: Wood
Use: Warship
Tonnage: ~ 60 tons
Owner: British Government
Nationality: British

Final Voyage

Master: William Reid
Date of Loss: July 19, 1769
Disaster Type: Ashore & burned
Cause: Intentional
Final Status: Total loss
Location: On the north part of Goat Island

Narrative

Newport Mercury - July 24, 1769 P3

Last Monday morning, the 17th instant, the armed sloop **LIBERTY**, *commanded by Captain William Reid, arrived here and brought in a brig and a sloop belonging to Connecticut, taken in the Sound, without this colony, on suspicion of the brig's having done some illicit act & that the sloop had some contraband goods on board; but as no proof appeared, against the brig, she reported her cargo at the Custom House here; and on Wednesday, no prosecution having been entered against either of them, Capt. Packwood went on board his brig in order to get his sword and some necessary apparel, which the commanding officer on board (one of the* **LIBERTY**'*s men) refused to let him bring away, and its said, offered him violence, which reduced Captain Packwood to the necessity of drawing his sword, to force his way into his boat, whereupon the officer called to the* **LIBERTY**'*s people to fire on Capt. Packwood as he was going ashore, which they did, and a brace of balls supposed went very near but did not hurt him; they then attempted to fire several more guns upon him, which happily all snapped or flashed and could not be discharged. This attempt of violence by the* **LIBERTY**'*s people, whose commander had never condescended to exhibit his commission to the governor of this colony, so enraged a number of persons that, the ensuing evening having met Captain Reid on the Long-Wharf, they obliged him to send for his men on shore in order to discover the man who first fired at Captain Packwood; upon which Capt. Reid sent for all his hands, except his mate. Afterwards a number of persons, unknown, went on board the* **LIBERTY**, *sent the mate away, cut her cables and let her drive ashore at the point, where they cut away her mast, scuttled her, and carried both her boats to the upper part of this town and burnt them.*

LIBERTY

The response to this article was posted in the adjacent column of the same issue of the Mercury:

By the Honorable Joseph Wanton, Esquire - Governor, Captain General, and Commander in Chief, of and over the English Colony of Rhode Island, and Providence Plantations, in New England, in America:

A PROCLAMATION

Whereas Charles Dudley, Esq., Collector and Surveyor, and John Nicholl, Esq., Comptroller, of his Majesty's Customs for the colony aforesaid, have this day presented unto me a memorial, setting forth that a number of people on the nineteenth instant, in the evening, being assembled in a riotous and tumultuous manner, did, with threats against his life, compel Capt. William Reid, Commander of the sloop ***LIBERTY*** *in the service of the revenue, lying in the harbor of Newport, to order the people who had the keeping and charge of his vessel, to come on shore, after which a number of men boarded the said sloop, and set at liberty a sloop brought into this port by the said William Reid, laden with prohibited goods and under seizure, and she was afterwards carried away to the great prejudice of his majesty. And that they then proceeded to destroy the said sloop* ***LIBERTY****, by cutting away her mast and rigging, and scuttling her so that she sunk; and burnt her two boats. I have therefore thought fit, by and with the advice of such members of his majesty's council, as could conveniently be called together, to issue this proclamation, hereby directing and requiring all the officers of justice in this colony, to use their utmost endeavours to inquire after and discover the person's guilty of the aforesaid crimes that they may be brought to justice.*

Newport Mercury - July 31, 1769 P3

Last Saturday afternoon the sloop ***LIBERTY*** *was floated by a high tide , drifted over to Goat Island; and is grounded at the north end, very near where the pirates were buried; what this prognosticates we leave to the determination of astrologers.*

Newport Mercury - August 7, 1769 P3

Last Monday evening, just after the storm of rain, hail and lightning, the ***LIBERTY*** *sloop, which we mentioned in our last to have drifted to Goat Island, near where the pirates were buried, was discovered on fire, and she continued burning for several days, till almost entirely consumed.*

The burning of the **LIBERTY** which, ironically enough, was built as an American vessel and previously owned by John Hancock before being taken by the British, represents one of the earliest events that led ultimately to the American War of Independence.

Research Sources

1. Newport Mercury, July 24, 1769 P3
2. Newport Mercury, July 31, 1769 P3
3. Newport Mercury, August 31, 1769 P3
4. "History of the Destruction of the Gaspee" by John Russell Bartlett (1861)
5. "A History of American Privateers" by Edgar Stanton Maclay (1899)
6. "Ships and Shipmasters of Old Providence" (1919)
7. The drawing is of the Armed Sloop SACHEM of the Continental Navy

GASPEE

A popular, artist's rendition of the night of June 9, 1772 - His British Majesty's schooner **GASPEE** aground and burned.

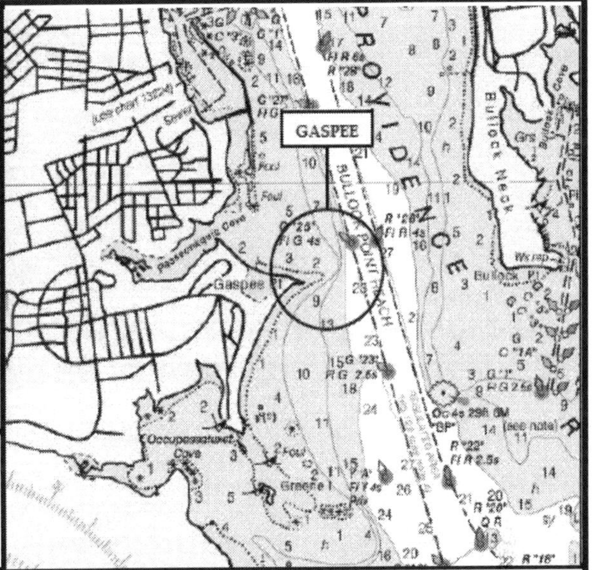

The Vessel

Type: Schooner
Construction: Wood
Use: Revenue ship
Dimensions: 49′ x 19′ x 7′
Tonnage: 102
Launched: Unknown prior to 1764
Owner: British Navy
Nationality: British
Official No.: N/A
Home Port: Newport, RI

Final Voyage

Port of Departure: Newport, RI
Port of Destination: In pursuit of the American sloop HANNAH
Master: William Dudingston
Cargo: N/A
Date of Loss: June 9, 1772
Disaster Type: Stranding
Cause: Pilot error
Final Status: Total loss
Location: Gaspee Point, Providence River

Narrative

There are few Rhode Islanders who have not heard of the British schooner **GASPEE** and the story of how those being pursued by her, through skillful sailing, she was run ashore on the west side of the river, below Providence. The story begins several months prior to the loss of the vessel. Historical records indicate that the schooner arrived in Newport in March of 1772, *"to prevent breaches of the revenue laws, and to stop the illicit trade, so long and successfully carried out in the colony"*. It seems that as good as the Rhode Islanders were at smuggling cargos past the British forces, the **GASPEE** managed to capture enough of them that she was beginning to be more than an annoyance to the locals. On that fateful day in early June, the packet HANNAH left Newport bound for Providence and shortly thereafter Captain Dudingston decided to give chase. He ordered Captain Lindsey of the HANNAH to "come to" but Lindsey calculated that a good breeze, his local knowledge of bay waters and his sailing ability would see him to reach his destination before the revenuer could catch him. Afternoon turned into early evening as the vessels raced northward with the **GASPEE** gaining despite her master's lack of familiarity of the bay. As the vessels approached Providence, Lindsey saw an opportunity and brought his smaller vessel in close to what was then called Namquit Point [now Gaspee Point] and at the last moment changed tack, heading northeastward. Dudingston had no time or, more importantly, not enough distance between him and shore, to make the comparable course alteration and ran

GASPEE

hard ashore on the extreme tip of the point. One of the local residents, Mr. John Brown, quickly observed that the stranding occurred just a couple of hours after high tide and the ebbing tidal flow would make it impossible for the stranded schooner to free herself for several hours. This presented, *"an opportunity ... to put an end to the trouble and vexation she daily caused. Brown directed one of his shipmasters to collect eight of the largest longboats in the harbor, with five oars each; to have the oars and rowlocks well muffled, to prevent noise, and to place them at Fenner's Wharf ..."* It is said that he sent a man along the main street beating a drum, and informed the inhabitants of the fact that the **GASPEE** was aground. He invited *"those persons who felt disposed to go and destroy that troublesome vessel to repair to Mr. James Sabin's house* [across the street from Fenner's Wharf]" Apparently there were enough men to man all of the boats with a sea captain acting as the steersman for each. Captain Dudingston, although inexperienced, was savvy enough to post a guard on the schooner in expectation of an attack by the rebels. At around midnight, his worst fears were realized when a sentry aboard the **GASPEE** spotted the small fleet of longboats and challenged them from his position near the bow of the British vessel. The noise brought Dudingston to the deck where he repeated the sentry's warning for the men in the long boats to keep away. The attacking fleet continued their approach and, although it is not clearly stated which side fired first, shots were fired by men on both sides. The captain of the **GASPEE** was struck by musket fire as the Americans continued to approach and the men of the attacking force quickly climbed aboard the helplessly stranded vessel. The crew followed their captain into the cabin and other areas below deck but surrendered on demand of the Rhode Islanders. Dudingston was severely wounded but the Americans tended to him and brought him off the vessel with the rest of the crew as prisoners and took him to Pawtuxet. Although it is not stated exactly who called for the burning of the schooner, Captain Abraham Whipple was the overall commander of the expedition. The schooner burned to the waterline and was lost. Needless to say, the British were not happy with this action and put pressure on the Governor of Rhode Island to find and punish the scoundrels. The governor posted a reward of *"one hundred pounds, sterling money of Great Britain, to any person or persons, who shall discover the perpetrators of said villainy, to be paid immediately upon the conviction of any one or more of them."* No one ever claimed the reward and none of the local citizens were ever captured, jailed or held for trial. The leaders of the colony expressed *"extreme regret"* to the king and his court but, alas, there seemed to be a severe case of amnesia when it came to identifying even one of the conspirators. The remains of the **GASPEE** simply faded away over the years and to this day have not been relocated though many have tried and failed.

Although little is known of the subsequent career of Captain Dudingston, it is know that he survived to the age of 76 or 77 and achieved the rank of Admiral in the British Navy. Whether the injury aboard the **GASPEE** in any way improved his career opportunities is not known.

Research Sources

1. "A History of the Destruction of His Britannic Majesty's Schooner Gaspee" by John Russell Bartlett (1861)
2. "A History of American Privateers", by Edgar Stanton Maclay (1899)
3. "Ships and Shipmasters of Old Providence" (published by the Providence Institute of Savings, 1919)
4. "British Warships In the Age of Sail, 1714-1792", by Rif Winfield (2007)
5. Photo courtesy of the Providence Public Library

DIANA

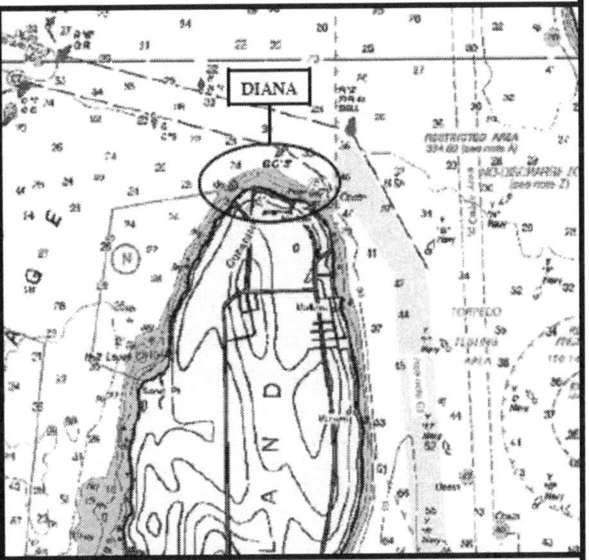

The Vessel

Type: Armed Sloop
Construction: Wood
Use: Tender to HMS ROSE
Owner: By parties in Providence but had been seized by the British for use as a tender
Nationality: British (at time of incident)
Home Port: Newport, RI

The Event

Port of Departure: Newport, RI
Mission: Intercept shipping in West Passage
Date of Incident: June 15, 1775
Disaster Type: Stranding
Cause: Chased ashore
Status: Pulled Off
Location: North end of Conanicut Island

Prelude to the Conflict

On June 14, 1775, Nicholas Cooke, Deputy Governor penned the following letter to Captain James Wallace, the commander of His Majesty's Ship ROSE, then on station at Newport, *"Long have the good people of this colony been oppressed by your conduct in interrupting their lawful trade, and preventing the importation of the provisions necessary for their subsistence. The acts of the British parliament, already filled with restrictions of trade, offensive in the highest degree, seem by you to be thought too lenient. Not controlled by those you affect to call your masters, you have detained the persons and taken away the property of his Majesty's American subjects, without any warrant from the acts of trade, by which you have greatly impeded the intercourse between this and the other colonies, as well as between the different parts of this colony. The inhabitants expecting the interposition of the lawful authority of the colony, have born these outrages with a patience almost criminal; the legislatures have heard their complaints, and in consequence of an act passed by the General Assembly this day, I demand of you the reason of your conduct towards the inhabitants of this colony, in stopping and immediately restoring their vessels; and I also demand of you that you immediately restore the two packets belonging to some inhabitants of the town of Providence, and all other vessels belonging to the inhabitants of this colony, which you have taken, and unjustly detain..."* The response to this letter was brief and to the point, but not what the colonists were hoping for, *"I have received your letter of the 14th. Although I am unacquainted with you, or what station you act in, suppose you write in behalf of some body of people. Previous to my giving an answer, I must desire to know whether or not you, or the people on whose behalf you write, are not in open rebellion to your lawful Sovereign, and the acts of the British legislature?*

DIANA

The Conflict

Newport Mercury - June 19, 1775 P3

Last Thursday one of the Providence packets, which had been arbitrarily seized by, and detained as a tender to the men-of-war in this harbor, was sent up the bay, 'tis supposed, to take a vessel which, 'twas reported had gone up the back side of Conanicut, but unluckily she met with two armed vessels, which fired upon her so warmly that she was obliged to turn tail to, but not being able to get off, the people stuck her ashore on the north end of Conanicut, and left her; she was immediately got off, and carried away, most probably to be delivered to her proper owner. This happened just before sunset.

Note: Over the years, several historians have claimed that the tender discussed in the newspaper account was the **DIANA**. Since the account does not specifically name the packet to be this vessel, there is at least a possibility that the vessel involved was not the **DIANA** but regardless of her identity there can be no doubt that this incident took place as described.

The Significance of the Conflict

Several states lay claim to being the birthplace of the US Navy and among them is the state of Rhode Island. The specific details of the first naval engagement between American and British forces are as noted in the newspaper account above but, as might be expected, there is more to the story, and criteria to be met, if these vessels qualify to be considered in the running for the claim. It is said that a single vessel cannot be considered to constitute a navy...there must be at least two vessels. According to a report addressed to Congress at a later date, Abraham Whipple of Providence was selected by the Rhode Island General Assembly on June 15, 1775, to take command of the Rhode Island Navy, the first American Navy of the Revolution. Whipple was a captain in the employ of John Brown, a leading merchant from Providence, who on June 12th had volunteered one of his vessels, the sloop KATY, to be chartered for this purpose. A second vessel, a row galley named WASHINGTON, completed the naval force and together the two wasted no time in taking the fight to the British forces stationed in the waters of Narragansett Bay. The run in between a tender to the HMS ROSE, previously seized by and under control of the British, and the KATY, accompanied by the WASHINGTON, was probably more accidental than planned, but led to the same effect as if they had both known of each others location in advance. Shots were fired from the American sloop which led to a decision on the part of the British to run their vessel ashore and abandon her and, thus, a battle can be considered to have been fought. The details of claims by other states to the title of being the birthplace of the federal navy is not the focus of this story and, ultimately, the winner may be determined elsewhere but it is clear that with the assignment of the sloop KATY and the WASHINGTON, and the appointment of Commodore Whipple, that the state of Rhode Island has , at the very least, solid, traceable evidence necessary to be considered.

Research Sources

1. Newport Mercury, June 19, 1775 P3
2. Rivington's New York Gazetter, June 29, 1775 P2
3. "History of Newport County" by Richard M. Bayles (1888)
4. "Who Was Commodore Whipple?" (Internet)
5. "First American Revolution Navy Ships" (Internet)
6. "Our Young Navy" (Internet)

HMS GLASGOW

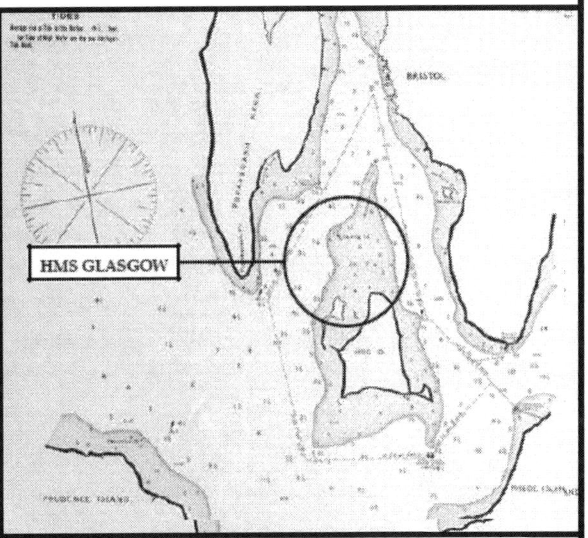

The **HMS GLASGOW** was a sixth rate ship similar to the unidentified vessel of the same rig pictured above.

The Vessel

Type: 6th rate Ship
Construction: Wood
Use: Warship
Dimensions: 109′ x 30′ x 9′
Tonnage: 451
Launched: Hull, England in 1757
Owner: British Navy
Nationality: British
Home Port: Boston, MA

The Event

Port of Departure: Newport, RI
Port of Destination: Bristol, RI
Master: Tyringham Howe
Date of Incident: October 7, 1775
Disaster Type: Stranding
Cause: Navigational error
Status: Got Off
Location: On the extreme northwest point of the island inside Poppasquash Point, Bristol

Maintaining an Army of Occupation

On December 6, 1776 a British fleet arrived off Newport, Rhode Island, with the intention of capturing the town and, thus, controlling the entrance to Narragansett Bay, one of the most strategically well suited bodies of water on the eastern seaboard. Several thousand soldiers moved into the town and seized control with little or no resistance from the locals and settled in for what would become a thirty-five month occupation. But taking the town was the easy part. Once settled in, there were the issues of finding a place to house and feed the soldiers. To supply the troops with food was the role of the victualers who, during that period, preceded the force and made contracts with local residents to provide such provisions as were needed. The larger the force, the more difficult the task. And when contracts could not be made for what the troops needed, they felt obligated to result to deadly force and take what they needed. The following article appeared in the New York Gazette and Weekly Mercury on October 16, 1775. *NEWPORT, October 9. – By the motions of some of the men of war and transports in this harbor, last Monday, it was suspected they intended to take off live stock from the farms on the south part of this island, called Brenton's Neck, the ensuing night; whereupon a number of persons* [American rebels] *went down in the evening and brought off about 1,000 sheep and between 40 and 50 head of cattle from several farms.* This type of clandestine activity was not unusual and often prompted a response from the occupiers such as the event which indirectly brought about the incident to the ship **HMS GLASGOW**. On October 7th a small fleet of British vessels left Newport on a foraging expedition to the upper

HMS GLASGOW

part of the bay. The small fleet comprised 16 vessels which boldly sailed into the harbor at Bristol to address their needs. What follows is a published letter from an eyewitness to the event written to correct an earlier newspaper account said to be incorrect in detail, *"Having observed in the last Newport Mercury an imperfect account relative to the conduct of his Majesty's ships, under the command of Capt. Wallace at Bristol, last Saturday night, I embrace this opportunity to give you a true and particular detail of facts that took place, from their anchoring in the harbour till they left the town. On Saturday the 7th instant, P.M. appeared in sight of the harbour, a very formidable fleet consisting of 16 sail, viz. three men-of-war, one bomb ketch, and other armed vessels, all which, excepting the* ***GLASGOW*** *(who ran ashore at Pasqash point), drew up in a line of battle, from one end of town to the other; soon after they had moored, a barge came from the ROSE to the head of a wharf, with the Lieutenant, who asking if there were any gentlemen on the wharf, William Bradford being present, answered yes; whereupon the Lieutenant informed him, Captain Wallace had a demand to make on the town, and desired two or three of the principal men, or magistrates of the town, would go on board his ship, within an hour, and hear his proposals, otherwise hostilities would be commenced against the town; the above gentleman replied as a magistrate, that, in his opinion, Captain Wallace was under a greater obligation to come ashore, than for the magistrates to go on board his ship to hear them; and added that if Captain Wallace would come to the head of the wharf the next morning, he should be treated as a gentleman, and the town would consider of his demands; with this answer the Lieutenant returned on board the ROSE. The inhabitants being made acquainted with the above conversation, repaired to the wharf, and waited with the utmost patience, for a reply from Capt. Wallace, till an hour had expired, when the whole fleet began a most heavy cannonading, and the bomb vessel to bombard, and heave shells and carcasses into the town; which continued, without interruption, an hour and a half. In the meantime Col. Potter in the hottest of the fire, went upon the head of the wharf, hailed the ROSE, went on board and requested a cessation of hostilities, till the inhabitants might choose a committee to go on board and meet with Capt. Wallace; which request was complied with, and six hours were allowed for the above purpose. Col. Potter returned and made a report to the committee of inspection who chose a select committee to hear Capt. Wallace's demands, which after they had gone on board, Capt. Wallace informed were a supply of 200 sheep and 30 fat cattle. This demand, the committee replied, it was impossible to comply with, for the country people had come in and drove off their stock, having only a few sheep and some milk cows. After some hours had expired, during the negotiation, without coming to any agreement, Capt. Wallace told them, I have only one proposal to make, "if you will promise to supply me with 40 sheep, at or before 12 o'clock, I will assure you that another gun shall not be discharged." The committee seeing themselves reduced to this distressing alternative, either to supply their most inveterate enemy with provisions or devour to the flames the town … reluctantly chose the lesser, by agreeing to supply them with 40 sheep at the time appointed, which was punctually performed. ...*

The newspaper spelling of Poppasquash Point (derived from the name Papoose Squaw Point) was illustrative of a common error of the time. Also, other sources indicate that the actual location of the stranding of the **HMS GLASGOW** was on the northwestern point of the island inside the point. The ship came off without injury at the rising of the tide.

Research Sources

1. New York Gazette and Weekly Mercury, October 16, 1775 P3
2. New York Gazette and Weekly Mercury, October 23, 1775 P3
3. "History of Newport County, Rhode Island, 1638-1887" by Richard M. Bayles (1888)
4. "Revolutionary Defences in Rhode Island" by Edward Field (1896)
5. "British Warships in the Age of Sail, 1714-1792" by Rif Winfield (2007)

HMS DIAMOND

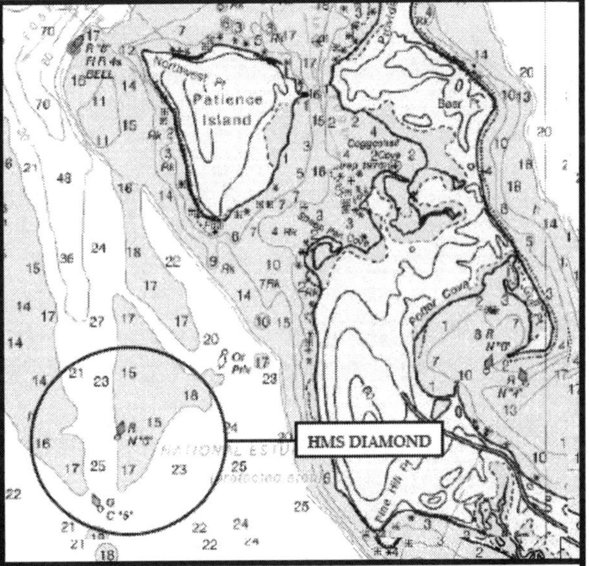

The Vessel

Type: 5th rate Frigate
Construction: Wood
Use: Warship
Dimensions: 130′ x 35′ x 12′
Tonnage: 709
Launched: Hull, England in 1774
Nationality: British
Home Port: Newport, RI

The Event

Owner: British Navy
Date of Incident: January 2, 1777
Disaster Type: Stranding
Cause: Unknown
Status: Got off
Location: On a shoal about ½ mile southwest from Patience and a little more southeast from Warwick Neck

Esek Hopkins, Commander-In-Chief, Continental Navy

The story of Esek Hopkins, Commander-In-Chief of the Continental Navy and the stranding of the British frigate **HMS DIAMOND** provides an example of some of the less-than-honorable actions taken during the development of a military force in a newly formed nation. The following comes mostly from a biographical work on the life of Hopkins published in 1898. *It was not long after the British forces took possession of Newport that an incident occurred which brought down upon Hopkins much criticism from the officers of his fleet, as well as from the people in the state. ... It was the second day of January, 1777 at about 1 o'clock in the afternoon, while the WARREN was lying off Field's Point, at the entrance of Providence Harbor, an orderly from Colonel Brown, who was located at Warwick, came on board and delivered to Hopkins a message containing the information that a British war vessel was aground near Warwick Neck. ... When the news was received, the ship PROVIDENCE lay about a mile below the point, and the sloop PROVIDENCE lay against the Pawtuxet shore, about four miles still farther to the southward. As soon as Hopkins received this information, he endeavored to get down the river to investigate the situation. Captain Allen Brown, a pilot, was at that time on board the WARREN* [and] *being consulted as to the advisability of taking the ships down to the point where the grounded vessel lay, informed Hopkins "the wind was so far westerly and blowed so hard that the ships could not be carried down." ... Hopkins therefore did not venture with either of the ships, but taking the WARREN's pinnace with twenty-two men, went to the PROVIDENCE (sloop), Capt. Whipple, taking Captain Brown, the pilot, with him. Upon arriving on board the sloop and finding her fully manned, they immediately got*

HMS DIAMOND

under weigh and proceeded down the river toward the stranded vessel. As the sloop drew down on her it was discovered that she was the frigate **DIAMOND**, *and that she lay "on a shoal which runs off S.W. from Patience about half a mile from that island and a little more than southeast from Warwick Neck." There was about eleven feet of water at low tide, and as the tide was about half way down she did not careen. Lying about a mile and a half off, about southwest by south, was a fifty-gun ship with her top sails loose, her "anchor apeak," which as the wind was, could have floated her within pistol shot of the* **DIAMOND**. *Hopkins was of the opinion that on account of the severity of the wind she did not "come to sail". From his knowledge of the river and bay, with the gale then blowing, he felt it would be unwise to order his ships down to the* **DIAMOND** *and even if the wind had not blown so hard and the ships could have been brought down, he afterward said he should not have done so, for "the enemy's ships could have come to sail with any wind that we could and a great deal better as they lay in a wide channel and we in a very narrow and very crooked one". Arriving off Warwick Neck, Hopkins went ashore to the fort, where he was informed by Col. Bowen that he had sent for two eighteen pounders, and, after remaining there a half hour, until the guns arrived, Hopkins went back to the sloop. What subsequently took place is best told in Hopkins' own words, "I went aboard the sloop and we dropped down under the ships stern a little more than a musket shot off it being there a little after sunset. We fired from the sloop a number of shot which she returned with her stern chasers; the ship careened at dusk about as much as she would have done had she been under sail. After they had fired from the shore about twenty six shots they ceased and soon after hailed the sloop and said they wanted to speak with me. I went ashore and was informed they were out of ammunition. I offered them powder and stuff for wads but we had no shot that would do. They sent to Providence for powder and shot and I went aboard the sloop and sent some junk ashore for wads. Soon after they hailed again from the shore and I went to see what they wanted, and gave Captain Whipple orders not to fire much more as I thought it would do but little execution, it being night and could not take good aim with the guns. When I got ashore the officer that commanded them desired that I would let them have some bread out of the sloop which I sent the boat off for but the people not making the boat well fast, while they were getting the bread she drifted away and I could not get aboard again. The ship by lighting got off about 2 o'clock the same night".*

Apparently Hopkins did not think too much about this incident but others saw this as an opportunity to rid themselves of him and filed a formal complaint that the commander had been derelict in his duty and was openly disrespectful of the Congress. On March 26, 1777 the matter was taken up by the Marine Committee and without any discussion the matter was resolved by calling for the immediate suspension of Esek Hopkins from his command of the American Navy. The officers and others who filed the complaint were not entirely successful however, as the members of the Marine Committee, although not strong supporters of Hopkins, found the complaint to be of a questionable character and decided to formally question the principal complainant, Lieutenant Richard Marvin, with the result that he was terminated from the service on April 3rd. But as members of the committee still had issues with Hopkins, they took advantage of this complaint and on the following January (1778) the commander's suspension was ended when he was summarily discharged from the service. Hopkins was not going to leave quietly, however, and later that month he decided to bring suit against his accusers. That case could not be scheduled until June of 1778 and the trial lasted just five days but in the end, Hopkins did not prevail and was not restored to his former role.

Research Sources

1. "Esek Hopkins, Commander-In-Chief of the Continental Navy" by Edward Field (1898)
2. "British Warships in the Age of Sail, 1714-1792" by Rif Winfield (2007)

HMS CERBERUS

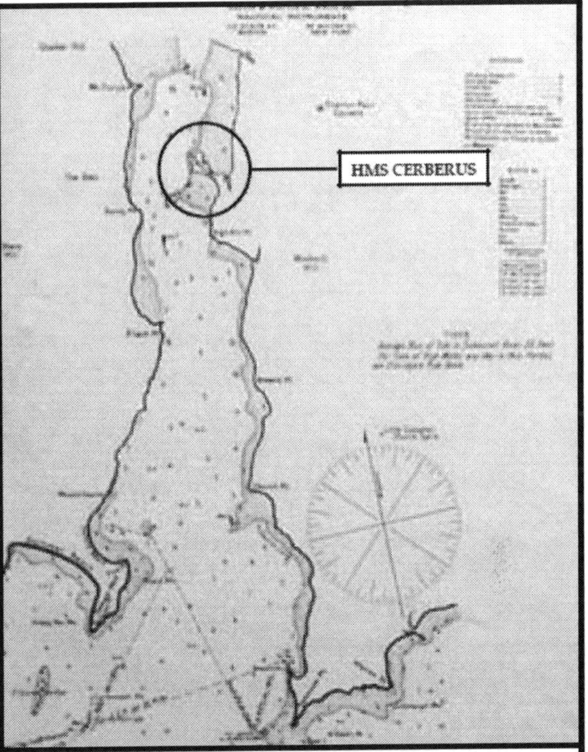

The HMS ACTIVE shown in the painting was a sister ship to **HMS CERBERUS**. Both were 6th rate ships of the Coventry class and served the British during the Revolutionary War. The 28-gun ship was stationed in Newport where she was finally lost, but not at this time.

The Vessel

Type: 6th rate ship
Construction: Wood
Use: Warship
Dimensions: 118′ x 33′ x 10′
Tonnage: 593
Launched: East Cowes, England in 1758
Owner: British Navy
Nationality: British Home Port: Newport, RI

The Event

Master: John Simmonds
Cargo: N/A
Date of Incident: January 10, 1777
Disaster Type: Attacked
Cause: War
Status: Repaired
Location: On her station, off Fogland Ferry, in the Sakonnet River

Narrative

Hartford Courant - January 27, 1777 P3

Providence, Jan. 18

On Friday morning, last week, a party of our troops from Seconnet, with one 18 and one 12 pounder, drove the ***CERBERUS*** *man of war from Fogland Ferry; she returned the fire briskly for some time, and slightly wounded one of our men; but was at length obliged to put to sea, and is since arrived at Newport. By certain accounts received from thence, we learn that she was considerably damaged in her hull, and had 6 men killed and a number wounded.*

The **CERBERUS** was repaired and returned to service but the rest of her career was short. Just 18 months after this incident, while on station off the Portsmouth shore and near Dyer Island, she was intentionally destroyed by her crew when the French fleet entered Narragansett Bay.

HMS CERBERUS

Research Sources

1. Hartford Courant, January 27, 1777 P3
2. "History of Newport County, Rhode Island, 1638-1887" by Richard M. Bayles (1888)
3. "British Warships in the Age of Sail, 1714-1792" by Rif Winfield (2007)

UNIDENTIFIED

A modern day replica of a 1776 vintage sloop like the UNIDENTIFIED vessel lost on the Point Judith shore in 1777.

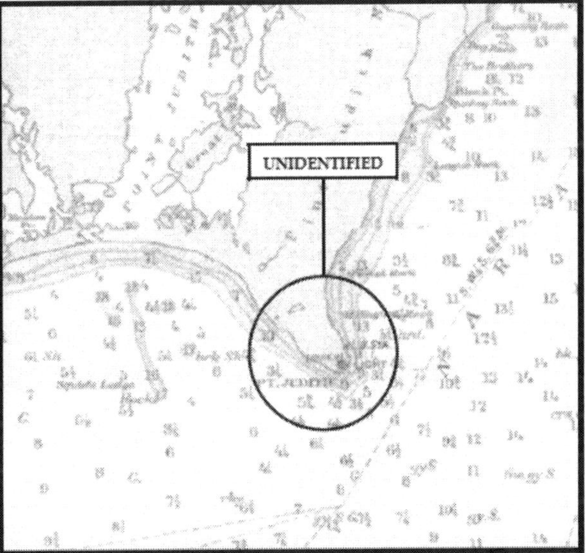

The Vessel

Type: Sloop
Construction: Wood
Use: Merchant
Nationality: American
Port of Departure: Turks Island, West Indies
Port of Destination: Providence, RI
Master: John Therlo

The Event

Cargo: salt, lead, iron, cotton-wool, etc.
Date of Incident: January 26, 1777
Disaster Type: Ashore & burned
Cause: Act of war
Status: Unknown but probably lost
Location: On the Point Judith shore (probably on the eastern side of the neck)

Narrative

The story of the loss of an unidentified merchant sloop on Point Judith is found in the Records of the Colony of Rhode Island & Providence Plantations published about a century after the event:

Whereas Messrs. Christopher Whipple and John Therlo preferred a petition to this assembly, setting forth, that on the 26th day of January last, being bound from Turks Island to the port of Providence, with a cargo of salt, lead, iron, cotton-wool, &c., they were steering for the harbor of Newport, not knowing the enemy were in possession thereof, until they discovered their shipping; that they sent a boat on shore to make inquiry, and being informed that they were part of the enemy's fleet, they put the vessel about, and steered for the Eastern Sound, being pursued by two of the enemy's ships; that in order to escape them, they again out about, and steered for the Western Sound; when they presently discovered eleven sail of the enemy's fleet coming down the Sound and standing for Newport, who fired upon them; that still being pursued by the two vessels aforesaid, they were reduced to the necessity of running the vessel aground, on Point Judith shore; that in order to save their effects from falling into the hands of the enemy, they cut away their mast, and got the sails and some of her rigging ashore, with two bags of cotton-wool, and a number of other articles, when the enemy getting possession of the vessel, set her on fire about seven o'clock, in the evening, and immediately left her; upon which, the said John Therlo, with some assistance, extinguished the fire about two o'clock, the same night, and when about getting the salt on shore, a quantity of which was saved; as was also a quantity of the iron, cotton-wool, part of rum, a cask of porter, and a number of other articles, which are now in the hands of Stephen Potter of South Kingstown...

UNIDENTIFIED

Research Sources

1. Records of the Colony of Rhode Island and Providence Plantations, Vol. VIII (printed by order of the General Assembly—edited by John Russell Bartlett—1863)

TWO BROTHERS

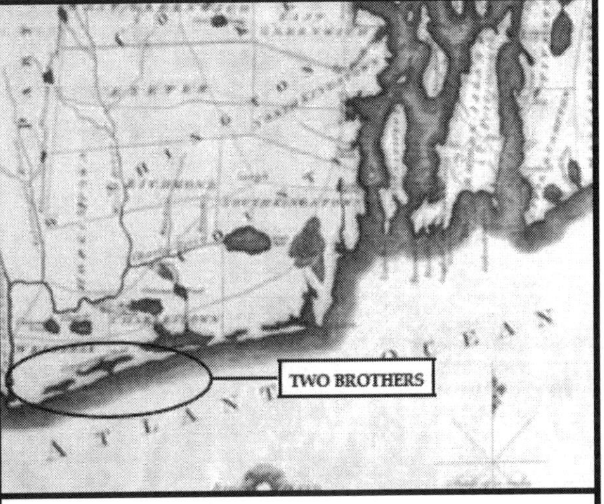

The Vessel

Type: Schooner
Construction: Wood
Use: Merchant
Tonnage: 150
Nationality: American
Port of Departure: West Indies
Port of Destination: Connecticut

The Event

Master: Lt. William Leeds (prize master)
Cargo: provisions
Date of Incident: February 3, 1777
Disaster Type: Stranding
Cause: Run ashore to prevent capture
Status: Got Off
Location: Near Westerly

Narrative

The incident to the schooner **TWO BROTHERS** was not unlike many others which occurred at a time when the value of vessels and their cargoes was great. Captured vessels and their cargoes were known as prizes and the common practice of the captor was to put a few of his men, known as a prize crew, aboard to bring the vessel to a friendly port where they could be legally "condemned", sold and the proceeds distributed. First mention of the stranding of the **TWO BROTHERS** came from an address delivered by William P. Sheffield before the Rhode Island Historical Society in 1882 which simply had the following information, *"March 11, 1777 – the TWO BROTHERS, with a cargo of provisions, was driven on shore at Westerly"*. Researching the newspapers of the day, the following was found.

Providence Gazette and Country Journal - March 15, 1777 P3

State of Rhode Island and Providence Plantations, King's County

In obedience to an act of the General Assembly, I hereby give notice that the court created for the trial of prize causes in said state, which was to have been holden at the state house in South Kingstown, in said county, on the 11th day of March, A.D. 1777, for trial of the justice of the capture of the schooner **TWO BROTHERS**, *her appurtenances and cargo, is adjourned to the second day of April A.D. 1777, at said state house, at the hour of ten in the forenoon, when and where the parties concerned are notified to attend; and pursuant to said act of assembly, the town sergeants or constables of said county are hereby required then and there to make their returns to me, with the names of the jurors who have been drawn to attend said trial, upon penalty of ten pounds for failure therein; and each juror so drawn is hereby required to appear and serve upon said trial, as he could avoid being fined for non-appearance.*

TWO BROTHERS

Armed with two bits of information, that the vessel was run ashore and that she had been captured, the search continued for the rest of the story. As it turned out, the details would be found with a history of the Connecticut Privateer sloop AMERICAN REVENUE which had been moderately successful along the eastern coast of the United States before turning her attention to the Caribbean. ... *The AMERICAN REVENUE now apparently moved somewhat to the south. Her next prize was the schooner* **TWO BROTHERS** *(John Salter) which was captured on 27 December 1776 or 3 January 1777. The 150-ton* **TWO BROTHERS** *was bound from Cork, Ireland to Jamaica, with a cargo of beef, pork, butter, bread, flour, cheese, fish, oats and salt. A prize master, Second Lieutenant William Leeds, and a prize crew of seven men were put aboard. On 3 February 1777 the* **TWO BROTHERS** *was approaching the coast, having closed on Gardiner's Island, when she was sighted and chased by a patrolling British warship, HM Frigate NIGER. The prize master ran her ashore near Westerly, Rhode Island. The crew jumped out and put a warp from the schooner to the shore, pulled her up tight, and began unloading the cargo. NIGER moved in closer, laying down a heavy fire on the schooner, and driving the prize crew to abandon her. A barge with twelve sailors rowed from the warship and got aboard the* **TWO BROTHERS**. *Rhode Island troops under Colonel Stanton and militia under Colonel Noyes, stationed in Westerly to defend the town, hurried down to the beach with two field pieces, and returned fire to the warship. The boarding party, unable to get the schooner unstuck, set her on fire in the cabin and returned to the NIGER. The prize crew re-boarded the* **TWO BROTHERS**, *put out the fire and watched the British sail away. The schooner was brought up to Westerly. Both troops and prize crew now claimed the prize. On 11 February the two colonels, Stanton and Noyes, filed a libel in the Rhode Island admiralty court against the* **TWO BROTHERS**. *The next day the agents for the AMERICAN REVENUE also filed a libel. The trial was held at South Kingston, Rhode Island on 2 April, 1777. The court condemned the schooner and awarded her to the privateer. When the colonels decided to appeal the verdict, the owners were permitted to sell the prize on giving bond to return the monies if the verdict was overturned.* **TWO BROTHERS** *was sold for Ł4038.16.4. After court costs the owners and crew divided Ł2698.12.4.* The subsequent career and final fate of the schooner **TWO BROTHERS** is not known.

Research Sources

1. Providence Gazette & Country Journal, March 15, 1777 P3
2. "An Address Delivered by William P. Sheffield, Before the Rhode Island Historical Society in Providence, February 7 A.D. 1882" (1883)
3. American War of Independence At Sea (Internet)

TRYALL

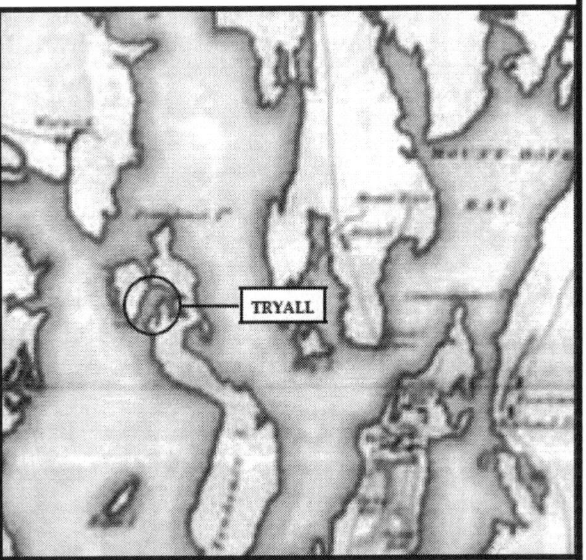

The Vessel

Type: Schooner
Construction: Wood
Use: Warship
Owner: British Navy
Nationality: British
Home Port: Unknown

Final Voyage

Date of Loss: February 14, 1777
Disaster Type: Ashore & burned
Cause: Probably pilot error
Final Status: Total loss
Location: Between Prudence Island and Patience Island

Narrative

When the British occupied Newport in December of 1776 maritime activities in Narragansett Bay changed for the worse for the American "rebels". The British intended to show the colonists exactly who was in charge, but most Americans, though occupied, did not lose sight of their goal of freedom. Although the entrance to the bay was under the control of their enemy, Rhode Islanders continued to resist, sending privateers and warships out to capture and destroy enemy ships as often as they could. Just two months into the occupation an opportunity came to show that the Americans were willing to "mix it up" in terms of a fight, if that was what they needed to do to be free. Although the loss of the schooner **TRYALL** (first not identified at all and later as the TRYAL) was not due to a battle, American forces headed to the scene of her stranding as soon as it was known and it is due to their presence that the vessel became a loss to the British rather than maybe having been pulled off and returned to service.

Providence Gazette and Country Journal - February 22, 1777 P3

On Friday last week, one of the enemy's schooners, of 8 carriage guns, and 12 swivels (supposed to be the ST. LAWRENCE) came to anchor near Warwick Neck; a shot being fired at her from the shore, she immediately slipped her cable and in endeavoring to run between Patience and Prudence islands, got aground. Intelligence being received her of her situation, the sloop PROVIDENCE was immediately sent to take possession of her; but on the sloop's approach the enemy took to their boats, leaving a train that communicated with the magazine, and when the sloop had got within a mile of her, she blew up; the cable and anchor have been since secured.

TRYALL

In a letter from Commodore Esek Hopkins to the Continental Marine Committee the following is excerpted, ... *This day about half past 3 o'clock in the afternoon I received a message from Colonel [John] Waterman, that a large armed schooner, one of his majesty's fleet, was ashore on the northern part of Prudence - I immediately put men out of the WARREN on board the sloop PROVIDENCE, and dispatched her under the command of Captain John B. Hopkins - they got near her about sunset, when the schooner's people put fire to and quitted her - and we suppose by the time she blew up, that they had fixed a train to go off about the time they expected our people to board her - however, she is effectually destroyed which perhaps may make them more cautious of coming where they are not well acquainted - I hear the said schooner was built in England for the business. ...*

As we know there are two sides to every story and, in most cases, they can disagree from a different perspective. In this instance, however, the British version generally matches that of the American reports. The following is from the master's log of HMS DIAMOND. This log entry starts from the day before the incident but is included in its entirety for clarity, *Remarks on board his Majesty's Ship DIAMOND. February 77, Thursday 13th - AM - weighed the small Br* [bower or bow anchor] *and stood further to the northward and let go the anchor again in 13 fathom and veered to half a cable, Bristol Church steeple NNE½E, the south part of Prudence Island SSW off shore 1 mile. PM - John Carter and John Smith deserted when cutting of wood on shore on Prudence Island – At 8 sent the* ***TRYALL*** *schooner with our cutter, a petty officer and 10 marines - first part fresh breezes and squally weather; middle and later, moderate and fair - at half past 3 the officer and marines returned without success. The master of the schooner coming with them informs of her being ashore between Patients* [Patience] *and Prudence Islands. At 4 discovered a large armed sloop coming down from Providence. Made the signal to the CENTURION for the gundola - The sloop hauled towards where the schooner was. At ½ past 4 observed a large fire between Prudence and Patients Island which proved to be the* ***TRYALL*** *on fire.*

Not far away the HMS CERBERUS lay at anchor off Hope Island. Her captain's journal reported the incident and aftermath as follows: . *February 77, Friday 14th - Fresh breezes and clear - at 1 PM observed the* ***TRYAL*** *schooner aground between Patience and Providence - sent the boats to her assistance. At 5 set her on fire finding it impracticable to get her off. Brought her crew and part of her stores onboard. Saturday 15 - AM - sent the boats to pick up what was to be found. At 10 the boats returned with three 3-pounders, 4 swivels, some bayonets, cutlasses, iron hoops & 20 pigs of ballast. Fresh breezes and clear. PM - sent the officers and some of the people belonging to the schooner on board the DIAMOND.*

Research Sources

1. Providence Gazette and Country Journal, February 22, 1777 P3
2. "History of Newport County, Rhode Island, 1638-1887" by Richard M. Bayles (1888)
3. "Naval Documents of the American Revolution", Vol. 7 (1976)
4. "British Warships In the Age of Sail, 1714-1792", by Rif Winfield (2007)

SPITFIRE

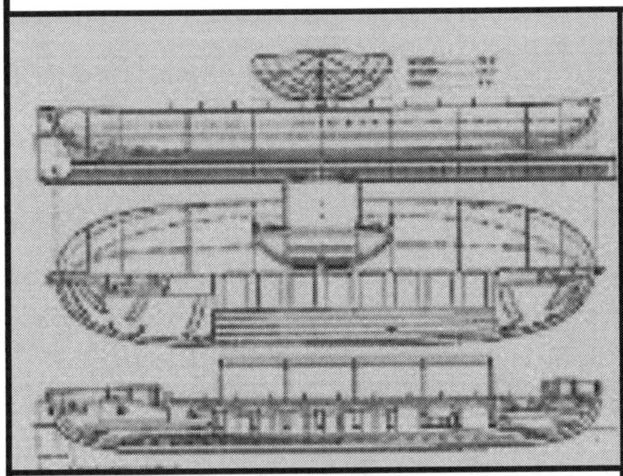

An American Revolutionary era galley. Designed to be rowed, the vessel was armed for defense or offensive action.

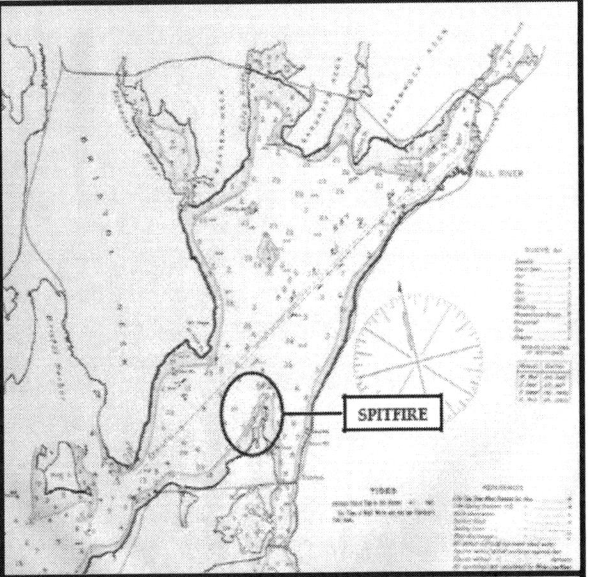

The Vessel

Type: Galley
Construction: Wood
Use: Warship
Launched: Providence, RI in 1776
Owner: Continental Navy
Nationality: American
Official No.: N/A
Home Port: Providence, RI
Master: Isaac Tyler

Final Voyage

Port of Departure: Providence, RI
Port of Destination: Portsmouth, RI
Cargo: Unknown
Date of Loss: March 13, 1777
Disaster Type: Ashore & burned
Cause: War Loss
Final Status: Total loss
Location: At or near Common Fence Point after coming through Bristol Narrows

Narrative

In the "History of Newport County, Rhode Island 1638-1887" by Richard Bayles there is a reference to the loss of an unnamed galley off the northern end of Aquidneck Island, "*On the 15th of March an attack was made by the Americans with a fire ship and two galleys on an English man- of-war, which, according to the German account, ended in the loss of one of the galleys, burned to save it from the Hessians, and the escape of the other, with the loss of the burning vessel.*" Like many early references, there is some truth and some confusion about this account which required a further search of details. In "Revolutionary Defences in Rhode Island" by Edward Field the details of the event become a little more clear, "*Commencing at the north end of the island is Common Fence Point. Here on the evening of the 13th of March, 1777, the row galley* ***SPITFIRE*** *commanded by Captain Isaac Tyler, grounded in the night, or, as the entry in the records of the Council of War says, "struck the bottom". Near her at the time was the row galley WASHINGTON. The captain of the* ***SPITFIRE*** *endeavored to get the assistance f the WASHINGTON to haul him off, but this aid was not forthcoming, on account of differences between the two commanders. When morning dawned, the position of the* ***SPITFIRE*** *was discovered by one of the enemy's boats patrolling the bay. The* ***SPITFIRE*** *had been abandoned so it was a comparatively easy task to take possession of her. This was done, and as it was difficult to float her, she was set on fire. The responsibility for this loss was made the subject of a searching investigation by the Council of War.*" The third and final rendition of this incident comes from an Internet site named "British Soldiers, American Revolution" which gives the following

SPITFIRE

information, *"On 21 February 1777, an American galley called the* **SPITFIRE** *supported a party of American troops that landed on the island, a second landing that week. ... Three weeks later on the night of 13-14 March, the* **SPITFIRE** *was passing through the narrows at Bristol Ferry, today the site of the Mount Hope Bridge. Movements like these were usually done at night to minimize the danger of detection by British sentries, but nighttime navigation was itself hazardous. The* **SPITFIRE** *ran aground. British artillery crews supported by soldiers on temporary service with the gunners, were highly adept at rapid deployment of their field artillery pieces and had strategically positioned them where they could be moved to repel landings. The immobilized American galley presented an excellent opportunity to use this capability, and field pieces were moved to the shore to engage the* **SPITFIRE**. *Realizing the hopelessness of their situation, the crew of the galley abandoned it and made for the safety of the Bristol shore. Although the vessel was now defenseless against the British artillery, the solid iron ball and shot fired by those guns could damage the ship but not destroy it completely. Being aground already, it could not be sunk. It was essential to deprive the Americans of a valuable hull that could be refitted, so complete destruction was essential. The galley had to be burned. Rather than wait for boats to be brought to the scene (boats were scarce along the shoreline, because they could too easily be used for clandestine activities), a British private soldier took action. Henry Pickles went into the water and swam to the galley. The exact location of the grounded galley is not known, but this swim could have been as much as a half mile in an area with significant currents. We also do not know whether Pickles set fire to the galley himself, or brought a line that was used to haul it closer to the British shore. Either way, the* **SPITFIRE** *was consumed by fire and completely destroyed.*

Research Sources

1. "History of Newport County, Rhode Island, 1638-1887" by Richard M. Bayles (1888)
2. "Revolutionary Defences in Rhode Island" by Edward Field (1896)
3. "The Navy in the American Revolution" by Charles O. Paullin (1906)
4. "British Soldiers, American Revolution" (Internet)

WASHINGTON

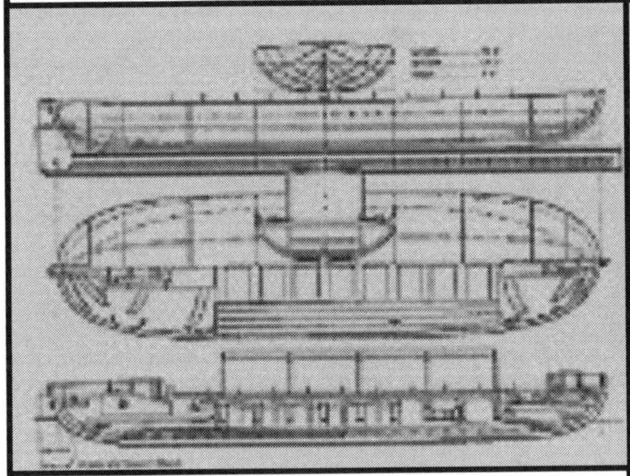

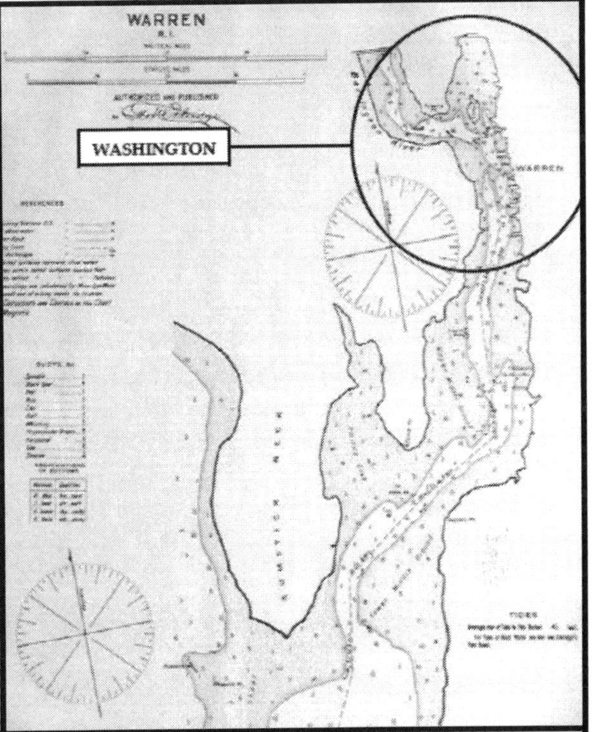

The **WASHINGTON** started out as an armed row galley as in the drawing above but in later years, after this event, was altered to a schooner rig. Such an alteration, although not common, was not unheard of in this period.

The Vessel

Type: Galley
Construction: Wood
Use: Warship
Launched: Providence, RI in 1776
Nationality: American
Home Port: Providence, RI

The Event

Owner: Continental Navy
Date of Incident: April 2, 1777
Disaster Type: Burned & sunk
Cause: Explosion
Status: Rebuilt
Location: At Warren

Narrative

Like most early historical events, the story of this disaster came from research into multiple sources of information, most of which at least agree on the basic details. In this case, the local newspapers supplied the first clue.

Providence Gazette and Country Journal - April 5, 1777 P3

Wednesday last one of the gallies belonging to this state unfortunately blew up near Bristol, by which accident eight men were killed.

The next source of information is the "History of Newport County, Rhode Island 1638-1887" by Richard M. Bayles where the following note was found, *"On the 2nd of April the row galley **WASHINGTON** blew up near Bristol and eight men perished."*

From "Ships and Shipmasters of Old Providence" the following details were found in a biographical sketch of Joseph Carlo Mauran, "... *The earliest mention of his activities is in the*

WASHINGTON

*Providence Gazette of May 10, 1777, when it is noted that Commodore Sir Peter Barker sends word from Chatham of the activities of various ships commanded by Esek Hopkins. Captain Mauran was then the commander of the ship BLAIZE CASTLE, and the following July was given the command of the armed galley **WASHINGTON** carrying ten four-pounders, fourteen swivel guns, and eighty men. A year later the vessel was destroyed by the British at Warren, and Captain Mauran, though dismissed from the service, was recommended as a good and faithful sea officer to all ye friends of ye American states. He was exonerated of all blame for the ravage of Warren by the Brit*

The final source of information concerning this incident is "The History of Warren, Rhode Island In the War of the Revolution" where the following information was discovered, "*At a later date* [after December 2, 1776] *a guard of sixteen men was stationed at Warren, and the row-galley **WASHINGTON** was sent to protect the entrances to Warren and Kickemuit Rivers. On the 2nd of April, 1777, an explosion occurred on board the galley by which eight lives were destroyed. The vessel was, however, afterward repaired, schooner rigged, and put in service again. The bodies of the unfortunate victims of this accident were buried on the west shore of Kickemuit river near the "narrows" of the stream, not far from the scene of the disaster"*.

Research Sources

1. Providence Gazette and Country Journal, April 5, 1777 P3
2. "Records of the State of Rhode Island and Providence Plantations Vol. VIII" by John Russell Bartlett (1863)
3. "History of Newport County, Rhode Island, 1638-1887" by Richard M. Bayles (1888)
4. "The History of Warren, Rhode Island In the War of the Revolution, 1776-1783" by Virginia Baker (no date)
5. "Ships and Shipmasters of Old Providence" (1919)

HAMPDEN

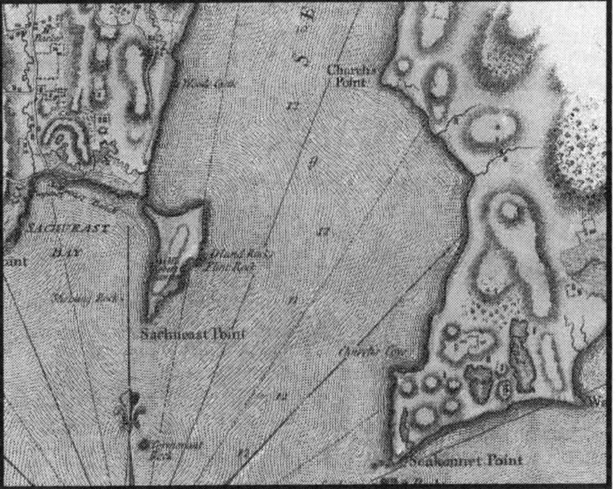

The Vessel

Type: Brig
Construction: Wood
Use: Privateer
Nationality: American
Official No.: N/A
Home Port: Providence, RI
Port of Departure: Providence, RI
Port of Destination: cruise to capture vessels

The Event

Master: probably Ezekiel Burroughs
Date of Incident: August 27, 1777
Disaster Type: Attacked
Cause: War
Status: Escaped
Location: Sailed down the Sakonnet River in company with Ship Oliver Cromwell; escaped to sea during the engagement

Narrative

The story of the brig **HAMPDEN** is directly intertwined with the Ship OLIVER CROMWELL. On August 27, 1777 the two vessels, in company, passed through the narrows at the head of the Sakonnet River bound for the ocean to cruise in search of enemy vessels to capture. Between them and open water there were a number of British vessels to be passed and, in typical Rhode Island privateer fashion, the plan was to sneak by them at night. They knew that the greatest threat would come from the British Sloop KINGSFISHER which lay at her station off Fogland Ferry, in the upper part of the river. The plan did not work out so well for the Americans but fortunately for the **HAMPDEN**, the enemy's attention went to the OLIVER CROMWELL which was intentionally put ashore by her crew when, according to the British version, they should have been more than a match for the KINGSFISHER. Regardless of that assessment, the master and crew of the **HAMPDEN** took the opportunity to leave the area with great dispatch and lived to continue in her privateering ways for some time.

Research Sources

1. "Newport Harbor and Lower Narragansett Bay, R.I. During the American Revolution" by Elizabeth Covell (1933)
2. American War of Independence At Sea (www.awiatsea.com)
3. "American Privateer ship Oliver Cromwell (1776) from http://threedecks.org

OLIVER CROMWELL

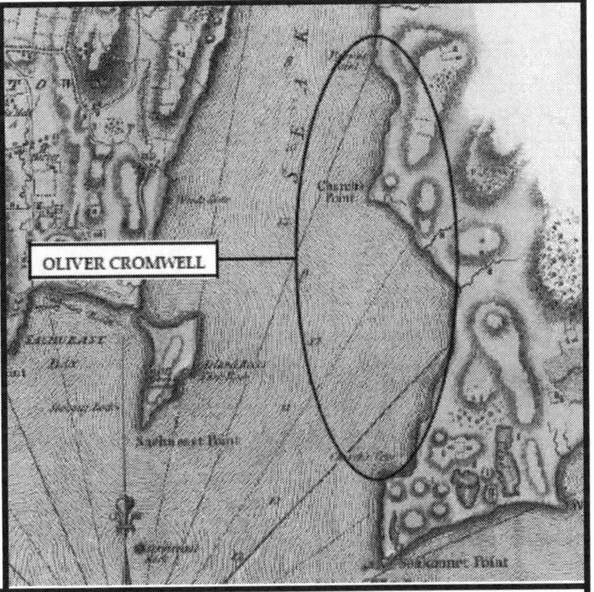

The Vessel

Type: Ship
Construction: Wood
Use: Privateer
Tonnage: 160
Launched: Taunton River, MA in 1776
Owner: Nicholas Brown & William Russell
Nationality: American
Home Port: Providence, RI

Final Voyage

Port of Departure: Providence, RI
Port of Destination: cruise to capture vessels
Master: Samuel Chase, Jr.
Date of Loss: August 27, 1777
Disaster Type: Ashore & burned
Cause: War Loss
Final Status: Total loss
Location: North of Sakonnet Point

Narrative

During the Revolutionary War years in Rhode Island, numerous vessels were launched for the purpose of privateering, that is, to search out and capture or destroy enemy vessels. Although these vessels did not formally belong to a navy, they served the purpose for which they were used. One of these, the ship **OLIVER CROMWELL** had a very short career marked by a fiery end. In Bayles, "History of Newport County, Rhode Island, 1638-1887" the author references this event as follows, *"On the 2d of September a new privateer of 20 guns, from Providence, attempting to run the blockade, was chased ashore by the British vessels and burned".*

Further research brought the full story to light in a website which deals exclusively with the American war of independence and the actions at sea. The story reads as follows, *Rhode Island Privateer Ship* ***OLIVER CROMWELL*** *was commissioned under Commander Samuel Chace, Jr. on 21 November 1776. She seems to have been a new ship, of about 160 tons, and was fitting out up the Taunton River when the British invaded Rhode Island in December 1776 and occupied Newport.* ***OLIVER CROMWELL*** *was recommissioned on 4 August 1777, again under Chace (now spelled Chase).* ***OLIVER CROMWELL*** *was a new vessel and "well fitted", armed with twenty 6-pounders on the gun deck, two 3-pounders on the quarterdeck and carried sixteen swivel guns. Although she was designed to carry between 190 and 200 men as her regular crew, she had only twenty-three men aboard on the night of 26 August. The* ***OLIVER CROMWELL*** *and the Continental Navy Brigantine HAMPDEN both attempted to break*

OLIVER CROMWELL

out past the British blockade in Narragansett Bay on the morning of 27 August. It was a very dark nighwith a heavy fog. The chosen route was out of the Taunton River and down the Sakonnet River, guarded only by HM Sloop KINGFISHER (Commander Alexander Graeme). At 0400 the British battery at Fogland Ferry discerned a brig passing by. She was almost past the battery before any shots were fired. The gunners managed to fire at her twice before she made off. The gunfire awakened the sleeping KINGFISHER, which discovered a large ship near her, with a full press of sail set. KINGFISHER slipped her anchor and got under way, firing her bow chaser at the **OLIVER CROMWELL**. *Chace, with no men to fight back, altered course and ran the ship hard ashore to the north of Sakonnet Point. KINGFISHER hustled up and anchored nearby. KINGFISHER then began firing into the ship which forced the Americans to abandon the ship and row ashore in their boats.*

KINGFISHER sent her boats to the **OLIVER CROMWELL**. *Ashore the American crew rallied and kept up a "continual" but ineffective fire on the British boarding party. The British intended to refloat the ship. However, it was ebb tide, she was driven ashore and all her sail was set. The boarding party found a light burning in the light room of the magazine. Unable to float their prize, the British set her on fire and she blew up about 0500. Not a single shot had been fired from the* **OLIVER CROMWELL**. *The fight with the* **OLIVER CROMWELL** *effectively covered the HAMPDEN, which got away.*

Research Sources

1. "History of Newport County, Rhode Island, 1638-1887" by Richard M. Bayles (1888)
2. American War of Independence At Sea (www.awiatsea.com)
3. "American Privateer ship Oliver Cromwell (1776) from http://threedecks.org

UNIDENTIFIED

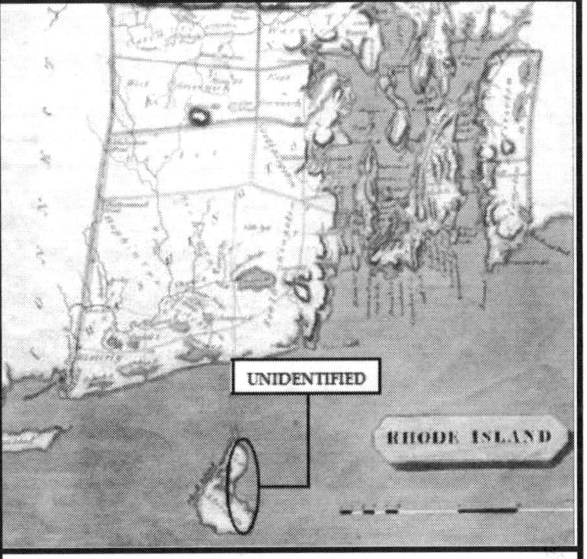

The Vessel

Type: Schooner
Construction: Wood
Use: Merchant
Nationality: American
Official No.: N/A
Port of Departure: West Indies
Port of Destination: New London, CT

Final Voyage

Cargo: rum, sugar and "warlike stores"
Date of Loss: September 1, 1777
Disaster Type: Ashore & burned
Cause: War
Final Status: Total loss
Location: Probably on the eastern beach at Block Island

Narrative

During the years of the occupation of Newport by British forces, numerous warships patrolled waters all along the eastern seaboard but from Rhode Island spent most of their time between New York and Nova Scotia. The HMS CERBERUS was one of those British vessels that sailed the waters off Rhode Island and made several captures. The following is an excerpt from the log of the CERBERUS relative to the capture and destruction of a coastal merchant vessel. *September, 1777, Monday 1 - Block Island 4 Lgs* [4 leagues] *at 6 AM saw a sloop off Montauk, weighed and gave chace* [chase]. *Moderate breezes and fresh winds [PM] at 2, Gay Head [Martha's Vineyard} north northeast 5 Lgs; at 4 run the chace on shore, who proved to be a schooner loaded with rum, sugar & warlike stores; anchored within gunshot of her & kept a constant fire upon a body of armed men lurking about the beach while our boats went and burned the vessel; had 1 man killed and 1 wounded. ½ past 6 weighed and came to sail.*

"Naval Documents of the American Revolution"

A project of epic proportions, the compilation of primary source information relative to the navy during the American Revolution was undertaken by the Secretary of the Navy's Advisory Committee on Naval History. The idea of the project had been envisioned for years but various other commitments stood between the concept and the physical creation of the reference. As luck would have it, though it would be years before the physical preparation of materials would begin, the collection of data from sources all across the United States and Europe continued and

UNIDENTIFIED

the amount of primary source material continued to grow over the years. Finally, in 1964, the first of what has been predicted to be a 15-volume set went to press. Since then, there have been a total of eleven volumes published, Number 11 arriving in 2005. Each volume ranges from just over 1,100 pages of documentary material to more than 1,600 pages. To date, the eleven published volumes cover the period from December 1, 1774 to March 31, 1778 with more to come. Primary source materials which have been selected for publication include letters, log book excerpts, newspaper articles, written assignments to various naval officers, etc., and this material comes from both parties to the conflict presenting the researcher with the opportunity to see an event or events from more than a single perspective. The information is well organized chronologically for ease of understanding and sources are very well documented. This is, without a doubt, one of the most comprehensive collections of information from the period for the specific subject material.

Research Sources

1. "Naval Documents of the American Revolution", Vol. 9 (1986)

ADMIRAL PARKER

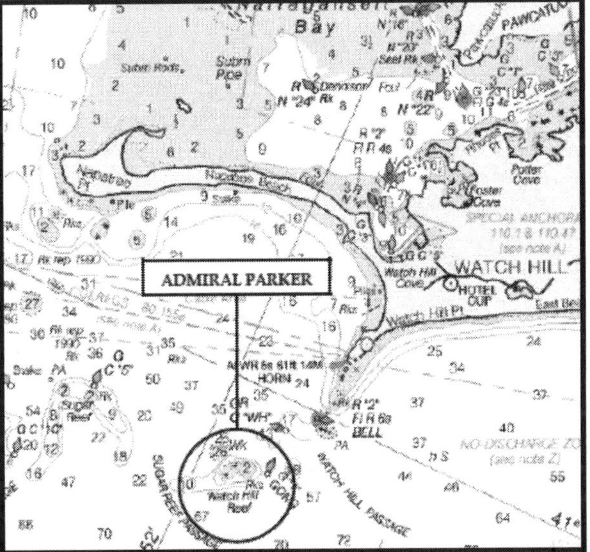

The Vessel

Type: Schooner
Construction: Wood
Use: Tender
Owner: British Navy
Nationality: British
Port of Departure: Gardiner's Island, NY
Port of Destination: Newport, RI

Final Voyage

Master: Lt. Deane
Cargo: N/A
Date of Loss: September 22, 1777
Disaster Type: Ashore & burned
Cause: Pilot error
Final Status: Total loss
Location: On Watch Hill Reef

Narrative

New London Gazette - September 26, 1777 P2

Last Monday a fleet of twenty-one sail of shipping came out of Gardiner's Bay and went down the Sound, bound to Newport, among which was 7 or 8 ships. The same day, a ship, burthen about 200 tons, prize to Capt. Conklin, arrived at Stonington; one was from the Bay of Honduras, bound to England… About an hour after the above prize came to anchor, Capt. Conklin (who was bound in) was chased by a man-of-war, and a schooner of 12 guns, belonging to the above fleet; when the latter, endeavouring to take a short course, and cut off Capt. Conklin from the land, ran on Watch Hill Reef, at about a mile distant from Capt. Conklin, who came to anchor within Watch Point; a brisk fire was kept up between the two vessels, for several hours; the man-of-war came to anchor just without the schooner, in order to protect her from Capt. Conklin. The schooner remained in this situation until the next morning, when her people set her on fire in the hold, and were directly taken off in the man-of-war's boat. Several articles were brought out of her by a boat that went on board after she was quitted by her people; but the boat tarried only a few minutes, and immediately after they left her, the magazine taking fire, she blew up. Her guns, it is said, will all be saved. One man was found dead by the side of the vessel. Captain Conklin received no damage.

Providence Gazette and Country Journal - September 27, 1777 P3

Monday afternoon a British frigate and a schooner of 14 guns, chased a small privateer sloop in the Western Sound; the privateer outsailed them, and came to anchor near Watch Hill, in this state, when the

ADMIRAL PARKER

schooner attempting to approach her, ran on a reef of rocks at high water, where it is supposed she bilged; She was briskly fired on from some cannon on the shore and hulled several times; when the hands quitted the deck, and retreated into the hold. The frigate, which lay off and on, but dared not approach very near, sent her boats in the night, took off the men and burnt the vessel.

New London Gazette - October 3, 1777 P3

All the guns which belonged to the schooner mentioned in our last to be burnt at Watch Hill Reef, are saved, together with her anchors, a number of neat small arms, &c.

Although the newspaper accounts and most records of British warships of the era do not list this vessel by name, an Internet site called "American War of Independence at Sea" names the schooner to be the **ADMIRAL PARKER**.

Research Sources

1. New London Gazette, September 26, 1777 P2
2. Providence Gazette and Country Journal, September 27, 1777 P3
3. New Haven Journal, October 1, 1777 P3
4. New London Gazette, October 3, 1777 P3
5. Boston Independent Chronicle and Universal Advertiser, October 9, 1777 P2
6. American War of Independence at Sea (Internet site)

HMS SYREN

Pictured is the British 6th rate frigate HMS ACTIVE of the same size as the **HMS SYREN** lost on Point Judith.

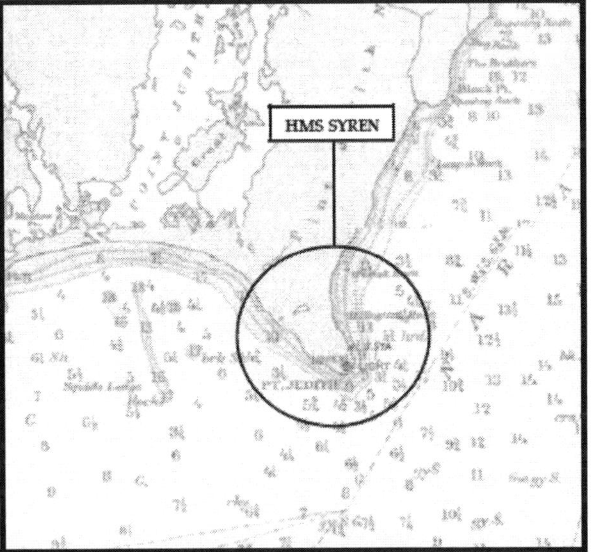

The Vessel

Type: 6th Rate Frigate
Construction: Wood
Use: Warship
Dimensions: 120′ x 33′ x 10′
Tonnage: 603
Launched: Chatham,, England in 1773
Owner: British Navy
Nationality: British

Final Voyage

Home Port: Newport, RI
Master: Tobias Furneaux
Date of Loss: November 6, 1777
Disaster Type: Stranding
Cause: Storm
Final Status: Blown up
Location: At or near Point Judith

Narrative

On July 29th, 1815 the following account appeared in the Newport Mercury. It speaks of the exploits of one Bailey Brooks, a deep-sea diver who spent much of the summer of that year retrieving items of interest from shipwrecks. This article speaks to the lost frigate **HMS SYREN**.

Newport Mercury - July 29, 1815 P3

Ship News

Arrived here on Saturday last, sloop MARY-ANN, Captain Jeffers, with the diving-bell, from Point Judith, having on board a quantity of iron knees, and an anchor weighing upwards of 3,000 wt. taken from the wreck of the British frigate ***SYREN****, sunk there during the Revolutionary War.*

In researching the loss of **HMS SYREN** the following account was found in the Rhode Island Historical Society Collections, Vol. XVII, No. 1, January, 1924. The article was written by William David Miller and entitled, "The Capture of His Majesty's Ship Syren":

During a gale on the morning of November 6, 1777, the British frigate ***SYREN****, sailing in company with ship SISTERS and the tender TWO MATES, was driven ashore near Point Judith and was captured by the battery of artillery stationed at that place assisted by members of the Second Regiment of the Kings County Militia under Col. Charles Dyre. The SISTERS and the TWO MATES shared a like fate although*

HMS SYREN

it appears that the SISTERS had been floated prior to her capture. The ***SYREN*** *was a frigate of twenty-eight guns and was manned by a crew of one hundred and sixty-six officers and men, her captain being Tobias Furneaux. No reference can be found to the details of the other two vessels. The following depositions, made by men called up shortly after the ships went aground, give an interesting account of the incident: "Edward Lock of South Kingston declareth, that on the sixth day of November A.D. 1777 in the morning of said day I marched complete in my arms to Point Judith Point, where lay two ships aground and a schooner afloat, & after a smart engagement I with others took said schooner, sometime after that ye same day, I saw at said Point Judith Pain Peckham and Martin Murphy and Jo. Pain with gun in his hand. We remained there with others till some time in ye evening of the same day till Colonel Charles Dyer appeared there & soon after he came, Col. Sands and Captain Samuel Potter told us as we and our guns were wet, we had better go from said point & dry ourselves & guns & refresh ourselves & return as soon as we could conveniently – agreeable to said directions we left said point, dry'd ourselves & guns & refreshed ourselves & myself & said Jn. Pain Peckham returned to said point early next morning with our guns and I saw said Martin Murphy at said point said morning, & then we all went to work in helping ye prisoners on shore & in unloading said ships and worked their several days." ... The landing of the prisoners was completed without interruption and they were sent to Providence under escort, a small number being later transferred to Newport for exchange. On December 26, 1777, Captain Furneaux was granted a parole... The unloading of the supplies and gear took a longer time and in the meantime, word having been received by the British, four ships had been dispatched from Newport. Upon their arrival several boats were put off containing a demolition party. This party were successful in laying and firing charges on board the* ***SYREN****. A passage from the journal of Bartholomew James – later Rear Admiral – gives the following account of this action. "On the following day I brought her (the tender LADY PARKER) out of the harbor (Newport), and was directed to proceed to sea in her company with his Majesty's ships FLORA, LARK and PIGOT tender, and go to the assistance of the* ***SYREN*** *frigate, who with a transport, had run on shore at Point Judith, and whose people were made prisoners by the rebels. At ten o'clock in the night the two frigates anchored about two miles off the shore, and the rebels commenced a fire upon us from three eighteen pounders. Four boats were then manned and equipped with combustibles, under the first lieutenant of the CHATHAM, who was sent to command the second boat, the second lieutenant of the LARK the third, and myself the fourth. We left the ships at eleven o'clock and rowed towards the* ***SYREN****, amidst a heavy fire from the enemy of cannon and musketry and found a heavy sea running alongside of her, that her masts were made a stage to walk from the ship on shore, and that they had got out a quantity of her stores and provisions. In this situation we boarded her, and each of the officers, as directed by the admiral, carried his basket of combustibles into the ship and fired her in different places; though our retreat was necessarily so precipitate, that we were obliged to get into the first boat we could find and put off with all speed, as the fire had communicated to her guns, which were then going off both sides; and we completely destroyed her without any accident...*

Research Sources

1. Newport Mercury, July 29, 1815 P3
2. "History of the State of Rhode Island" by S.G. Arnold (1860)
3. "History of Newport County" by Richard M. Bayles (1888)
4. "Revolutionary Defenses in Rhode Island" by Edward Field (1898)
5. "The Capture of His Majesty's Ship Syren" by William David Miller (1924)
6. "Newport Harbor and Lower Narragansett Bay, Rhode Island During the Revolutionary
7. Way" by Mrs. Elizabeth Covell (1933)
8. "Shipwrecks of the Western Hemisphere" by Robert F. Marx (1971)
9. "Shipwrecks – An Encyclopedia of the World's Worst Disasters as Sea" by David Ritchie
10. "The Sailing Navy, 1775-1854 " by Paul H. Silverstone (2001)
11. "British Warships In The Age of Sail, 1714-1792" by Rif Wenfield (2007)

SISTERS

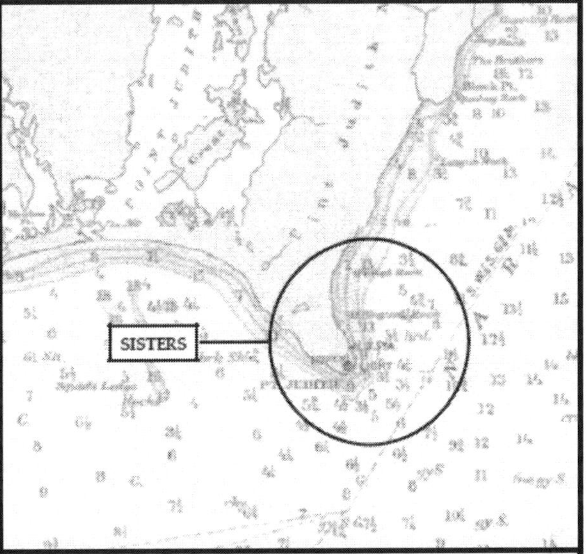

The Vessel

Type: Ship
Construction: Wood
Use: Transport
Owner: British Navy
Nationality: British

Final Voyage

Date of Loss: November 6, 1777
Disaster Type: Stranding
Cause: Pilot error or storm
Final Status: Total loss
Location: At or near Point Judith

Narrative

Details of the loss of the British transport ship **SISTERS** are somewhat lacking and come from a number of unusual sources. The first is a brief notation from the Frederick McKenzie diary as excerpted in a paper read before the Newport Historical Society in 1932 which, in part, reads, *"Nov. 7* [1777] *- The SYREN Frigate, a transport ship, and a schooner, were by mismanagement run ashore upon Point Judith. It was impossible (as our ships did not at once put out upon signals of distress), to rescue them. The Captain and crew of the SYREN were obliged to surrender to the Rebels. One of our own sloops rescued the people of the transport...".* The second source is a letter from one Pelham Winslow to Edward Winslow, Jr. written on December 2, 1777 and printed as part of the proceedings of the Massachusetts Historical Society in 1886. This letter reads, in part, *"Captain Ben Smith arrived here* [New York] *this day from Madeira; he touched at Newport ... and has wrote you by Mr. Sheaffe, who sailed in company with Captain Smith but is not yet arrived. ... Captain Smith further informs me that a few days before he sailed from Newport a flag of truce arrived from Providence, with forty or fifty sailors lately belonging to his Majesty's ship SYREN who, with a tender and a transport ship were sometime past drove ashore from Point Judith in a heavy gale of wind. The vessels were lost but the people got ashore and were made prisoners. ..."* The third and final source of this incident comes from an entry in "The Historical Magazine and Notes and Queries Concerning the Antiquities, History and Biography of America" published in New York in 1860. Under a date of December 7th is the following entry, *"At 2 o'clock this afternoon returned the two frigates who informed that the SYREN and the* ***SISTERS****, transport, with a schooner had run on shore at Point Judith, and all the men made prisoners."*

SISTERS

Research Sources

1. "Newport Harbor and Lower Narragansett Bay, Rhode Island During the American Revolution" by Mrs. Elizabeth Covell (published in the Bulletin of the Newport Historical Society, Number 86, January, 1933)
2. "Proceedings of the Massachusetts Historical Society, Vol. II—Second Series" (published by the society in 1886)
3. "The Historical Magazine and Notes and Queries Concerning the Antiquities, History and Biography of America" (published in New York in 1860)

TWO MATES

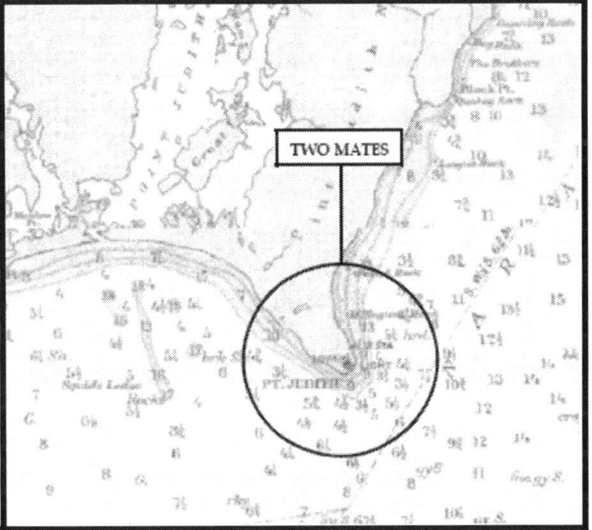

The Vessel

Type: Schooner
Construction: Wood
Use: Transport?
Owner: British Navy
Nationality: British

Final Voyage

Date of Loss: November 6, 1777
Disaster Type: Stranding
Cause: Pilot error
Final Status: Some salvage
Location: At or near Point Judith

Narrative

Searching for information on maritime incidents in the earliest years is a most challenging task. In the 1860's the Rhode Island Secretary of State, John Russell Bartlett, compiled information concerning political events that took place during the one hundred and fifty year period from 1636 to 1792. This was published as "Records of the State of Rhode Island and Providence Plantations in New England" and filled ten volumes. Within these volumes there are several references that support the story of the loss of the schooner **TWO MATES** which went ashore along with the HMS SYREN and the transport ship SISTERS in early November of 1777. Apparently the involvement of the state had to do with money that was not paid to those who were involved with the salvage efforts and subsequently made sale of their "booty" to other parties. In part the records read as follows:

Whereas, the prize ships SYREN and SISTERS; and the prize schooner ***TWO MATES****, together with their guns, stores, cargoes and appurtenances, which were captured in this state, have been mostly sold by the captors, who are not empowered by law to call special courts, in order to collect from the purchasers the moneys due on sales of the said prizes; and the said moneys remain in the hands of said purchasers and the captors, and the costs and charges of the trial and condemnation of the said prizes, and the other expenses thereof, remain unpaid; and as no distribution can be made among the said captors until said moneys be collected, be it therefore enacted by this General Assembly, and by the authority thereof it is enacted, that all the accounts of the sales of the said prizes, or authentic copies of said accounts, be immediately delivered to the sheriff of the county of Kings, by the person or persons who are possessed of the same. ...* Each of the persons referenced to as captors or purchasers was to be required to take the following oath, *"You ... do solemnly swear that you have not, by any ways or means whatsoever, directly or indirectly, by yourself, or by any person or persons, for, by or under you, taken, secreted, concealed or embezzled, any*

TWO MATES

article or articles of the goods, effects or things of any kind whatsoever, whichever belonged to the prize ship SYREN, or the prize ship SISTERS, or the prize schooner **TWO MATES**, *or to the stores, tackle, furniture, cargo or appurtenances of either of the said vessels, which were lately taken near the shore of Point Judith; and that if you know of any person or persons, who have taken, secreted, concealed or embezzled, any of the aforesaid goods or effects, you will give information to the sheriff of Kings county, or to the agent or agents of the captors, of all you know, and of all you have been informed of, by any other person or persons, relating to such concealment.*

That this was an important issue to the state is supported by subsequent action taken by the General Assembly whereby one Beriah Brown was appointed to collect the moneys due from the several persons who purchased any of the effects from the vessels. Ultimately it was discovered that the purchasers of the materials from these three vessels were named Broome and Babcock. The final act to this story is documented as follows: *... the said Messrs. Broome and Babcock are willing to pay the same* [moneys due from the sale] *unto Peter Phillips, Esq., one of the agents for the captors, provided they could do the same without being guilty of a breach of the aforesaid act, empowering the said Beriah Brown to collect the moneys aforesaid.*

There can be no doubt that the vessels did, in fact, run ashore on Point Judith and they were at least partially stripped of the salvageable materials from all three. Whether or not the hulls of these vessels were left to be destroyed by the elements or were pulled off the rocks at Point Judith is not clearly stated but further word of them beyond their capture and condemnation as war prizes has not surfaced within the records of the day.

Research Sources

1. "Records of the State of Rhode Island and Providence Plantations in New England", Volume VIII (edited by John Russell Bartlett and printed by the order of the General Assembly)
2. "Newport Harbor and Lower Narragansett Bay During the American Revolution" by Mrs. Elizabeth Covell (a paper read before the Newport Historical Society, Nov. 21, 1932)

HMS TRITON

The Coventry class ACTIVE (pictured) was just a bit smaller than the modified Mermaid class ship **HMS TRITON**.

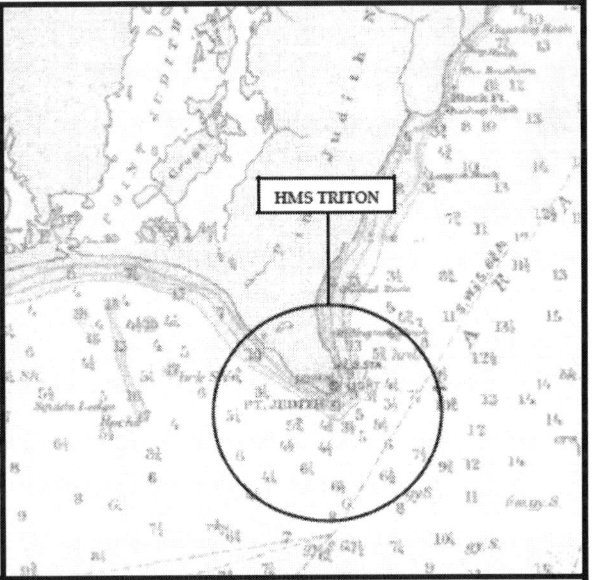

The Vessel

Type: 6th rate Ship
Construction: Wood
Use: Transport
Dimensions: 124′ x 33′ x 11′
Tonnage: 620
Launched: Bucklers Hard, England in 1773
Owner: British Navy
Nationality: British

The Event

Master: Skeffington Ludwidge
Cargo: Unknown
Date of Incident: November 10, 1777
Disaster Type: Stranding
Cause: Unknown
Status: Probably got off
Location: Near Point Judith

Narrative

On November 6, 1777 an incident occurred at Point Judith by which three British vessels, two ships and a schooner, ran ashore at Point Judith. The ships were lost but it was hoped that the schooner would come off. These vessels, the HMS SYREN, SISTERS and TWO MATES (see separate data sheet for each) were, in fact, all lost near the point. In researching this incident, information has been found indicating that there was yet another transport vessel which got ashore in the vicinity just a few days later, the **HMS TRITON**. Information concerning this vessel and event has been much more difficult to come by, perhaps because of the great deal of attention given to the HMS SYREN which was reported as the leading ship of the convoy traveling from Newport to Long Island, New York at the time of the disaster on the 6th.

Research into the vessel indicates that there was a 6th rate ship named **HMS TRITON** and she was in American waters at the time of this incident. In "British Warships In the Age of Sail, 1714-1792" by Rif Winfield, the TRITON left England, bound for North America in March of 1776. She is said to have been in the St. Lawrence (Canada) from sometime in 1777 to 1778. This generalized timeline leaves room for a stranding in the vicinity of Point Judith to have taken place and if this was, as could be supposed, a non-fatal or even minor stranding, that could be the reason that so little attention was paid to the event, but it would be surprising, to say the least, that there would not be at least a log entry indicating the incident to a ship of this size.

HMS TRITON

Research Sources

1. Providence Gazette and Country Journal, November 15, 1777 P3
2. "Shipwrecks in the Americas" by Robert Marx (1987)
3. "Shipwrecks—An Encyclopedia of the World's Worst Disasters at Sea" by David Ritchie
4. "British Warships In the Age of Sail, 1714-1792" by Rif Winfield (2007)

SALLY

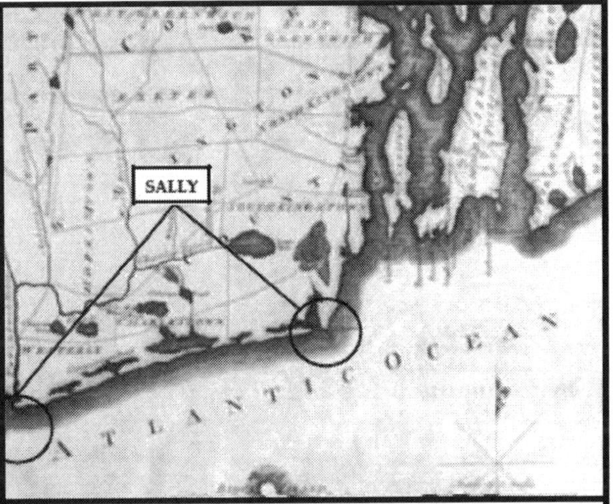

The Vessel

Type: Brig
Construction: Wood
Use: Merchant
Tonnage: 50
Launched: Providence, RI in 1770
Owner: Benjamin Bowers
Nationality: American
Home Port: Bristol, RI

Final Voyage

Master: John Voce
Cargo: Unknown
Date of Loss: January 12, 1778
Disaster Type: Stranding
Cause: Chased ashore
Final Status: Total loss
Location: On Wicopesset Reef (off Watch Hill) or at Point Judith

The Mystery of Sally

The loss (or not) of the vessel **SALLY** provides a good example of the confusion of early records. The initial clue that there was an incident came from a snippet concerning a captain in the American Continental Navy named Daniel Aborn. Aborn was reported to have been master of a sloop named **SALLY** reported as chased ashore by the British warship HMS UNICORN on January 12, 1778. Local customhouse records revealed that there was, indeed, a sloop of this name from Providence under the command of a Daniel Aborn. However, in the newspapers of the time, the following conflicting information was found.

New London Gazette - January 16, 1778 P2

New London, January 16.

... *Sabbath evening* [the 11th] *a brig from Providence, bound to this port, was drove on Wicopesset Reef by two British ships, who hulled her 16 times, and fired a great number of shot through her rigging but the brig soon after got off and put into Stonington.*

A few weeks later the following notice of a public auction appeared in a New York newspaper.

New York Gazette and Weekly Mercury - February 2, 1778 P3

PUBLICK AUCTION

... *One 10 inch cable, 60 or 70 fathom, half worn; the lower mast and one top mast, laying on the beach at Jerusalem South, Long Island* [an error in location as Jerusalem is immediately to the west of Point Judith on the coast of Rhode Island]; *also, what other part of the Brig* ***SALLY****, that can be found.*

SALLY

So the questions are, what was the vessel's rig, where did this incident actually take place, and what was the outcome? Probably the only facts which are agreed upon are the date of the incident, the cause of the event (that she was driven ashore due to enemy activity) and the name of the vessel. The custom house records show a 50-ton brigantine named **SALLY** that was registered in Bristol, Rhode Island at this time but not after January of this year and a 20-ton sloop of the same name registered in Providence. There is no confusing one rig for the other in terms of the number of masts and rigging configuration. Perhaps somewhere in the corner of an old attic or basement or in correspondence from an early ancestor, the details of the event are hidden and will someday be revealed to bring this mystery to a conclusion.

Research Sources

1. New London Gazette, January 16, 1778 P2
2. New York Gazette and Weekly Mercury, February 2, 1778 P3
3. "American War of Independence - At Sea" (concerning Daniel Aborn)
4. Providence Custom House records

UNIDENTIFIED

A facsimile of the US Continental sloop PROVIDENCE circa 1776.

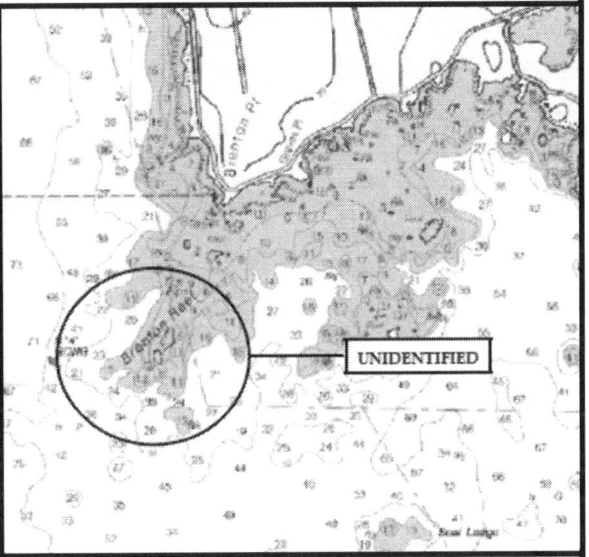

The Vessel

Type: Sloop
Construction: Wood
Use: Merchant
Nationality: American
Port of Departure: Surinam, South America
Port of Destination: New London, CT

The Event

Cargo: molasses, coffee and sail cloth
Date of Incident: January 17, 1778
Disaster Type: Stranding
Cause: Unknown
Status: Probably got off
Location: Brenton Reef

Narrative

In the ninety-eighth bulletin of the Newport Historical Society (1933), Mrs. Elizabeth Covell published a paper entitled "Newport Harbor and Lower Narragansett Bay, Rhode Island During the American Revolution". This paper is based on the diary of a British officer named Frederick McKenzie who was stationed in Newport during most of the city's occupation by the British and has offered perhaps the best record of events which survived that period. For January 18, 1778 he noted the following:

Last night a rebel sloop came ashore on Brenton's Reef. She was from Surinam for New London, laden with molasses, coffee and sail cloth. Our troops were sent out and secured her crew of eight, and took possession of her. Lord Howe signified that this sloop was Genl Pigot's property, as Lord of the Manor. 'Tis supposed she will prove worth £800 or £1000.

Research Sources

1. "Newport Harbor and Lower Narragansett Bay, Rhode Island During the American Revolution" by Elizabeth Covell (1933)

COLUMBUS

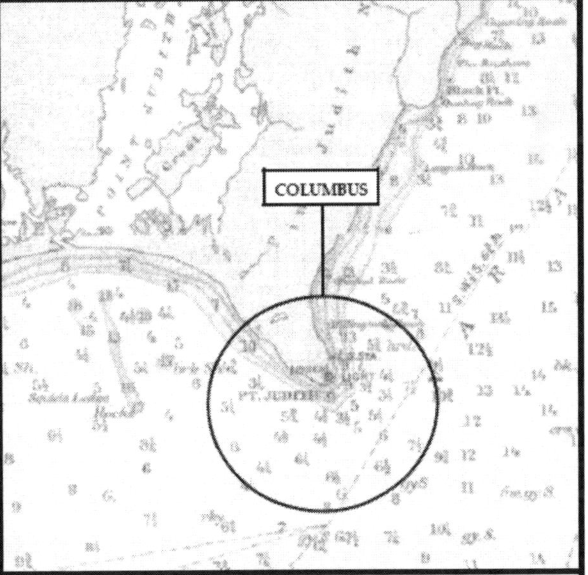

The Vessel

Type: Frigate
Construction: Wood
Use: Warship
Tonnage: 200
Launched: Philadelphia, PA in 1774
Owner: US Continental Navy
Nationality: American
Home Port: Providence, RI

Final Voyage

Port of Departure: Providence, RI
Master: Hoysted Hacker
Date of Loss: March 28, 1778
Disaster Type: Ashore & burned
Cause: War
Final Status: Total loss
Location: At Point Judith

Narrative

On November 21, 1932, Mrs. Elizabeth Covell presented a paper to the Newport Historical Society entitled, "Newport Harbor and Lower Narragansett Bay, Rhode Island During the American Revolution". In part, this paper was based on information from the diary of a British officer named Frederick McKenzie who was stationed in Newport during its occupation. The following information is an excerpt from this paper, "*Mar. 24 [1778] - Lord Howe, in the EAGLE of 64 guns, sailed out of the harbour today for the Delaware; on the 28th the fleet will sail for Philadelphia. On the 28th the LARK Frigate, stationed off Greenwich, perceived a vessel coming down, and made the signal whereupon the MAIDSTONE and SPHYNX put to sea to intercept her; the rebel vessel came past the SOMERSET lying in the Narragansett Passage, who gave her many shot; outside the two frigates were ready for her so she was obliged to run on shore within Point Judith. The wind dying down, our ships were not able to approach, so the rebels were able to get out her stores, and bring some guns to protect her. As the wind came in the afternoon, the frigates worked up and burned her. She proved to be the* ***COLUMBUS****, a Continental Frigate of 36 guns. The rebels saved all the powder on board, but the ship was entirely destroyed.*

In the book, "History of Newport County, Rhode Island 1638-1887" by Richard M. Bayles, the following confirming information is found, "... *On the 16th of February [1778], the frigate WARREN, Captain John B. Hopkins, taking advantage of a snowstorm, ran the blockade of the British*

COLUMBUS

Squadron, giving and taking fire as she passed and got safely out to sea. The frigate ***COLUMBUS*** *made a similar attempt on the 27th of March, but was unable to get through and, driven ashore at Point Judith, was burned by the British the next day.*

At least one other source repeats this story again, but it is possible that it was based on one of these earlier accounts. With early reference materials, it was not unusual for information to be copied repeatedly from a single source. The most credible source for information on events of this type during the Revolutionary period is the McKenzie Diary information.

Research Sources

1. "Newport Harbor and Lower Narragansett Bay Rhode Island During the American Revolution," by Elizabeth Covell (Bulletin of the Newport Historical Society, Number Eighty-Six, January, 1933)
2. "History of Newport County, Rhode Island 1638-1887," by Richard M. Bayles, 1888
3. "History of the State of Rhode Island and Providence Plantations, Vol. II, 1700-1790" by Samuel Greene Arnold, 1860
4. Dictionary of American Naval Fighting Ships

UNIDENTIFIED

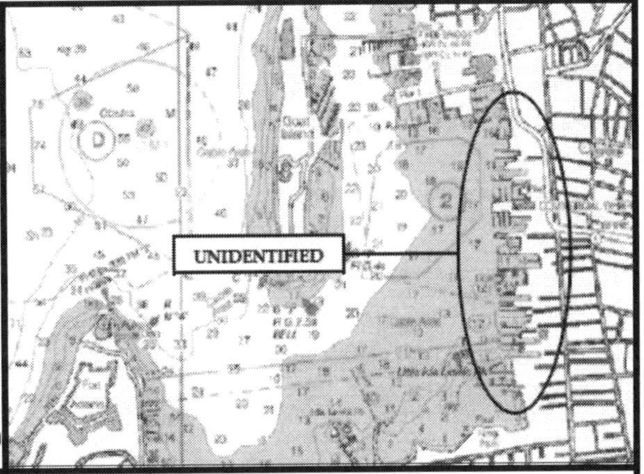

The Vessel

Type: Schooner
Construction: Wood
Use: Tender
Owner: British Navy
Nationality: British
Home Port: Newport, RI

Final Voyage

Port of Departure: Newport, RI
Date of Loss: April 30, 1778
Disaster Type: Sunk
Cause: Result of leaks from battle
Final Status: Probably raised
Location: At an unspecified wharf in Newport

Narrative

Though the British occupied Newport for a number of years during the Revolution and did their best to control shipping to and from Narragansett Bay by the Americans, the fact is that vessels did manage to sneak in and out with some degree of frequency. This was the scenario that took place at the end of April, 1778 when the armed frigate PROVIDENCE ran the British blockade outbound to Europe. In the "History of Newport County, Rhode Island, 1638-1887" by Richard M. Bayles is the following reference, " *On the night of the 30th Captain Abraham Whipple took out the frigate PROVIDENCE in the dark and a heavy storm, and ran the blockade of the British squadron, firing his broadsides as he passed and sinking one of the tenders. He carried dispatches to France and returned safely to Boston.*"

Providence Gazette and Country Journal - May 2, 1778 P3

PROVIDENCE, May 2

Thursday evening the PROVIDENCE frigate, in the service of the United States, Abraham Whipple, Esq., Commander , sailed from this port on a cruize.

Providence Gazette and Country Journal - May 9, 1778 P2

Captain Whipple in the PROVIDENCE frigate, who sailed from this port last week, in his passage down the bay was fired upon by the LARK frigate, which lay near Warwick Neck, and had got under way; Capt. Whipple returned the compliment with a broadside, and we since learned killed 3 and wounded 17 of the LARK's crew; her hull and rigging were likewise much damaged. The JUNO frigate, the lowermost of the enemy's ships, fired a broadside at the PROVIDENCE as she passed, and received another, but with what effect we have not yet learnt. Capt. Whipple likewise poured a broadside into a tender that got under sail, and shattered her so much that the enemy were obliged to haul her to a wharf at Newport, where she sunk. The enemy's ships did not follow Captain Whipple to sea, as was reported.

UNIDENTIFIED

Research Sources

1. Providence Gazette & Country Journal, May 2, 1778 P3
2. Providence Gazette & Country Journal, May 9, 1778 P2
3. "History of Newport County, Rhode Island, 1638-1887" by Richard M. Bayles (1888)

ATTACK ON WARREN

Vessels Involved

UNIDENTIFIED - A vessel identified only as a small American privateer was set fire during the attack by British forces in the Warren River, but the local inhabitants managed to put the fire out before much damage had been done

UNIDENTIFIED - Two vessels identified only as guindalos [they may have meant galleys] were destroyed in the Warren River (or at the village of Kickemuit) during the attack

UNIDENTIFIED - A large number of flat bottom boats (one estimate was that there were 125 boats involved) were destroyed by British
forces in the Warren River (or at the village of Kickemuit) during the attack

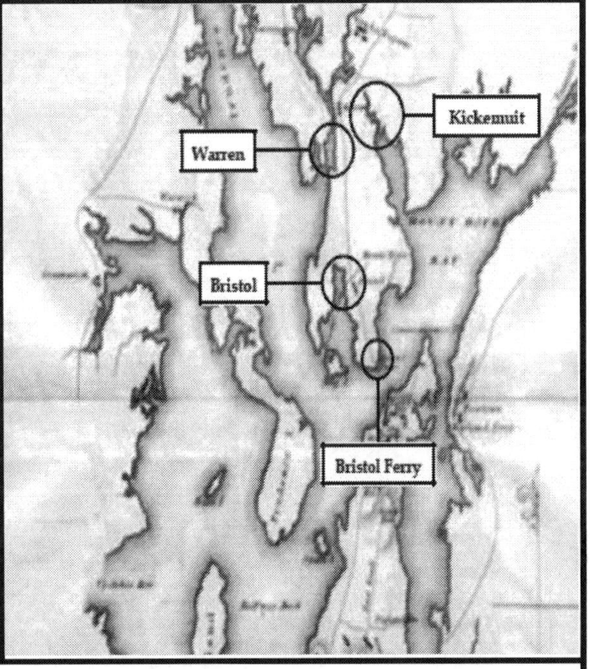

The British Attack Warren

In the late spring of 1778, British forces occupying Narragansett Bay heard rumors of a planned assault on Aquidneck Island (then referred to as Rhode Island) and decided to send a fleet of small boats with troops to deny the rebels the opportunity. One of the closest points to the island was at Bristol Neck just a short distance from the Portsmouth shore. On the neck are the towns of Bristol and Warren and the village of Kickamuit. The town of Warren became the focal point for an expedition whose goal was to ensure that there would be no assault. Newspaper accounts reported conflicting details in very general terms.

Providence Gazette and Country Journal - May 30, 1778 P3

... Sunday night last some of the enemy's shipping came up the bay from Rhode Island undiscovered; in the morning, at day-break, they landed about 500 men between the towns of Bristol and Warren, and marched immediately through Warren to Kickemuit, where a number of flat bottomed boats and a galley were repairing, which they burnt, together with a corn mill, then returning to Warren, they entered several houses, greatly insulting the inhabitants, most of which they plundered of clothing, bedding, furniture, &c. They afterwards set fire to the Meeting House, Parsonage, and several other houses, which were consumed, and a small magazine of military stores destroyed; they also set fire to a new privateer sloop in the harbor, but the flames were extinguished before she was much damaged. They then began their retreat by the road leading to Bristol, which they entered, burning, plundering and destroying whatever their haste would permit, not sparing the Episcopal Church. ... Intelligence of their descent arrived here about eight o'clock in the morning, when the inhabitants turned out with great spirit, and by orders marched straight towards Bristol. Col. Barton, by direction from the Hon. General Sullivan, went forward to rally the scattered inhabitants, and hang upon the enemy's rear to give time, if possible, for the main body to come up. He collected about 20 men and pursued the enemy toward Bristol Ferry, near which he came up with and attacked the rear with great bravery, until badly wounded by a musket ball he was obliged to retire from the field. The enemy's boats arrived in time to embark them, before it was possible for General Sullivan, with the troops, to get up. Had they remained an hour longer in the town, their retreat would have been effectually cut off.

ATTACK ON WARREN

Boston Gazette and Country Journal - June 1, 1778 P4

... Early on Monday morning last a detachment of the enemy, from Rhode Island, landed at Warren, where, after destroying two houses, a number of boats, two guindalos & a small privateer, they proceeded to Bristol, burnt the church, and several houses, took a Col. and a party of men posted there, and made a precipitate retreat to the island. The militia of the adjacent towns mustered but were too late to check them.

Two non-newspaper accounts of this attack are of interest. The first is from the American perspective and is taken from the "History of Newport County, Rhode Island, 1638-1887".

... On the night of Sunday, the 25th of May, General Pigot sent a fleet of small vessels up the bay from the Newport anchorage to break up the preparations which were making for a descent on the island. Six hundred men were embarked under command of Lieutenant Colonel Campbell, and landed at day-break between the towns of Bristol and Warren. They marched at once through Warren to Kickemut River, where they burned a number of flat bottomed boats and a galley, which were being repaired. On their return through Warren they entered the houses, plundered the inmates of clothing, bedding and furniture, and then set fire to the Meeting House, parsonage and other houses and destroyed a magazine of military stores. They also set fire to a new privateer sloop in the harbor, which was not, however, seriously injured. The other non-newspaper account of the attack presents the British perspective and is taken from the diary of Frederick McKenzie, a British officer who was stationed in Newport for most of the occupation and who kept a detailed diary of events. McKenzie wrote for May 25th, *About 500 men marched from Newport last night to Arnold's Point, (opposite Hog Island), and were embarked. They proceeded to the FLORA, which lay opposite, and from thence up the bay and round Papasquash Point, to the Warren River, where they landed, undiscovered., about half past three in the morning. They proceeded to Warren; at Kickemuit Bridge they found 125 boats, mostly large flat bottom; a sloop, a store house and a corn mill; all of which, together with some houses, the bridge and some gun carriages were burnt and totally destroyed. At Warren powder and other military stores were discovered in a house which was set fire to by which means the church and many houses were burnt. After this the troops returned by way of Bristol; as by now the alarm had become general, they were fired on from behind walls, trees and houses by about 300 rebels; notwithstanding which they entered Bristol, where military stores, the church and about 20 of the principal houses were burnt, and several guns destroyed. The troops re-embarked near Bristol; 69 prisoners were brought over with them from Windmill Hill, and marched from thence to Newport. The troops returned in the boats to Newport, where they landed about 4 in the afternoon. During the expedition about 40 cannon were destroyed. The destruction of the armed vessels and so many boats must undoubtedly prevent the rebels from making up an attempt on this island for a considerable time. Prisoners brought in belonging to a Col. Topham's Regiment stationed at Howland's Ferry say the people of the country are much alarmed and discontented; and that great blame is thrown on Genl. Sullivan for neglecting to place proper guards on their boats.*

Research Sources

1. Providence Gazette & Country Journal, May 3, 1778 P3
2. Boston Gazette & Country Journal, June 1, 1778 P4
3. Providence Gazette & Country Journal, June 13, 1778 P3
4. "History of Newport County, Rhode Island, 1638-1887" by Richard M. Bayles (1888)
5. "Newport Harbor and Lower Narragansett Bay, Rhode Island, During the American Revolution", by Mrs. Elizabeth Covell (1932)

ATTACK ON FALL RIVER

Vessels Involved

UNIDENTIFIED - Nine (9) large boats were captured and burned on the shore in the vicinity of Fall River, MA

UNIDENTIFIED - A British galley covering the retreat of the attacking force was driven ashore on Rhode Island (northern end of Portsmouth) and abandoned

UNIDENTIFIED - A British sloop covering the retreat of the attacking force was driven ashore on Rhode Island (northern end of Portsmouth) and abandoned

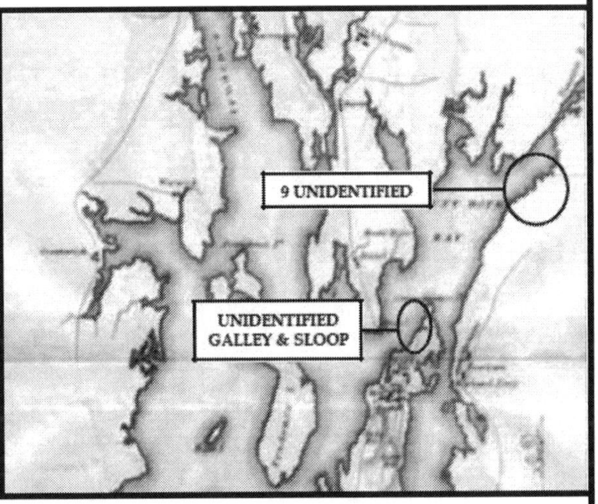

The British Attack Fall River

A week after an assault on Bristol Neck during the spring of 1778, British forces decided to make another attack to further limit the American rebels ability to be able to launch an attack on "Rhode Island" (the island that we know as Aquidneck Island).

Providence Gazette and Country Journal - June 6, 1778 P3

Sunday morning last, about day-break, a party of British troops from Rhode Island, consisting of 150 men, under the command of a Major Ayres, landed at the mouth of Fall River, with design to burn Freetown, and the mills. They set fire to the lower mill, and a house that stood on the shore, but the town and upper mills, by the vigilance of 25 of the inhabitants, were saved. Apprized of the enemy's intention, they took up the bridge and posted themselves behind a wall that commanded it, from whence they kept up so brisk a fire on the enemy, that after an engagement of near an hour and a half, they were compelled to retire, leaving behind them one killed and another mortally wounded. Five muskets and as many hats have been since found, and from every circumstance it appears that their loss was considerable. The militia turned out with great alacrity, and repaired to the place of action; but the precipitate retreat of the enemy deprived those spirited fellows of an opportunity to revenge the injuries they have repeatedly received, and of treating the detestable conflagrators as they justly deserved. The enemy's boats and shipping, in pulling down the river, received considerable annoyance from our fort on Bristol Neck; a galley that came up to cover them, from the well directed fire of the fort, was driven on the Rhode Island shore, the men obliged to abandon her; and a sloop that attempted to assist her shared the same fate.

Providence Gazette and Country Journal - June 13, 1778 P3

The enemy, in their account of the late unsuccessful expedition against the mills, at Fall River, acknowledge they had two privates killed, and a lieutenant and four privates wounded.

Two other non-newspaper accounts of this attack are of interest. The first is from the American perspective and is taken from the "History of Newport County, Rhode Island, 1638-1887".

On Sunday morning, the 31st of May, the British made a dash at Fall River. One hundred and fifty men under Major Ayres, were landed at daybreak at the mouth of the river and burned a mill and house on the shore, but were prevented from going inland, where they proposed to burn Freetown and the mills, by Colonel Durfee who, with twenty-five men covered the bridge from behind a wall until the militia came up.

ATTACK ON FALL RIVER

Two British vessels, a galley and a sloop, covering the retreat, were driven on the Rhode Island shore and abandoned. The boats and vessels were warmly received as they passed down the river by a hot fire from the fort on Bristol Neck. The other non-newspaper account of the attack presents the British perspective and is taken from the diary of Frederick McKenzie, a British officer who was stationed in Newport for most of the occupation and who kept a detailed diary of events. McKenzie wrote for May 31st, *The General and the Commodore having determined to attempt destroying some saw mills, and a quantity of plank for building boats, which they had upon Fall River., the PIGOT Galley, a gunboat and the boats of the FLORA, JUNO, VENUS, ORPHEUS, and KINGFISHER with 100 men of the 54th Regiment were ordered for this service. At 12 o'clock last night they passed through the Bristol Ferry, unperceived by the rebels, and proceeded up Mount Hope Bay. On approaching the shore near Fall River, they were fired on by a guard of about 40 men, but pushed and dispersed the enemy. They the proceeded and burned one saw mill, a corn mill, 9 large boats, and about 15,000 feet of plank. The rebels gathering, our men returned to the boats and re-embarked.*

It is interesting to see how one incident is viewed from each side. From the perspective of the Americans, the incident was of a valiant defense of their property. From the perspective of the British, the incident was a successful attack on rebel positions resulting in destruction that would limit the chances of the rebels to launch a successful attack on Newport. From a historical perspective, this was simply a skirmish in which both sides had limited success and losses given the value of the sloop and galley that had to be abandoned.

Research Sources

1. Providence Gazette & Country Journal, June 6, 1778 P3
2. Providence Gazette & Country Journal, June 13, 1778 P3
3. "History of Newport County, Rhode Island, 1638-1887" by Richard M. Bayles (1888)
4. "Newport Harbor and Lower Narragansett Bay, Rhode Island, During the American Revolution", by Mrs. Elizabeth Covell (1932)

ALARM

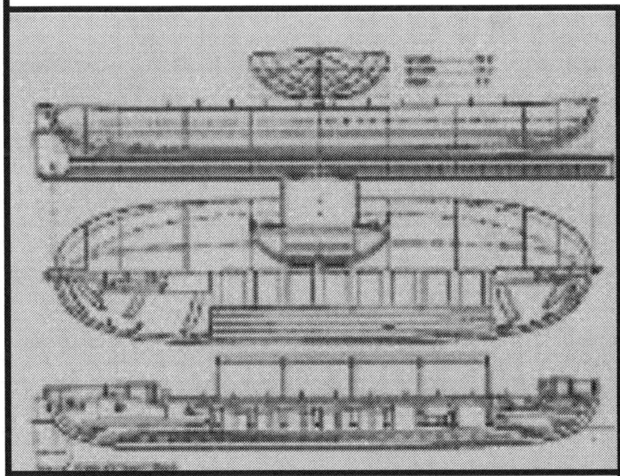

Although most of the warships used in the Revolutionary War were sailing vessels, there were also numerous rowed galleys like the **ALARM**. They carried a small number of troops and cannon.

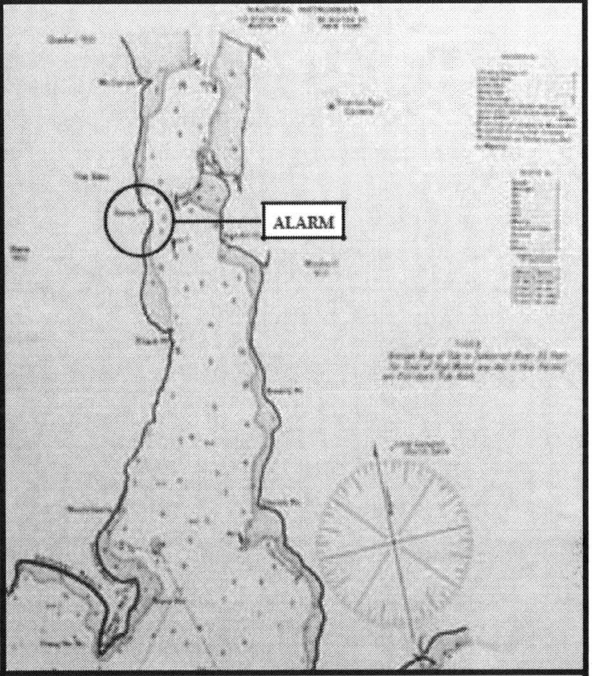

The Vessel

Type: Galley
Construction: Wood
Use: Warship
Dimensions: 72′ x 19′ x 6′
Launched: Near New York City, NY in 1770
Owner: British Navy
Nationality: British
Official No.: N/A
Home Port: Newport, RI

Final Voyage

Port of Departure: N/A Port
of Destination: N/A Master:
Lt. Philip d'Auvergne
Cargo: N/A
Date of Loss: July 30, 1778
Disaster Type: Ashore & burned
Cause: War—Intentional
Final Status: Total loss
Location: Off Sandy Point (now McCorrie Pt.)

Narrative

In the late summer of 1778 a plan was formed by the Americans in collaboration with the French to oust the British from their entrenched position at the mouth of Narragansett Bay. This plan was for a joint naval and land operation which would come to be known as The Battle of Rhode Island. The French fleet, under the command of Count D'Estaing, approached Rhode Island near the end of July with rumors of a large British fleet of ships not too far behind them. French ships entered the bay through each of the three passages, the East Passage (or Sakonnet River), the West Passage (between Conanicut Island and the western shore of the bay) and via the direct approach to Newport. At the time there were three vessels stationed in the Sakonnet River, the **ALARM** and SPITFIRE (both galleys) and the sloop KINGFISHER. (see separate data sheets for the SPITFIRE and the KINGFISHER). Each of these was stationed at a strategic point on the river but as word of the approaching warships reached them, their commanding officers were faced with making the decision of fight or flee. In the case of the **ALARM**, her master decided to run her ashore and burn her rather than have her be captured by the enemy.

ALARM

There are numerous references to the loss of the galley **ALARM**. In "Our French Allies" by Edwin Martin Stone, the galley was noted as carrying 10 guns and that her station was at Fogland Ferry in the East Passage. It was also noted that she had been burnt at Sandy Point. A paper entitled, "The Battle of Rhode Island" by ex-governor Charles W. Lippitt was published in October, 1915, in a bulletin of the Newport Historical Society. Although it does not mention the **ALARM** by name, it provides an overview of the events and a statistical account of the vessel losses by the British. In another bulletin of the Newport Historical Society, in 1933, there is a lengthy article entitled, "Newport Harbor and Lower Narragansett Bay, R.I. During the American Revolution", by Elizabeth Covell. Based on the diary of Frederick Mackenzie, an officer of the British army based in Newport for most of the occupation, the information offers invaluable insight into the events of the time. The **ALARM** is listed as one of numerous vessels that spent time in Newport between 1776-1779. In addition, the following entry came from this diary for 1778, *July 30.—... Two French frigates had come into the Seconnet, and two into the Narragansett Passage. The two in Seconnet, sailing up to Black Point, orders were given to set fire to the KINGFISHER, which was immediately done. The galleys also were set on fire. I think our people were too precipitate in burning the vessels. ...* In "Sailing Ships of the Old Navy" by Michael Phillips (1995), "The Sailing Navy 1775-1854" by Paul Silverstone (2006) and "British Warship in the Age of Sail 1714-1792" by Rif Winfield (2007) details of the vessel can be found.

An Interesting Commemorative Stamp

It is not unusual for stamps to be produced to commemorate important historical events or people. In researching the loss of the British galley **ALARM**, it was discovered that a stamp had been created to pay tribute to this event. It seems a bit odd that a commander deciding to run his vessel ashore and set fire to it to prevent capture would be considered noteworthy enough to earn this distinction but the criteria used are not clear. The stamp is a local British stamp but the issue date is not.

Research Sources

1. Connecticut Courant , August 11, 1777 P3
2. New York Gazette and Weekly Mercury, August 24, 1777 P2
3. "Our French Allies" by Edwin Martin Stone (1884)
4. "The Battle of Rhode Island" by ex-governor Charles W. Lippitt (1915)
5. "Newport Harbor and Lower Narragansett Bay, R.I. During the American Revolution" by Elizabeth Covell (1933)
6. "Sailing Ships of the Old Navy" by Michael Phillips (1995)
7. "The Sailing Navy 1775-1854" by Paul H. Silverstone (2006)
8. "British Warships In the Age of Sail 1714-1792" by Rif Winfield (2007)

HMS KINGFISHER

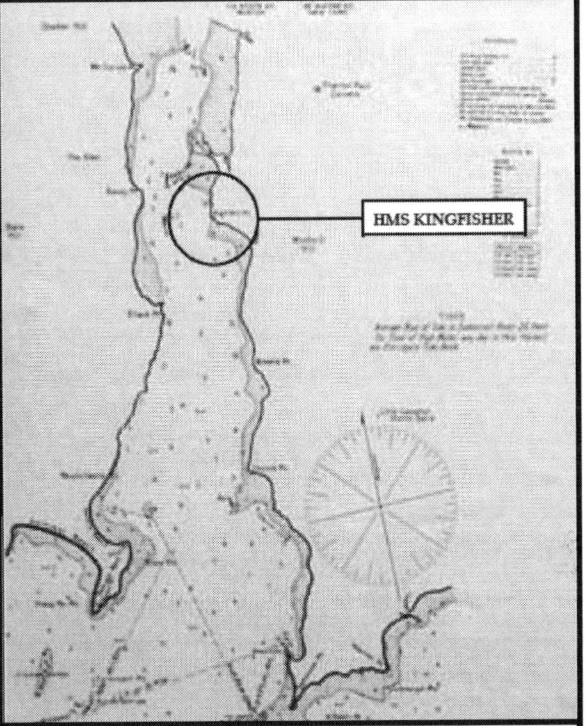

During the American Revolution and the occupation of Newport, there were a large number of warships, including the sloop **HMS KINGFISHER** stationed around Aquidneck Island.

The Vessel

Type: Sloop
Construction: Wood
Use: Warship
Dimensions: 96′ x 26′ x 12′
Tonnage: 302
Launched: Chatham, England in 1770
Owner: British Navy
Nationality: British
Home Port: Newport, RI

Final Voyage

Port of Departure: Her station off Fogland, in the Sakonnet River (drifting down river)
Master: Lt. Hugh Christian
Date of Loss: July 30, 1778
Disaster Type: Ashore & burned
Cause: War—Intentional
Final Status: Total loss
Location: A little north of Sandy Point, off High Hill, Tiverton

Narrative

New York Gazette and Weekly Mercury - August 24, 1778 P2

Providence, August 1

Wednesday last, to the joy of every good subject, the fleet of his most Christian Majesty, the great and wise ally of these states, commanded by Admiral Count D'Estaing, arrived off Point Judith. ... On Thursday two French ships of the line came up the west side of Conanicut, and took their stations above the north end of that island; several shot were fired at them as they passed, and a few returned; the enemy's ships which lay there got under sail on the near approach of our friends, and entered Newport Harbour by the east side of Conanicut. ... The ***KINGFISHER*** *of 16 guns, with two gallies (see separate data sheets), were blown up by the enemy in Seconnet River, on the approach of two other French ships. The Britons ... are in great consternation; and a few days will ... produce events of utmost importance.*

HMS KINGFISHER

In the "History of Rhode Island", published in 1853, Rev. Edward Peterson referred to the loss of the **KINGFISHER** but misidentified her as a man-of war. "Our French Allies" published in 1884 described the vessel correctly as an 18-gun sloop but misidentified her station as being at the mouth of the Sakonnet River and identified the location of the disaster as being a little north of Sandy Point. Thirty years later, ex-governor Charles Lippitt touched on the subject in a more general manner mentioning the number of British vessels destroyed when the French fleet of Count D'Estaing approached Newport. After another two decades, in 1933, Mrs. Elizabeth Covell presented a paper to the Newport Historical Society based on the diary kept by a British Army officer stationed in Newport during the occupation. Frederick Mackenzie, that officer, specifically mentioned the **KINGFISHER** by name and further confirmed the location of her stranding. In "Campaign on Rhode Island" by Erick A.O.D. Taylor, a much more detailed account of the incident was presented, *"D'Estaing arrived off Newport on July 29th... At 5 P.M. on that day two French ships, AIMABLE and ALEMENE, sailed up the Seaconnet, anchoring off Third Beach. These ships remained there until 3 P.M. on the 30th at which time they pushed their way up to Fogland Ferry, exposing themselves to the fire of the battery at that place. The French proceeded slowely, taking soundings as they went. Before them, above the battery, lay the galleys LAMB* [misspelling of the name of the galley ALARM] *and SPITFIRE* (see separate data sheets on each galley) *and the 16-gun corvette* ***KING FISHER****. The French ships were now supported by the French corvette STANLEY. After night fell the French would approach and seize the ships. However, the wily British were abandoning their boats and had set them alight, hoping the strong-running tide would drift them against the French. ...from ashore they watched (****KINGFISHER****) float seaward, lighting like a torch the farther banks where even then the Americans were encamping. The French cutters approached and grappled her. After putting a man (M. De Dorset) aboard she grounded and then exploded."* In "The Sailing Navy 1775-1854" by Paul Silverstone (2006) and "British Warship in the Age of Sail 1714- 1792" by Rif Winfield (2007) details of the British sloop **KINGFISHER** are presented that help to complete the picture of this vessel.

Research Sources

1. Connecticut Courant , August 11, 1777 P3
2. New York Gazette and Weekly Mercury, August 24, 1777 P2
3. "History of Rhode Island" by Rev. Edward Peterson (1853)
4. "Our French Allies" by Edwin Martin Stone (1884)
5. "The Battle of Rhode Island" by ex-governor Charles W. Lippitt (1915)
6. "Newport Harbor and Lower Narragansett Bay, R.I. During the American Revolution" by Elizabeth Covell (1933)
7. "Campaign on Rhode Island" by Erick A.O.D. Taylor
8. "Shipwrecks in the Americas" by Robert Marx (1987)
9. "The Sailing Navy 1775-1854" by Paul H. Silverstone (2006)
10. "British Warships In the Age of Sail 1714-1792" by Rif Winfield (2007)

SPITFIRE

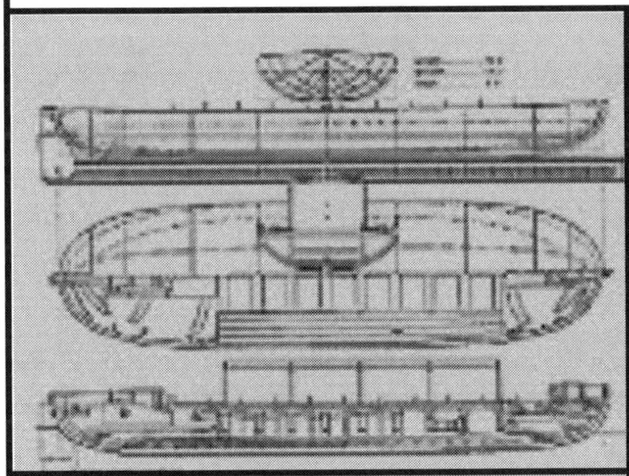

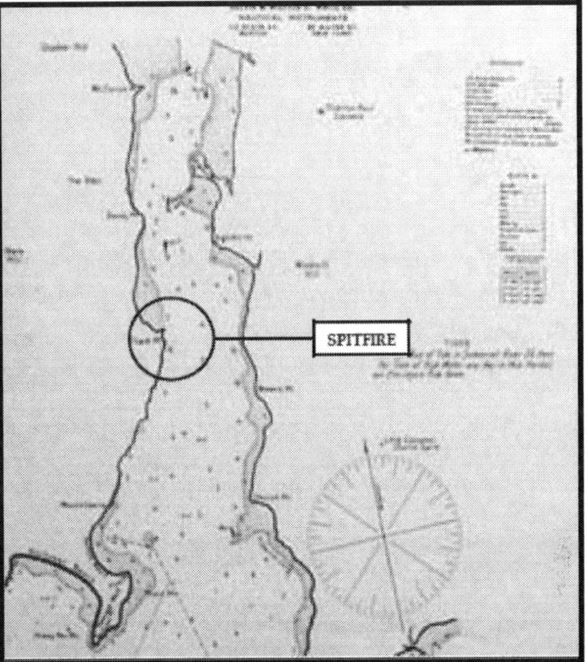

During the 1770s, a number of American vessels were sold to the British. The **SPITFIRE**, of Boston, may have had another name as galley of the same name was built in Providence and lost in 1777.

The Vessel

Type: Galley
Construction: Wood
Use: Warship
Owner: British Navy
Nationality: British
Home Port: Newport, RI

The Event

Master: Lt. James Saumarez
Date of Incident: July 30, 1778
Disaster Type: Ashore & burned
Cause: War—Intentional
Status: Raised
Location: At Black Point, Sakonnet River

Narrative

The arrival of a large fleet of French ships on July 30, 1778, although not a surprise to the British force occupying Newport, was not a pleasant sight for his majesty's troops to see. Major General Robert Pigot, commanding the Aquidneck Island invaders, was aware that the French were coming and was aware that his own country, Great Britain, was also in the process of sending a fleet to protect his troops and fortify their position. But the British fleet was late and would not arrive until nearly mid-August while the French, under the command of Admiral the comte d'Estaing, arrived first. Added to this mix was a force of Americans, under the command of Major General John Sullivan, ready to coordinate a land attack with an seaborn attack from the French in an effort to retake the city of Newport and wrest control of the waters of Narragansett Bay from Pigot. On duty at the time in the East Passage (Sakonnet River) were three vessels, the galley ALARM (see separate data sheet), the sloop-of-war HMS KINGFISHER (see separate data sheet) and the galley **SPITFIRE**. The three vessels were not stationed together but were not far from each other. As word of the approaching warships reached them, they each had to make the decision of whether to face the enemy vessels, initially two French frigates, or take all the necessary steps to ensure that their vessels and crews would not fall into the hands of the enemy. The **SPITFIRE** was run ashore and burned to prevent her capture but was later raised.

SPITFIRE

There are numerous references to the incident involving the galley **SPITFIRE**. In "Our French Allies" by Edwin Martin Stone the galley was noted as carrying 8 guns and that her station was south of Little Sandy Point and near the Portsmouth shore. It was also noted that she had been burnt at Sandy Point. In a bulletin of the Newport Historical Society published in 1933 there is a lengthy article entitled, "Newport Harbor and Lower Narragansett Bay, R.I. During the American Revolution", by Elizabeth Covell. Based on the diary of Frederick Mackenzie, an officer of the British army based in Newport for most of the occupation, the information offers invaluable insight into the events of the time. The **SPITFIRE** is listed as one of numerous vessels that spent time in Newport between 1776-1779. The following entry came from this diary for *1778, July 30. – ... Two French frigates had come into the Seconnet, and two into the Narragansett Passage. The two in Seconnet, sailing up to Black Point, orders were given to set fire to the KINGFISHER, which was immediately done. The galleys also were set on fire. I think our people were too precipitate in burning the vessels. ...* In "Campaign on Rhode Island" by Erick A.O.D. Taylor, the galley named **SPITFIRE** is noted as one of those set fire when the French fleet entered the East Passage. "British Warship in the Age of Sail 1714-1792" by Rif Winfield (2007) provides details of the vessel itself and named her commander.

Subsequent to the attack and the stranding of the galley, the SPITFIRE was raised and refitted and was later taken by the Americans in action during the following year.

Research Sources

1. Connecticut Courant , August 11, 1778 P3
2. New York Gazette and Weekly Mercury, August 24, 1778 P2
3. "Our French Allies" by Edwin Martin Stone (1884)
4. "Newport Harbor and Lower Narragansett Bay, R.I. During the American Revolution" by Elizabeth Covell (1933)
5. "Campaign on Rhode Island" by Erick A.O.D. Taylor
6. "British Warships In the Age of Sail 1714-1792" by Rif Winfield (2007)

NEWPORT UNDER SEIGE—SAKONNET RIVER

Vessels Involved

ALARM - Galley - 72′ x 19′ x 6′ - purchased near New York City in 1770 (said to be an ex-East Indiaman named MOUNTFIELD but this cannot be confirmed) - sailed for the British under command of Lt. Phillip d'Auvergne - stationed at Fogland Ferry (see separate data sheet)

HMS KINGFISHER - British Swan class Sloop - 96′ x 26′ x 12′ - 302 tons - launched at Chatham, England in 1770 - sailed, when lost, under command of Lt. Hugh Christian - stationed off Fogland Ferry (see separate data sheet)

SPITFIRE - Galley - probably comparable in size to the ALARM - purchased at Boston on January 25, 1778 - sailed, when lost, under command of Lt. James Saumarez - stationed south of Little Sandy Point and near the Portsmouth shore (see separate data sheet)

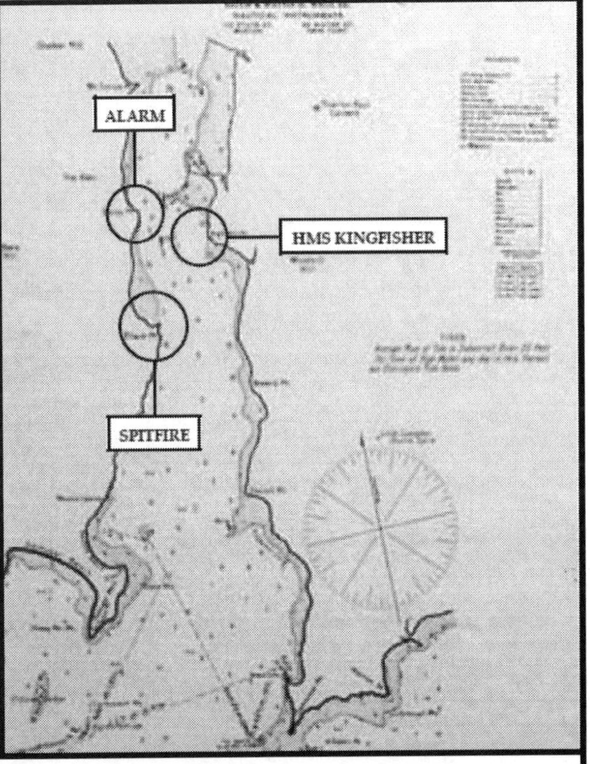

French Participation in the American Revolutionary War

When Great Britain went to war with the Americans not all European governments believed that the British would prevail in a armed conflict thousands of miles from home. Some tacitly supported the king while carefully watching events transpire. The French, unhappy with the British, provided unofficial aid to the Americans in the early part of the war, using third party vessels to send guns and ammunition to them. In early 1778, however, the tide was turning and as it became clear that the British might not be victorious, France formally recognized the United States followed by the king of England's issuance of a declaration of war on France. The following is excerpted from Bayle's "History of Newport County, Rhode Island, 1638-1887", "... *French assistance followed quickly the recognition of American independence and the treaty of alliance. Marie Antoinette, the queen, herself persuaded the king, Louis XVI, to order a naval expedition to the American coast. The squadron, consisting of twelve ships of the line, four frigates and four thousand troops, was placed under the command of the Count d'Estaing, an ambitious and promising officer. ... The fleet left Toulon the 13th of April, 1778, and passed the Straits of Gibraltar on the night of the 17th to 18th of May. On the 20th the captains of the vessels opened their sealed instructions and learned their destinations. ... It was hoped that the great secrecy with which the expedition had been organized would result in the surprise and defeat of Lord Howe's squadron which held the mouth of the Delaware. ... But the French fleet was badly composed for concerted action, the vessels being of unequal speed, and land was not seen until July. On the 8th of this month, eighty-seven days after departure from Toulon, the French fleet anchored at the mouth of the Delaware. ... [Sir Henry] Clinton, under orders from England, had evacuated Philadelphia on the 22nd of June, and both army and fleet were safe in the harbor of New York. Pilots were sent aboard the French vessels and d'Estaing set sail [for New York}.. The American pilots were unwilling to venture with the larger vessels which drew from twenty-three to twenty-five feet of water across the New York bar... The alternative offensive operation was an attempt to capture the British*

NEWPORT UNDER SEIGE – SAKONNET RIVER

garrison on Rhode Island. A plan was concerted between Washington and d'Estaing and [Major General] Sullivan was notified to be prepared. ... On the 22d of July the French fleet raised anchor and set sail to the southward but soon changed their course. The plan agreed upon was that General Sullivan should land on the north end of Rhode Island under cover of the guns of the French fleet, while d'Estaing should also force the passage of the main channel and take the fortifications of the town of Newport in reverse. On the 29th of July the French fleet arrived off Brenton's Ledge, three miles below Newport, and dropped anchor at the mouth of the great middle channel. ... The next day General Sullivan, who had already exchanged letters with the French admiral, went on board the LANGUEDOC, and a plan of operation was agreed upon. The FANTAQUE and SAGITTAIRE were ordered to watch the Narragansett or western passage while the frigates AIMABLE, ALEMENE and the corvette STANLEY should anchor in the eastern passage where the water was too shallow for the heavier ships. The retreat of the English vessels lying in the bay was thus cut off. The frigates, pushing up the eastern or Seconnet passage, anchored in front of the battery at Fogland ferry, but before fire opened from the guns, the British man-of- war, the KINGFISHER, of sixteen guns, and two galleys were set on fire by their crews; their shotted guns went off in all directions, and their magazines exploded to the confusion and consternation of friend and foe.

Thus, the first phase of the attack on the British occupying forces at Newport began. There were other actions (see separate data sheets) to vessels of his majesty's fleet stationed in Newport and at other areas along the west side of Aquidneck Island, but the action in the Sakonnet River was the first in the overall campaign. Unfortunately for the Americans and the French, this campaign was not entirely successful due, in part, to the weather as a storm arrived within the week along with Lord Howe's fleet from New York City, causing the departure of the French from Rhode Island waters, at least for now.

Research Sources

1. "History of Rhode Island" by Rev. Edward Peterson (1853)
2. "History of Newport County, Rhode Island. 1638 to 1887" by Richard M. Bayles (1888)
3. "The Battle of Rhode Island" by ex-governor Charles W. Lippitt (1915)
4. "Newport Harbor and Lower Narragansett Bay Rhode Island During the American Revolution" by Mrs. Elizabeth Covell (Newport Historical Society Bulletin, January, 1933)
5. "Campaign on Rhode Island" by Erick A.O.D. Taylor
6. "British Warships In the Age of Sail 1714-1792" by Rif Winfield (2007)

HMS CERBERUS

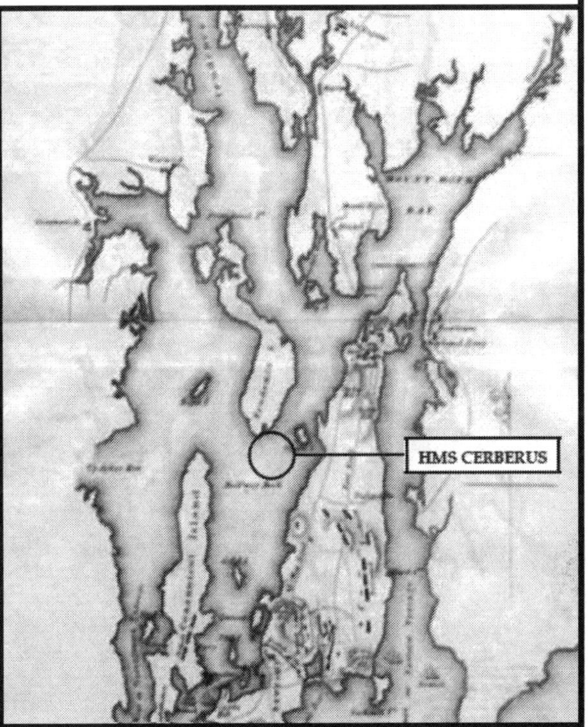

The **HMS CERBERUS**, like the vessel in the painting above, was a 6th rate ship and carried 28 guns when she went into battle. At the time of her loss she was run ashore & burned to prevent capture by the approaching French fleet.

The Vessel

Type: 6th rate Ship
Construction: Wood
Use: Warship
Dimensions: 118′ x 33′ x 10′
Tonnage: 593
Launched: East Cowes, England in 1758
Owner: British Navy
Nationality: British
Home Port: Newport, RI

Final Voyage

Master: John Simmonds (or Symonds)
Cargo: N/A
Date of Loss: August 4, 1778
Disaster Type: Burned & sunk
Cause: War-Intentional
Final Status: Total loss
Location: South of Dyer and near the Portsmouth shore (location shown is where her remains have been found)

Narrative

Boston Independent Chronicle and Universal Advertiser - August 13, 1778 P2

PROVIDENCE, August 8.

... Wednesday last, on the appearance of two French men-of-war on the east side of Conanicut, the enemy ran four of their frigates, and a galley, ashore on Rhode Island, and soon after burnt them, with their stores, provisions, &c. We since learn that the vessels destroyed are the LARK, ORPHEUS and JUNO, of 32 guns each, the ***CERBERUS****, of 28, and the PIGOT galley. A small privateer landed a number of men the same day on Rhode Island, and brought off four boats belonging to the above mentioned frigates, having on board small arms, clothing, &c. ... on Wednesday, three persons made their escape from Newport; they inform that the enemy have sunk 11 transports between Goat and Rose Islands, and that they have destroyed all the farming utensils on Rhode Island.* The following entry was taken from the diary of Frederick Mackenzie, a British army officer who was stationed in Newport during the occupation, " *Aug. 4 - This morning the two French ships in the Narragansett Passage stood round the*

HMS CERBERUS

north point of Conanicut. On seeing them the ***CERBERUS*** *endeavored to get down to the town, but finding she would be cut off, Capt. Symmons ran her on shore behind Redwood's and set her on fire. The ORPHEUS, LARK and PIGOT galley, observing the French ships coming up between Prudence and this island, were immediately run on shore; also the JUNO off Coddington Cove, the ORPHEUS at Almy's Point, and the LARK and PIGOT at Freeborn's Creek, where they were set on fire; all blew up late in the evening. The explosion was very great, as the LARK had 76 barrels of powder in the magazine. The house of one Wilcox, in the swamp was set on fire thereby, and totally consumed. Some books and papers from the ORPHEUS were found some three miles from the place where she blew up. It was a most mortifying sight to us to see so many fine ships destroyed in so short a time without any loss on the part of the enemy.*

There are a number of other reference sources (listed below) which provide similar evidence or details regarding the overall campaign or specifications relative to the vessel itself but, in general, the details above tell the story of what transpired on that August day in 1778. (for an overview of this event, involving HMS CEREBUS, HMS LARK and HMS ORPHEUS, see the multi-wreck data sheet entitled, "Newport Under Siege—Portsmouth")

Research Sources

1. Boston Independent Chronicle and Universal Advertiser , August 13, 1778 P3
2. Massachusetts Spy, August 20, 1778 P3
3. "History of Rhode Island" by Rev. Edward Peterson (1853)
4. "Our French Allies" by Edwin Martin Stone (1884)
5. "History of Newport County, Rhode Island 1638-1887" by Richard M. Bayles (1888)
6. "The Battle of Rhode Island" by ex-governor Charles W. Lippitt (1915)
7. "Newport Harbor and Lower Narragansett Bay, R.I. During the American Revolution" by Elizabeth Covell (1933)
8. "Campaign on Rhode Island" by Erick A.O.D. Taylor
9. "Shipwrecks in the Americas" by Robert Marx (1987)
10. "Sailing Ships of the Old Navy" by Michael Phillips (1995)
11. "The Sailing Navy 1775-1854" by Paul H. Silverstone (2006)
12. "British Warships In the Age of Sail 1714-1792" by Rif Winfield (2007)

HMS LARK

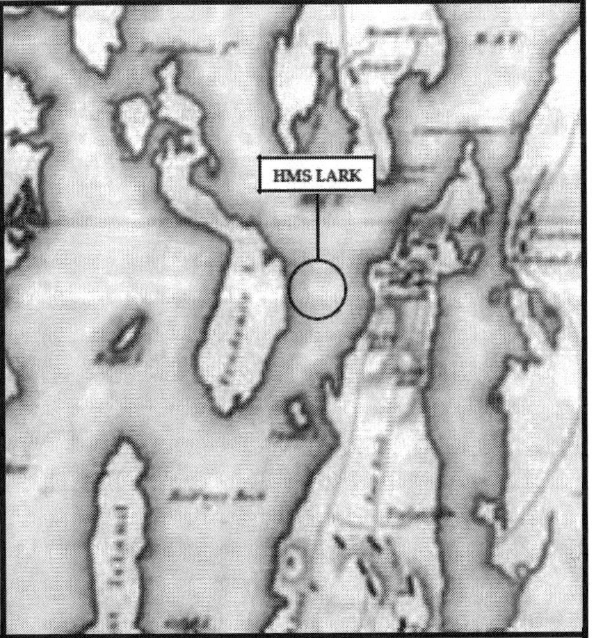

HMS LARK was a fifth rate ship which carried 32 cannon and a complement of 210 men when set fire and abandoned.

The Vessel

Type: 5th rate ship
Construction: Wood
Use: Warship
Dimensions: 126′ x 34′ x 12′
Tonnage: 680
Launched: Rotherhithe, England in 1762
Owner: British Navy
Nationality: British
Home Port: Newport, RI

Final Voyage

Port of Departure: Newport, RI
Master: Richard Smith
Date of Loss: August 4, 1778
Disaster Type: Burned & sunk
Cause: War—Intentional
Final Status: Total loss
Location: Near the Portsmouth shore, midway between Arnolds Point and Coggeshall Point, Portsmouth

Narrative

During the Battle of Rhode Island, American and French forces were involved in a joint effort to rescue the residents of Newport from the British army of occupation which had been in control of the town since December of 1776. As a French fleet approached the town, a number of British warships including the **HMS LARK** were destroyed rather than be captured to be used against them. But it wasn't long before local salvagers went to work to save what they could from the wrecks. The following article appeared just two months after the attack.

Providence Gazette and Country Journal - October 10, 1778 P3

State of Rhode Island and Providence plantations. A libel is filed before me, by William Turner Miller, Esq., Shubel Burr, Merchant, and William Barton, Esq.., for themselves and all others concerned, setting forth, that upon the fifteenth day of August, A.D., 1778, the said William Barton and others, in a large flat bottomed boat, upon the seas, near the shores of Rhode Island, captured and took and have brought into the county of Bristol, in said state, for trial and adjudication, one 18 inch cable,, one 17 inch cable, two large cannon, about 900 iron hoops, about one ton of wrought iron, a quantity of copper, lead, cannon shot,

HMS LARK

musket balls, flints, tallow, one ton of junk, an iron caboose, a cap for a ship's mast, a number of ship's blocks and dead eyes, a ship's buoy, a quantity of clothing, &c. all which articles appertained to ships of war, owned by the British King, stationed near the said island, and there lately burnt by his own subjects. The justice of said capture will be tried at the maritime court of said state, appointed to be holden at Warren, in said county, on the ninth day of November, A.D. 1778, at the house of Ebenezer Cole, Inn holder, at the hour of ten in the forenoon. This notice of said trial is given, that the owner, or any persons concerned therein, may appear in said court, if they see cause, and show cause, if any they have, why the said cables, cannon &c. should not be condemned. John Foster, Judge of said court.

The result of this court action is not known but given the sentiment of the Americans at the time, which would certainly include members of the court, it would seem likely that the materials were found to be reasonably attained and the fairly captured property of the men named. (for an overview of this event, involving HMS CEREBUS, HMS LARK and HMS ORPHEUS, see the multi-wreck data sheet entitled, "Newport Under Siege—Portsmouth").

Research Sources

1. Boston Independent Chronicle, August 13, 1778 P2
2. Providence Gazette and Country Journal, October 10, 1778 P3
3. "History of Rhode Island" by Rev. Edward Peterson (1853)
4. "Our French Allies" by Edwin Martin Stone (1884)
5. "History of Newport County, Rhode Island, 1638-1887" by Richard M. Bayles (1888)
6. "The Battle of Rhode Island" by ex-governor Charles W. Lippitt (1915)
7. "Newport Harbor and Lower Narragansett Bay, R.I. During the American Revolution" by Elizabeth Covell (1933)
8. "Campaign on Rhode Island" by Erick A.O.D. Taylor
9. "Shipwrecks in the Americas" by Robert Marx (1987)
10. "Shipwrecks—An Encyclopedia of the World's Worst Disasters at Sea" by David Ritchie
11. "The Sailing Navy 1775-1854" by Paul H. Silverstone (2006)
12. "British Warships In the Age of Sail 1714-1792" by Rif Winfield (2007)

HMS ORPHEUS

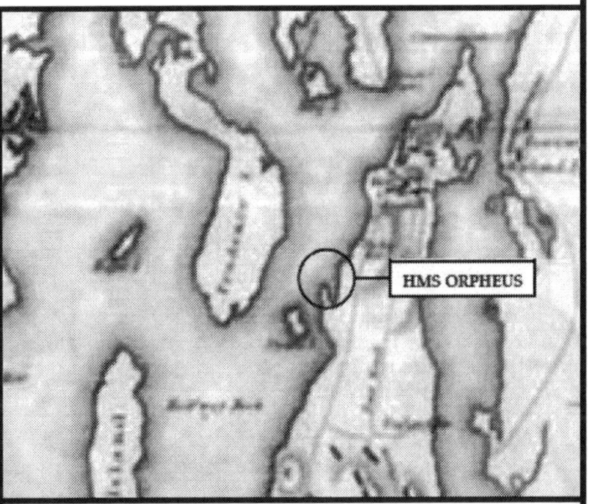

The Vessel

Type: 5th rate ship
Construction: Wood
Use: Warship
Dimensions: 130′ x 35′ x 12′
Tonnage: 708
Launched: Harwich, England in 1773
Owner: British Navy
Nationality: British
Home Port: Newport, RI

Final Voyage

Master: Charles Hudson
Cargo: N/A
Date of Loss: August 4, 1778
Disaster Type: Ashore & burned
Cause: War—Intentional
Final Status: Total loss
Location: Near Coggeshall Point on the Portsmouth shore

Narrative

In the early 1970′s, an archaeology student located the remains of three British warships that had rested on the floor of Narragansett Bay for nearly two centuries. The historical significance of this find was readily apparent but there was not enough funding to properly perform an underwater archaeological expedition.. The vessels were the HMS LARK, HMS CERBERUS and the **HMS ORPHEUS**. Although the story of how the vessels got there has been told before, it deserves a retelling in the news of the day. (for an overview of this event see the multi-wreck data sheet entitled, "Newport Under Siege—Portsmouth"; separate data sheets can be found for HMS LARK and HMS CERBERUS).

Boston Independent Chronicle and Universal Advertiser - August 13, 1778 P2

PROVIDENCE, August 8.

… Wednesday last, on the appearance of two French men-of-war on the east side of Conanicut, the enemy ran four of their frigates, and a galley, ashore on Rhode Island, and soon after burnt them, with their stores, provisions, &c. We since learn that the vessels destroyed are the LARK, ***ORPHEUS*** *and JUNO, of 32 guns each, the CERBERUS, of 28, and the PIGOT galley. A small privateer landed a number of men the same day on Rhode Island, and brought off four boats belonging to the above mentioned frigates, having on board small arms, clothing, &c. … on Wednesday, three persons made their escape from Newport; they inform that the enemy have sunk 11 transports between Goat and Rose Islands, and that they have destroyed all the farming utensils on Rhode Island.*

HMS ORPHEUS

Other British Vessels Named HMS ORPHEUS

According to Internet sources the HMS ORPHEUS lost during the Revolutionary War was only the first of a number of British vessels to carry that name over the years. A complete list includes all of the following naval vessels.

- *A modified Lowestoffe class frigate* [this one] *launched in 1773 and burnt to avoid capture in Rhode Island in 1778.*
- *A 32-gun 5th rate ship launched in 1780 and wrecked in the West Indies in 1807.*
- *A 36-gun 6th rate ship launched in 1809 which lasted only a decade and was broken up in 1819.*
- *A 22-gun, Jason class, screw corvette launched in 1860 and wrecked in New Zealand in 1863.*
- *An M-class destroyer launched in 1916 and sold for scrap in 1921.*
- *An Odin class submarine launched in 1929 and lost with all hands in a depth-charge attack off Tobruk in 1940.*
- *An Oberon class submarine launched on 1959 and sold for scrap in 1994.*

Research Sources

1. Boston Independent Chronicle, August 13, 1778 P2
2. Massachusetts Spy, August 20, 1778 P3
3. "Our French Allies" by Edwin Martin Stone (1884)
4. "History of Newport County, Rhode Island, 1638-1887" by Richard M. Bayles (1888)
5. "The Battle of Rhode Island" by ex-governor Charles W. Lippitt (1915)
6. "Newport Harbor and Lower Narragansett Bay, R.I. During the American Revolution" by Elizabeth Covell (1933)
7. "Campaign on Rhode Island" by Erick A.O.D. Taylor
8. "Shipwrecks in the Americas" by Robert Marx (1987)
9. "Shipwrecks—An Encyclopedia of the World's Worst Disasters at Sea" by David Ritchie
10. "The Sailing Navy 1775-1854" by Paul H. Silverstone (2006)
11. "British Warships In the Age of Sail 1714-1792" by Rif Winfield (2007)

NEWPORT UNDER SEIGE – PORTSMOUTH

Vessels Involved

HMS CERBERUS - British Coventry class 6th rate ship - 118′ x 33′ x 10′ - 593 tons - launched at East Cowes, England in 1758 - sailed, when lost, under command of John Simmonds (or Symonds) - stationed south of Dyer Island, Portsmouth (see separate data sheet)

HMS LARK - British Richmond class 5th rate Ship - 126′ x 34′ x 12′ - 680 tons - launched at Rotherhithe, England in 1762 - sailed, when lost, under command of Captain Richard Smith - stationed midway between Arnold's Point and Prudence Island (see separate data sheet)

HMS ORPHEUS - British modified Lowestoffe class 5th rate ship - 130′ x 35′ x 12′ - 708 tons – launched in Harwich, England in 1773 - sailed, when lost, under command of Capt. Charles Hudson - stationed between northern end of Prudence Island and Calf Pasture Point (see separate data sheet)

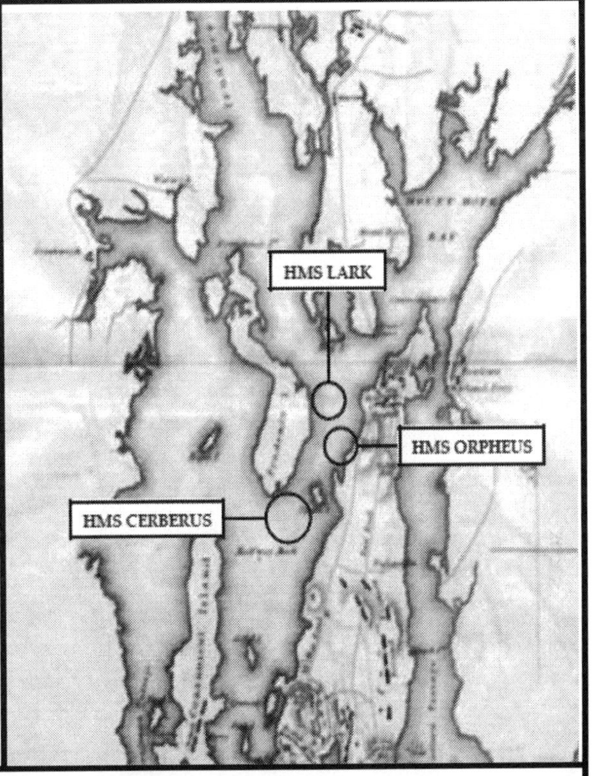

The French Attack Newport

When Count d'Estaing and the French fleet arrived off Narragansett Bay on July 29th, 1778 to coordinate with American forces in an attack on Newport, little did he know what would transpire over the next 10 days. After a strategy session held aboard the LANGUEDOC, while anchored off Brenton Reef, the French commander determined to split his force and send three ships up the eastern passage (Sakonnet River), two ships up the western (or Narragansett) passage and take the remaining vessels in through the main channel approaching Newport. After his vessels entered the eastern passage, the next phase of the campaign began. The following is excerpted from Richard M. Bayle's "History of Newport County, Rhode Island, 1638-1887", *"At daylight on the 5th of August, the SAGITTAIRE and FANTASQUE sailed up the western passage, doubled the point off Conanicut Island and dropped anchor in the middle channel. Four British frigates, the* ***LARK, ORPHEUS*** *and JUNO, thirty-two guns, the* ***CERBERUS****, twenty-eight, and the corvette FALCON, sixteen, were run ashore on Rhode Island and burned on their [French] approach to Tammany Hill".* **LARK, ORPHEUS** and **CERBERUS**, were located off the western shore of the island at Portsmouth. The others mentioned were located close to Newport and their stories are told in separate data sheets. It has been conjectured over the years whether the captains were ordered to burn and sink their vessels or whether they did so on their on. That practice, destruction versus capture was not uncommon at that time as a sound vessel in the hands of the enemy could easily be used against their original masters. Nearly two centuries after this campaign, the remains of these wrecks were located by a student of Archaeology from the University of Rhode Island and an era which had been of little interest to any other than historians suddenly became the subject of great local and international interest. Nearly four decades have passed since then and the sites remain the subject of study by new generations of archaeologists using the latest technology to learn as much as possible from these sites.

NEWPORT UNDER SEIGE—PORTSMOUTH

Research Sources

1. "History of Rhode Island" by Rev. Edward Peterson (1853)
2. "History of Newport County, Rhode Island. 1638 to 1887" by Richard M. Bayles (1888)
3. "The Battle of Rhode Island" by ex-governor Charles W. Lippitt (1915)
4. "Newport Harbor and Lower Narragansett Bay Rhode Island During the American Revolution" by Mrs. Elizabeth Covell (Newport Historical Society Bulletin, January, 1933)
5. "Campaign on Rhode Island" by Erick A.O.D. Taylor
6. "British Warships In the Age of Sail 1714-1792" by Rif Winfield (2007)

HMS JUNO

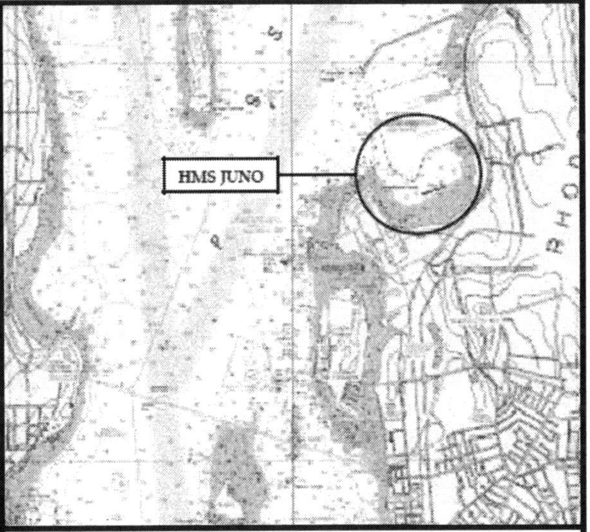

The Vessel

Type: 5th Rate Frigate
Construction: Wood
Use: Warship
Dimensions: 128′ x 34′ x 11′
Tonnage: 667
Launched: Deptford, England in 1757
Nationality: British
Home Port: Newport, RI

Final Voyage

Owner: British Navy
Master: Hugh Dalrymple
Date of Loss: August 4, 1778
Disaster Type: Burned & sunk
Cause: Set fire & exploded
Final Status: Total loss
Location: Coddington Cove, Newport

The Battle of Rhode Island - The Arrival of the French Fleet

During the occupation of Newport by British forces (December, 1776 to October, 1779) there were numerous vessels stationed at the port at one time or another. One list shows nearly 90 vessels involved. When the French fleet, under Admiral d'Estaing, arrived at Narragansett Bay to support American forces in a combined siege on Newport, there were a handful of British warships stationed at various locations in Narragansett Bay and the Sakonnet River tasked with the defense of the force of some 7,000 British soldiers ashore. The vessels most well known to be associated with the effort were the frigates CERBERUS, **JUNO**, LARK, ORPHEUS and FLORA, the sloops KING'S FISHER, and FALCON, and the galleys ALARM, PIGOT and SPITFIRE. These vessels were strategically positioned and not in the immediate proximity of one another which made each particularly vulnerable if challenged by more than a single French warship. **HMS JUNO**, a fifth rate frigate carrying 32 guns, was stationed in the center of the West Passage, about half way between the Jamestown West Ferry and Conanicut Point. In that position she would have been one of the first of the British vessels to see the French sailing in. D'Estaing's plan was to sail up the West Passage side, pass around the northern point of Conanicut Island and then sail in a southeasterly direction toward Newport. History tells us that **HMS JUNO** turned and ran toward Coddington Cove where she was set fire and exploded just offshore. It is not confirmed that the destruction was intentional or through battle but local legend leans toward the self destruction theory. There is no record of salvage for this vessel.

HMS JUNO

Narrative

Each of the following sources has some information about the event although all do not agree.

"Our French Allies" - *The frigate **JUNO**, stationed in the center of the West Passage, about halfway between Jamestown West Ferry and Conanicut Point; burnt at Coddington Cove.*

"History of Rhode Island" by Reverend Edward Peterson - *Three British frigates lay at anchor on the east side of Prudence. ... They weighed anchor and sailed with the design of getting under protection of the battery at Tammany Hill. ... A number of British vessels lying at Coddington Cove were set on fire as soon as the burning of the frigate was discovered.*

"Newport Harbor and lower Narragansett Bay R.I. During the American Revolution" by Elizabeth Covell [Newport Historical Society, 1933] - [the entries herein are from the diary of one Frederick Mackenzie, an officer in the British Army] *August 4th - This morning the two French ships in the Narragansett passage stood round the north point of Conanicut. The ORPHEUS, LARK and PIGOT, observing the French ships coming up between Prudence and this island, were immediately run on shore; also, the **JUNO**, off Coddington Cove...*

"History of Newport County, Rhode Island 1638-1887" by Richard M. Bayles - *On the 2nd of August all the live stock which had been driven in from Portsmouth and Middletown, and all carriages, carts, wheelbarrows, shovels, pickaxes, axes and saws were this day and the next taken from the inhabitants. Trees were cut down and thrown across the road to delay the march of the enemy. ... On the 5th of August ... on the appearance of the French fleet four frigates were blown up near Coddington Point.*

It is clear that the **HMS JUNO** was run ashore and destroyed in the shoal waters off Coddington Point. There is no indication that any salvage was attempted on this vessel except that one source indicates by the amount of bounty paid that the cannon on almost all were saved.

Research Sources

1. "Our French Allies" by Edwin Martin Stone (1884)
2. "History of Rhode Island" by Edward Peterson (1853)
3. "History of Newport County, Rhode Island 1638-1887" by Richard M. Bayles (1888)
4. "Newport Harbor and lower Narragansett Bay During the American Revolution" by Elizabeth Covell for the Newport Historical Society (1932)
5. "Campaign on Rhode Island" by Eric A. O'D Taylor
6. "Shipwrecks, An Encyclopedia of the World's Worst Disasters at Sea" by David Ritchie
7. "The Sailing Navy 1775-1854" by Paul H. Silverstone (2006)
8. "British Warships In the Age of Sail" by Rif Winfield (2007)
9. Rhode Island Ocean Special Area Management Plan (2010)
10. Correspondence with D.K. Abbass Ph.D.

PIGOT

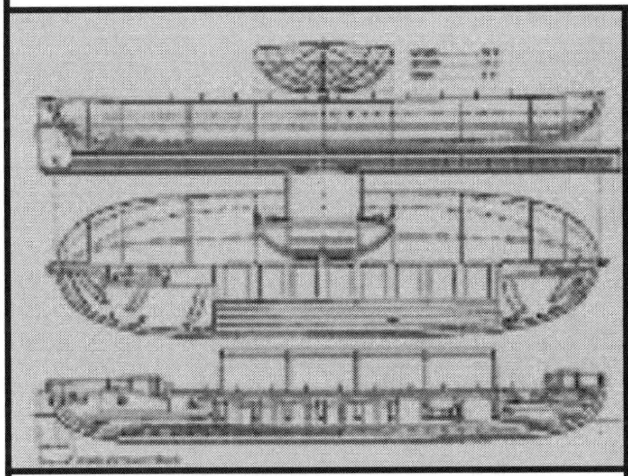

Pictured is a Revolutionary era galley. This one is of American design and it could be a match to the British galley PIGOT assigned to protect Newport.

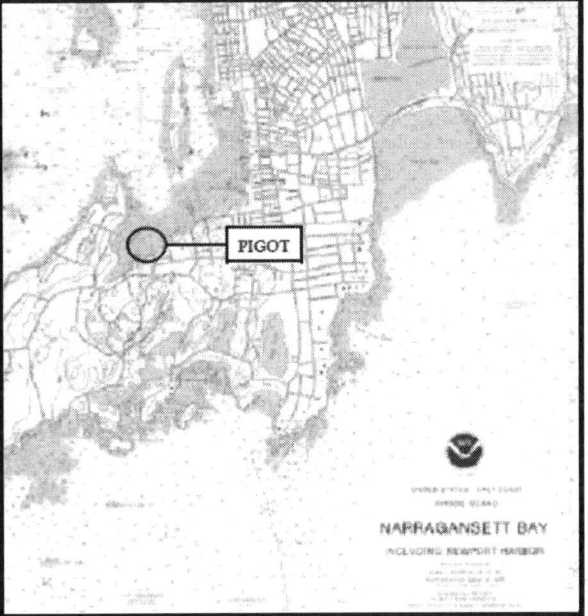

The Vessel

Type: Galley
Construction: Wood
Use: Warship
Owner: British Navy
Nationality: British
Home Port: Newport, RI

The Event

Date of Incident: August 4, 1778
Disaster Type: Ashore & burned
Cause: To prevent capture
Status: Repaired
Location: A little south (from Fort Adams), near the shore on the opposite side of the cove

The Battle of Rhode Island - Inconsistencies

The interpretation of historic records is a lengthy and often frustrating task. Take, for example, the British galley **PIGOT**. The galley appears on a lengthy list of vessels which were stationed in Newport at one time or another during the British occupation. Depending on the source material, this vessel was either recently built or was purchased in North America by the British. Regardless of its origin, this vessel appears to be one of those assigned to protect the occupying forces at the port. The next inconsistency, and one that is more germane to this incident, is the location where she was stationed when the French fleet under D'Estaing arrived to aid in the liberation of the Americans on Aquidneck Island. One source puts the galley on station off the west shore of the island, near Freeborn Creek. Another has her assigned to duty at the mouth of the Sakonnet River. A third has her stationed near Brenton Point (in this case, the point where Fort Adams is located). There is a possibility that all three are correct with the missing element being the date of the specific assignment. For sake of argument, it will be accepted that she was located at or near the third location mentioned. As the French fleet approached, the British vessels were directed to do their best but under no circumstances should they let their vessels be captured. This has sometimes been interpreted as an order to scuttle and burn if outgunned and in threat of capture. The **PIGOT** was run ashore and set on fire but apparently not too badly damaged for she was returned to service and, in fact, was captured by forces of the Continental Navy off the coast of Rhode Island in October of the same year.

PIGOT

Narrative

Each of the following sources has some information about the event although all do not agree.

"Our French Allies" - ***PIGOT****, galley, stationed near Brenton's Point (Fort Adams), burnt a little south, near the shore, on the opposite side of the cove.*

"Newport Harbor and lower Narragansett Bay R.I. During the American Revolution" by Elizabeth Covell [Newport Historical Society, 1933] - [the entries herein are from the diary of one Frederick Mackenzie, an officer in the British Army] *August 4th - This morning the two French ships in the Narragansett passage stood round the north point of Conanicut. The ORPHEUS, LARK and* ***PIGOT****, observing the French ships coming up between Prudence and this island, were immediately run on shore; also, the JUNO, off Coddington Cove, the ORPHEUS at Almy's Point and the LARK and* ***PIGOT*** *at Freeborn's Creek, where they were set on fire...*

"Captain's Contentious" by Louis Arthur Norton (2009) - *... the British continued to use the stronghold at Newport to command much of eastern Narragansett Bay. The most effective British naval defense was a stout two-hundred-ton galley called the* ***PIGOT****, stationed at the mouth of the Sakonnet River, the gateway to many Rhode Island eastern shore communities. The galley had a crew of forty five, and girded with heavy antiboarding nets, the vessel was a formidable floating battery. ... When French ships bombarded Newport on 25 July, the British frigate FLORA ... was heaved down onto the beach so that its keel and bottom could be shaved of barnacles and sea grass. As a result of the French cannon bombardment ashore, the helpless FLORA was heavily damaged and declared unserviceable. The recently built British galley* ***PIGOT*** *was armed with twelve 8-pounders salvaged from the now-useless FLORA.*

Obviously, the **PIGOT** was run ashore and set ablaze but was not badly damaged for she was back in action in short order serving the British forces who had not been displaced from their occupation of Newport at this time. Several months later, **PIGOT** was captured and taken into the Continental Navy.

Research Sources

1. "Our French Allies" by Edwin Martin Stone (1884)
2. "Newport Harbor and lower Narragansett Bay During the American Revolution" by Elizabeth Covell for the Newport Historical Society (1932)
3. "The Sailing Navy 1775-1854" by Paul H. Silverstone (2006)
4. "British Warships In the Age of Sail" by Rif Winfield (2007)
5. "Captains Contentious" by Louis Arthur Norton (2009)

HMS FALCON

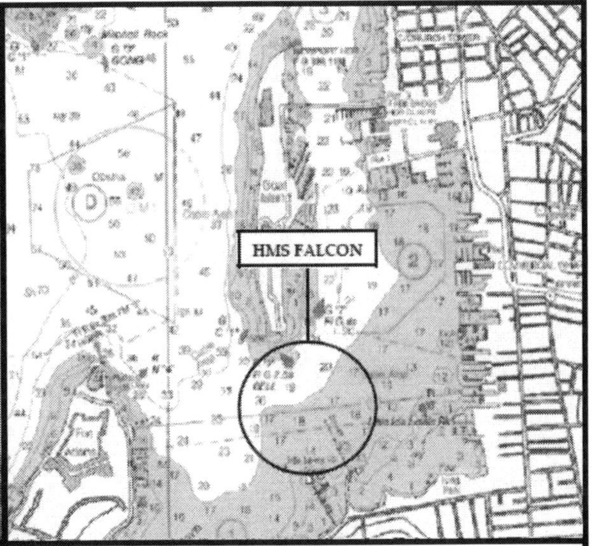

The Vessel

Type: Sloop
Construction: Wood
Use: Warship
Dimensions: 95′ x 27′ x 13′
Tonnage: 305
Launched: Portsmouth, England in 1771
Nationality: British
Home Port: Newport, RI

The Event

Owner: British Navy
Master: Cmdr. Henry Harmood
Date of Incident: August 5, 1778
Disaster Type: Sunk
Cause: Intentional (as a blockship)
Status: Raised
Location: Near the south end of Goat Island, Newport

The Battle of Rhode Island - The British Defense of Newport

British forces occupied the city of Newport from December of 1776 until October of 1779. In the latter part of the summer of 1778 the French, who were sympathetic to the American cause, sent a fleet of ships to assist in a combined land and sea attack on the British in Newport. The plan to coordinate such an attack would have been most difficult in an age when communication would have been carried out by small dispatch vessels and couriers. While the American troops were preparing for the land portion of an attack the British troops in Newport were preparing to meet both forces on both fronts. To help defend the city, a number of transport vessels were sunk in the waters around Goat Island. The weather became an unanticipated wild card and the attack was delayed for several days. A number of French vessels were driven offshore in the storm but several were able to force their way into Narragansett Bay and lay siege to the city. Orders were given by the leaders of the occupying forces to the effect that British vessels should be run ashore, if circumstances warranted, so as to prevent capture as their loss would be preferable to their being captured. Still other vessels were sunk as blockships to prevent the enemy from being able to sail directly into the inner harbor. The sloop **HMS FALCON** was one of the vessels sunk in Newport Harbor, off the southeastern part of Goat Island. After the departure of the French, the sloop was raised, refitted and recommissioned. Her new master, Commander Richard Lock, had a short career on this vessel as she was reported to have foundered with all hands in a storm off the coast in late September, 1778.

HMS FALCON

Narrative

The following notes are from some of the sources of information that have been recorded over the years that have recorded the Battle of Rhode Island and the occupation of Newport by the British.

"Our French Allies" - *The HMS FLORA and the* ***FALCON****, an 18-gun sloop, were sunk with their armaments while the other eight British vessels on station here were burnt and all their munitions of war went to the bottom.* ***FALCON*** *was stationed between Goat Island and the Dumplings and was sunk near the south end of Goat Island.*

"History of Rhode Island" by Reverend Edward Peterson - *The* ***FALCON*** *and FLORA, frigates, were sunk; the latter at Fort Wolcott Wharf and they were never afterward able to float her.* [There is some confusion as to the type and final fate of these vessels, depending on the source material.]

"Newport Harbor and lower Narragansett Bay R.I. During the American Revolution" by Elizabeth Covell [Newport Historical Society, 1933] - [the entries herein are from the diary of one Frederick Mackenzie, an officer in the British Army] *August 8th - Soon after the French fleet anchored within the harbor, the General gave orders for all houses and buildings within reach of our (British) guns to be set on fire; this was done and about 20 were burnt. While the French were coming in, the orders were given to scuttle and sink the FLORA and* ***FAULCON****, the former between the Long Wharf and Goat Island and the latter off the SE end of Goat Island.*

It is clear that the **HMS FALCON** was sunk and not burned. It also seems clear that the sloop was later raised although the indication that she was lost at sea just six weeks after this incident suggests a very rapid refit.

Research Sources

1. Notes from "Our French Allies" by Edwin Martin Stone (1884)
2. "History of Rhode Island" by Edward Peterson (1853)
3. "Newport Harbor and lower Narragansett Bay During the American Revolution" by Elizabeth Covell for the Newport Historical Society (1932)
4. "The Sailing Navy 1775-1854" by Paul H. Silverstone (2006)
5. "British Warships In the Age of Sail" by Rif Winfield (2007)
6. Rhode Island Ocean Special Area Management Plan (2010)

LORD SANDWICH

The barque EARL OF PEMBROKE in this painting was built in Whitby, England in 1764. A few years later she would be renamed ENDEAVOUR and participate in the first circumnavigation of the world with Captain James Cook. Renamed the **LORD SANDWICH**, she may have served as a troop transport and prison ship in Newport.

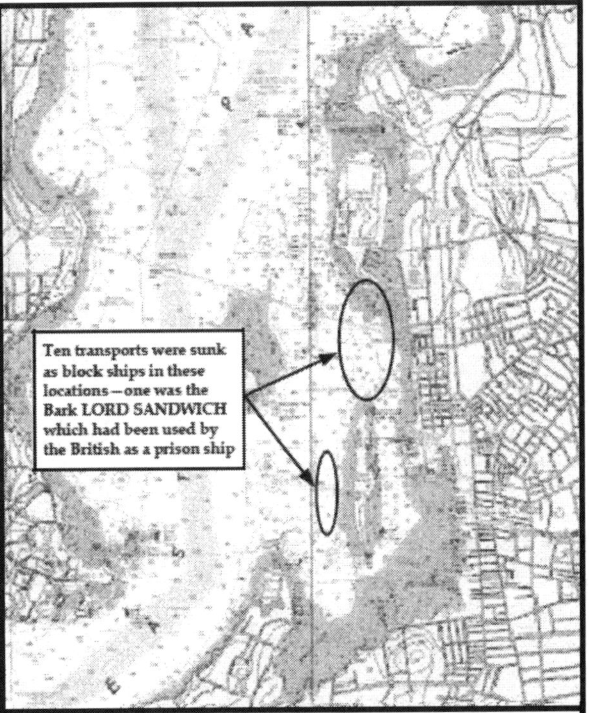

The Vessel

Type: Bark
Construction: Wood
Use: Transport/Prison Ship
Dimensions: 97′ x 29′
Tonnage: 368
Launched: Whitby, England in 1764
Owner: British Navy
Nationality: British
Home Port: Newport, RI (when lost)

Final Voyage

Date of Loss: August 3-6, 1778
Disaster Type: Sunk
Cause: Intentional to block access to Newport Harbor by approaching French forces
Final Status: Total loss
Location: Vessels were sunk between north end of Goat Island and "Blue Rocks" and some to the west of Goat Island. A possible site for this vessel is at 41-30.149 N, 71-19.830W

Narrative

Of all of the vessels lost in the waters off Newport, there is none less intriguing than the British bark **LORD SANDWICH**. The story of her loss is well known and is well documented. During the early years of the Revolutionary War the city of Newport was occupied by British forces. In the summer of 1778 rumors were rampant that a French fleet of warships was going to come to the aid of the Americans and would force the British to give up their hold on Newport. News of the imminent arrival of this fleet reached Newport at the end of July and despite a significant number of troops in the city, there were only a limited number of British warships stationed around Aquidneck Island and in Narragansett Bay and it was important to leave them at their stations to give the alarm should the French fleet attempt to sneak up on the city through other than a direct approach. Captain John Brisbane, the British Commander at Newport, decided that it would be a good idea to block the approach to the inner harbor by sinking some of his surplus vessels. Ten identified vessels, including the **LORD SANDWICH** were sunk.

LORD SANDWICH

The Prison Ship Lord Sandwich

The incident to the **LORD SANDWICH** is straightforward, but what is less certain is the history of the vessel and the possibility that this vessel might be the same vessel known a dozen years earlier as HM Bark ENDEAVOUR. A great deal of research has been done to prove the link between the two named vessels and there is a strong argument to support the accuracy of that possibility. But is that argument strong enough? The bark EARL OF PEMBROKE was built in Whitby, North Yorkshire, England in 1764. In late March of 1768, she was purchased for service by the British government to be used in the upcoming voyage of James Cook. She was renamed ENDEAVOUR. After returning to England at the end of a successful circumnavigation of the globe, the ENDEAVOUR was put into store ship service and assigned to supply the Falkland Islands. In September of 1774, the ENDEAVOUR was "paid off" and in the following March was sold to J. Mather, a private shipper, according to the Lloyds Register of 1775-1776. In December of 1775, the navy requested Mather and others to each provide a vessel for use as troop transports to the American colonies. Mather selected the ENDEAVOUR for that purpose but on December 6th of that year, she failed survey and was not accepted for that service. Later in that month, Mather renamed the ENDEAVOUR to be the **LORD SANDWICH** and he again submitted the vessel for use as a transport; again, the vessel was found to be unacceptable for service. Mather seemed determined to have this ship accepted for service so he had the **LORDSANDWICH** repaired and for a third time submitted her for transport service. On February 4th the **LORD SANDWICH** was accepted. The bark sailed, with troops, to New York in 1776 and later correspondence from Lord Howe in New York indicates that the **LORD SANDWICH** was among the vessels dispatched to Newport with her troops. Once at Newport she served, at least for a time, as a prison ship according to the diary of Frederick Mackenzie, a British officer who was stationed there. The rest of the story is clearly known. What is not clear is whether or not the **LORD SANDWICH** accepted for use as a troop transport was the vessel formerly known as ENDEAVOUR. The argument to support that they were the same is strong. The transport bark **LORD SANDWICH** is noted at various stages in the story to be of the same tonnage as the ENDEAVOUR, but the likelihood of her being sufficiently repaired from a condition that failed survey twice to one that was acceptable for use, all within the period of one month, at least raises the question that she might not be the same vessel. The name **LORD SANDWICH** was not that uncommon and the vessel accepted for use as a transport could have been another of that name. That said, there is no doubt that there was a **LORD SANDWICH** and it was sunk somewhere outside Newport's inner harbor. Perhaps, the remains of this historic vessel will be found and the bark's former identity confirmed; only time will tell.

Research Sources

1. The Diary of Frederick Mackenzie
2. Providence Daily Journal, March 11, 1999
3. Providence Daily Journal, April 7, 1999
4. Providence Daily Journal, August 10, 1999
5. Correspondence with D.K. Abbass Ph.D.
6. "Endeavour and Resolution Revisited", Journal of the Newport Historical Society, Vol. 70
7. "Preliminary Report on the Australian National Maritime Museum's participation in the Rhode Island Marine Archaeology Project's search for HMB *Endeavour* August 2002"
8. Various Internet sites regarding the HM Bark Endeavour, Lord Sandwich, etc.

(There are various versions of the final status of HMS ENDEAVOUR as postulated by marine historians. This document represents an intensive investigation by the author on this vessel and is believed to be authoritative.)

NEWPORT UNDER SEIGE

Vessels Involved

BETTY - 234 tons - Long, Master

BRITANNIA - 374 tons - Trousdale, Master

EARL OF OXFORD - 231 tons - Johnson, Master

GOOD INTENT - 241 tons - Harrison, Master

GRAND DUKE OF RUSSIA - 671 tons - Holman, Master

LORD SANDWICH—368 tons—Blanchard, Master (see separate data sheet)

MALAGA - 205 tons - Chien, Master

RACHEL AND MARY - 320 tons - Rowbotham, Master

SUSANNA - 254 tons - Spencer, Master

UNION - 261 tons - Bryson, Master

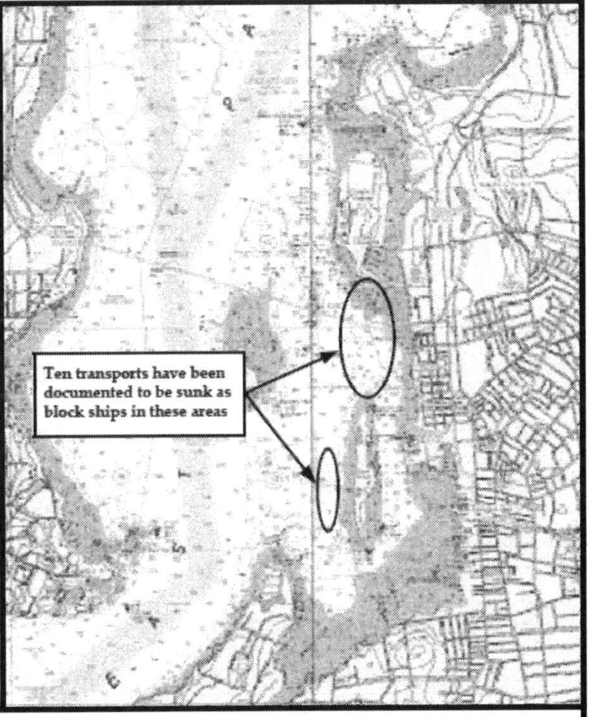

Narrative

December, 1776 was a bad month for Newporters as British forces began to land in the town, marking the beginning of an active occupation of the port city that would continue for almost three years, their final departure not occurring until the latter part of 1779. For some time prior to the actual occupation of the city British ships had been arriving in Narragansett Bay and the increasing number of troops caused great anxiety for the local residents who were forced to "contribute" livestock and other commodities needed to support the unwelcome visitors. In late November, 6,500 troops on 60 transports gathered in New York for the planned occupation of Newport giving them complete control of Narragansett Bay. The troops were commanded by Sir Henry Clinton, while command of the fleet was assigned to Admiral Sir Peter Parker. On the 7th, the British fleet entered the bay via the West Passage, sailing up to and around the northern point of Conanicut Island before heading toward Aquidneck Island. On the 8th, some troops were landed on Long Wharf, Newport, and the main body at Greensdale in Middletown. The American forces, in anticipation of the landing, hastily left the island presenting little or no resistance to the occupiers. The British commander, Clinton, left Rhode Island in early January, 1777 and command of the troops passed to the Honorable Hugh Earl Percy who remained in charge for just three months. Percy returned to England in April, 1777 passing command to General Prescott. Skirmishes involving local American patriots were common and, in fact, General Prescott himself was captured in July resulting in the appointment of General Sir Richard Pigot who was sent to Newport from New York for that purpose. In October, 1777 the size of the British occupation forces at Newport was estimated at about 4,000 men plus the men who manned the British ships in the bay. Some warships but mostly transport vessels, sailed to and from Narragansett Bay during this time, resulting in a fluctuation of the size of the force. Although the British occupied Newport, they were unable to accomplish their original plan of using Newport as a base of operations for an attack on Boston from the south. The British did consider but did not make an attack on Providence, but the warships stationed at Newport and around Aquidneck Island were used offensively in at least once case when in May of 1778

NEWPORT UNDER SEIGE

several were dispatched to thwart an attempted attack on Newport by American forces. The summer months o f 1778 approached bringing with them rumors that a fleet of ships from France was to be sent to the aid of the Americans. General Pigot responded by rebuilding forts on Brenton Point, Goat Island, Rose Island and Conanicut Island. There can be little doubt that there was concern by Pigot of an attempt to release the British grasp on Narragansett Bay. On July 29th word was received of the sighting of the French fleet. For some reason, the fleet, commanded by Count d'Estaing, decided to come to anchor off the reef [probably Brenton Reef] perhaps awaiting all of the vessels to arrive. Preparations for an attack on Newport were undertaken when, surprisingly, the French fleet set sail and headed away from the bay. The purpose of this move has never been clearly explained but they were gone for two days before returning to Rhode Island Sound on August 2nd. On August 3rd General Pigot ordered five or six transports to be sunk *"from the north end of Goat Island to the town"* to obstruct the entrance to the harbor on that side. Three others were held ready to sink at the south entrance. On the 5th of August *"four transports were sunk in the morning on the west side of Goat Island."*

Over the years these sunken vessels have been sought after by divers and archeologists for their historical significance. One of these, the HMS LORD SANDWICH, may have even greater significance if proven to have originally been named HMS ENDEAVOUR, a vessel used by Captain James Cook in his circumnavigation of the world.

Of late, there is yet another possible twist to the story. One might expect that following the departure of the French fleet and after hostilities of the war had ended, that the merchants of Newport would seek to clear away these obstructions to shipping seeking to enter Newport harbor, and that well may be the case. Recently, the following entry in the Newport Mercury of January 4, 1845 was discovered.

Newport Mercury, January 4, 1845 P1

A Chronological Account of all material occurrences from the first settlement of Rhode Island - 1780

... The wrecks of the British Vessels, sunk in the harbor of Newport were sold by the state to individuals and most of them raised, among them was the Frigate FLORA which lay sunk near the fort...

The specific mention of the Frigate FLORA definitely links this newspaper tidbit to the vessels in question. What remains to be found is definitive proof of which vessels may, indeed, have been raised from their watery graves to be disposed of in some unspecified location less intrusive to the shipping traffic normally found in and around Newport. That proof will be elusive.

Research Sources

1. "Preliminary Report on the Australian National Maritime Museum's participation in the Rhode Island Marine Archaeology Project's search for HMB *ENDEAVOUR* August 2002"
2. Information compiled from ADM 106/3404 and ADM 49/127 (D.K. Abbass, 1999)
3. "History of Newport County, Rhode Island. 1638 to 1887" by Richard M. Bayles (1888)
4. "Newport Harbor and Lower Narragansett Bay Rhode Island During the American Revolution" by Mrs. Elizabeth Covell (Newport Historical Society Bulletin, January, 1933)
5. Newport Mercury, January 4, 1845 P1
6. The Diary of Frederick McKenzie

GRAND TURK

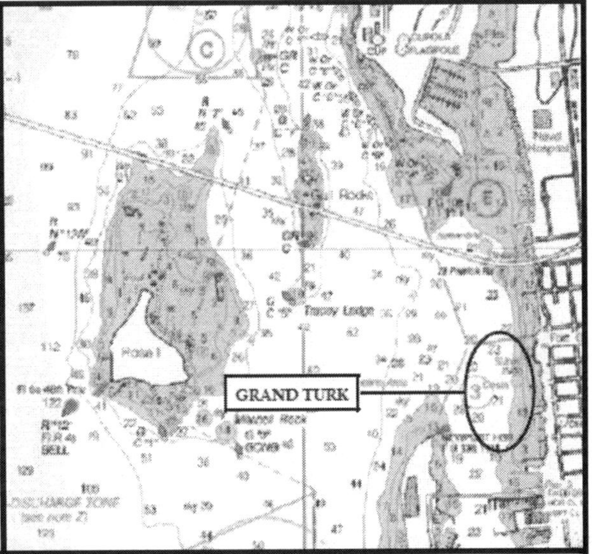

The Vessel

Type: Ship
Construction: Wood
Use: Transport
Owner: British Navy
Nationality: British
Home Port: Newport, RI

The Event

Date of Incident: August 8, 1778
Disaster Type: Ashore & sunk
Cause: Intentional – to block harbor entrance
Status: Unknown but probably saved
Location: Between Goat Island and the North Battery at Newport

Narrative

Connecticut Courant - August 18, 1778 P3

New London, August 14

We hear that a thousand troops from New York were at the east end of Long Island a few days ago collecting provisions for the British Army. Our accounts from Rhode Island, are , that last Saturday ten sail of Count D'Estaing's fleet which were lying below the town of Newport, went up the east side of Conanicut, and anchored above the ferry and as they passed the town the enemy kept up a brisk fire from their batteries, which was returned from the ships with great spirit, and we hear that the enemy had 12 men killed at one of their batteries, but that two men only were wounded in the fleet. That in the afternoon of the same day the enemy burnt eight dwelling-houses which were situated just without their lines, about two miles north of the town, some of them were valuable buildings and at night they burnt a large ship which lay partly aground on the north side of Fort Island; she is supposed to be an old Indiaman which had been used for a transport and afterwards armed for a ship of war.

With some minor differences this story agrees with that documented in the diary of Frederick McKenzie, a British officer, who was stationed in Newport during the occupation by British forces from late in 1776 until the latter part of 1779. The large ship referred to is identified in that diary as the **GRAND TURK**. It is interesting to note the conjecture that the ship may have been a former Indiaman as a search of the vessels of that trade has resulted in only two ships of that name, one built in 1781 and the other, quite a bit larger, that was not built until 1790.

GRAND TURK

The McKenzie Diary and the Transport Grand Turk

Frederick McKenzie is best known to us as the single most important chronicler of day-to-day life in Newport during the three years of occupation by the British. Of particular interest was his willingness to comment on the activities of both parties, British and American, and his attention to detail. In 1934, a local historian, Elizabeth Covell, of Newport, presented a paper to the Newport Historical Society based on the diary that McKenzie kept. Among the items of interest is a list of all British vessels that were stationed in Newport at some time during the occupation. On this list appears the ship **GRAND TURK**, identified as a transport. Specifically from the McKenzie diary comes the following excerpt for Aug. 8, 1778: " *Soon after the French Fleet anchored within the harbour, the general gave orders for all houses and buildings within reach of our guns to be set on fire; this was done and about 20 were burnt. While the French were coming in, the orders were given to scuttle and sink the FLORA and FAULCON, the former between the Long Wharf and Goat Island, and the latter off the southeast end of Goat Island. The* ***GRAND TURK*** *transport, formerly an East Indiaman, was run on shore between Goat Island and the North Battery."* It is clear that there was a large ship that was involved as the French fleet approached Newport but its true identity and final fate are yet to be confirmed.

Research Sources

1. Connecticut Courant, August 18, 1778 P3
2. "Newport Harbor and Lower Narragansett Bay Rhode Island During the American Revolution" by Mrs. Elizabeth Covell (Newport Historical Society Bulletin, January, 1933)
3. The Diary of Frederick McKenzie

HMS FLORA

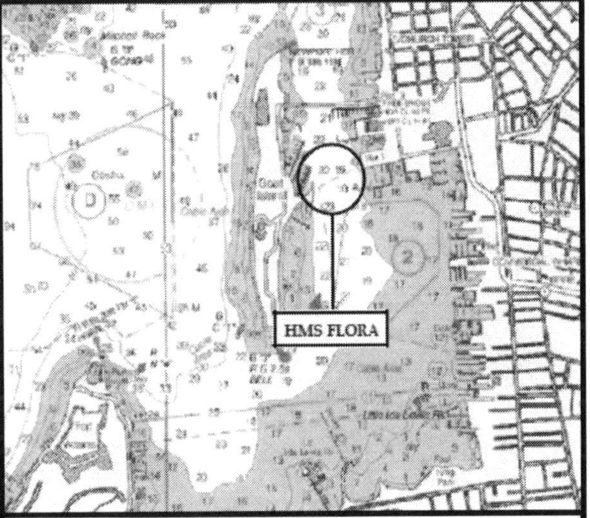

The Vessel

Type: Frigate
Construction: Wood
Use: Warship
Launched: Deptford, England in 1780
Owner: Royal Navy
Nationality: British

Final Voyage

Date of Loss: August 8, 1778
Disaster Type: Sunk
Cause: Intentional (to prevent capture)
Final Status: Raised
Location: Between Long Wharf and the wharf at Fort Wolcott on Goat Island

The Battle of Rhode Island - An Overview

British forces occupied the city of Newport from December of 1776 until October of 1779. The local residents were unable to break free of the grip of the military forces during this period and we can only imagine the anger and frustration that they experienced. But there was a glimmer of hope when in the latter part of the summer of 1778 it was learned that the French, who were sympathetic to the American cause, agreed to mount an attack on the British in Narragansett Bay. It was determined that a coordinated land and sea attack would be most effective but apparently neither side could keep a secret and while the Rhode Island troops were massing for an attack the British troops were reinforcing their positions outside Newport both on the land side and to seaward. A number of transports were sunk in the waters around Goat Island for further defense from the approaching French fleet of Count D'Estaing. Coordination of the attacking forces became an issue and the weather an unanticipated wild card. The attack was delayed for several days and several of the French ships were driven offshore by the natural effects of the storm. Nonetheless, the remnants of the French fleet were finally able to force their way into Narragansett Bay and lay siege to the city of Newport. The British, having a number of vessels at strategic positions within the bay, decided that they were not going to be able to successfully defend their position and were most concerned that their vessels should fall into the hands of the Americans to be used against them. Orders were given and almost all of the British vessels were directed to run their vessels ashore and set afire as their loss would be preferable to their capture. The frigate **HMS FLORA** was one of the vessels sunk in Newport Harbor but not burned. Although it took almost a year, she was eventually raised and rebuilt.

HMS FLORA

Narrative

The following notes are from some of the sources of information that have been recorded over the years that have recorded the Battle of Rhode Island and the occupation of Newport by the British. Note that there is a certain amount of diversity in the information which is pertinent only to the sinking of the **HMS FLORA**.

"Our French Allies" - ***FLORA** was a frigate of 32 guns. She and the FALCON, an 18-gun sloop were sunk with their armaments while the other eight British vessels on station here were burnt and all their munitions of war went to the bottom. **FLORA** was stationed south of Rose Island but was sunk in Newport Harbor south of Long Wharf.*

"The Battle of Rhode Island" by ex-Governor Charles W. Lippitt [Newport Historical Society Bulletin #18] - ... *August 6, eleven of the French ships approached Newport and under a heavy cannonade passed the town and its batteries. The only British frigate remaining in the harbor [**FLORA**] and a number of transports were burned in the greatest haste.*

"History of Rhode Island" by Reverend Edward Peterson - *The FALCON and **FLORA**, frigates, were sunk; the latter at Fort Wolcott Wharf and they were never afterward able to float her. About a year after the British evacuated the island, and the Americans took possession, the **FLORA** was floated, fitted for sea, and sent to France.*

"Newport Harbor and lower Narragansett Bay R.I. During the American Revolution" by Elizabeth Covell [Newport Historical Society, 1933] - *[the entries herein are from the diary of one Frederick Mackenzie, an officer in the British Army] August 8th - Soon after the French fleet anchored within the harbor, the General gave orders for all houses and buildings within reach of our (British) guns to be set on fire; this was done and about 20 were burnt. While the French were coming in, the orders were given to scuttle and sink the **FLORA** and FAULCON, the former between the Long Wharf and Goat Island and the latter off the SE end of Goat Island.*

It is clear that the frigate **FLORA** was sunk and not burned. It is also clear that she was later raised. Although some of the details vary, the basic facts are confirmed. From another source two other interesting facts have come. First, that the **FLORA** was eventually sunk for good in 1809. The second interesting fact is that this frigate was the first of her class when built and apparently the change was to accommodate an upgrading of her armament from 12-pounder cannon to 18-pounder cannon which made her a bit more formidable than others of her size which carried the lighter weaponry.

Research Sources

1. "Memoirs of Rhode Island", Rhode Island Republican, September 12, 1838
2. Notes from "Our French Allies" by Edwin Martin Stone (1884)
3. Newport Historical Society Bulletin #04 (October, 1912)
4. Newport Historical Society Bulletin #18 (October, 1915)
5. "History of Rhode Island" by Edward Peterson (1853)
6. "Newport Harbor and lower Narragansett Bay During the American Revolution" by Elizabeth Covell for the Newport Historical Society
7. Sailing Ships of the Old Navy 1750-1840 - Fa to Fu (Internet Source)

ACQUILLON

A painting entitled "French Frigate Engaged in Battle". Perhaps the battle between D'Estaing and Lord Howe was similar to this action.

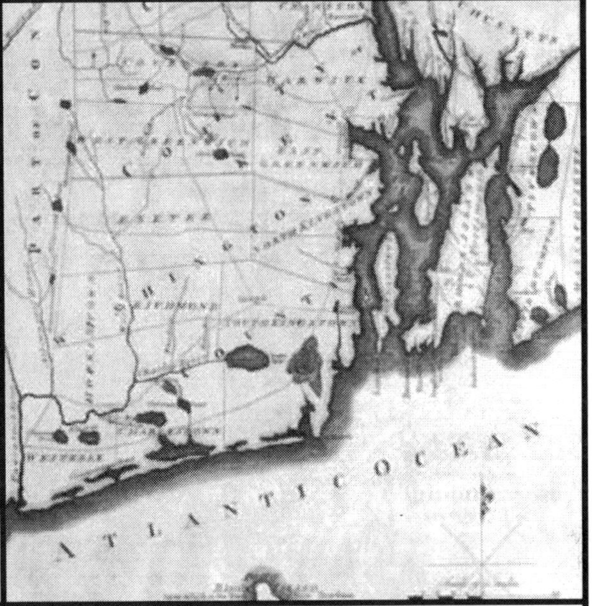

The Vessel

Type: Frigate
Construction: Wood
Use: Warship
Owner: French Navy
Nationality: French

Final Voyage

Date of Loss: August 14, 1778
Disaster Type: Sunk
Cause: In battle or storm
Final Status: Total loss
Location: Somewhere off Newport

A Battle Off Rhode Island

At the end of July, 1778 a fleet of French vessels arrived off the coast of Rhode Island causing the British forces that occupied Newport to destroy a number of their vessels to prevent capture. But before the French could do more to aid in what was to be a combined operation with American revolutionary forces, a fleet of British ships under the command of Lord Howe arrived from New York to do battle with the French. The following account from "A Naval History of the American Revolution," by Gardner Allen written in 1913 describes the campaign.

... D'Estaing remained off Sandy Hook eleven days and is said to have captured during that time twenty British vessels bound into New York. July 22 he sailed for Newport, having been requested by Washington to cooperate with General Sullivan in an attack on that town. On the 29th the French fleet appeared off Newport and a few days later occupied the eastern and western channels of Narragansett Bay. ... Unfortunately Sullivan did not get ready for the movement against Newport until August 8. D'Estaing then ran into the central channel of the bay, under fire from the batteries at the entrance, and anchored the main body of his fleet north of the harbor. The attack was planned for the 10th. On the 9th the British fleet appeared off Point Judith, where it anchored. Howe had sailed from New York August 1, having been reinforced by several ships of Admiral Byron's fleet, which had been scattered by a storm on its passage from England. Howe now had with him one seventy-four, seven sixty-fours, five fifties, two forty-fours, six frigates, and several small vessels. Although his force was thus considerably increased, he was still somewhat weaker than his adversary, and seems to have no intention of attacking. Under the circumstances, however, D'Estaing preferred the open sea, and early the next morning, August 10, the

ACQUILLON

wind having shifted to the north during the night, he cut his cables and ran out of the bay. Upon observing this movement of the French, Howe got under way, and the two fleets spent the next twenty- four hours maneuvering for the weather-gauge, or, according to D'Estaing's account, the British fleet fled before the wind, attempting to get back to New York, with the French in pursuit. This continued until late on the afternoon of the 11th, and the leading French ships were just overhauling the British rear, when the wind, which had been increasing, became a violent gale, which soon scattered the vessels of both fleets, each ship being engaged in a struggle with the elements. "At half-past three in the morning" of the 12th, says D'Estaing in his report, "the bowsprit broke, then the foremast, then the main-top, then the mizzenmast; finally, the mainmast fell. Our rudder broke next. The last misfortune was the greatest of all. We were now only a floating mass with nothing to steady us and nothing to guide us." This was the plight of the Admiral's flagship, the LANGUEDOC, of ninety guns. The storm continued unabated until the afternoon of the 13th, when it subsided. Before night the LANGUEDOC and another dismasted French ship were attacked by two British ships, but darkness put an end to the encounter. The next day most of the French fleet came together and anchored for temporary repairs. The British made their way back to New York. D'Estaing, having completed necessary repairs, bore away for Rhode Island August 17, and appeared again before Newport on the 20th. It was then decided that the fleet could be thoroughly refitted at no place nearer than Boston, and D'Estaing therefore sailed again on the 22d, to the great disappointment of Sullivan, who was forced to abandon his campaign against Newport.

From the diary of Frederick Mackenzie, a British officer stationed in Newport at the time, a similar account is found. Mackenzie noted that on the 9th, *At 12 o'clock a fleet hove in sight to the southward increasing in number until 35 sail appeared, standing directly for the harbor. It was our fleet under the command of Lord Howe, from New York. It lay at anchor overnight. The next day the French fleet got in motion, and kept up a prodigious fire as they passed our batteries, which was returned, but the ships were too far away for either side to do too much damage. As soon as Lord Howe saw them coming he made sail. His reasons for thus retiring before the French fleet are not known to us.* On the 12th he noted, *Heavy rain all night and day, with strong gale at northeast. ... The inhabitants say they have not had so severe a storm for three or four years past.* An entry on the 14th states, *Five dead bodies and part of a wheel and tiller rope supposed to belong to one of the French ships, was found yesterday on the shore of Brenton's Neck.*

In 1853, Peterson's "History of Rhode Island" noted the following as having been reported in Mackenzie's diary under the date of August 22, 1778, *With respect to the French fleet, it is reported that the* ***ACQUILLON****, a frigate is lost, the TONNANT, of 84 guns, missing, and the rest of the fleet shattered and damaged.*

Researching the composition of the French fleet during this campaign shows nothing of a vessel of this name and, in fact, it does not appear that the French navy ever had a vessel of this name built, captured or purchased. Nonetheless, it would appear that the wreckage that came ashore represents a vessel lost or at least badly damaged. Could this material have come from Count D'Estaing's LANGUEDOC? It is possible but will take more in-depth research to confirm.

Research Sources

1. "History of Rhode Island" by Reverend Edward Peterson (1853)
2. "A Naval History of the American Revolution" [Vol. I] by Gardner Allen (1913)
3. "Newport Harbor and Lower Narragansett Bay, Rhode Island, During the American Revolution" by Mrs. Elizabeth Covell (Newport Historical Society Bulletin, No. 86, 1933)

MINERVA

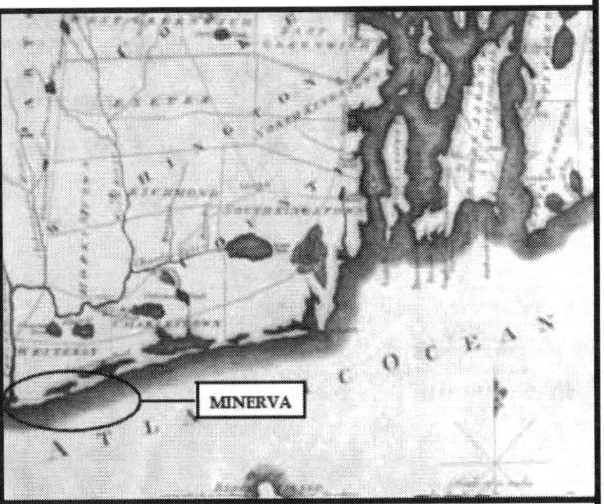

The Vessel

Type: Ship
Construction: Wood
Use: Transport
Tonnage: 300
Owner: British Navy
Nationality: British
Home Port: Bath, ME

Final Voyage

Date of Loss: Fall/Winter, 1778
Disaster Type: Stranding
Cause: Unknown
Final Status: Total loss
Location: Somewhere along the shore of King's County (probably off Westerly), Rhode Island

Narrative

During the Revolutionary War years British warships and their support vessels were a constant presence in Rhode Island waters. And one might expect that with the large number of vessels present there would be accidents, some minor and others of a more serious nature. But documenting these events, given the remoteness of the colony, was difficult and often resulted in gaps in the information. The incident with regards to the probable loss of the British ship **MINERVA** provides an excellent example of this. According to one source, this ship was possibly lost on October 21, 1778 off Westerly. This could not be confirmed through the local news of the time. But the following legal announcement was posted in late January, 1779.

Providence Gazette and Country Journal - January 30, 1779 P3

State of Rhode Island and Providence Plantations

*A libel filed before me, by William Channing, Esq., Attorney General, for and in behalf of said state, against the British ship called the **MINERVA**, of the burthen of three hundred tons, and the British sloop called the MISS NORTH, of the burthen of forty tons, their furniture, appurtenances, and cargos, which have lately been shipwrecked, and driven on the shores of said state, in the county of King's County, and by a warrant from his excellency the Governor, and a warrant from the offices of the Superior Court of said state, have been taken into custody by the sheriff of said county, whereupon the said William prays, that the said ship and sloop, their appurtenances, and cargoes, may be adjudged forfeited and confiscated, for the use of said state. Another libel is also filed before me, by Nathan Babcock, of Westerly, in said county, for himself, against the aforesaid ship, her appurtenances and cargo; who prays that the same may be adjudged forfeited and confiscated, for his use. The claims of the said libellants respectively, will be tried at*

MINERVA

the maritime court of said state, appointed to be holden at the state house in South Kingstown, in said county, on the fifteenth day of February, A.D. 1779, at the hour of ten in the forenoon. This notice of said trial is given, that the owner or owners, or any person or persons concerned, may appear at said court and show cause, if they have any, why the said vessels, their appurtenances and cargoes respectively, should not be adjudged and condemned, agreeable to the prayer of one of the other said libellants. JOHN FOSTER, Judge of Said Court.

The following account notes a vessel wrecked in this area two months after the October date.

Providence Gazette and Country Journal - December 19, 1778 P3

Providence, December 19

... Extract of a letter from a gentleman in the southern part of this state, dated December 14, 1778. "Last night a large transport was driven ashore at Westerly. Her cargo consists of 30 or 40 of the enemy's troops, two puncheons of rum, and some other articles."

It is possible that both news items relate to the same vessel though the December account does not mention the sloop. One thing is quite certain, it was a trying time for shipmasters. For now, this incident with two possible dates will be considered to be one and the same event. The final fate of the vessel or outcome of the libel suit is not known.

Research Sources

1. Providence Gazette and Country Journal, December 19, 1778 P3
2. Providence Gazette and Country Journal, January 30, 1779 P3
3. "Shipwrecks in the Americas" by Robert Marx (1987)

PIGOT

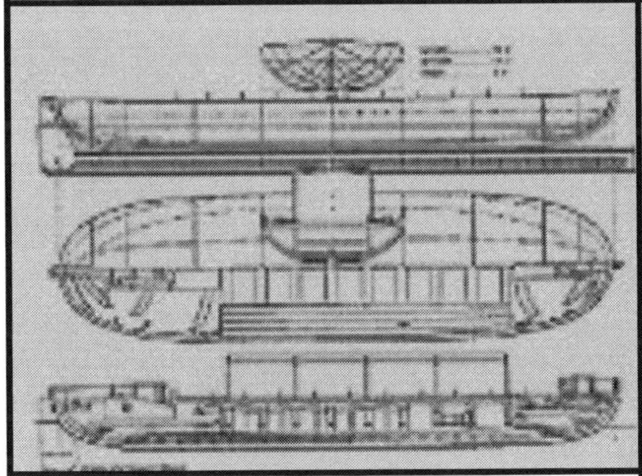

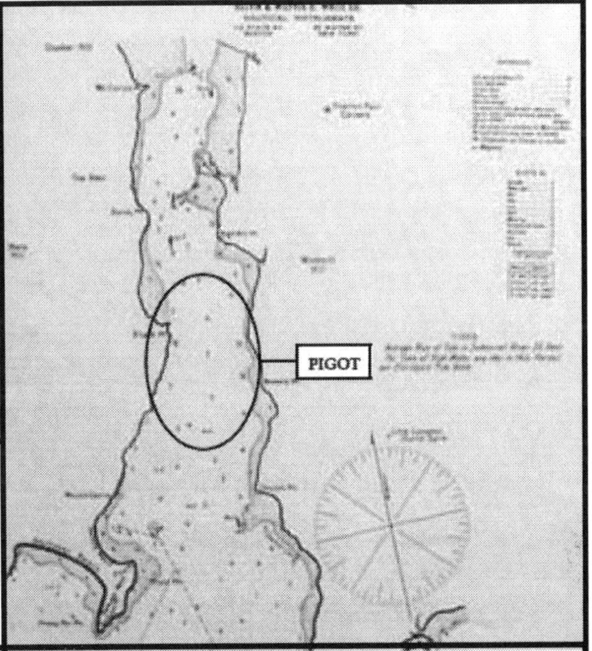

The origin of the Galley **PIGOT** is not clearly known but she was a purchased American vessel (July 19, 1778). Less than a month later she was burned in Newport but was later returned to duty.

The Vessel

Type: Galley
Construction: Wood
Use: Warship
Owner: British Navy
Nationality: British
Home Port: Newport, RI

The Event

Master: Lt. William Dunlap
Date of Incident: October 29, 1778
Disaster Type: Captured
Cause: War loss
Status: Taken to Connecticut and condemned
Location: Lower part of Sakonnet River

Narrative

Providence Gazette and Country Journal - November 7, 1778 P3

Providence, November 7

Extract of a letter from Major Talbot, to the Hon. Major-General Sullivan, dated Stonington, October 29, 1778. "I sailed from Providence in the sloop HAWK on Sunday the 25th Instant, with the troops you were pleased to put under my command, for the purpose of capturing the ***PIGOT*** *galley, then lying on the east side of Rhode Island; but the wind being small, came to anchor the same evening under Rocky Island. The next day we got through Bristol Ferry to Mount Hope. Wednesday night at ten o'clock made sail, and ran through Howland's Ferry; when we had got as far as Fogland Ferry, hauled down all sail, and drifted through under bare poles, to prevent any firing from the enemy's battery on Rhode Island, which might have alarmed the galley. We happily passed the battery undiscovered, and at half past one in the morning were within a small distance of the* ***PIGOT****. We were immediately hailed, and the marines on her quarter fired upon us. We reserved our fire, till we had run our jib boom through her fore shrouds, then threw in a volley of small arms, loaded with musket and buck shot. The seamen on deck soon ran below, calling for the master, and those below never ventured on deck; my men immediately ran out upon the jib boom, from which they boarded, and carried her without the loss of a man. We soon after came to sail, and arrived the same day in this harbour. The* ***PIGOT*** *mounts 8 twelve-pounders, and had 45 men on board; her nettings*

PIGOT

were eight feet above our gunwale. The captain behaved with great resolution, and defended the sides of his vessel in his shirt and drawers for some time, without a single man to assist him. My men all behaved well, Lieut. Helme, of Col. Topham's Regiment, behaved with the greatest spirit, and was the first man on board the **PIGOT**.*" The prisoners taken in the* **PIGOT** *galley were conducted here on Monday last, and sent on board the prison ship in the river.*

Almost a century later, in 1860, the story was retold by Samuel Greene Arnold in volume 2 of his "History of the State of Rhode Island and Providence Plantations. His account clarifies some of the confusion in the letter from Talbot.

... The east passage was blockaded by the **PIGOT** *galley, a stout vessel of two hundred tons, armed with eight twelve-pounders, defended by strong boarding-nettings, and having a crew of forty-five men. Talbot determined to take her. In a small sloop called the HAWK, equipped with two three-pounders and a corps of sixty men, under Lieutenant Baker, selected from the troops then quartered in Providence, he embarked on his perilous expedition. A headwind detained him the first night in the river, but the next day he passed in safety the British battery at Bristol Ferry, and anchored in Mount Hope Bay to await a favorable wind. The following day he proceeded alone to Little Compton to reconnoiter, and finding the* **PIGOT** *armed at all points, he obtained fifteen more men under Lieutenant William Helme of Topham's regiment. The next night being very dark, and the wind favorable, they made sail until near the fort at Fogland Ferry, where they lowered sail and silently drifted with the tide, under bare poles, past the battery. It was so dark that they had to send out a boat with muffled oars to find the galley. This done they crowded sail and bore down upon the enemy. A volley of musketry greeted their approach, and was answered by a discharge of small arms from the HAWK; but before the* **PIGOT** *could bring her cannon to bear, the jibboom of the HAWK tore through the nettings and caught in the foreshrouds. Lieutenant Helme, followed by his command, ran along the bowsprit, and boarded the enemy. Her crew were driven below, the commander alone fighting gallantly on deck. The galley was taken without the loss of a man on either side, and the HAWK with her prize bore away for Stonington.*

Epilogue

The capture of the British galley **PIGOT** was a big deal, especially for Major Talbot who was promoted to the rank of Lieutenant-Colonel and was presented with what was described as a "genteel silver-hilted sword". Further, once the condemnation proceedings were completed, he assumed command of the vessel and proceeded to sail the New England coast and capture other enemy vessels. The galley itself, for reasons unstated, continued in service only until early 1780.

Research Sources

1. Providence Gazette and Country Journal, November 7, 1778 P3
2. "History of the State of Rhode Island and Providence Plantations" Vol. II by Samuel Greene Arnold (1860)
3. "The Navy of the American Revolution" by Charles Oscar Paullin (1906)
4. "British Warships in the Age of Sail 1714-1792" by Rif Winfield (2007)

RENOWN

The fourth rate ship HMS ACTIVE is representative of the class of vessel to which the **HMS RENOWN** belonged. The attack on this vessel during the winter of 1778 showed the ingenuity of the American rebels in waging war.

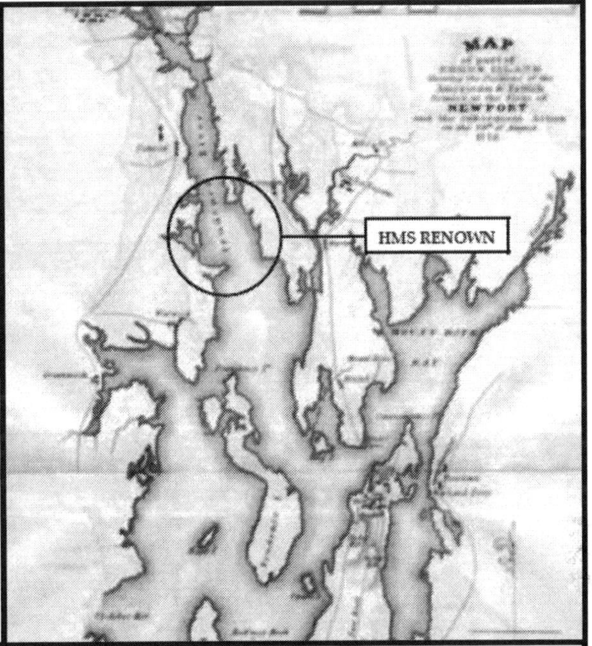

The Vessel

Type: 4th rate ship
Construction: Wood
Use: Warship
Dimensions: 119′ x 40′ x 17′
Tonnage: 1,050
Launched: Southampton, England in 1774
Owner: British Navy
Nationality: British
Home Port: Providence, RI

The Event

Master: George Dawson
Cargo: N/A
Date of Incident: Winter, 1778
Disaster Type: Attacked
Cause: Act of War
Status: Undamaged
Location: At anchor somewhere in the Providence River

A Novel Plan of Attack

Normally unusual incidents are not difficult to track down though there often are a number of different versions of the story. This one is the exception, for although numerous sources were checked, only one version could be found. The story represents unusual ingenuity on the part of the American rebels and their plan could have been a major event in the Revolutionary War had it been successful. The story is taken from a book entitled, "A History of American Privateers" by Edgar Stanton Maclay.

... Stimulated by his successes against the ASIA and the PIGOT, [Lieutenant Colonel] *Talbot soon formed a plan for destroying the 50-gun ship* ***RENOWN****, which the enemy, late in 1778, stationed off Rhode Island. An old, high-sided merchant ship, of about 400 tons, was carried down the river a few miles below Providence, and a stage was built on her deck, as if for carrying cattle. This stage was calculated to be about seven feet higher above the surface of the water than the upper tier of guns in the* ***RENOWN****, and was spread out over the sides in order to facilitate boarding when the two vessels lay close together, and its height would not only enable the men to command the decks of the enemy, but place them above the fire of their guns. To drive the enemy from their upper decks, the colonel provided a great number of stout earthen pots, each of which held three pounds of dry gunpowder and three hand grenades ready charged.*

RENOWN

These fire pots were securely closed, and then, to preserve them from any ready charged. These fire pots were securely closed, and then, to preserve them from any accidental wet, covered with sheep or lamb skin, with the wool on the outside. Over all were laid two pieces of slow match that were so long that when lashed on with a cord made a handle to hold it by, while the ends of the match hung below the pot as much as twelve inches. By repeated experiments the colonel found that any man of common strength could throw these pots to a distance of forty feet with considerable certainty. Their fall on the deck would infallibly break them and scatter the contents, when the fire of the slow match would communicate with the loose powder, and in an instant with the grenades. It was the colonel's design, in real action, to station one hundred men in a convenient part of his ship with one of these fire pots in each hand. He conceived that the explosion on the enemy's decks of two hundred pots, containing together six hundred pounds of dry powder, and the successive bursting of six hundred hand grenades, would in the night, when assisted by musketry fire from two hundred men and the shouts and huzzas of all, produce a terrible scene of destruction and alarm at the first outset, drive the enemy from their quarters, so that the boarding party might, without great difficulty, succeed in getting possession of the quarter deck of the man-of-war. Talbot also counted on, as a considerable item in the success of this enterprise, the reported lack of discipline aboard the ***RENOWN****, he having learned from some prisoners who had been detained aboard this craft that her officers were especially negligent at night. On the evening selected for the attempt, the American vessel dropped six miles farther down the river, while a body of nearly four hundred men marched along the shore, abreast of her, ready to embark and take part in the attempt when all was ready. Unfortunately for the projectors of this daring scheme, the weather that night suddenly came on very cold, the ice forming so rapidly in the river as to prevent the land force from getting aboard, and when morning dawned it was found that the river was frozen over, holding both the* ***RENOWN*** *and the merchantman immoveable all that winter.*

Once the ice broke up sufficiently to release the RENOWN, she was moved to a location off Newport where she could be protected by the guns on the fort at Goat Island.

Research Sources

1. "A History of American Privateers" by Edgar Stanton Maclay (1899)
2. "British Warships In the Age of Sail 1714-1792" by Rif Winfield (2007)

HERMIONE

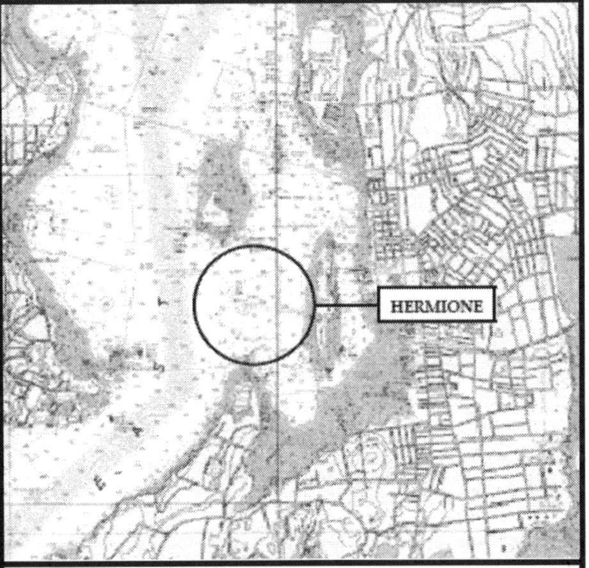

The Vessel

Type: Ship's boat
Construction: Wood
Dimensions: 42' long
Owner: French Navy
Nationality: French

The Event

Date of Incident: April 13, 1781
Disaster Type: Sunk
Cause: Accident
Status: Probably retrieved
Location: Newport Harbor

The French Frigate Hermione

Although the name of the French frigate **HERMIONE** is not immediately recognizable to students of Newport's maritime history, this vessel was involved in one of the most significant events that took place during the revolutionary era. When she set sail from Rochefort, France on March 11, 1780 she carried the French general La Fayette who arrived in Newport some seven weeks later for meetings with General Washington to advise the American commander that more than 5,000 French reinforcements and five frigates were being sent to support the American forces in their efforts to attain freedom from British rule. **HERMIONE** remained in port for a short time before proceeding on to Boston but during this short stay suffered a terrible accident which resulted in the loss of a number of her crew. The incident was not to the vessel herself but rather to her boat which can be seen

between the foremast and mainmast on the model above. The frigate, built in 1779, was over 140 feet long and nearly 1,200 tons, more than large enough to carry a boat that was itself more than forty feet in length.

HERMIONE

Narrative

Newport Mercury - January 25, 1845 P1
An Account of all material Occurrences from the 1st settlement of Rhode Island – 1781

On the 13th of April a boat belonging to the French Frigate ***HERMIONE*** *accidentally sunk in the harbor of Newport, by which eleven men were unfortunately drowned.*

It seems somewhat ironic that having survived a trip across the Atlantic, these sailors met with such an accident when only a short distance from shore.

Research Sources

1. Newport Mercury, January 25, 1845 P1
2. Information on French Frigate HERMIONE (1779) from the Internet
3. Photo of the reconstructed longboat of the frigate from the vessel reconstruction website

Section II - The 1800s and Beyond

The years following the American Revolution through the years when the United States became involved in World War I were notable for the expansion of our country in size and population and as America grew, the development of commerce grew with the resultant increase in the number of ships. This period was not free of disputes with other countries and the varied interests among our own citizens also led to trouble and strife. During this era there was a war with Great Britain, in 1812, a major American Civil War in the 1860s and, as the 19th century ended, a war with Spain.

Also, this period saw the growth in size of sailing vessels to sizes never before imagined and to their eventual decline as steam powered vessels became the predominant group. Government vessels often led that change, but experimentation with new technology often led to unexpected and disastrous incidents. After the Civil War, emphasis on the US Navy was increased and with that came a concentrated effort on their part for the development of a variety of specialized craft. Along with technological advances in shipbuilding came similar advances in the areas of safety (lighthouses and lightships) and salvage so that many, if not most of the vessels involved in incidents during this period were raised, repaired, rescued and often returned to service. In terms of military or paramilitary disasters during this time in Rhode Island waters, maritime disasters were much more frequently caused by weather and mechanical incidents rather than by act of war.

REVENGE

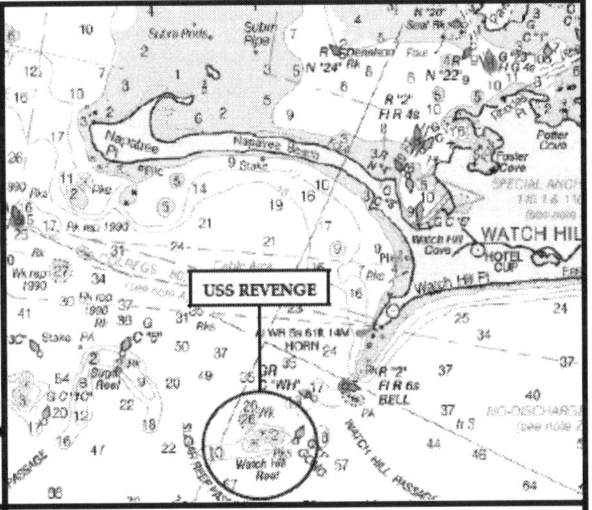

The Vessel

Type: Schooner
Construction: Wood
Use: Warship
Dimensions: 70′ length
Owner: US Navy
Nationality: American
Official No.: N/A
Home Port: New London, CT

Final Voyage

Port of Departure: Newport, RI
Port of Destination: New London, CT
Master: Lt. Oliver Hazard Perry
Date of Loss: January 9, 1811
Disaster Type: Ashore & sunk
Cause: Pilot error
Final Status: Total loss
Location: By the spindle on Watch Hill Reef

The Event

In early 1811, a young lieutenant Oliver Hazard Perry was assigned the task of surveying Newport Harbor in Rhode Island with the goal of having better charts. His was to be a one week trip and return to home base at New London. His vessel, the US schooner **REVENGE** never made it back. The following was reported on in the news of the time.

Newport Mercury - January 12, 1811 P3

Ship News—Port of Newport

... We learn with regret that the U.S. schooner ***REVENGE****, Lieut. Perry, which sailed from this port on Tuesday afternoon last for New London, went ashore on Wednesday morning on Watch Hill Reef, and soon afterwards went to pieces. The officers and crew were saved.*

Newport Mercury - January 19, 1811 P3

... We are sorry to find that the report mentioned in our last, of the loss of the U.S. schooner ***REVENGE****, is confirmed by the following extract from the New-London Gazette of Wednesday last. "Loss of the U.S. schooner* ***REVENGE****" On Wednesday morning last, the U.S. schooner* ***REVENGE****, of 14 guns, Lieut. Perry, in proceeding from Newport for this port, unfortunately struck on Watch Hill Reef and in a few hours went to pieces. The sails, rigging, 6 cannon, and almost every article of value was saved. The remainder of the cannon, it is said, , will be got up without much difficulty. At the time the* ***REVENGE*** *struck, the fog was so thick that the jib-boom could not be seen from the quarter deck. There was a branch pilot on board.*

REVENGE

A Surprise Discovery

Fifty years after its loss, the remains of the **REVENGE** were accidentally relocated when a salvage firm, in search of another distressed vessel, found her remains.

Newport Daily News - February 12, 1863 P2

Sub-Marine Operations at Watch Hill – A company from Boston have been in our vicinity for two or three weeks past, waiting the opportunity to examine the remains of the schooner EBEN SAWYER, from New Bedford, bound to New York, with a valuable cargo of sperm oil, yellow metal, &c., recently wrecked upon Watch Hill Reef. Most of the oil was saved at the time. The weather proved unfavorable until one day last week, when the operator made his first examination of the premises. In about two hours he discovered the remains of three distinct old wrecks, lying in about 42 feet of water, in a large basin beyond the ledge, forming an eddy where the water was unaffected by the strong tidal currents in that vicinity. One of these were the remains of the United States schooner ***REVENGE****, Oliver H. Perry, Commander, wrecked on her passage from Newport to New London, more than 50 years ago, the copper still remaining on her bottom.*

The accidental discovery of Perry's schooner was apparently only of interest due to its historic relationship to her commander and no action was taken beyond the reporting of the find. For the second time, the location of the vessel was left to be forgotten to all but historians.

Two Centuries After The Event

On Thursday, January 6, 2011, two local divers announced to the world that the remains of the **REVENGE** had been rediscovered, this time intentionally. The divers apparently became interested in locating her remains after reading a book written by a local author and set out with enthusiasm and a metal detector to see what they could find. They first found a cannon, then before long had located a half dozen more plus an anchor and other metal objects. The find was reported to the Naval History & Heritage Command, the arm of the Navy which oversees this type of operation, who subsequently made plans to perform a survey of the area and wreckage to see if the divers' claim can be supported. Only time will tell if their find is the historic vessel claimed and what action, if any, will be taken to retrieve or preserve the artifacts.

The Vessel Itself

The schooner **REVENGE** was originally built in Baltimore and was called the RANGER. She was sold to the Navy in December of 1806 and was first assigned as a naval vessel in February of 1807 to Commodore John Shaw and was used under his command in the Mississippi River.

Research Sources

1. Newport Mercury, January 12, 1811 P3
2. Rhode Island American and Daily Advertiser, January 15, 1811 P3
3. Newport Mercury, January 19, 1811 P3
4. Newport Daily News, February 12, 1863 P2
5. Newport Mercury, November 19, 1921 P8
6. "Westerly and Its Witnesses" by Frederic Denison (1878)
7. "Shipwrecks off the Shores of Westerly" by Margaret Carter (1973)
8. Dictionary of American Naval Fighting Ships

ESSEX

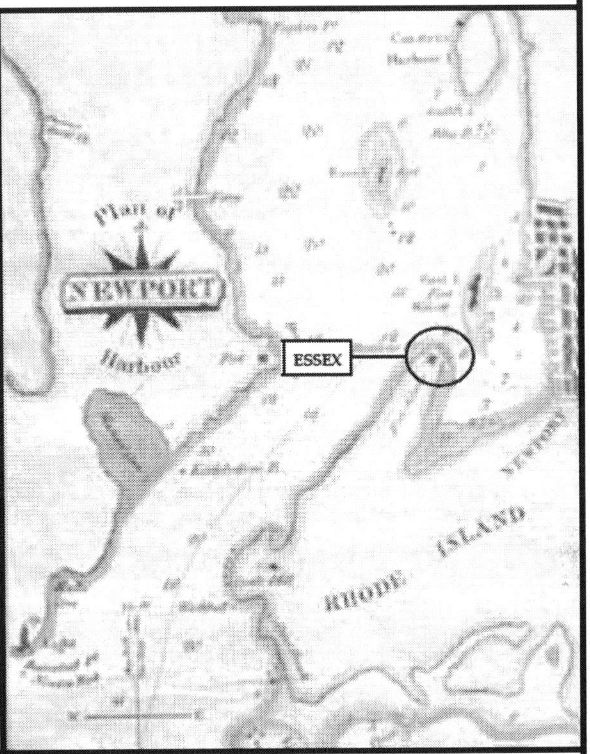

There were only 23 vessels that made up the United States Navy during the War of 1812. The frigate ESSEX was built by a private subscription in 1799 in Salem, MA and given to the navy that year.

The Vessel

Type: Frigate
Construction: Wood
Use: Warship
Dimensions: 140′ x 31′ x 12′
Tonnage: 860
Launched: Salem, MA in 1799
Owner: US Navy
Nationality: American
Home Port: Washington, DC

Final Voyage

Port of Departure: Hampton Roads, VA
Port of Destination: Newport, RI
Master: David Porter
Cargo: N/A
Date of Loss: December 24, 1811
Disaster Type: Stranding
Cause: Storm
Final Status: Got off
Location: Fort Adams, Newport

Narrative

Newport Mercury - November 19, 1921 P8

Notes and Queries – 1812

Great damage was done to the shipping on the coast by the storm of the 24th of December, 1811. The U.S. frigate PRESIDENT, Com. Rogers, lay at the Long Wharf in Newport during the gale, and made it out in safety. The frigate ***ESSEX****, Capt. Porter, went on shore near Fort Adams, and the sloop of war HORNET, Capt. Dent, rode out the gale.*

Newport Mercury - November 28, 1811 P3

The U.S. Frigate ***ESSEX****, Capt. Porter, arrived at this port on Monday last from Hampton Roads – We learn that the* ***ESSEX*** *will remain in this harbor during the winter. … The late snowstorm was the most severe that has been experienced here for many years.*

ESSEX

Rhode Island American - December 31, 1811 P3

The U.S. Frigate ***ESSEX****, Capt. Porter, arrived at this port on Monday last from Hampton Roads – We learn that the ESSEX will remain in this harbor during the winter.*

Rhode Island American - January 3, 1812 P3

The United States ships PRESIDENT, ***ESSEX****, and ARGUS, lately arrived at Newport, dragged their anchors in the late storm, but we are happy to hear received no material damage.*

Research Sources

1. Newport Mercury, December 28, 1811 P3
2. Rhode Island American, December 31, 1811 P3
3. Rhode Island American, January 3, 1812 P3
4. Newport Mercury, November 19, 1921 P8
5. American Merchant Marine at War, www.USMM.org

US GUNBOAT NO. 46

The most distinctive aspect of a gunboat of this era is the bow mounted cannon. Shown is a US gunboat that was built and sunk in 1776 in Lake Champlain. Recovered in 1935, it now resides at the Smithsonian Museum.

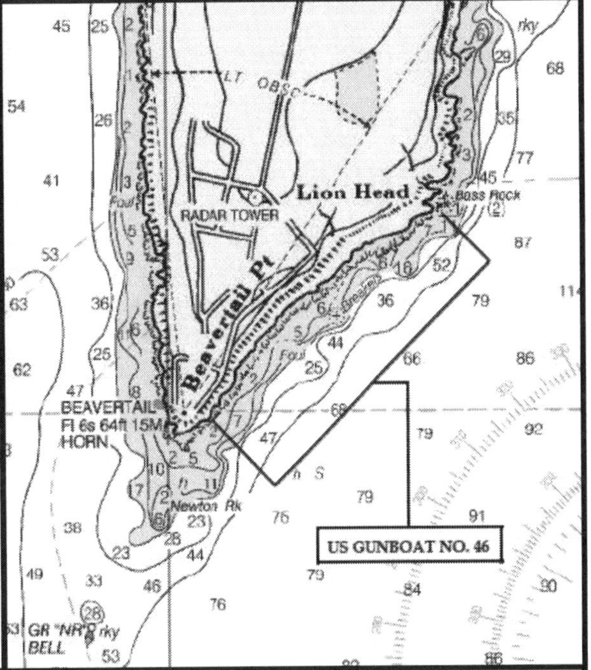

The Vessel

Type: Boat
Construction: Wood
Use: Gunboat
Dimensions: 47′ x 18′ x 5′
Launched: New York City, NY in 1806
Owner: U.S. Navy
Nationality: American

Final Voyage

Master: Lt. Samuel G. Blodget
Date of Loss: September 29, 1812
Disaster Type: Sunk
Cause: Storm
Final Status: Total loss
Location: Near the lighthouse on the south end of Conanicut Island, east side of the island

Narrative

Newport Mercury - October 3, 1812 P3

Distressing Accident

It is with regret that we announce the loss of the ***U.S. GUN-BOAT NO. 46****, during the severe gale on the evening of the 29th ult., together with her Commander Lieut. Samuel G. Blodget, and eight of the crew. It appears from a statement of a gentleman of this town, who was on board the Gun-Boat and witnessed the distressing scene, that she was lost on the south part of the island of Conanicut, near the lighthouse, when in the act of veering, having missed in stays twice – we are also assured, to the honor of Lieut. Blodget, that he behaved with the utmost coolness and decision and sacrificed his own life in providing for the safety of his crew, as no persuasion could induce him to quit his vessel until they had made the attempt to save themselves, and was in this situation washed overboard at the same instant with the gentleman above referred to who, with two officers and seven men, providentially escaped a watery grave. Lieut. Blodget was in the 28th year of his age – He entered the Navy very early in life, and was esteemed a brave officer. The following are the names of the unfortunate seamen who were drowned, viz. – Dennis M'Stay, Thomas Joice, Jonas Fisk, John Dutcher, Samuel Holly, Morris Smith, John Howard, Josiah Simmons.*

US GUNBOAT NO. 46

Columbian Phenix - October 10, 1812 P3

Marine and Naval Intelligence

GUN-BOAT NO. 46 was cast away on Conanicut during the severe gale on the evening of the 29th ult. when in the act of veering, having missed in stays twice, by which casualty the commander, Lieut. S.G. Blodget, an esteemed officer, and 8 seamen, unfortunately perished.

Newport Mercury - November 19, 1921 P8

Notes and Queries—1812

*The **U.S. GUNBOAT NO. 46**, Lieut. Samuel G. Blodget, was upset in a severe gale on the 29th of September, near the lighthouse near the south end of Conanicut. Lieut. Blodget and eight of his men were drowned. Lieut. Blodget was in the 28th year of his age.*

Aftermath of the Disaster

The following letter from Master Commandant Oliver Hazard Perry (who was in command of the ten gunboats at Newport at the time) to Secretary of the Navy Hamilton was sent from Newport, Rhode Island on November 10, 1812.

*Sir, With the assistance of Mr. Palmer, the proprietor of the Diving-bell, I have been so fortunate as to regain gun, anchors, cables & small quantity of the shot &c. of the late **US GUNBOAT NO. 46**. Mr. Palmer charges the department with one-third of the value for salvage, which with your permission I will cause to be paid him—his vessel was considerably exposed in this business, and he has exerted himself to save as much of the public property as possible—the gun above referred to is a 32 pounder, and is at present on Fort Wolcott, loaned to the US.—for which I have the commanding officer's receipt until your pleasure is known. Respectfully [&c], O.H. Perry*

Research Sources

1. Newport Mercury, October 3, 1812 P3
2. Rhode Island Republican, October 6, 1812 P3
3. Providence Gazette, October 10, 1812 P2-P3
4. Columbian Phenix, October 10, 1812 P3
5. Newport Mercury, November 19, 1921 P8
6. "The Naval War of 1812 - A Documentary History, Volume 1" - edited by William S. Dudley

WHAMPOA

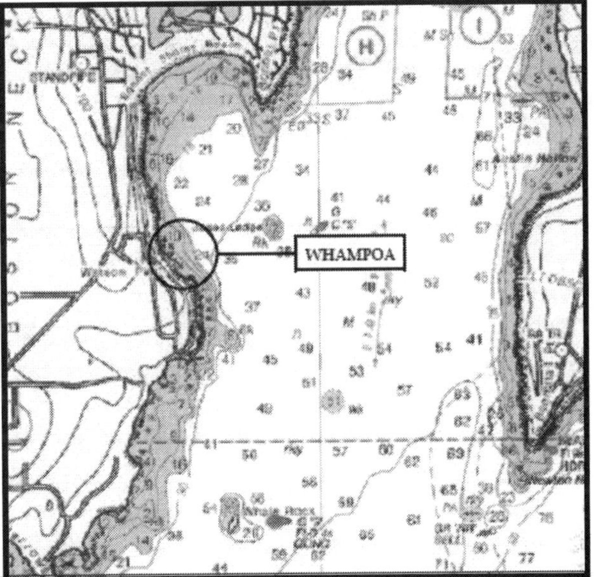

The Vessel

Type: Ship
Construction: Wood
Use: Merchant
Owner: Mr. De Roy & others
Nationality: American
Home Port: New York City, NY
Port of Departure: L'Orient, France
Port of Destination: New York City, NY

Final Voyage

Master: Daniel Waterman
Cargo: brandy, wines and silks
Date of Loss: April 28, 1813
Disaster Type: Ashore & burned
Cause: War
Final Status: Total loss
Location: Near Watson's Pier, north from Narragansett Pier

Narrative

Newport Mercury - May 1, 1813 P3

On Wednesday morning last, the ship **WHAMPOA**, *Daniel Waterman master, owned by Messrs. De Roy, Bayard & McEvers, and others, of New-York, was chased on shore near Watson's pier, in the West Passage, about three miles within the lighthouse, by the British frigate ORPHEUS. The* **WHAMPOA** *carried 8 six-pounders and was 28 days from L'Orient, bound to New York, with a cargo of brandy, wine and silks. As soon as she struck on the rocks she was scuttled and her masts cut away by order of the captain. The frigate came to anchor about two miles off, with her broadsides toward the ship, and immediately sent a boat with a number of men to burn her; but being warmly received and several of the men killed or disabled by the fire from the ship, the boat returned to the frigate, which instantly manned and sent 3 of her boats to renew the attack. Further resistance being vain, (as the frigate kept up a constant fire and the boats were approaching) the captain and crew escaped to the shore, and the enemy entered the ship and set her on fire. The frigate remained at anchor until satisfied that the* **WHAMPOA** *was effectually fired, when she made sail and stood to the eastward. As soon as the alarm was given of the approach of the enemy, the Artillery Company commanded by Col. B. Fry, and the several companies of militia in this town, were immediately under arms; and the third company of militia, commanded by Capt. B. Pearce, crossed over to the west side of Conanicut, where they were soon after followed by the Artillery Company with two field pieces. Here they were compelled to remain several hours, in the utmost*

WHAMPOA

impatience, waiting for the ferry-boat, which all that time was detained on the opposite shore. The sloop DEFIANCE, of Providence, was then lying at anchor about a mile from the shore. Capt. Pearce sent off two of his men to her in a crazy canoe in the hope of prevailing upon the captain the carry the company across, but, instead of complying, he hoisted sail and stood up the bay. As soon as it was possible Capt. Pearce crossed the ferry, and hastened to the place where the ship was stranded. She had been burning several hours; and those who were present considering all attempts to extinguish the flames to be fruitless and desperate, had forsaken her, and retired to the walls out of the reach of her guns; some of which had gone off as the fire reached them. Capt. Pearce was informed of this by the people under the walls, who added further that there was a large quantity of powder on board which was every moment expected to take fire. He was not however to be deterred from making some attempt to rescue the property, and immediately the boats were manned from his company and sent off to the ship, which they entered, and by their indefatigable exertions at length succeeded in extinguishing the flames. The preservation of a great proportion of the ***WHAMPOA****'s valuable cargo has been the consequence of these exertions – 131 pipes of brandy with a number of casks and cases of goods, have already been secured and brought to this town. - The* ***WHAMPOA****'s cargo consisted of 174 pipes brandy, 39 boxes merchandize, 32 casks vinegar and 18 boxes wine. The company did not return to Newport until the following morning. Had they met with no impediment to their march their ardent wishes would have been gratified by their arriving at the scene of action in time to have encountered the enemy and prevented the ship being fired, as we have no doubt they would. …*

Newport Mercury - November 19, 1921 P8

Notes and Queries

The ship ***WHAMPOA****, Capt. Waterman, of New York, was chased on shore near Watson's pier, in the West Passage, within the lighthouse, by the British frigate ORPHEUS. The* ***WHAMPOA*** *carried 8 six-pounders and was 28 days from L'Orient, with a cargo of brandy, wine and silks. As soon as she struck on the rocks she was scuttled and her masts cut away by the crew. The frigate came to anchor about two miles off, with her broadsides toward the ship, and sent her boats to burn her, which, after an obstinate resistance, they effected, losing one of the Lieutenants and having several men wounded. The captain and crew escaped to the shore. On the alarm being given at Newport, the Artillery Company and several companies of militia proceeded to the west side of Conanicut; here they were detained for several hours being unable to cross the ferry until the departure of the enemy. The 3rd company of the militia, Capt. Pearce, proceeded to the ship and were very instrumental in saving great part of the cargo.*

Research Sources

1. Newport Mercury, May 1, 1813 P3
2. Boston Daily Advertiser, May 5, 1813 P3
3. Connecticut Gazette, May 5, 1813 P3
4. Newport Mercury, May 20, 1915 P8
5. Newport Mercury, November 19, 1921 P8
6. Sailing Ships of the Royal Navy (Internet)
7. Niles Weekly Register, March 15, 1813 P1

HOLKER

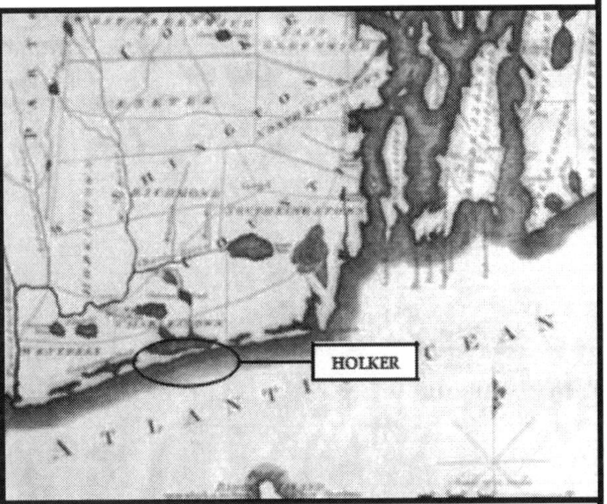

The Vessel

Type: Brig
Construction: Wood
Use: Privateer
Owner: Unknown
Nationality: American
Official No.: N/A
Home Port: New York City, NY

Final Voyage

Master: Rowland
Date of Loss: May 10, 1813
Disaster Type: Stranding
Cause: War (Chased Ashore)
Final Status: Went to pieces
Location: Near the halfway house between Point Judith and Watch Hill

Narrative

As was the case during the Revolutionary War, the use of privateers continued during the War of 1812. Because these vessels were privately owned, it is often difficult to get details on the vessel itself but the details of the loss of the brig **HOLKER** (also found spelled HOLKAR) can be found from both sides of the engagement.

New York Columbian - May 12, 1813 P2

The Holkar lost

Our correspondent at New London writes, under date of the 10th inst., Monday, in a postscript: "I have broken the seal to communicate, that information has just been received here (which I believe may be relied on) that the private armed brig ***HOLKAR****, belonging to New York, was this morning run on shore on Narragansett Beach, by a British frigate, supposed to be the ORPHEUS, and that 6 of the men belonging to the brig were drowned in attempting to land. It is said that the brig will be got off by the enemy." We wish we could find room to hope the brig thus lost was some other than the* ***HOLKAR****. As it is, however, she has not been an unprofitable servant, having probably cleared herself two or three times. The loss of any of her brave crew is to be regretted. Capt. John Harris, in a fishing smack, arrived through the Sound this afternoon, having witnessed the destruction of the* ***HOLKAR****. He left Newport on Monday morning, and saw the frigate in chase of the brig. About sun an hour high, at high water, the brig grounded near the Halfway house, on Narragansett Beach, and the ship sheered in towards her, and came to anchor. She then opened her broadside on the privateer, and continued her fire until 2 o'clock P.M. by which time the brig was cut down to the water's edge, her masts going over with all sails set, and her hull above water being shot away by piece-meal. The men got ashore in her boats, Capt. H. supposed.*

HOLKER

One hundred and eight years later, in a compilation of history of the War of 1812 in Rhode Island, the following newspaper account was found.

Newport Mercury - November 19, 1921 P8

1813

...

*The Brig **HOLKER**, Captain Rowland, of eighteen guns, from a cruise, was chased on shore by the ORPHEUS, Frigate, on Charlestown Beach, between Point Judith and Watch Hill. The ORPHEUS came to anchor a mile from the shore and manned her boats to take possession of the brig; the officers and crew of the **HOLKER** escaped to the shore, with the exception of nine men drowned, several of them prisoners. The militia, under Gen. Joseph Eaton, assembled and fought bravely in defense of the **HOLKER**; the British, after keeping possession ten hours, finding she could not be got off, abandoned the attack. The brig afterwards bilged and went to pieces. A vessel which spoke the ORPHEUS a few days after was informed that they had several men killed in attempting to get off the **HOLKER**.*

On the other side...in a history of the HMS ORPHEUS there is a brief mention confirming the incident, ... *The 20-gun American privateer **HOLKAR** was destroyed off Rhode Island on 11 May.*

Research Sources

1. New York Columbian, May 12, 1813 P2
2. Newport Mercury, November 19, 1921 P8
3. "Sailing Ships of the Royal Navy" (Internet)

USRC VIGILANT

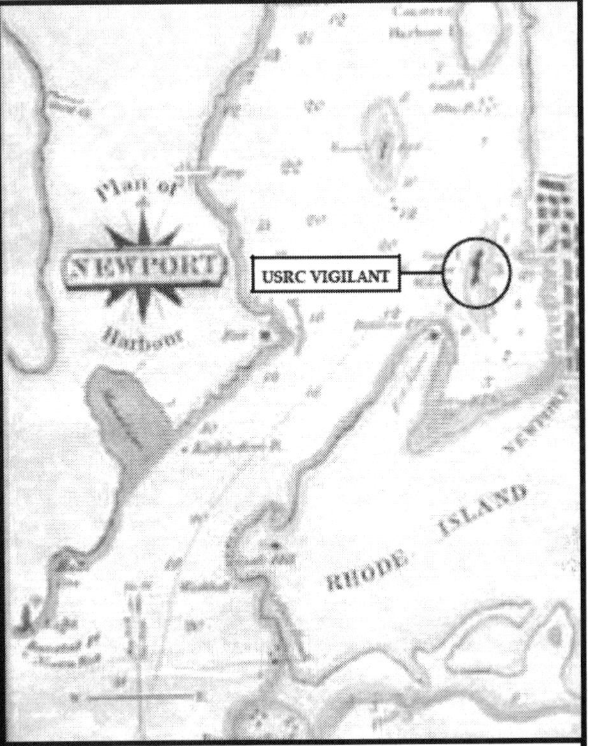

The Vessel

Type: Schooner
Construction: Wood
Use: Revenue Cutter
Dimensions: 60′ x ? x 10′
Tonnage: 65
Launched: Newport, RI in 1812
Nationality: American
Home Port: Newport, RI

The Event

Owner: US Revenue Cutter Service
Date of Incident: September 23, 1815
Disaster Type: Stranding
Cause: Storm
Status: High & dry
Location: On Fort Wolcott, Goat Island, Newport

Narrative

New York Columbian - September 29, 1815 P2

The Hurricane. The height and violence of the sea at Providence and Newport, produced a greater calamity in these towns than any other yet heard of. The loss of property in the former place is estimated at five millions of dollars; but, at Newport, the loss of lives and houses carried off in the flood , the promiscuous spectacle of carriages, buildings, bales, timber and vessels, all afloat together, represented the ancient deluge in miniature. The tide rose about 4½ feet higher than ever known… Ship COMET carried on Fort Wolcott, 'high and dry;' the revenue cutter shared the same fate.

USRC VIGILANT

New York Gazette - September 29, 1815 P2

... Ship COMET was driven on Fort Wolcott, high and dry'. The revenue cutter shared the same fate.

Newport Mercury - September 30, 1815 P2 & P3

AWFUL AND DESTRUCTIVE STORM

On Saturday last this town was visited by one of the most awful and destructive storms ever experienced here; sweeping away and laying prostrate almost everything in its course. The gale commenced early in the morning at N.E. and continued increasing in violence (the wind varying from N.E. to S.E. and S.W.) until about 11 o'clock A.M. when it began to abate, and about one o'clock all danger from the wind and tide was over, and the afternoon was fair and mild—forming a striking contrast with the war of the elements which had existed but a few moments before. ... The Revenue Cutter ***VIGILANT****, dragged her anchors, and went ashore on Fort Wolcott, but fortunately sustained no damage.*

Newport Mercury - October 14, 1815 P3

... The elegant Revenue Cutter ***VIGILANT****, which drove high and dry on Fort Wolcott in the late severe gale, has, by the great assistance afforded by the commanding officer and men of the garrison, been got off without experiencing any injury.*

Research Sources

1. New York Columbian, September 29, 1815 P2
2. New York Gazette, September 29, 1815 P2
3. Newport Mercury, September 30, 1815 P2 & P3
4. Newport Mercury, October 14, 1815 P2
5. "The Revenue Cutter Service: Nine Cutters and the War of 1812", by Scott E. Walden, 2008
6. Painting - US Revenue Cutter VIGILANT circa 1813, courtesy of US Coast Guard History

BRENTON REEF (LV-11)

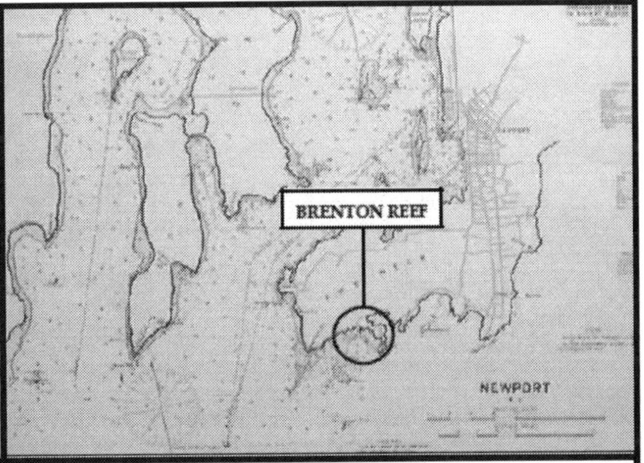

The Vessel

Type: Schooner
Construction: Wood
Use: Lightship
Dimensions: 104′ x 24′ x 9′
Tonnage: 320
Launched: Baltimore, MD in 1853
Owner: US Lighthouse Service
Nationality: American
Home Port: Newport, RI

Final Voyage

Port of Departure: N/A
Port of Destination: N/A
Cargo: N/A
Date of Loss: October 19, 1865
Disaster Type: Stranding
Cause: Storm
Final Status: Got off
Location: On Price's Neck

Narrative

New York Times - October 21, 1865 P2

THE GALE

Reports from the Eastward

Providence, R.I., Friday, Oct. 20. The effects of the gale last night were very severe on the coast. Brenton's Reef light-ship went ashore on Price's Neck about 9:30 o'clock last night. One man swam ashore. We have no further particulars as yet.

New York Herald - October 21, 1865 P4

The Gale at the Eastward

Brenton's Reef light-ship went ashore on Price's Neck about half-past nine last night. One man swam ashore. We have no further particulars as yet.

New York Herald - October 21, 1865 P8

Information has been received that the Brenton's Reef Lightship broke away from her moorings last night at 9 o'clock. and went ashore on Price's Neck, on the south side of Rhode Island. She will be replaced, or the Relief Light ship substituted at the earliest practicable moment, of which due notice will be given.

By order of the Lighthouse Board, L.M. Powell, LH Inspector, 3d dist. October 20, 1865

BRENTON REEF (LV-11)

The Lightships of Brenton Reef

In all there were four lightships (not including relief vessels from time to time) assigned to the station at Brenton Reef. A brief history of each is below:

LV-14 - The first lightship assigned to this station was a 91-foot long sloop rigged vessel built in 1852. This 159-ton vessel carried a single lantern and had a bell and horn for fog warning. Both of the latter items were hand powered. The LV-14 served at Brenton Reef for three years but continued in service until retired in 1872.

LV-11 - The second lightship assigned to this station was a 104-foot long schooner rigged vessel built in 1853. This 320 ton vessel carried two lanterns and like her predecessor had a hand operated bell and horn for fog warning. The LV-11 served at Brenton Reef for forty-one years but continued in service until retired in 1925. At the time of her retirement, LV-11 was more than 70 years old and was considered the oldest vessel in the Lighthouse Service.

LV-39 - The third lightship stationed outside the dangerous reef was a 119-foot long schooner rigged vessel built in 1875. The vessel registered 387 tons and carried two lanterns as had the previous lightship. This lightship was the first ever to be fitted with a 12″ steam whistle at the time of construction. She also carried a hand operated bell. The LV-39 served at Brenton Reef for thirty-eight years and retired at the end of her service on this station in 1935.

LV-102 - The fourth and final lightship assigned to this station was a 101-foot long vessel built in 1916. This lightship was a 360 ton steel hulled craft equipped with a single lantern and a 6″ air siren for foggy days. The LV-102 served at Brenton Reef from 1935 until 1962 and retired in 1963.

In 1962, LV-102 was replaced with an 87-foot tall tower, the second to be erected on the east coast of the United States. The theory of replacing floating lightships with permanently anchored tower structures was sound but the structures were not. Although the Brenton Tower survived for twenty-seven years, it was not replaced with another. Modern technology, particularly in the field of satellites, brought to a close the need for either a floating light or fixed light tower to protect commercial and non-commercial vessels.

Research Sources

1. New York Times, October 21, 1865 P2
2. New York Herald, October 21, 1865 P4
3. New York Herald, October 21, 1865 P8
4. Photo courtesy of US Coast Guard archives
5. www.ShipbuildingHistory.com

JULIA

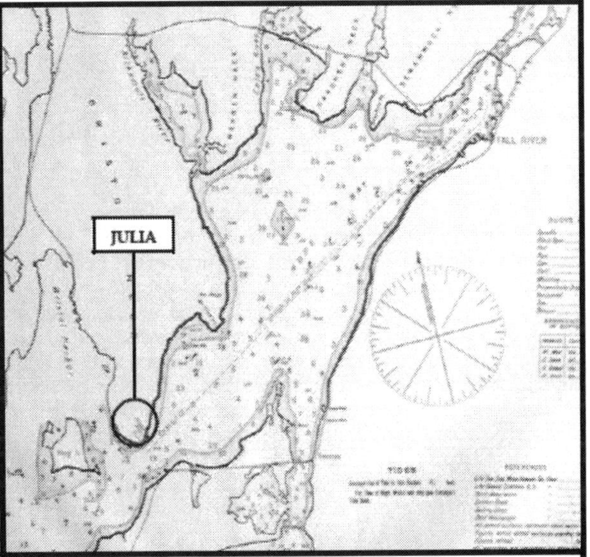

The Vessel

Type: Schooner
Construction: Wood
Use: Lightship
Dimensions: 40′ x 15′ x 6′
Tonnage: 20
Nationality: American
Official No.: 13483
Home Port: Newport, RI

The Event

Owner: John Coggeshall
Master: John Coggeshall
Cargo: N/A
Date of Incident: December 15, 1870
Disaster Type: Stranding
Cause: Storm
Status: Got off
Location: On Bristol Ferry

Narrative

New York Herald - December 19, 1870 P10

Shipping News - Notice to Mariners

*Schr **JULIA**, of Newport, used as a light vessel on the southeast part of Hog Island, for the steamers of the Narragansett Steamship Company, parted her moorings during the heavy blow of the 15th inst. and went ashore at Bristol Ferry.*

New York Herald - December 20, 1870 P10

Shipping News - Marine Disasters

*Schr **JULIA**, of Newport, acting as a light boat on Hog Island Point, which was driven ashore in the gale of the 15th in Narragansett Bay, was got off and towed to Newport on the 16th.*

Apparently the shoal at Hog Island was of sufficient importance to eventually warrant its own lightship. In the photo above, the schooner rigged lightship LV-12 is shown on her station. But it took a long time to correctly protect mariners from the shoal. In 1869 the Lighthouse Board asked Congress for an appropriation to build a lighthouse to replace the small lightship. The appropriation was denied. Twenty six years later, they decided that a lightship would suffice at that location. In 1899, Congress finally appropriated funding for a lighthouse, and built it in 1901.

JULIA

The Julia

According to the custom house records, the **JULIA** had been purchased from the United States government. She may have been a British sloop rigged vessel of this name which had been operating out of Nassau, in 1863 until captured and placed in the service of the U.S. Navy. She was sold at Key West in 1865. Interestingly, she had been under the command of an Acting Master's Mate L.C. Coggeshall. Is it coincidence or could L.C. Coggeshall and John Coggeshall be related and the purchase of her been encouraged by her former master to his relative who could, with little difficulty, have changed her rig to a schooner?

Research Sources

1. New York Herald, December 19, 1870 P10
2. New York Herald, December 20, 1870 P10
3. Merchant Vessels of the United States - 1869
4. Dictionary of American Naval Fighting Ships
5. Newport Custom House records

BRENTON REEF (LV-11)

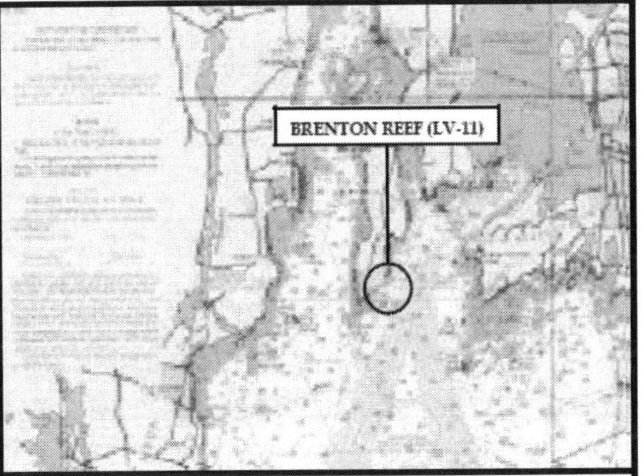

The Vessel

Type: Schooner
Construction: Wood
Use: Lightship
Dimensions: 104′ x 24′ x 9′
Tonnage: 320
Launched: Baltimore, MD in 1853
Owner: US Lighthouse Service
Nationality: American
Home Port: Newport, RI

Final Voyage

Port of Departure: N/A
Port of Destination: N/A
Cargo: N/A
Date of Loss: December 3, 1873
Disaster Type: Adrift
Cause: Storm
Final Status: Towed in
Location: Drifted from her station to rocks off Beavertail

Narrative

New York Times - December 4, 1873

THE BRENTON'S REEF LIGHT-SHIP ADRIFT

Providence, Dec. 3. – The steamer NEWPORT, of the Fall River Line, Capt. A.G. Simmons, commander, in making her Eastern passage, and upon reaching the station for the Brenton's Reef lightship, outside of Newport Harbor, found the buoys at their anchors, but no light-ship in sight. A dense fog prevailed, but hearing the faint sound of a bell to the northward, and believing it to be from the light-ship, the steamer was headed to the northward and careful progress made until the light-ship was overtaken at Beaver Tail, just as she was nearing the rocks which line the coast in that vicinity. The NEWPORT took the light-ship in tow to a safe anchorage in the outer harbor of Newport, and proceeded on her passage, arriving at Fall River at 7:20 o'clock A.M. – three hours late.

LV-11 was generally a lucky lightship and survived for more than 70 years. While on station at Brenton Reef she ran ashore on Price's Neck in a storm in 1865, broke loose in this incident in 1873, and was run down, but not sunk, by the British steamer CURLEW in 1890.

Research Sources

1. New York Times, December 4, 1873
2. Photo courtesy of US Coast Guard archives
3. www.ShipbuildingHistory.com

JOSEPH HENRY

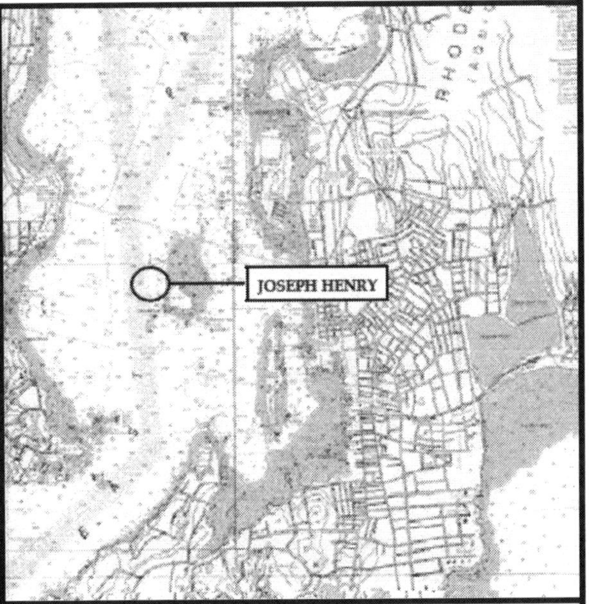

The Vessel

Type: Schooner
Construction: Wood
Use: Target Practice
Dimensions: 70′ x 20′ x 2′
Launched: Baltimore, MD in 1853
Owner: U.S. Government
Nationality: American
Home Port: Newport, RI

Final Voyage

Master: Lt. Kinsley
Cargo: N/A
Date of Loss: September 24, 1875
Disaster Type: Ashore & sunk
Cause: Collision
Final Status: Raised
Location: On the west side of Rose Island, Newport Harbor

Narrative

Like the topsail schooner in the sketch above, the schooner **JOSEPH HENRY** spent a number of years in the employ of the US Coast Survey. At some point in time, probably after she had served for two decades, she was transferred or put on loan to the Naval Torpedo Station where she served as an assisting vessel in torpedo testing operations.

New York Times - September 25, 1875

A COLLISION IN NEWPORT HARBOR

The Naval Steamer Nina Crushes in the Side of the Schooner Joseph Henry

Newport, R.I., Sept. 24. This forenoon the United States steamer NINA, stationed at the torpedo station, went outside with the class of Lieutenant Commanders on board. The schooner ***JOSEPH HENRY****, recently ordered to the station for torpedo practice, followed, having on board the Lieutenants of the station for the purpose of having a mock battle with the NINA, the latter having the Harvey torpedo in tow. The NINA was to make every effort to strike the* ***JOSEPH HENRY*** *with a dummy Harvey torpedo. The NINA was chasing the schooner on the wind, and the latter, in order to avoid her tacked across the NINA's bow, but finding that she was coming into too close quarters, wore across her bow instead. The NINA, not expecting her to hold her wind, attempted to pass under her stern, but the schooner in wearing across her bow prevented it. The engineer, to prevent the collision, which was inevitable, was ordered to stop and reverse the engine, which was done, but it was too late to prevent the NINA striking. She struck her about*

JOSEPH HENRY

abreast the mainmast, crushing her side in and causing her to leak rapidly. Lieut. Swinburn, on board the schooner, was knocked overboard by the shock, but was quickly rescued from his perilous position by a boat from the NINA. The schooner stood off for the west side of Rose Island, where she was beached in seven feet of water. The NINA followed her and as soon as she struck, sent a boat alongside, and took off the Lieutenants and crew. She was stripped of her sails and rigging, but it is not expected that the vessel will be worth raising, she being very old and rotten in some places, and valued at about fifteen thousand dollars.

Newport Daily News - September 25, 1875 P2

A COLLISION IN THE BAY

*An accident occurred during the torpedo practice yesterday which narrowly escaped serious results. The NINA and the ex-coast survey schooner **JOSEPH HENRY** went outside yesterday noon for a little practice with a dummy Harvey torpedo which the NINA was to try to get under the **JOSEPH HENRY**. The steamer was chasing the schooner on the wind with the torpedo in tow and the schooner, to avoid the torpedo, started to back across the bow of the steamer, and finding there was not room enough wore around. The NINA intended to pass under the schooner's stern, but the wearing of the schooner brought the two vessels too close, and the engineer of the NINA was ordered to stop and reverse his engine. For some reason the engine would not reverse and the NINA struck the **JOSEPH HENRY** about amidships cutting her side down to the water's edge. Lieutenant Swinburne, who was on the schooner, was knocked overboard by the shock, and picked up by a boat from the NINA. Lieut. Kinsley, who was in command of the schooner, climbed on board the NINA when she struck, supposing the schooner would go down at once. Lieut. Randall, who was second in command on the schooner, headed her for Rose Island intending to beach her, as the hole was on the weather side, but one of the sailors let go of the anchor too soon and she lies where her deck is under water at high tide. Her sails and rigging have been stripped off. The hull is so old and rotten that it is probably not worth raising. Her officers and crew were taken off by the NINA which closely followed her.*

Newport Daily News - September 29, 1875 P2

*Waters and Mitchell have contracted to raise the schooner **JOSEPH HENRY** which was sunk by a collision with the U.S. Steamer NINA on Friday last.*

Newport Daily News - September 30, 1875 P2

*The government schooner **JOSEPH HENRY**, which has been raised, has been found worth repairing.*

Apparently the decision to repair the **JOSEPH HENRY** was sound. The schooner returned to duty spending most of the next decade in the service of the torpedo station. And what is ironic is that the final chapter in the career of this vessel involved another torpedo, but this time it was not a dummy torpedo and not an accident...but that is another story.

Research Sources

1. New York Times, September 25, 1875
2. Newport Daily News, September 25, 1875 P2
3. Newport Daily News, September 29, 1875 P2
4. Newport Daily News, September 30, 1875 P2
5. NOAA History — Coast & Geodetic Survey Ships

GENERAL JESSUP

Pictured is FERRY LAUNCH NO. 132, smaller than the GEN. MONROE, the successor to the **GENERAL JESSUP**. In the newspaper account it mentions a sail on the **JESSUP** implying an unusual rig on the earlier steam powered ferry.

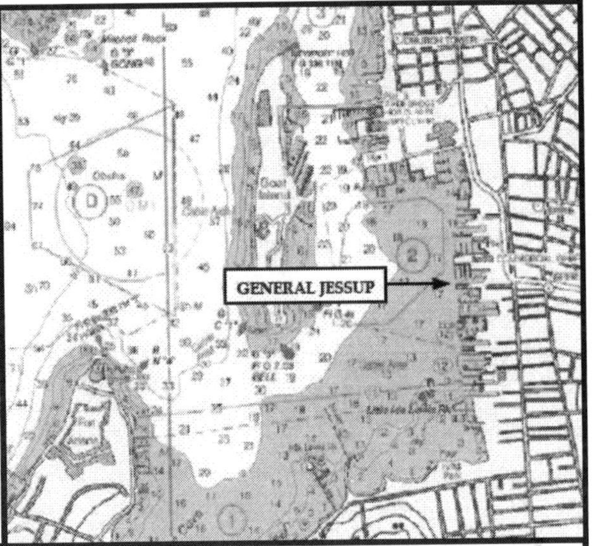

The Vessel

Type: Steamship
Construction: Wood
Use: Ferry
Owner: US War Department
Nationality: American
Home Port: Newport, RI

The Event

Date of Incident: December 29, 1876
Disaster Type: Sunk
Cause: Storm
Status: Repaired
Location: At Perry Mill Wharf, Newport Harbor

Narrative

Over the years a number of vessels belonging to the U.S. government served as support vessels to Fort Adams, providing ferry service from the Perry Mill Wharf, in downtown Newport, across the harbor to the fort. One of the earliest was the **GENERAL JESSUP** about which little is known. What is known is that the winter of 1876 was not kind to the little steamer as two storms, just weeks apart, did damage to and then sank the vessel. The first event was reported in the Hartford Daily Courant on December 21st.

Hartford Daily Courant - December 21, 1876 P1

NEWS AND NOTATIONS

*... The steam launch **GENERAL JESSUP**, belonging to Fort Adams, Newport Harbor, was nearly lost Monday night. Her propeller was lost, and in a violent storm the boat tossed about for hours. Finally a life boat crew saved the persons on board.*

According to the executive documents of the House of Representatives for the year 1877-78 (specifically the report of the Chief Signal Office), *December 18 and 19, 1876 – A large fleet of vessels remained in port* [Newport]. *The steam launch **GENERAL JESSUP**, of Fort Adams, broke her shaft and screw.*

But this was just the first of her problems for less than two weeks later she was caught by another storm when at her moorings and this time the damage was a bit more severe...the vessel ended up on the bottom of Newport harbor as noted in the newspaper account of the storm.

GENERAL JESSUP

Newport Daily News - December 30, 1876 P2

THE STORM

The Wind Blows a Hurricane With Torrents of Rain and Driving Sleet—High Sea—The Vessels in the Harbor—The Steamers—The Fort Launch Sunk

The wind blew a hurricane last night and was accompanied first by sleet and afterwards by torrents of rain. The sidewalks were in a wretched condition and the few who ventured out, experienced no little difficulty in walking. No such weather has been seen here for a long time. Early in the afternoon the storm signal was out and a large fleet of vessels put in for a harbor. Among them a propeller from Providence to New York. The steamer NEWPORT did not leave Fall River for New York until this forenoon, and the OLD COLONY did not leave New York. The Providence boat was half an hour late. The sea ran very high and broke over vessels at the docks. The Providence Press Company's boat was swamped at her moorings. ... During the gale the steam launch ***GENERAL JESSUP****, which was moored immediately north of Cottrell's shipyard, and was to be taken on the ways for repairs, early this morning, was blown from her anchorage, the wind having veered to the southwest at about eleven o'clock, blowing a severe gale. Her position was considered at nightfall a perfectly safe one, the engineer and captain being on board in charge of her. Her sail having been broken by the storm she went ashore at the Perry Mill Wharf where she sank, but the tide having receded she was high and dry this morning, having suffered much damage. As her screw was detached, having been lost a few days since, it was of course impossible to manage her. The engineer escaped drowning by climbing the smoke stack.*

The report of the Chief Signal Officer offers the following details, *December 29 and 30, 1876—A hurricane which was accompanied by sleet and afterward by rain. A large number of vessels put into the harbor for shelter on account of the signal. The steam launch* ***GENERAL JESSUP*** *was sunk at her moorings in the harbor, and the engineer escaped drowning by climbing the smokestack. The New York steamers delayed departure until the storm was over. Some minor accidents occurred in the harbor.*

Details relative to the vessel itself and its final fate have not been found at this time.

Research Sources

1. Hartford Courant, December 21, 1876 P2
2. Newport Daily News, December 30, 1876 P2
3. Report of the Secretary of War, 44th Congress, 1st session, House of Representatives
4. Index to the Executive Documents of the House of Representatives for the Second Session of the Forty-Fifth Congress, 1877-'78, Volume VI—Report of the Chief Signal Office

UNIDENTIFIED

USN FERRY LAUNCH NO. 132 was in similar service to the **unidentified** ferry launch in collision in Newport Harbor.

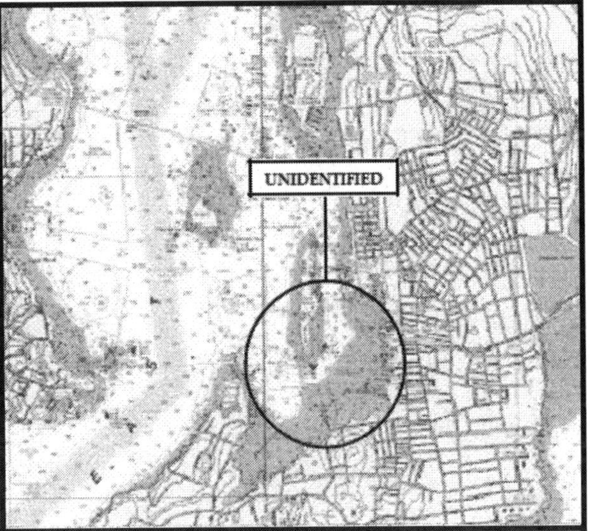

The Vessel

Type: Steamship
Construction: Probably Wood
Use: Ferry Launch
Owner: U.S. Navy
Nationality: American
Home Port: Newport, RI
Master: Coxswain Daniel Rielly

The Event

Port of Departure: Her pier in Newport
Port of Destination: Torpedo Station, Goat Isl.
Date of Incident: November 23, 1883
Disaster Type: Damaged
Cause: Collision
Status: Beached
Location: Inner Newport Harbor

Narrative

Newport Mercury - December 1, 1883 P1

As the EOLUS was passing through the harbor last week Friday, on her 5 o'clock trip out, she struck the Torpedo launch just aft of amidships. The launch was on her trip to the station. Several vessels were riding at anchor between the two moving boats, preventing the officers of the EOLUS from seeing the launch. They heard the latter blow one whistle which signified that she would go to the right. Captain Wightman of the EOLUS answered the whistle and stopped the engine, but as the launch came in view she was right on them, passing her bows. The launch, though leaking badly, reached the station where she was beached. The EOLUS was not damaged at all, and continued on her course. Each consider the other to blame.

New York Times - November 28, 1883

INVESTIGATING A COLLISION

Providence, R.I., Nov. 27. The collision between the steamer EOLUS and the launch of the torpedo station at Newport was the subject of an official investigation to-day. The board consisted of Lieut.- Commanders Newell and Jewell, and Lieuts. Judd and Washburn Maynard. Coxswain Daniel Reilly, Fireman Canfield, Mate Boyd and Watchman Harrington testified for the Government, they having been on the launch at the time of the collision. They testified that the EOLUS was to blame. Capt. Wightman, of the EOLUS testified that he answered the launches whistles and did all in his power to prevent the collision, and that it appeared to him as if the launch was following him up. The board finally decided that the EOLUS was to blame and so reported to Capt. Selfridge, who will transmit the result to the Navy.

UNIDENTIFIED

Some Newport Torpedo Station Steam-Launches

The Naval Torpedo Station in Newport had many thousands of workers over the years who needed transportation to and from Goat Island, Rose Island and Gould Island every day. Over the years there were a number of steam launches employed by the station to provide various services. According to the report of the Secretary of the Navy for the second session on the Forty-Fourth Congress, the following steam launches were assigned to duty at the Torpedo Station and were reported to be in the condition stated:

- *Steam Launch No. 1 (BILLOW) is in use as a ferry launch, is in good condition, runs economically, and is admirably adapted for her purpose.*
- *Steam Launch No. 2 (WAVE) is used for torpedo experiments; is old, in not very good condition, nor is it well adapted for torpedo purposes. It answers very well as a relief boat to the ferry-launch.*
- *Steam Launch No. 3 (RIPPLE,) experimental launch, is now fitted with a propeller designed by Lieut. Barber, U.S.N. This boat was in use by the frigate CONGRESS until sunk in the North River, where it lay for seven months; and, as may be supposed, is not now in first-rate condition, and is only useful as a boarding boat to men-of-war on their arrival and for the exchange of officer's visits.*
- *Steam Launch No. 4 (FOWLER) has just been returned to the station, after an absence of about two years. This boat was long experimented with with the Fowler wheel, but is now returned with the Mallory wheel. The hull only of this boat, which is of steel, is in good condition.*
- *Steam Launch No. 5 (SUCCESS) is an English built so-called life-boat launch; is in excellent condition, being fitted with Herreshoff's boiler and engines. The launch is fitted for torpedo purposes as a service launch.*
- *Steam Launch No. 6 (LIGHTNING) was contracted for through John B. Herreshoff and would be 55 feet long and 6 feet wide, fitted with a safety-coil boiler, and a pair of engines with the combined capacity of 60 horse-power, which would run the boat at 19 miles an hour. This suggests that her intended use was not as a ferry.*

Although this information was a few years prior to the collision between the EOLUS and the unidentified vessel, it seems likely that the steam ferry launch involved in the incident was the BILLOW. It is also possible that it was another steam launch, perhaps the WAVE, or the SPRAY which was built in 1879.

Research Sources

1. New York Times, November 28, 1883
2. Newport Mercury, December 1, 1883 P1
3. Newport Mercury and Weekly News, December 1, 1933 P1
4. Report of the Secretary of the Navy for the Second Session of the Forty Fourth Congress

WAVE

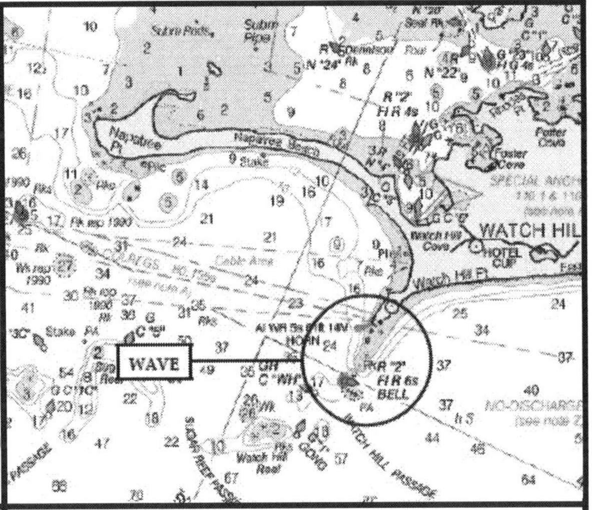

The Vessel

Type: Schooner
Construction: Wood
Use: Government service
Owner: A. Robinson
Nationality: US Government
Official No.: N/A
Home Port: Unknown

The Event

Port of Departure: Newport, RI
Port of Destination: New London, CT
Date of Incident: August 19, 1884
Disaster Type: Stranding
Cause: Pilot error
Status: Got off
Location: On the rocks at Watch Hill Point

Excerpt from US Life Saving Service Annual Report—1885

*August 19 - At about 10 o'clock in the forenoon the schooner **WAVE**, a small vessel belonging to the government, bound from Newport, Rhode Island, to New London, Connecticut, while attempting to pass through the narrow channel inside the buoy off Watch Hill Point, coast of Rhode Island, struck on the rocks at the point. The Watch Hill Station (Third District,) a third mile distant, was closed for the summer, but the keeper, who was out fishing, seeing this vessel's situation, went to her assistance. By the time he got alongside her sails had been lowered and the crew were endeavoring to heave her afloat. Finding they did not succeed, the keeper advised them to hoist their sails again, and by that means the schooner was forced off the reef. He then piloted her into the channel, and saw her safely on her course up Fisher's Island Sound.*

Research Sources

1. Excerpt of the US Life Saving Service Annual Report - 1885
2. "Storms and Shipwrecks of New England" by E.R. Snow
3. "Encyclopedia of American Shipwrecks" by Bruce Bermen
4. "Shipwrecks off the Shores of Westerly", by Margaret Carter (1973)

JOSEPH HENRY

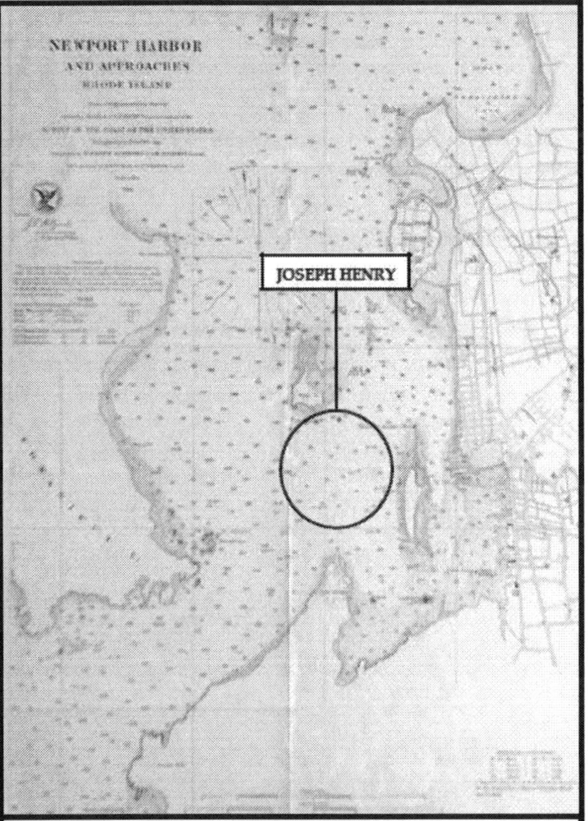

The Vessel

Type: Schooner
Construction: Wood
Use: Target
Dimensions: 70′ x 20′ x 2′
Launched: Baltimore, MD in 1853
Nationality: American
Home Port: Newport, RI

Final Voyage

Owner: U.S. Government
Date of Loss: August 24, 1884
Disaster Type: Sunk
Cause: Torpedo test
Final Status: Total loss
Location: Outside Goat Island, Newport

Narrative

Newport Mercury - August 30, 1884 P1

PRESIDENT ARTHUR IN NEWPORT

His Movements—Other Government Officials—Torpedo Experiments, Etc.

... At about one o'clock Tuesday afternoon the United States steamer DESPATCH, with President Arthur on board, arrived and was received with salutes from the steamers of the North Atlantic squadron, the Torpedo Station, Fort Adams and the schoolship NEW HAMPSHIRE. She came into the inner harbor and dropped anchor just in front of the Torpedo Station. A cold, drizzling rain was falling and the President did not leave his vessel during the afternoon... Wednesday dawned clear and beautiful and the presidential party was astir at an early hour. At about 10 o'clock President Arthur was landed at Ferry Wharf in his barge and, taking a carriage, was driven to the Ocean House and other places on the Avenue, returning to the wharf about 11 o'clock. In the meantime some twenty-five or thirty ladies and gentlemen, who were to be the guests of the President on a short trip up the river, had assembled at the landing where they waited

JOSEPH HENRY

for the President… The various ships of the North Atlantic Squadron and the Fish Commission steamer ALBATROSS, with Secretary Chandler on board, had already sailed, and as soon as things could be made ready the DESPATCH followed. After about three hours of target practice, the vessels all returned to their anchorage here. Thursday was devoted to a visit to the Torpedo Station. It was to be a great day for that Institution and a large number of distinguished guests had been invited, both by Captain Selfridge, commander of the station, and by President Arthur. A synopsis of what was going to be done in the way of experiment, included the President's reception on the island with a salute of twenty-one torpedoes and the blowing up of the hull of the old schooner ***JOSEPH HENRY****. These being the leading features of interest to the citizens who were not included among the invited guests, at 11 o'clock, the time when the president was expected to land at the island, the wharves and house-tops were covered with anxious spectators. About half an hour later the president left the DISPATCH for the island. He was received by Captain Selfridge and, with his guests, escorted to an elevation near the headquarters. After reaching this place of prominence the twenty-one torpedoes arranged in a line along the front of the Station for the presidential salute were exploded. It was one of the most successful torpedo salutes ever fired and the beautiful sight was witnessed by thousands of people. The Presidential party... was then conducted to the chemical laboratory, where the mode of manufacturing gun cotton and the various other explosives was duly explained and all questions satisfactorily answered. Gun cotton was shown to be absolutely harmless in itself, it being impossible to explode it, but when placed with fuluate of mercury, it is readily detonated with an electric spark. They were then shown through the electrical and machinery buildings and thence to the dock where very successful experiments were made with the Lay- Haight torpedo. The Selfridge Gun Cotton Contact Torpedo was then sent out to blow up the old hull, but owing to some deviation in the steering, it passed too far to the bow of the wreck and failed to do its work. The party then went on the TRIANA and was taken outside where some very successful torpedo target shooting was indulged in. The torpedoes were lashed to spars extending out from the side of the vessel and the targets were empty casks which were floating in the water. After devoting some time to these experiments the party returned to the dock where the Selfridge Contact Torpedo was again sent on its mission of destruction. This time it was eminently successful, the wreck being completely demolished, and the President and Secretary Chandler hastened to congratulate the inventor. The party then broke up and the President returned to the DESPATCH. Yesterday at about nine o'clock the various naval vessels under the command of Rear Admiral Luce, left their moorings for the open ocean where they maneuvered in review before the President. … Today, if the weather be suitable, there will be a sham naval battle and a landing at Coaster's Harbor Island.*

After thirty years of service to the US government, the schooner **JOSEPH HENRY** certainly went out with a bang. Ironically, nearly ten years earlier, in 1875, the same vessel was sunk after collision with another government steamer while engaged in a "war game" in almost the same area of the harbor. At the earlier date the torpedo being tested was a Harvey torpedo and was not armed...but that's another story.

Research Sources

1. Newport Mercury, August 30, 1884
2. Sketch is from the cover of Harper's Weekly, September 13, 1884
3. Popular Science, January, 1900 (article about the development of torpedoes)
4. NOAA History – Coast & Geodetic Survey Ships

USS BOSTON

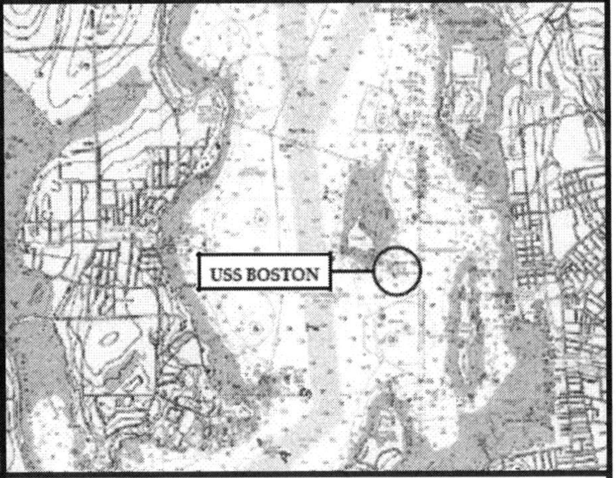

The Vessel

Type: Cruiser
Construction: Steel
Use: Warship
Dimensions: 283′ x 42′ x 17′
Tonnage: 3189
Launched: Chester, PA in 1884
Owner: U.S. Navy
Nationality: American
Home Port: New York City, NY

Final Voyage

Port of Departure: Upper Narragansett Bay
Port of Destination: Rose Island anchorage
Master: James O'Kane
Date of Loss: August 3, 1889
Disaster Type: Damaged
Cause: Navigational error
Final Status: Repaired
Location: Struck a rock (believed to be Mitchell Rock) off Rose Island in returning to anchorage

The ABCD Fleet

After the end of the Civil War the United States found that they had many more vessels than men as the lure of peacetime employment was greater than remaining in the employ of the War Department that no longer had a war. The result was a large number of surplus vessels and the decision to sell many of those to foreign governments. By the early 1880's, the United States Navy had few vessels left and even fewer that were of the caliber of other navies of the time. As things for the Navy looked bleak, some in Congress realized the error of this path and decided to begin building a modern, state-of-the-art Navy which would restore the United States to its leadership position among the major countries of the world. In 1883 the legislature authorized the construction of four steel hulled cruisers that would, in theory, become the foundation of a new fleet. But, as is the case with many good ideas, the financial side of the plan often does not meet the needs of the idea. However, that being said, the commitment was made for these four ships, dubbed the "ABCD Fleet" because their names began with the first four letters of the alphabet. Although not built in that order, these vessels were the protected cruisers ATLANTA, BOSTON and CHICAGO and the dispatch boat DOLPHIN. Once all had been built they became known as the Squadron of Evolution and for nearly a year steamed to ports in Europe, the Mediterranean and South America, a symbol of the new and improved US Navy. But each vessel had to pass a series of sea trials to confirm speed, maneuverability, and other qualities. It was on return from running one of these tests that the BOSTON was involved in a minor incident with a rock in Narragansett Bay. A thorough investigation of the events followed.

USS BOSTON

Narrative

New York Times - August 14, 1889 P8

CAPT. O'KANE EXPLAINS

HOW IT WAS THE CRUISER BOSTON STRUCK A ROCK

A court of inquiry to ascertain why the **BOSTON** *ran on the rock near Newport, on Aug. 3, was convened yesterday at the Brooklyn Navy Yard. The court consists of Capt. N.H. Kirkland, Capt. J.N. Miller, Capt. J.A. Howells, and Judge Advocate Lieut. J.H. Nichols.*

Their instructions from the Navy Department are to examine into the causes of the accident and to make such suggestions as they think proper in regard to it. The scope of the inquiry may go so far as to include the question of the employment of local pilots on United States vessels or of regularly-appointed United States pilots. As it is now the war vessels are navigated by chart, under directions of the Captain and navigator.

Capt. James O'Kane of the **BOSTON** *was the only witness examined yesterday afternoon. He said that the* **BOSTON** *had been in Newport Harbor and vicinity from early morning till 4:30 o'clock in the afternoon engaged in performing the turning and speed evolutions required by the Board of Examiners, who were on board. "After the completion of the speed trial," said Capt. O'Kane, "the board informed me they were through for the day. I directed the ship be run into her former anchorage after having gone around Gould Island to work off surplus steam. The ship followed the course of a measured mile in the southerly direction, till the Spindle, on the end of Goat Island, was at a safe distance - 200 or 250 yards - for rounding. The navigator asked if he had not better pass the stern of two coal hulks lying in midchannel. I said, 'You had better pass the stern and then round her up to the wind,' meaning then to let the anchor go."*

"The helm was put hard a-port and in turning the ship touched upon a rock, which I would not say was Mitchell Rock unless a search was made. The ship passed over the rock, heeling considerably, but with no apparent strain. She rapidly came up head to the wind and was anchored."

Capt. O'Kane said the general appearance of surrounding objects at the time of touching was one of perfect safety. The ship was, perhaps, a little nearer Rose Island than ships usually turn, but knowing the steering qualities of the Boston, he had no concern. The ship would have passed the spot where the coal hulks were, and anchored had they not been there. The tide was, in his opinion, a moderate flood.

In reply to questions by the Judge Advocate, Capt. O'Kane said that the engines were moving slightly when the vessel struck. She had been slowed down. The helm was put in starboard in time to pass around when the spindle was bearing north. He was steering by land, not by compass. ...

The investigation of this "minor" incident continued for four days with the key witnesses being asked questions to determine if there was any action necessary for the overall betterment of the service. The report was not public and would be delivered to the Secretary of the Navy but in the opinion of the local reporter covering the story, the captain would be exonerated.

Research Sources

1. Newport Mercury, August 10, 1889 P1
2. New York Times, August 14, 1889 P8
3. New York Times, August 15, 1889 P8
4. New York Times, August 16, 1889 P8
5. Naval History and Heritage Command
6. Merchant Vessels of the United States - 1897

BRENTON REEF (LV-11)

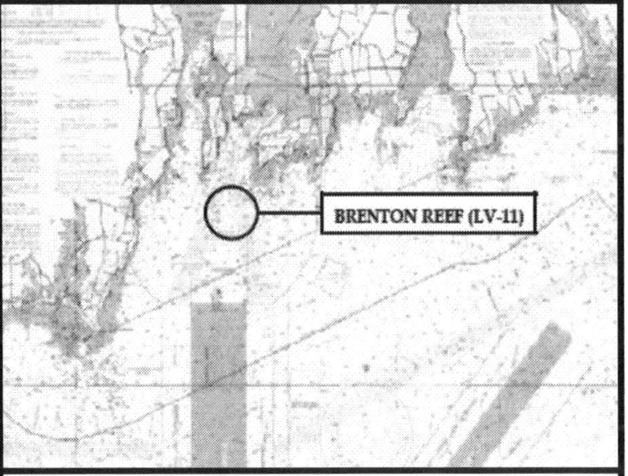

The Vessel

Type: Schooner
Construction: Wood
Use: Lightship
Dimensions: 104′ x 24′ x 9′
Tonnage: 320
Launched: Baltimore, MD in 1853
Owner: US Lighthouse Service
Nationality: American
Home Port: Newport, RI

Final Voyage

Port of Departure: N/A
Port of Destination: N/A
Master: Edward Fogerty
Date of Loss: November 26, 1890
Disaster Type: Damaged
Cause: Collision
Final Status: Repaired
Location: On her station off Brenton Reef, Newport

Narrative

New York Times - November 27, 1890 P5

Telegraphic Brevities

***BRENTON'S REEF** lightship was run into yesterday morning by the British Steamer CURLEW, St. John, for Providence. Twelve feet of the lightship's port bow and bulwarks were carried away and three streaks of the bow broken.*

Newport Mercury - November 29, 1890 P1

*British Steamer CURLEW, from St. John, for Providence, run into **BRENTON REEF** lightship Wednesday morning, carrying away about twelve feet of the latter's bulwarks and stanchions. The captain of the lightship immediately came ashore and telegraphed particulars of the accident to the department.*

Lightships have been the victim of collisions for as long as they have been stationed at or near dangerous points near major port cities. The incident with the **BRENTON REEF** lightship and the steamship CURLEW is the only incident of this type to have taken place while a lightship was on station outside the entrance to Narragansett Bay.

Research Sources

1. New York Times, November 27, 1890 P5
2. Newport Mercury, November 29, 1890 P1

GEN. MONROE

The FERRY LAUNCH NO. 132 owned by the US Army is similar to but smaller than the steam launch **GEN. MONROE** used to transport personnel to Ft. Adams

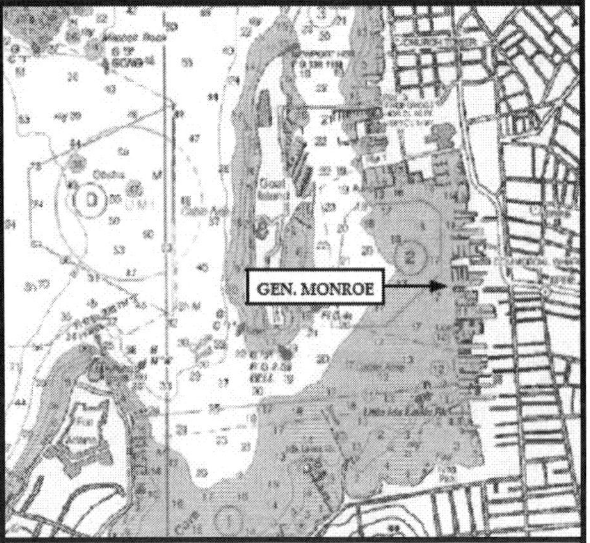

The Vessel

Type: Steamship
Construction: Wood
Use: Launch
Dimensions: 83′ x 16′ x 6′
Tonnage: 62
Launched: New York City, NY in 1875
Owner: U.S. Army
Nationality: American
Home Port: Newport, RI

Final Voyage

Port of Departure: N/A
Port of Destination: N/A
Master: Not Aboard
Cargo: N/A
Date of Loss: January 6, 1891
Disaster Type: Sunk
Cause: Leak
Final Status: Raised
Location: At Perry Wharf, Newport

Narrative

New York Times - January 7, 1891 P3

A GOVERNMENT LAUNCH SUNK

*Newport, R.I., Jan. 6. - The United States launch **MONROE**, running between Fort Adams and this city, sank at her dock here this morning and two men asleep aboard had a narrow escape. The cause of the sinking is unknown. Captain John Waters will raise her.*

Newport Mercury - January 10, 1891 P1

The Fort Launch Sunk

*Steam launch **GEN. MONROE**, plying between the city and Fort Adams, sank at her moorings at Perry Wharf at an early hour Tuesday morning, since which time Capt. Waters has been working to float her. The cause of her sinking is not known, the first indication of her liability to do such a thing being the discovery, by the two men who sleep on board, that the water was nearly up to their berths. Capt. Waters succeeded in pumping the water out of the craft Thursday, but the vessel still refused to float and he has now rigged a derrick with which to lift her stern when the water shall again be pumped out – probably today.. The vessel must have got a bad hole in her from some cause, as she filled in fourteen minutes after the pumps were stopped, Thursday.*

GEN. MONROE

Research Sources

1. New York Times, January 7, 1891
2. Newport Mercury, January 10, 1891
3. Merchant Vessels of the United States—1896 (list of Quartermasters Dept., U.S. Army)
4. Photo courtesy of US Naval Historical Center

GEN. MONROE

The FERRY LAUNCH NO. 132 owned by the US Army is similar to but smaller than the steam launch **GEN. MONROE** used to transport personnel to Ft. Adams

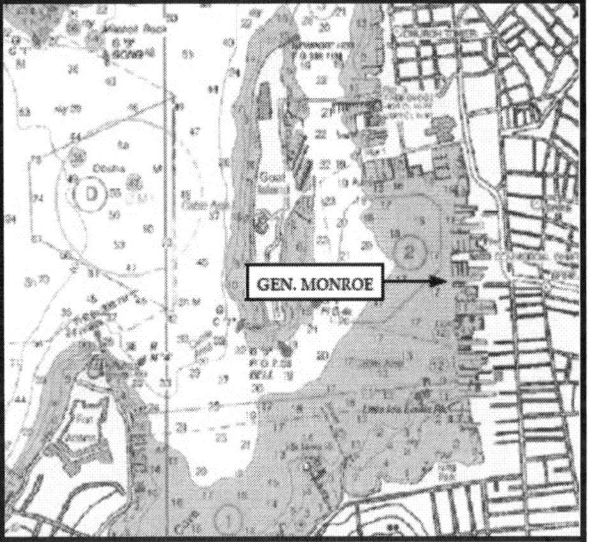

The Vessel

Type: Steamship
Construction: Wood
Use: Launch
Dimensions: 83′ x 16′ x 6′
Tonnage: 62
Launched: New York City, NY in 1875
Owner: U.S. Army
Nationality: American
Home Port: Newport, RI

Final Voyage

Port of Departure: N/A
Port of Destination: N/A
Master: Not aboard
Cargo: N/A
Date of Loss: September 7, 1895
Disaster Type: Sunk
Cause: Engineer error
Final Status: Raised
Location: At Perry Wharf, Newport

Narrative

Newport Mercury - September 14, 1895 P1

Too Much Water

*Steam launch **MONROE**, attached to Fort Adams, was sunk at her Perry Wharf slip early Saturday morning, through the carelessness of the man in charge who, after turning on the water to fill the boilers, went away, forgetting to shut it off. The result was that not only the boilers but the boat itself filled and then the whole business went to the bottom. The work of floating the craft was at once begun, but it was not accomplished until late Tuesday afternoon, it finally requiring the combined efforts of government tug ROCKET, the Reynolds tug AQUIDNECK, and the NO. 1 fire steamer to pump her out. She is now at the Old Colony docks for repairs and a complete overhauling.*

Just four years earlier, in 1891, this same launch had mysteriously sunk in almost the same spot.

Research Sources

1. Newport Mercury, September 14, 1895 P1
2. Merchant Vessels of the United States—1895
3. Photo courtesy of the US Naval Historical Center

CUSHING (TB-1)

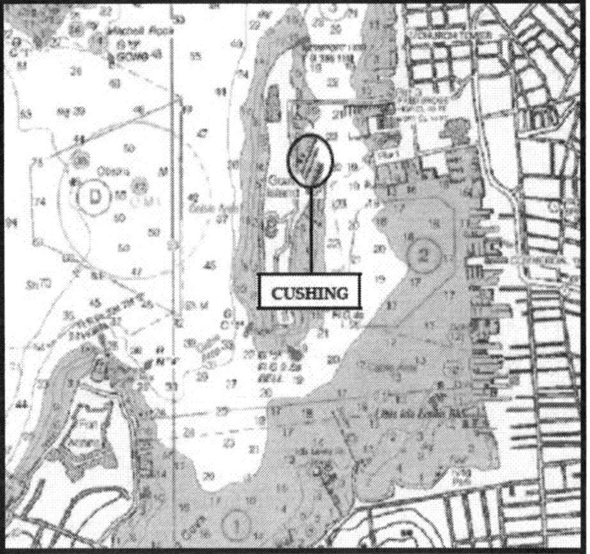

The **CUSHING** (TB-1) was the first of a number of purpose-built torpedo boats manufactured in the Herreshoff yard in Bristol, R.I. although not the first boat put to that use. An earlier torpedo boat was also built by Herreshoff and carried the name STILETTO. She was initially built to be a yacht but was purchased by the navy due to her outstanding speed.

The Vessel

Type: Steamship
Construction: Steel
Use: Torpedo Boat
Dimensions: 138′ x 14′ x 4′
Tonnage: 66
Launched: Bristol, RI in 1890
Nationality: American
Home Port: Newport, RI

The Event

Owner: U.S. Navy
Date of Incident: September 9, 1896
Disaster Type: Stranding
Cause: Storm
Status: Got off
Location: Near the torpedo boat STILETTO, just north of the new government pier at the Torpedo Station on Goat Island

Narrative

Boston Daily Globe - September 10, 1896 P5

TORPEDO BOATS ASHORE

Gale Forced the Stiletto Aground and the Cushing Attempted Rescue

NEWPORT, R.I., Sept. 9 - The torpedo boats ***CUSHING*** *and STILETTO are both aground near the torpedo station here. They arrived down the bay just before 1 o'clock from Bristol. In making her slip during a severe northeast gale which prevailed the STILETTO was forced ashore just north of the new government pier and the* ***CUSHING****, in trying to assist her was soon in the same predicament. Efforts by the station launch and a local tug to move the two boats were unavailing and have been abandoned for the present. Both are hard and fast with the tide falling. The STILETTO has a heavy list, and the* ***CUSHING*** *appears to be injured otherwise than from grounding.*

Research Sources

1. Boston Daily Globe, September 9, 1896
2. Merchant Vessels of the United States—1896
3. Dictionary of American Naval Fighting Ships
4. John Palmieri, Curator, Herreshoff Marine Museum
5. Norene Rickson, Librarian/Archivist, Herreshoff Marine Museum

STILETTO

The **STILETTO** (pictured) was not built as a torpedo boat but was purchased in 1887 by the navy for testing purposes.

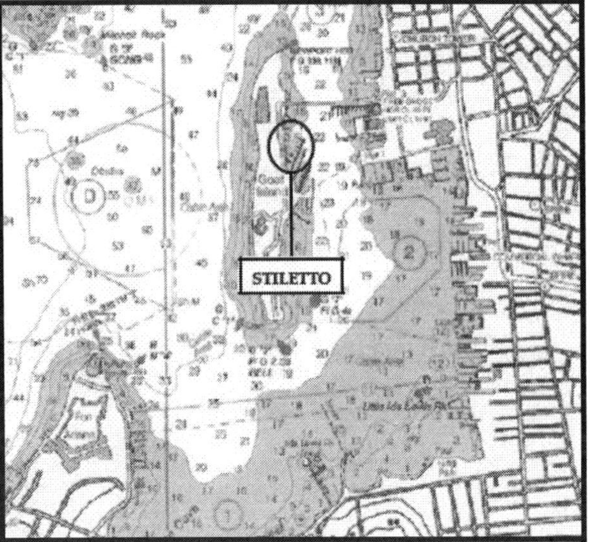

The Vessel

Type: Steamship
Construction: Wood
Use: Torpedo Boat
Dimensions: 94′ x 11′ x 5′
Tonnage: 31
Launched: Bristol, RI in 1885
Nationality: American
Official No.: 116040

The Event

Owner: U.S. Navy
Home Port: Newport, RI
Date of Incident: September 9, 1896
Disaster Type: Stranding
Cause: Storm
Status: Got Off
Location: Just north of the new government pier at the Torpedo Station on Goat Island

Narrative

Boston Daily Globe - September 10, 1896 P5

"WORST STORM ON RECORD"

Statement of Government Officer Well Borne Out by the Number of Wrecks and Disasters

PROVIDENCE, Sept. 9 - The northeast gale whipped everything around lively on the bay and south coast today and tonight. Much damage was done to small craft during the afternoon in this vicinity. At 6 tonight Captain Uriah B. Dodge, the government officer at the harbor, made this report, "Worst storm on record this year. It is blowing 72 miles from the northeast and increasing. Rain in torrents and phenomenally high; hurricane signals flying all the afternoon. ..."

TORPEDO BOATS ASHORE

Gale Forced the Stiletto Aground and the Cushing Attempted Rescue

NEWPORT, R.I., Sept. 9 - The torpedo boats CUSHING and ***STILETTO*** *are both aground near the torpedo station here. They arrived down the bay just before 1 o'clock from Bristol. In making her slip during a severe northeast gale which prevailed the* ***STILETTO*** *was forced ashore just north of the new government pier and the CUSHING, in trying to assist her was soon in the same predicament. Efforts by the station launch and a local tug to move the two boats were unavailing and have been abandoned for the present. Both are hard and fast with the tide falling. The* ***STILETTO*** *has a heavy list, and the CUSHING appears to be injured otherwise than from grounding.*

STILETTO

Research Sources

1. Boston Daily Globe, September 9, 1896
2. American Yacht List (1885)
3. Merchant Vessels of the United States—1896
4. John Palmieri, Curator, Herreshoff Marine Museum
5. Norene Rickson, Librarian/Archivist, Herreshoff Marine Museum
6. Photo courtesy of US National Archives and Records Administration

USS TEXAS

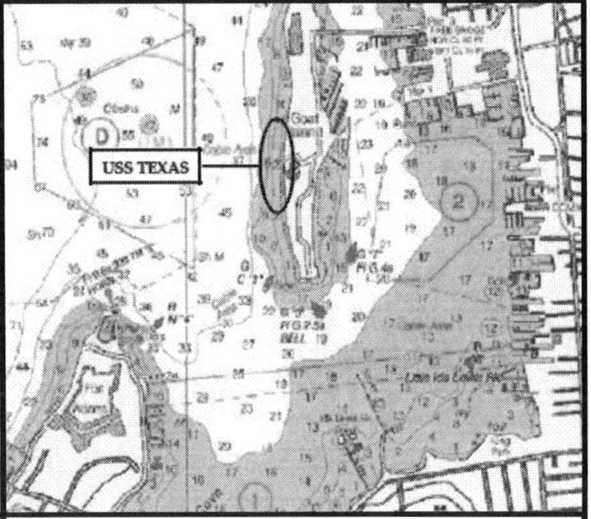

The **USS TEXAS** was a US Navy vessel launched in Norfolk, Virginia in 1892, commissioned in 1895, and ended her career when sunk in Chesapeake Bay as a target after decommissioning in 1911.

The Vessel

Type: Steamship
Construction: Steel
Use: Battleship
Dimensions: 308′ x 64′ x 22′
Tonnage: 6,315
Launched: Norfolk, VA in 1892
Owner: U.S. Navy
Nationality: American
Home Port: New York City, NY

The Event

Port of Departure: New York City, NY
Port of Destination: Newport, RI
Master: Captain Henry Glass
Date of Incident: September 16, 1896
Disaster Type: Stranding
Cause: Engine room error
Status: Pulled off
Location: On the west side of Goat Island, near the Torpedo Station

Narrative

New York Tribune - September 17, 1896 P1

THE TEXAS RUNS AGROUND

Battle-Ship Stuck In The Mud In Newport Harbor

*NEWPORT, R.I., Sept. 16.—The United States second-class battle-ship **TEXAS** tonight added another mishap to her already unfortunate career. In compliance with orders she was coming here for her torpedo outfit. She made the harbor shortly after 6 o'clock and at about 6:20 reached the torpedo station having first gone over toward the Jamestown shore, and then turned and come across the bay for anchorage. For some reason the ship's engines did not stop when they should and she kept forging ahead. Her anchor was dropped, but still she did not stop, and when too late her helm was thrown over with the hope of clearing the island. The water shoals rapidly here, and when she struck, with land on her port quarter, she ran her nose some two feet out of water and her stern was crowded under. Drawing twenty-three feet of water, with the tide three hours down, she was imbedded hard and fast in the heavy mud. It was just about dusk and signal rockets were at once sent up. A tug went to her assistance and pulled tight on the tow-line, but did not budge her. It was some time after the ship struck before her engines finally stopped. The tide was still falling but it is not believed that her position is serious as divers say her position is free from rocks. A larger tug was engaged to-night, and about 1 o'clock she will go out and make an attempt on the rising tide, which does not become high enough until nearly 4 o'clock. Some sailors say that it will require more than an ordinary tide and small tugs to haul her off. The crew seem to be lightening her forward as much as possible. The **TEXAS** came off at 1:40 a.m. by the assistance of four tugs, which set up a steady strain*

USS TEXAS

at two bells and got her off after slightly over half an hour's pulling. There was no rock under her and she is uninjured without doubt. Her going ashore was due to a misunderstanding of orders in the engine room. It is understood that the port engine was not reversed when it should have been. The ***TEXAS*** *was aground about seven hours.*

New York Tribune - September 18, 1896 P5

THE MISHAP TO THE TEXAS

Likely to be Investigated by a Court of Inquiry

Washington, Sept. 17. – Captain Glass telegraphed the Navy Department from Newport this morning that the ***TEXAS****, having run on the sand off Goat Island, had floated again and, so far as he could learn, was uninjured. A report by mail will follow. The favorable outcome of what might have proved a serious accident to the unlucky battle-ship* ***TEXAS*** *caused general satisfaction among the officials of the Navy Department this morning, and they were greatly relieved after the suspense of the night. The reports of the ship's striking on a bottom known to be so rocky as Newport Harbor having given rise to considerable fear that the vessel would be ruined. The career of the* ***TEXAS*** *ever since she existed only on paper had been so checkered that the superstitious thought her end had come. Her collapse in the Brooklyn dry-dock last year, followed by the "development of structural weakness" on her trial trip, caused her to be sent to the Norfolk Navy Yard last January, where her immersed hull was thoroughly rebuilt, costing over $200,000. During her six-months stay in the Norfolk dry-dock her frames and bottom were strengthened, and it was only about three weeks ago that she was pronounced complete and sent to join Admiral Bunce's squadron at Tompkinsville the day before Li Hung Chang arrived in America. Her cost, including repairs up to that time, had exceeded $4,000,000, although she had been designed originally to cost only $2,500,000. To fix the responsibility for yesterday's unfortunate occurrence will be the immediate effort of the Navy Department. The battle-ship MASSACHUSETTS, drawing at least two feet more water than the* ***TEXAS****, had just visited the Newport naval station and secured her torpedoes. She had scarcely given up her berth to the* ***TEXAS*** *when the latter vessel approached and struck. Captain Rodgers, of the MASSACHUSETTS, is known as one of the most cautious commanding officers in the service, and he stayed well out from shore and anchored in about sixty feet of water. It is believed that Captain Glass, also a cautious officer, concluded he could lie a little closer to the island than the MASSACHUSETTS. Fortunately, the tide was out and when it rose later in the night he was able to pull his ship off. The effort to blame the affair on a machinist is combated among naval officers who are friendly to the enlisted men. They say that in going into port all officers are on duty, and that an engineer officer or two of them must have been in charge of the engine room. Engineer officers, however, contend that they can only obey signals, and if the engines were kept going ahead when the stop signal had been given the signal must have been out of order and failed to act. …*

An investigation was held and Captain Henry Glass was acquitted of all blame. The chief engineer, Moore, was determined to be responsible for the accident due to the negligence of Assistant Engineer Hinds and Chief Machinist Hunley both of whom were reprimanded.

Research Sources

1. New York Tribune, September 17, 1896 P1
2. New York Tribune, September 18, 1896 P5
3. New York Tribune, October 25, 1896 PA9
4. Merchant Vessels of the United States—1896
5. Dictionary of American Naval Fighting Ships

STILETTO

The **STILETTO** (pictured) was built by the Herreshoff Manufacturing Company in 1885 and purchased soon after by the US Navy due to her outstanding speed.

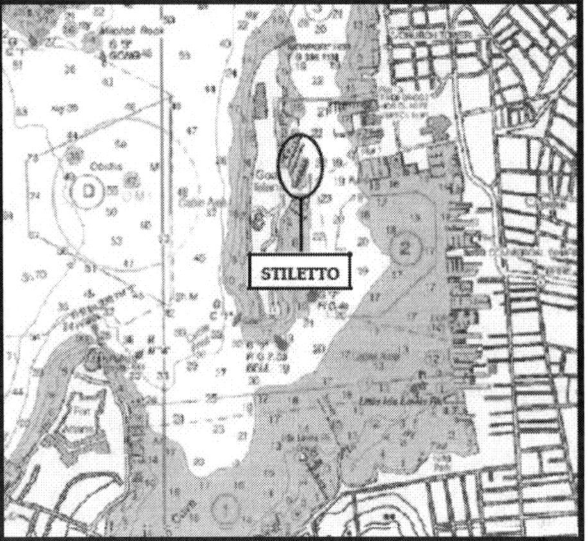

The Vessel

Type: Steamship
Construction: Wood
Use: Torpedo Boat
Dimensions: 94′ x 11′ x 5′
Tonnage: 31
Launched: Bristol, RI in 1885
Nationality: American
Official No.: 116040

The Event

Owner: U.S. Navy
Home Port: Newport, RI
Date of Incident: October 9, 1897
Disaster Type: Sunk
Cause: Boiler dropped into the hull
Status: Raised
Location: Alongside the large dock at the Torpedo Station on Goat Island

Narrative

Boston Daily Globe - September 10, 1897 P81

HOLE PUNCHED IN BOTTOM Torpedo Boat Stiletto Had to be Beached

Chain Broke as Boiler Was Being Taken Out for Repairs

It Nearly Fell Through Thin Plates - Boat on Marine Railway

*NEWPORT, RI, Oct. 9 - Torpedo boat **STILETTO** was sunk at the torpedo station this noon. This evening the force at the station succeeded in getting the vessel on the government marine railway for repairs. The accident by which the torpedo boat was sent to the bottom occurred while an attempt was being made to remove the boiler from the **STILETTO**. The vessel was alongside the large dock at the station, which is fitted with a huge derrick. There had been some doubt about the stability of the derrick to life heavy objects, and a few days ago it was thoroughly overhauled, the old gear removed and new substituted. This was completed on Thursday, and everything appeared to be in perfect order for the task of removing the **STILETTO**'s border. The chains were carefully affixed about the boiler and the signal to hoist was given. When the boiler was lifted a few feet above the deck of the vessel a sharp snap was heard, the chains broke and the boiler fell back into the hold of the vessel with a crash, followed by a thud that denoted that the boiler had found a resting place at the keelson. A hurried examination of the vessel was made and it was found that the torpedo boat was sinking rapidly. The pumps were started and the government steam launch BILLOW, which was lying at another dock, a few yards away, was hailed, and the latter hooked on to the **STILETTO** and started for the gravel beach, a few hundred feet away, to*

STILETTO

prevent the vessel from sinking in deep water. In this the men were successful, and as the stern of the torpedo boat struck the beach, the nose disappeared under water, which covered nearly the forward half of the vessel. A lighter was summoned from a shipyard, and after laboring an hour and a half the boiler was removed from the hold of the ***STILETTO*** *and carried to the dock at which the torpedo boat was stationed when the accident occurred. Meantime the station's divers were under water, patching up the holes that had been punched in the plates of the vessel, and when the repairs had been made the pumps were able to float the vessel and keep her on top of the water, while the government steam launches BILLOW, SPRAY and RIPPLE succeeded, after four hours hard work, in getting the torpedo boat upon the ways, when it was found that a good sized hole had been made in her plates near the keelson. No blame attaches to any of the officials, as every precaution had been taken to guard against accident; and the only cause that can be found for the mishap is that there was a defective link in the chain, which was so hidden in the finishing as to evade detection.*

Newport Daily News - October 11, 1897 P8

ACCIDENT TO THE STILETTO

Saturday the ***STILETTO****, the eldest and smallest of the navy's torpedo boats, met with a mishap at the torpedo station. Men were at work removing the boiler at the north wharf, when, after the boiler had been raised to the deck and was partially supported by timbers, a chain used in the work snapped, allowing the whole weight of the boiler to come on the joist, which slipped. The boiler slid into the hold and sprung some of the thin planks with which the bottom is sheathed, causing the boat to leak. As it was not known how seriously the hull might be injured, it was decided to beach the craft as a precautionary measure.*

This was done by one of the launches. Later Crowley's spile driver lifted the boiler, the hole was patched and the boat floated at high tide and was taken in on the marine railway. The chain which broke was a new one that was apparently able to stand the strain. The damage to the boat's planking is very slight.

Research Sources

1. Boston Sunday Globe, October 10, 1897 P81
2. Newport Daily News, October 11, 1897 P8
3. American Yacht List (1885)
4. Merchant Vessels of the United States—1896
5. John Palmieri, Curator, Herreshoff Marine Museum
6. Norene Rickson, Librarian/Archivist, Herreshoff Marine Museum
7. Photo courtesy of US National Archives and Records Administration

LEWISTON

An artists rendering of the night the hospital ship **LEWISTON** ran ashore on the breakwater at Point Judith.

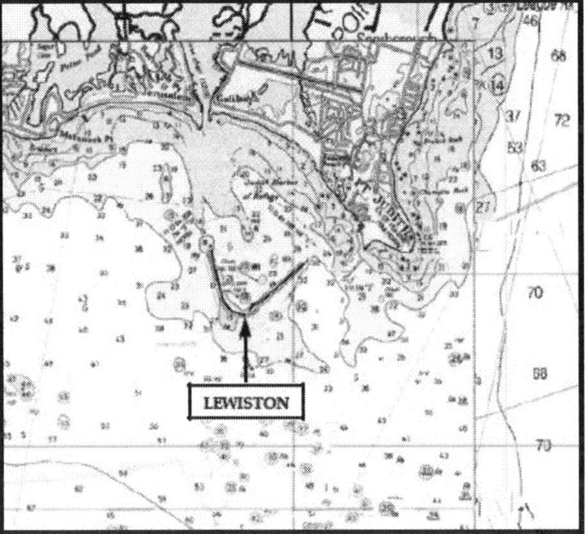

The Vessel

Type: Sidewheel Steamer
Construction: Wood
Use: Hospital Ship
Dimensions: 234′ x 33′ x 9′
Tonnage: 1127
Launched: New York City, NY in 1856
Owner: Bay State Steamboat Company
Nationality: American
Official No.: 15084
Home Port: Boston, MA

The Event

Port of Departure: Montauk Point, NY
Port of Destination: Boston, MA
Master: Charles Lyman
Cargo: 149 sick soldiers & nurses and 52 crew
Date of Incident: September 5, 1898
Disaster Type: Stranding
Cause: Fog
Status: Pulled off
Location: On the outside of the breakwater at Point Judith

Narrative

Naugatuck Daily News - September 6, 1898 P1

NEW ENGLAND NEWS

200 SICK SOLDIERS IN DANGER

Steamer Lewiston Ran Ashore Near Point Judith, R.I.

The steamer **LEWISTON**, *chartered by the Massachusetts Volunteer Aid Association, with nearly 200 sick soldiers on board, bound from Montauk Point to Boston, ran ashore near Point Judith last night and narrowly escaped being wrecked. One hundred and thirty-five of the men were placed in a lighter which fortunately was in the breakwater and were brought to Newport by a tug, landing at the Fall River line dock about midnight. The sick soldiers were in such an exposed place on the bare deck of the lighter during the trip of 16 miles across the bay from Point Judith that a number of men are not expected to reach Boston alive. As many as possible will be sent to Boston by a special train. The* **LEWISTON** *left Montauk Point yesterday morning with as many Massachusetts soldiers on board as she could carry. Her captain ran across the sound to New London, where a large quantity of fresh milk was obtained, and then she started for Boston. A heavy fog set in while the steamer was off Watch Hill.*

LEWISTON

Boston Daily Globe - September 6, 1898 P3

STEAMER LEWISTON BEACHED

Fifteen Feet of Water Ebbs and Flows in Her With the Tides

Newport, R.I., Sept. 20. – The ***LEWISTON*** *now lies beached inside the breakwater at Point Judith, near the Sand Hill Beach lifesaving station, in about fifteen feet of water. Her hull is full of water and the tide comes up level with her guards. Until an examination of her hull under the water line is made, it will be impossible to say whether she can be patched up within a short time or not. After the tug GAYNOR, towing the barge with the 118 sick from the* ***LEWISTON****, had left the breakwater for Newport last night, the steamer began to swing around with her port side to the rocks of the breakwater. The transfer of sick had been made none too quickly. As soon as the tug and barge had gone, the work of getting the* ***LEWISTON*** *off began. She was leaking but the water had not put her fires out and a full head of steam was up. As the tide rose, the bow of the steamer which was run up on the shelving side of the jetty when she struck, began to work free. The hawsers made fast to the rocks still held the steamer. Until all was ready they were not cast off. Captain Church of the Point Judith life-saving crew directed the work of getting the steamer free of the breakwater. It was 12:30 when the steamer finally swung free and started slowly astern, under her own steam. ... Only the hand of providence saved the ancient craft, which has tested the hardness of many New England rocks, from receiving her quietus in this exposed place. ...*

Excerpt from US Life Saving Service Annual Report – 1899

Sept. 5 - Am. str. ***LEWISTON*** *- Point Judith, Rhode Island - Collided with the breakwater and stranded during a thick fog while on her way from Montauk Point to Boston with 149 passengers – sick soldiers, doctors, and nurses – and 52 crew. Hearing her signals of distress, station crew pulled out in the surfboat and offered their services. They laid a plank walk from the vessel to a lighter lying inside the breakwater and assisted the soldiers to the lighter, which was then towed to Newport by a tug. The steamer's crew were nearly all on the breakwater and the master engaged another tug to float the vessel. Surfmen ran the line and the tug succeeded in getting her off and took her inside the breakwater. She was leaking so much that it was necessary to put her on the beach. Surfmen put the engineer's force on board and the vessel was laid ashore under her own steam. Station crew then transferred the men from the breakwater to the steamer and laid by until daylight. At 7 a.m. on the 6th, surfmen returned and transferred 45 of the crew to the beach, where they secured teams to take them to Wakefield, whence they were sent home by rail. At 1 p.m. keeper went on board and remained until the arrival of a wrecking outfit at 4 p.m. The* ***LEWISTON*** *was released on the 8th and towed to Providence.*

Research Sources

1. Boston Daily Globe, September 6, 1898 P1 & P3
2. Naugatuck Daily News, September 6, 1898 P1
3. North Adams Evening Transcript, September 6, 1898 P2
4. Newport Mercury, September 10, 1898 P1
5. Hartford Courant, September 7, 1898
6. Boston Daily Globe, September 7, 1898 P2
7. Boston Daily Globe, October 12, 1898 P9
8. Record of American and Foreign Shipping (1898)
9. American Lloyd's Register of American and Foreign Shipping (1872)
10. Merchant Vessels of the United States – 1897
11. Excerpt of the US Life Saving Service Annual Report - 1899

STILETTO

The **STILETTO** firing a torpedo from the single tube in her bow perhaps as she may have done during the maneuvers.

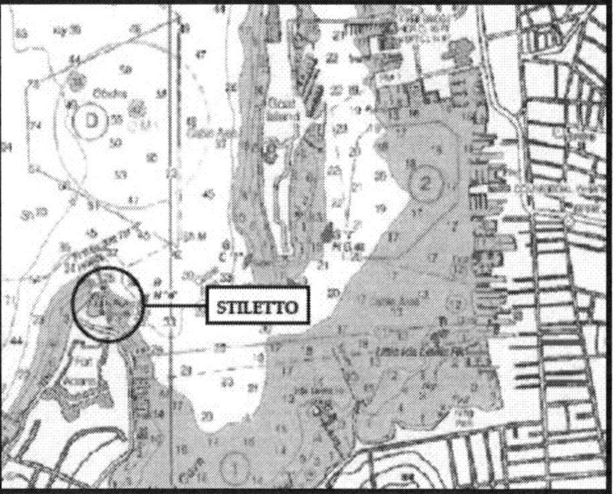

The Vessel

Type: Steamship
Construction: Wood
Use: Torpedo Boat
Dimensions: 94′ x 11′ x 5′
Tonnage: 31
Launched: Bristol, RI in 1885
Nationality: American
Official No.: 116040

The Event

Owner: U.S. Navy
Home Port: Newport, RI
Date of Incident: September 24, 1900
Disaster Type: Damaged
Cause: Collision with pier
Status: Repaired
Location: At the permanent dock at Fort Adams, Newport

Narrative

New York Times - September 2, 1900

NAVAL ATTACK ON NEWPORT

Imposing Spectacle in the Harbor When the Battleships Tried to Force An Entrance

NEWPORT, Sept. 24. - The long-talked-of naval manoeuvres off Newport were begun to-night with an attempt of a fleet of warships and torpedo boats to make an entrance to the bay. It is probable this force was unsuccessful, but it will not be known for two or three days, when the Committee of Arbitrament has heard the decisions of the umpire and the protests. As a spectacle, tonight's manoeuvre was a great success. Naval officers say they will derive much profit from it. The attacking force was in command of Capt. William M. Folger, and his flagship was the KEARSARGE. His fleet was composed of the battleships INDIANA and TEXAS, the gunboat SCORPION, and the torpedo boats PORTER, ROGERS, DAHLGREN, MORRIS, GWYN, and ***STILETTO****. The defenders were the cruiser NEW YORK, the battleship MASSACHUSETTS, and the gunboat LEYDEN. Forts Adams, Wetherell, and Greble also took part in the defense, the entire force being under Rear Admiral Farquhar. The torpedo boats furnished the feature of the attack. Lieut. Miller was in command of the flotilla, which was decided into two sections, and his flagship was the PORTER. The first section consisted of the flagship and the MORRIS, GWYN, and ROGERS. They rendezvoused at Whale Rock at 9 o'clock, and began the passage of Fort Greble. The force at the fort claim that they put out all the boats, but the umpires will have to rule on that.* The second section, including the torpedo boat **STILETTO**, approached via the East Passage where the MASSACHUSETTS was targeted. *The* ***STILETTO*** *had a bad accident. In the glare of the searchlight her navigator lost his bearings and the torpedo boat rammed the permanent dock at Fort Adams. Her bow was injured and her umpire, Lieut. Lincoln, was thrown overboard, but was picked up at once. Two of the*

STILETTO

crew of the boat were cut about the head. The running of the gauntlet of the forts by the big ships was a sensational affair. There was a long delay and many guns were fired by the forts on signal from the outposts before the first of the fleet was seen headed straight up the entrance. She looked as big as a house and was coming fast when she was picked up by the searchlight of Fort Wetherell and the firing at once began. It was the KEARSARGE. She at once turned on her powerful searchlights to bother the gunners, and opened fire as fast as her guns came in range. The picture she presented as she drew up so that she could use her raked fire broadside guns was one that will not soon be forgotten. It seemed to be one continuous blast of flame from her sides. She was under fire nine and a half minutes. After her came the TEXAS. She used no searchlights and fired but two guns to indicate the beginning and ceasing firing. She was under fire four and a half minutes. Next came the INDIANA using searchlights and only her turret guns. She was under fire nine minutes. Following her were the EAGLE and SCORPION, the latter of which made a very pretty picture with her broadside guns.

Newport Daily News - October 6, 1900 P8

THE STILETTO'S COLLISION UNAVOIDABLE

The naval court of inquiry which examined into the collision of torpedo boat ***STILETTO*** *with the dock at Fort Adams during the recent manoeuvres here has been submitted and approved and forwarded to the Navy Department. It finds that the collision was unavoidable owing to the blinding glare from the searchlights of the MASSACHUSETTS and NEW YORK just after the* ***STILETTO*** *had fired a torpedo at the MASSACHUSETTS and was making off. At this moment it would have been impossible to avoid ramming the MASSACHUSETTS had not the* ***STILETTO****'s helm been placed hard aport, and when this was done the craft was brought suddenly into collision with the dock. The board gives the items of damage, recommending the repairs, which will cost a few hundred dollars, and the substitution of a wooden bow for that carried away by the accident.*

Boston Daily Globe - October 6, 1900 P2

COLLISION UNAVOIDABLE

Court of Inquiry's Report on Stiletto's Accident at Newport

WASHINGTON, Oct. 5 – The report of the naval court of inquiry on the recent collision of the torpedo boat ***STILETTO*** *with the dock at Fort Adams during the Newport manoeuvres here has been submitted and approved and forwarded to the Navy Department. It finds that the collision was unavoidable due to the blinding glare from the searchlights of the MASSACHUSETTS and NEW YORK just after the* ***STILETTO*** *had fired a torpedo at the MASSACHUSETTS and was making off. At this moment it would have been impossible to avoid ramming the MASSACHUSETTS had not the* ***STILETTO****'s helm been placed hard aport, and when this was done the craft was brought suddenly into collision with the dock. The board gives the items of damage, recommending the repairs, which will cost a few hundred dollars, and the substitution of a wooden bow for that carried away by the accident.*

Research Sources

1. New York Times, September 2, 1900
2. Newport Daily News, October 6, 1900 P8
3. Boston Daily Globe, October 6, 1900 P2
4. American Yacht List - 1885
5. Merchant Vessels of the United States—1896
6. John Palmieri, Curator, Herreshoff Marine Museum
7. Norene Rickson, Librarian/Archivist, Herreshoff Marine Museum
8. Photo courtesy of US National Archives and Records Administration

SCORPION

The steam yacht SCORPION docked at an unknown port in 1898.

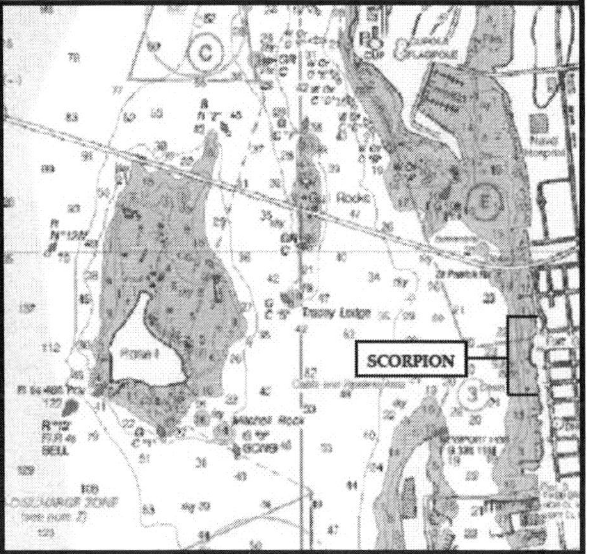

The Vessel

Type: Steamship
Construction: Steel
Use: Dispatch Boat
Dimensions: 210′ x 28′ x 11′
Tonnage: 426
Launched: South Brooklyn, NY in 1896
Owner: U.S. Navy
Nationality: American
Official No.: 116730

The Event

Home Port: US North Atlantic Squadron
Port of Departure: Block Island, RI
Port of Destination: Newport, RI
Date of Incident: July 23, 1902
Disaster Type: Stranding
Cause: Mechanical Failure
Status: Floated Off
Location: About 100 yards offshore, in the vicinity of Fort Greene, Newport Harbor

Narrative

Newport Mercury - July 26, 1902 P1

LOCAL MATTERS Struck at Fort Greene

Failing to respond to the signals sent to the engine room the United States dispatch boat ***SCORPION*** *went ashore near the site of Fort Greene on Wednesday. She struck on dangerous bottom and laid there for a number of hours before the tide rose sufficiently to permit of her removal. The vessel was coming into the harbor from the direction of Block Island and when headed in toward the shore the signal to reverse the engines was given. The engine failed to act and the* ***SCORPION*** *kept straight on toward shore. An anchor was let go but failed to hold and she finally struck about 100 yards from shore on a rocky bottom. Everything possible was done to get her off but without avail. After several government launches had struck on bottom is was decided to abandon the attempt to move her until the tide rose again. The SCORPION came off the rocks just as bells rung for 8. All stores forward had been carried aft and she was given as much trim by stern as possible. Then a kedge was run out and a strain taken. Just before she floated the crew went to mess and she was well afloat before they were summoned on deck. She was kedged out well clear of the rocks and over the anchor that had been let go to save her. There is reason to believe that a careful examination will reveal considerable damage to her hull.*

SCORPION

Ship's History - Dispatch Boat Scorpion

According to the Dictionary of American Naval Fighting Ships (DANFS) the dispatch boat **SCORPION** was the fourth naval vessel to carry that name. The following is an excerpt of her ships history:

The fourth ***SCORPION*** *was built in 1896 as SOVEREIGN, a two-masted schooner rigged, steel, steam yacht for M.C. Borden by John N. Robins, South Brooklyn, NY; purchased for the Navy on 7 April 1898; renamed* ***SCORPION****; and commissioned on 11 April 1898, Lt. Comdr. Adolph Marix in command. Following commissioning,* ***SCORPION*** *proceeded to Hampton Roads where she joined the Flying Squadron on 1 May and prepared for duty in the Caribbean. ...on 14 January 1899, she was decommissioned in preparation for conversion to a gunboat. Recommissioned on 22 August, she was assigned to Isthmian Canal Commission and ordered south. Into the Spring of 1900, she remained in the Caribbean as the Commission investigated the proposed canal routes. In June, she returned to the United States, operated off the northeast coast into the Fall, then resumed operations in the Caribbean. From November 1900 to May, 1901, she cruised off Hispaniola. In June, she arrived at Boston; and on 24 July she was again decommissioned. On 1 July 1902, the gunboat was recommissioned and assigned to the North Atlantic Squadron. For the next six years, she carried dispatches and personnel, conducted hydrographic surveys, and participated in exercises along the east coast and in the Caribbean, operating primarily off Santo Domingo during 1906 and 1907. Ordered to the Mediterranean in 1908,* ***SCORPION*** *sailed from Philadelphia on 22 October. ... Through the second Balkan War... in the summer of 1913 she continued to protect American interests* [in the Mediterranean]. *... During the first years of World War I,* ***SCORPION*** *was held at Constantinople and, on 11 April, 1917, after the United States had entered the war on the side of the Allies, she was interned. ... With the arrival of Rear Admiral Mark L. Bristol, High Commissioner to Turkey and Senior U.S. Naval Officer in Turkish waters,* ***SCORPION*** *assumed duties as flagship and dispatch vessel. ... Designated PY-3 in 1920, she shifted to Phaleron Bay, Greece, in November, 1923 and took up duties as station ship in the eastern Mediterranean. On 16 June, 1927, she departed the Mediterranean and steamed west. On 11 July, she arrived at Philadelphia, where she was decommissioned on 27 October 1927. Struck from the Navy list on 23 March 1929, she was sold to the Boston Iron and Metal Co. on 25 June of the same year.*

Research Sources

1. Newport Mercury, July 26, 1902 P1
2. Record of American and Foreign Shipping (1897)
3. Merchant Vessels of the United States—1902
4. Merchant Vessels of the United States—1920
5. Dictionary of American Naval Fighting Ships
6. Photo courtesy of the US Naval Historical Center

USS LEYDEN

Looking more like a coastal freighter than a tug, the **USS LEYDEN** (photo above) was just thirty-seven years old at the time of her loss on the rocky and desolate southern coast of Block Island.

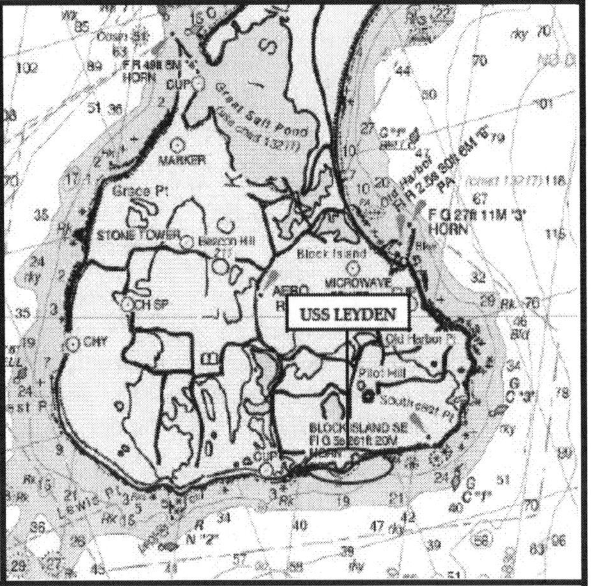

The Vessel

Type: Steamship
Construction: Steel
Use: Tug
Dimensions: 137′ x 26′ x 9′
Tonnage: 450
Launched: Chelsea, MA in 1866
Owner: US Navy
Nationality: American
Official No.: N/A
Home Port: Newport, RI

Final Voyage

Port of Departure: San Juan, Puerto Rico
Port of Destination: Newport, RI
Master: Lt. Chester Wells
Cargo: N/A
Date of Loss: January 21, 1903
Disaster Type: Stranding
Cause: Fog
Final Status: Total loss
Location: Under Mohegan Bluffs, near Southeast Light

Narrative

Boston Globe - January 22, 1903 P1

BREECHES BUOY SAVED 27 MEN

US Tug Leyden on the Rocks—Went Ashore at Block Island

Block Island, R.I., Jan. 21. - US Tug LEYDEN, bound from San Juan, P.R. for Newport, ran ashore on the south side of this island at noon today and is a total wreck. She is fast going to pieces. Six of her crew of 33 men left the wrecked tug in a small boat, which was dashed to pieces on the rocks a short distance from the shore. They were rescued by the lifesavers. The remaining 26 men and Lieut. Wells were taken off in the breeches buoy with great difficulty by the New Shoreham life-saving crew. Seaman Leylamb, who was in the small boat when it was demolished, swam until he was rescued but he is not expected to live as a a result of the injuries he received in the heavy sea. The call for help reached Capt. Littlefield at 1 o'clock, and he immediately set out with his crew and a complete set of apparatus. A persistent effort was made to cast a line aboard the tug and it was finally successful. At 2 o'clock the end of a hawser 1700 feet long was made fast to the foremast and the breeches buoy was put into operation. One by one the remaining members of the crew were drawn through the surf, and shortly after 3 o'clock the last man was hauled safely upon the shore. Lieut. Chester Wells, her commander, reports that during the night he picked up Shinnecock Light

USS LEYDEN

*and laid off until daylight, when he got Montauk Light. In a very short time the fog shut in very thick. He had intended to go two miles south of the light and as his patent log indicated that his position was correct, he proceeded. He shaped his course for Point Judith whistling buoy, all the while expecting to hear the fog whistle at the South light. He was running at the rate of six knots per hour when with a terrific crash the **LEYDEN** brought up on the rocks. A heavy southeast swell was running and the surf dashed high over the wrecked craft. She began to go to pieces in less than half an hour after she struck. The crew will be taken care of tonight at the life-saving station, and in the morning they will be sent to the mainland.*

*Washington, Jan. 21 – The **LEYDEN** was of the largest type of naval tug, schooner rigged and of 450 tons displacement. She was built in Boston in 1866, of iron, at a cost of about $100,000. She was 137 feet long, by 26 feet beam and drew 9½ feet of water. She had no double bottom, and made a speed of 10 knots an hour. Her commanding officer is Lieut. Chester Wells, Gunner Donnell was her executive officer. The **LEYDEN** was kept at the training station at Newport, RI before the maneuvers. For several years the **LEYDEN** was attached to the navy yard at Portsmouth, NH under command of mate John L. Vennard.*

Excerpt from US Life Saving Service Annual Report—1903

*Jan. 21 - New Shoreham, Rhode Island - U.S. str. **LEYDEN** - Stranded 200 yards from shore 1 mile west of the Southeast Light, Block Island in a thick fog, and was sighted at 12:40 p.m. by the light keeper, who notified the station keeper of the casualty by telephone. Surfmen called upon the crew of Block Island station to go to the scene, and then teamed their own surfboat and beach apparatus to the shore abreast the wreck, where the two crews united. Upon arrival they found that seven of the steamer's crew had attempted to land in a boat, which was dashed to pieces on the rocks by the heavy sea; the men, however, safely reached the shore with a line from the vessel being assisted by on-lookers. The surfmen sent the whip out by the steamer's line and soon rigged the breeches buoy and landed the twenty-nine men remaining on board without mishap, each as landed being taken to the keeper's dwelling for shelter. Afterwards the rescued men were taken to the life-saving stations, where such as needed dry clothing were supplied from the stores donated by the Women's National Relief Association and succored until the following day, when they left for Newport, Rhode Island. The vessel was a total loss.*

Research Sources

1. Boston Globe, January 22, 1903 P1
2. Newport Mercury, January 24, 1903 P1
3. Merchant Vessels of the United States—1902
4. Excerpts of the US Life Saving Service Annual Report - 1903
5. "Storms and Shipwrecks of New England" by E.R. Snow
6. "Shipwrecks of New England" - Internet site with list
7. Correspondence with researcher Joan Charles
8. Photo courtesy of US Naval Historical Center

A.D. BACHE

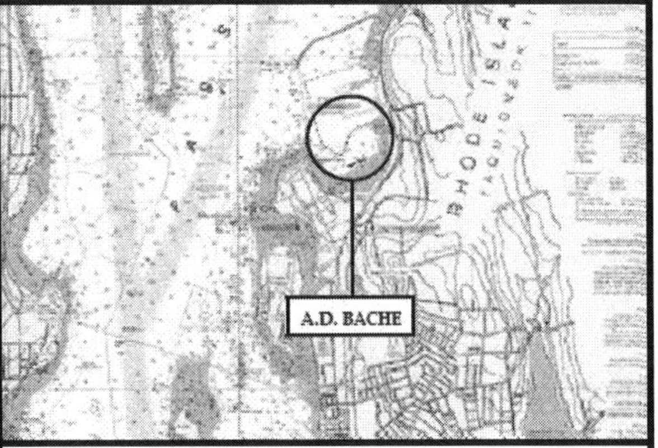

The Vessel

Type: Steamship
Construction: Iron
Use: Coast Survey
Dimensions: 153′ x 26′ x 9′
Tonnage: 252
Launched: Wilmington, DE in 1871
Owner: US Coast & Geodetic Survey
Nationality: American

Final Voyage

Cargo: N/A
Date of Loss: April 20, 1905
Disaster Type: Burned
Cause: Fire
Final Status: Repaired
Location: Somewhere in Coddington Cove, Newport

The BACHE Mysteries

In April of 1905 a fire occurred aboard the steamer **A.D. BACHE,** probably when she was at anchor, in Coddington Cove, north of Coasters Harbor Island in Newport. A search through the local newspapers of the time and other sources of data has yielded no details to accompany the notation of this event. That could indicate that the incident was a minor one or, since the **BACHE** was a government vessel, that no civilian participation was involved. But whether or not the incident occurred, a more interesting mystery involves the question of which vessel it may have affected. The original steamer **A.D. BACHE** was built in 1871 in Delaware and took her name from the superintendent of the U.S. Coast Survey between 1843 and 1867. The vessel led a long and distinguished career until she was nearly sixty years old. In 1901, one of two things happened. Either the original steamer **A.D. BACHE** was rebuilt at Shooters Island, NY or another vessel was built there and took the same name. The Merchant Vessels of the United States for 1901 notes that the **BACHE** measured 182 tons and was 147 feet in length. In the 1904 edition, she is shown as 252 tons and 153 feet in length with a notation that she was rebuilt in 1901 at Shooters Island. Regardless of whether the 1901 version was a new vessel or a newly rebuilt vessel, the Coast & Geodetic Survey vessel BACHE continued in service until 1927.

Research Sources

1. E-mail correspondence with Joan Charles (researcher)
2. E-mail correspondence with Albert E. "Skip" Theberge, Jr., NOAA Central Library
3. Merchant Vessels of the United States—1901 & 1904
4. Photo courtesy of NOAA, Office of NOAA Corps Operations

BRENTON REEF (LV-39)

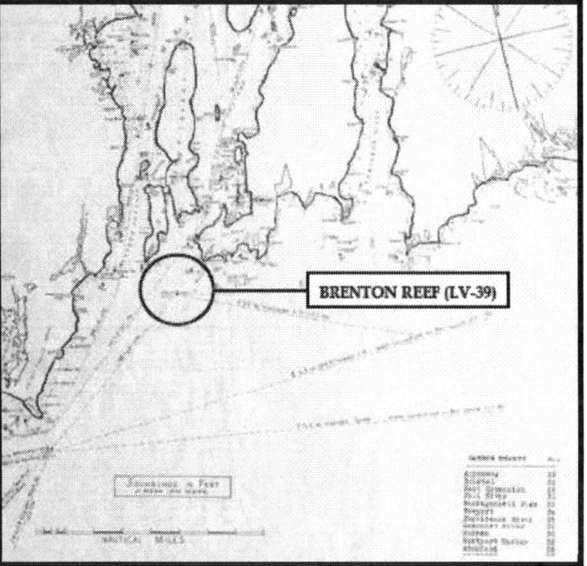

BRENTON REEF (LV-39) was one of four lightships and a stationary tower that have been stationed at the entrance to Narragansett Bay over the years.

The Vessel

Type: Schooner
Construction: Wood
Use: Lightship
Dimensions: 119′ x 26′ x 12′
Tonnage: 387
Launched: Pelham, NY in 1875
Owner: US Lighthouse Service
Nationality: American
Home Port: Newport, RI

The Event

Master: Edward Fogarty
Cargo: N/A
Date of Incident: August 24, 1905
Disaster Type: Damaged
Cause: Collision in fog
Status: Repaired
Location: While on her station off Brenton Reef at 41-25-54N 71-22-36W

Narrative

New York Times - August 27, 1905

IOWA SMASHES A LIGHTSHIP

Battleship in Collision at Brenton's Reef Station, Keeper Reports

NEWPORT, R.I., Aug. 26.– The battleship IOWA poked her nose into the Brenton's Reef Lightship while making her way towards this harbor last Thursday, it was learned today. That probability, it is inferred, is that the big warship was dangerously near running aground. After running into the lightship, according to the keeper, the IOWA drew away and made at once for harbor. The damage to the lightship was reported by Capt. Fogarty on his regular weekly visit to the shore. It will be necessary, he thinks, for a relief ship to take the station for a while. The collision with the lightship was the second mishap following the run out to sea this week of the battleship squadron of the North Atlantic fleet for maneuvers. The dense fog which hung off the coast interfered with the plans of the warships. The KEARSARGE on her return trip ran into the oil schooner N.S. GALLUP and towed her into port after taking off her crew. Capt. Fogarty says his vessel had a narrow escape from being sunk by the IOWA. It was 5 o'clock on Thursday afternoon, and the fog was so dense that it was impossible to see a ship's length ahead. The density of the fog obviously killed all sound, for those on the lightship heard no warning whistle from the battleship. It is believed that the battleship did not hear the lightship's bell, which was being struck repeatedly, or her fog whistle, which was sounding continuously. The IOWA was going about five knots an hour. The battleship

BRENTON REEF (LV-39)

struck the lightship on the bow and carried away the stem seven feet above the water line. The head stay and part of the rail and deck work were torn away. The blow was fortunately a glancing one, for the weight of the battleship had she struck head on, even at five knots speed,, would have sunk the signal vessel. After clearing from the lightship the IOWA headed toward the entrance to Newport Harbor, and was soon out of sight and hearing. Capt. Fogarty said he had reported the matter to Washington.

The **BRENTON REEF (LV-39)** spent almost sixty years in service before being retired in 1935. After retirement she served in several capacities including being a floating restaurant for a time. Her end came in 1975 when a century old and enroute to a shipyard in Beverly, MA. She foundered and sank to take on yet another role. After being lost for many years, her remains have been located and are visited by enterprising divers even today.

Research Sources

1. New York Times, August 27, 1905, 1865
2. "Lightships of the United States of America, Vol. I—Northeast" by Thomas Schoenwolff (2010)
3. "Rhode Island Lighthouse History" (Internet)
4. Photo courtesy of US Coast Guard Archives

USS ALABAMA (BB-8)

Pictured is the **USS ALABAMA** (BB-8) one of the earliest battleships of the post- Civil War US Navy. At 11,500 gross tons she made quite a hit, especially on that foggy day off the Rhode Island coast.

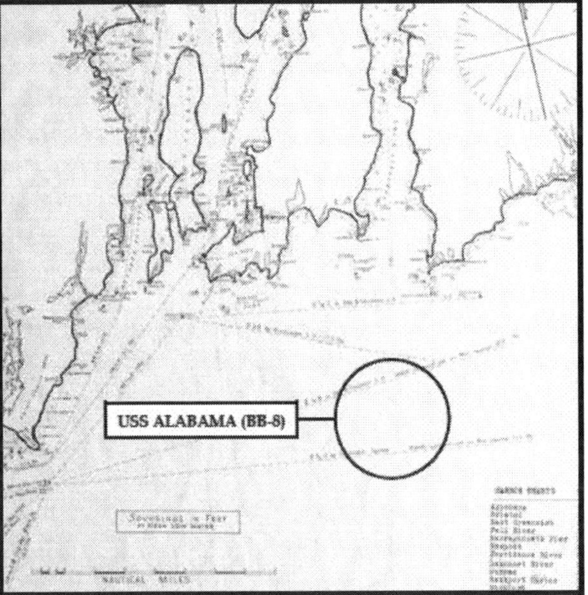

The Vessel

Type: Steamship
Construction: Steel
Use: Warship
Dimensions: 374′ x 72′ x 25′
Tonnage: 11,552
Launched: Philadelphia, PA in 1898
Owner: US Navy
Nationality: American
Home Port: Newport, RI

The Event

Port of Departure: Rockport, MA
Port of Destination: Newport, RI
Master: Captain Samuel P. Comly
Date of Incident: July 30, 1906
Disaster Type: Collision
Cause: Fog
Status: Repaired
Location: About 8 miles southeast from the Brenton Reef Lightship

Narrative

New York Times - August 1, 1906

BATTLESHIPS CRASH IN FOG AT NEWPORT

The Alabama hits the Illinois and Both Are Damaged

*NEWPORT, R.I., July 31.– Rear Admiral Robley D. Evans, commanding the North Atlantic Fleet, received reports in detail of a collision which occurred during a fog last night between the battleships **ALABAMA** and ILLINOIS about eight miles southeast of Brenton's Reef Lightship. The side of the ILLINOIS was scraped by the bow of the **ALABAMA**, and several plates of the forward part of the **ALABAMA** were dented. It is feared also that one or more of the six-inch guns on the two battleships were damaged. Rear Admiral Evans said tonight that he was satisfied that neither ship was injured below the waterline. The collision occurred between 8 and 9 o'clock last evening, when the second division of the battleship fleet was eight miles southeast of Brenton's Reef Lightship. Both the first and second divisions left Rockport, Mass., Monday morning for Newport. They sailed in single-column formation, with the first division in front, consisting of the battleship MAINE, the flagship of Rear Admiral Evans, and the battleships MISSOURI, KENTUCKY, and KEARSARGE. In the second division were the battleships **ALABAMA**, the flagship of Rear Admiral Charles H. Davis, the ILLINOIS, INDIANA and IOWA. The*

USS ALABAMA (BB-8)

fleet was making about 8 knots an hour on the run to Newport when the weather turned foggy, and orders were signaled to reduce the speed to 5 knots and keep the ships 400 yards apart. When the collision occurred, the first division ships were well into Newport Harbor, while the second was southeast of the lightship. In the thick fog the ***ALABAMA*** *and ILLINOIS came together at an angle, with the* ***ALABAMA*** *to starboard. The* ***ALABAMA*** *hit the ILLINOIS just abreast the forward turret, and the bow of the* ***ALABAMA*** *scraped the side of the ILLINOIS, crushing in the rail for some distance. Seaman Corbett was standing near a lifeboat on the ILLINOIS when the collision took place and was injured so severely by the fall of a boat davit that one of his legs had to be amputated tonight. On the ILLINOIS the gunwale on the starboard side forward was dented in, while the bill board on the bow of the* ***ALABAMA*** *was also damaged. The crews went to collision drill as soon as the accident happened. Officers of both ships say the discipline was of the highest order, although everyone feared that something very serious had occurred. On the bridge of the* ***ALABAMA*** *were Rear Admiral Davis, Capt. Samuel P. Comly, Commander of the vessel; Lieut. Commander H.F. Bryan, the navigating officer, and other officers. Capt. Gottfried Blockinger and Lieut. Commander A.H. Davis, the navigating officer, were on the bridge of the ILLINOIS. As soon as the fact of the collision became known to the other ships of the division the IOWA and INDIANA stood by the damaged ships, ready to give assistance in case it were needed. Rear Admiral Evans was informed almost immediately of the accident by Rear Admiral Davis, who sent him a wireless message. Admiral Evans ordered the division to anchor for the night in the vicinity of Brenton's Reef Lightship, and this afternoon the second division joined the first in Newport Harbor.*

The ***ALABAMA*** *met with a mishap on Jan. 7 this year as she was leaving New York Harbor. The KEARSARGE and KENTUCKY stranded in the lower bay and the* ***ALABAMA*** *struck the KENTUCKY on her starboard quarter, twisting her plate and breaking the doors on the gun port of the six-inch gun on the broadside battery. The* ***ALABAMA*** *had a hole knocked in her side, but proceeded on her way and repaired at the Norfolk Navy Yard. The KENTUCKY was so severely damaged that she had to return to Brooklyn Navy Yard.*

Research Sources

1. New York Times, August 1, 1906
2. Merchant Vessels of the United States—1906
3. Dictionary of American Naval Fighting Ships
4. Photo courtesy of the US Naval Historical Center

STILETTO

Only the quick action of the commander of the **STILETTO** (pictured) saved her.

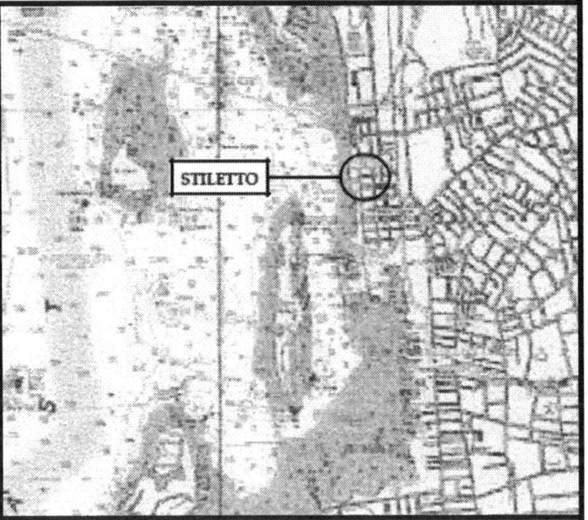

The Vessel

Type: Steamship
Construction: Wood
Use: Torpedo Boat
Dimensions: 94′ x 11′ x 5′
Tonnage: 31
Owner: U.S. Navy
Launched: Bristol, RI in 1885
Nationality: American
Official No.: 116040

The Event

Master: William T. Baxter
Home Port: Newport, RI
Date of Incident: May 18, 1908
Disaster Type: Ashore & damaged
Cause: Collision
Status: Pulled off and repaired
Location: Collision occurred off Breakwater Light, north end of Goat Island; the torpedo boat ran ashore near Walnut Street, Newport

Narrative

New York Times - May 19, 1908

TORPEDO BOAT IN COLLISION

Stiletto Barely Escapes Sinking Off Newport - Saved by Gunner Baxter

*Newport, May 18. The **STILETTO**, the oldest torpedo boat in the navy, was run into this morning by the torpedo station's steam launcher BREAKERS and was so badly damaged that it was necessary to beach her. She lay on the Newport sands all the afternoon with a large hole amidships on the port side, but this evening she was towed to the torpedo station for repairs. There was no loss of life, thanks to the good seamanship of Gunner William T. Baxter who was in command of the **STILETTO**. Baxter was taking a party of gunners up Narragansett Bay for exercise, a number of whom were seated in a launch which his vessel was towing. The BREAKERS suddenly rounded the lighthouse at the north end of the torpedo station and ran head on into the torpedo boat. Baxter at once turned loose the launch he was towing and gave his attention to saving the **STILETTO** and the men aboard of her. He instantly headed the vessel for the mainland of Newport, half a mile away, and ordered the engineer to crowd on all steam. Then he ordered the gunners to move over to the starboard side, and by thus placing their weight he lifted the port side sufficiently to check considerably the inrush of the sea into the fireroom. But their was no great margin of safety. The engine room filled with water so rapidly that the engines were stopped a minute or two before the vessel reached the beach. Baxter has been highly complimented to-night on his coolness and his doing the right thing at the right moment to save his vessel and the lives of his men.*

STILETTO

Newport Mercury - May 23, 1908 P1

Damaged in Collision

The old torpedo boat ***STILETTO*** *and the government launch BREAKER were in collision off Breakwater Light Monday morning and the former received injuries which necessitated running her ashore as quickly as might be. She was beached near the foot of Walnut Street but so rapidly was the vessel filling that all hands were summoned on deck to be ready to take to the water in case she should sink. The torpedo had a hole in her side about four feet high, which pretty nearly cut her in two. The BREAKER was coming from Rose Island and the* ***STILETTO*** *was going to Coddington Cove and the former came around the breakwater and crashed into the side of the torpedo boat. The* ***STILETTO*** *was immediately headed for shore and although the inrushing water put out the fires she reached the beach before enough water had entered to sink her.*

Newport Mercury - May 23, 1908 P5

Launch Rammed Torpedo Boat

A great hole was torn in torpedo boat ***STILETTO*** *amidship by a launch from the torpedo station at Newport, R.R., running into it. Following the accident the* ***STILETTO*** *headed for the beach opposite the Newport Harbor light at full steam. A launch from the torpedo station, from where the accident had been observed, hastened to the rescue, and the crew of the damaged boat were taken off immediately after the* ***STILETTO*** *reached shore. The launch with which the torpedo boat collided was not seriously damaged.*

Research Sources

1. New York Times, May 19, 1908
2. Newport Mercury, May 23, 1908 P1
3. Newport Mercury, May 23, 1908 P5
4. American Yacht List (1885)
5. Merchant Vessels of the United States—1911
6. John Palmieri, Curator, Herreshoff Marine Museum
7. Norene Rickson, Librarian/Archivist, Herreshoff Marine Museum
8. Photo from Conway's All the World's Fighting Ships 1860-1905

NERO

The naval collier **NERO** (pictured) began her career as the WHITGIFT, a British vessel built in 1895. She appeared in local waters for some time prior to WWI and had several mishaps including this stranding at Brenton Reef but survived.

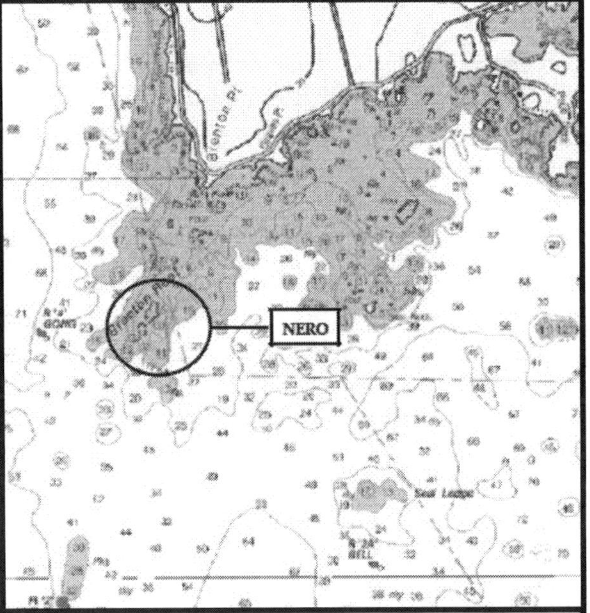

The Vessel

Type: Steamship
Construction: Steel
Use: Freighter
Dimensions: 312′ x 41′ x 22′
Tonnage: 6,360
Launched: Sunderland, England in 1895
Owner: US Navy
Nationality: American
Home Port: Newport, RI
Master: M. Kennedy

The Event

Port of Departure: Newport, RI
Port of Destination: Boston, MA
Cargo: None
Date of Incident: July 1, 1909
Disaster Type: Stranding
Cause: Pilot error
Status: Pulled Off
Location: Brenton Reef, on the rocks where the GEORGE W. HUMPHREY ran ashore and was lost in 1904

Narrative

Newport Daily News - July 1, 1909

COLLIER NERO AGROUND

Runs Ashore on Brenton's Reef But Lies Easily

Some Fog at the Time, But No Explanation Why She Was So Far Off Her Course

*Collier **NERO** ran aground on Brenton's Reef this morning at high water, about 8 o'clock, and is there yet. Fishing steamer VIGILANT, coming in, reported the accident to the Training Station. Fishing Steamers W.A. WELLS and STERLING sent boats to the ship to ask if aid could be given or any report made. Those on board paid no attention to the hail from the boats. Tugs SOLICITOR, RATTLER, HOKENDAUGUA and ROGER WILLIAMS went out and hailed the **NERO**, but received no reply. As a matter of fact, the captain of the **NERO** had no authority to engage a tugboat to help her out of his difficulties. The **NERO** lies about two thirds of the way out on the reef, and at the very rock, so the fishermen and Captain O'Neill of tug SOLICITOR say, on which fishing steamer GEORGE W. HUMPHREYS ran aground in 1904, and where her remains still rest. There was this difference. The*

NERO

*HUMPHREYS struck coming in and from the eastward, heading about northwest, while the **NERO** struck going out and from the westward, heading about south southwest. She ranges with the bell buoy on Castle Hill, which will enable one who knows the waters to see how far she was off her course as her course called for her making the lightship and where she struck was four miles to the eastward of that course. There was a little fog coming in at the time, but fishermen and others who were out had no trouble seeing their way and the lightship was blowing. Captain O'Neill of tug SOLICITOR was coming in with the swill scow when the **NERO** passed out. It was clear enough in the bay for him to see the ship above Gould Island, and as far out as Castle Hill as she passed out. There was a black streak of fog coming in and probably the **NERO** ran into this just before she struck, but why was she so far out of her course had not been explained up to noon except for surmises that in some way in taking her departure from Castle Hill a mistake was made. She was bound eastward but she could hardly have been expected to underrun her time so badly as to bring her into the middle of the reef, when in thick weather one would have expected her to run pretty close to the lightship before making the turn. Currents could hardly have caused the error since it was practically flood tide. The ship is not provided with wireless, and it was not until into this forenoon that tug CHICKASAW, of the Torpedo Station, reached the ship to make an investigation on which to base the report that must be made to Washington. Up to noon, other than the fact that the ship was on the reef, nothing was known at the naval stations here, but it was stated that cruiser CASTINE and collier BRUTUS, now at the coaling station, would pull on the **NERO** at high water this evening, when she will probably be floated. Captain Kenyon of the life saving station, was apparently the first to circulate the information of the distress of the vessel. The life saving station, like others along the coast, is taking its vacation and the crew is elsewhere. The captain, who was at once aroused by the distress signals, at once proceeded to acquaint himself as far as possible with conditions, and then began the use of the telephone to notify the naval stations. After this he started to assemble his crew, or rather a crew, since some of the regular members were to be reached, and toward noon was able to put out to the ship in his lifeboat. Before starting he reported the crew in no danger at present, as there was only a little chop on the sea. The Arbuckles, who are interested in floating ships by air, were notified. The captain of the RATTLER says that in his opinion the ship could be floated at high water by a powerful tug. She is light and when she tried to back out from the reef after the accident her wheel was so far out of the water that no power could be had. It was so choppy when the tugs were out that they did not dare run close to the ship for fear of grounding, but a small boat could easily carry lines on board for a big tug to pull. In the opinions of the captains who were out to the ship the present sea will not bother the **NERO** and unless her bottom is pierced there should be no trouble in floating her at high water. She lies on an even keel and is apparently easy. Captain Kenyon returned from the wreck with his life saving crew about 2:30 o'clock this afternoon having been sounding about the ship and learning the conditions existing. He reports that she should come off at high water tonight, almost of her own accord. While the rock is out of water 26 feet from her bow, there is a fathom or more under her stern at low water. The bottom appears to be quite smooth, and it is presumed that where she rests is also smooth, as she is not leaking. During the day, by use of her pumps, she discharged 500 tons of water ballast and things look quite favorable for her.*

Research Sources

1. Newport Daily News, July 1, 1909
2. New York Times, July 2, 1909
3. Merchant Vessels of the United States—1909
4. Dictionary of American Naval Fighting Ships
5. Photo courtesy of the US Naval Historical Center

IDA LEWIS

A 36′ McLellan Type E Motor Lifeboat. The **IDA LEWIS** was of this type and built by ELCO in 1909 as Hull No. 880.

The Vessel

Type: Gas Screw
Construction: Wood
Use: Lifeboat
Dimensions: 84′ x 26′ x 7′
Tonnage: 107
Launched: Bayonne, NJ in 1909
Owner: United States Life Saving Service
Nationality: American
Home Port: Newport, RI

The Event

Port of Departure: Newport Harbor
Port of Destination: Brenton Point Station
Master: Kenyon
Date of Incident: November 30, 1909
Disaster Type: Threatened
Cause: Mechanical failure
Status: Repaired
Location: Off the cove in the immediate vicinity of the Brenton Pont Life Saving Station

Narrative

Newport Daily News - December 1, 1909 P5

ALMOST WRECKED

New Power Lifeboat in Danger When Her Steering Gear Failed

Out Again This Morning, Her Crew Having A Rough Experience at Sea

The new power lifeboat IDA LEWIS narrowly escaped being wrecked Tuesday evening as she was returning to the station from this harbor. She had been here to have a leak in a gasoline feed pipe stopped, and it was about sunset when she attempted to negotiate the passage into the cove at the station, which is to be her berth. There was a heavy sea running and it was pretty lumpy about the entrance to the smooth water. Just as the boat was to wind its way between the rocks and was being tossed about the steering gear developed a defect, and but for the quick work of Captain Kenyon in securing control of the craft again, she would have piled up on the rocks, where the seas were lashing themselves into fine spray. A cogged segment is attached to the rudder head and on this plays a cog wheel operated by a long shaft extending to the captain's station, where he steers by a small wheel. A tiller is carried also, to be shipped in the event of need, in which case the gear is unshipped. Indications are that in allowing for this shifting the shaft supports have not been made so strong as they should be and the cogs disengage in the pounding of a sea.

IDA LEWIS

Similar difficulty has developed with the Provincetown boat. It will be remedied at once. Early this morning Captain Kenyon received a telephone message to go to Narragansett Pier, to take Lieutenant S.P. Edmunds, the inspecting officer and Superintendent Knowles to Block Island. A start in the lifeboat was made about 8 o'clock, in a heavy sea and a temperature down to 28 degrees. In the open boat, though clothed in oilskins, the crew became drenched and suffered from the cold. Captain Kenyon decided that the inspecting officer would not care to make the trip under such conditions, and that if he did it would be too much unnecessary hardship for the crew to go to the island and then return to its station for tonight in such weather. So he returned to the station, where the crew were glad to get into dry clothes. Word had been telephoned that the officers would arrive by public routes of travel rather than undergo the exposure which a trip at sea in a small boat, with a storm threatening, meant. On today's trip the steering wheel was not relied upon, but instead the tiller was shipped. Captain Kenyon found that, even with his great weight, the long stick was disposed to throw about the man who was handling it in a disagreeable manner.

Research Sources

1. Newport Daily News, December 1, 1909 P5
2. "Summary of Wooden Motor Lifeboat Types of the US Coast Guard" by Tim Dring (2007)
3. Photo from the Dring summary

WILLIAM A. WELLS

The typical menhaden fishing steamer in the sketch above was similar in design, if not in size, to the **WILLIAM A. WELLS**

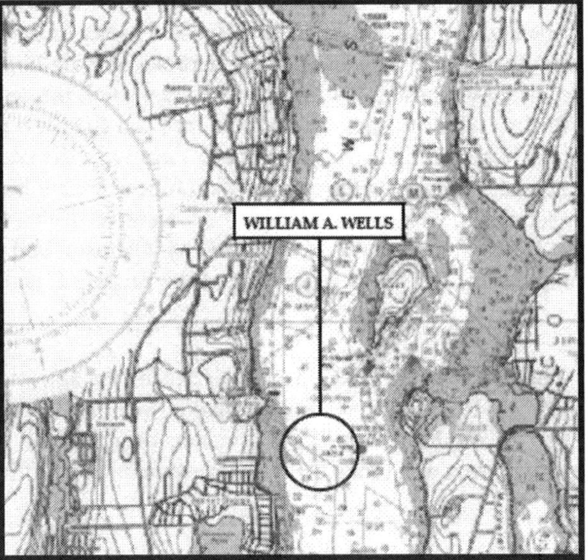

The Vessel

Type: Steamship
Construction: Wood
Use: Fishing
Dimensions: 76′ x 17′ x 8′
Tonnage: 68
Launched: Bristol, RI in 1873
Nationality: American
Official No.: 80352
Home Port: Newport, RI

The Event

Owner: Macomber and Nickerson Company
Master: Frank Macomber
Date of Incident: July 28, 1911
Disaster Type: Damaged
Cause: Struck by an artillery shell
Status: Repaired
Location: Close to the Narragansett shore, about 1¼ miles below Fort Greble, Dutch Island, West Passage

Narrative

Newport Daily News - July 28, 1911 P5

STRUCK BY A STRAY SHELL

Fishing Steamer William A. Wells Hit by a Shot from Fort Greble

Missile Goes Through the Deck and Water Tank and Lodges in the Keelson

Fishing steamer ***WILLIAM A. WELLS****, of Macomber & Nickerson's fleet, was struck by a stray shell from Fort Greble Thursday afternoon while proceeding down the west passage, but is still afloat. The worst of it was that it was a mortar shell and came right down through the deck and the iron water tank, and finally rested in the substantial structure of oak above the keel which is called a keelson and which on these big fishing steamers is no slight affair. Luckily, it was a sub-calibre shell which was fired. Had it been one of the 850-pound shells regularly fired from the mortars, that keelson would not have stopped it and the* ***WELLS*** *would probably have needed to be beached on the Narragansett shore. It was about 3:20 to 3:30, the* ***WELLS*** *was steaming close to the shore, perhaps a mile and a quarter below Fort Greble, the towing target was about a quarter of a mile off her port beam and about abeam, when the shot struck. Some of the men say they heard a whistling or shrieking as it came over the port quarter. It hit the forward house just port of the middle line and just forward of the big hatchway. It was coming straight down in the angle at which it was fired, which was quite high, and went through the woodwork of the forward house like so*

WILLIAM A. WELLS

much pasteboard. Also it went through the top and bottom of the big iron tank, and sank to rest in the keelson. An examination showed that the water was running out of the tank and it was disconnected from the other, which is on the starboard side. An examination showed the shell sticking in the keelson and it was removed. It is three inches in diameter, about a foot long and weighs 10 pounds. It was not an explosive shell else this story would have been different. The ***WELLS*** *returned to Newport and Captain Frank Macomber, who was on board, made a protest at the custom house. This morning one of the men from Fort Greble came over and learned what damage had been done. Repairs will be made by the Newport Shipyard, but the repairing of the iron tank will be something of a job. So far as can be remembered this is the first vessel to be hit by the target practice except a "touch" which the SWARFOOT received once while towing a target. As the captain of the* ***WELLS*** *stated today, he had often gone past while target practice was on and always found that it was so conducted that his craft was in no danger. It is entirely different off Sandy Hook, where the big gun practice is dangerous to passing craft. The shot which struck the* ***WELLS*** *was reported as "lost" by the plotters at Fort Greble. No splash was seen and there was nothing to show where the shell had fallen until the report that the fishing steamer had been hit was received. At the time the shot struck the steamer most of the crew of 22 were forward of the deck house, some in the rigging and some on the deck. No one was close to the line of the shell, which struck the steamer on the side nearest the fort and had not reached the middle line of the steamer until it struck the keelson. Many times, especially when the rapid-fire gun target practice was on, people out in boats, especially fishermen, have felt a trifle shaky about where the shots were going to fall but no one was ever in danger before this. There is probably more chance of variation in firing sub-calibre than the full-sized shells as the latter must go truer. Just so is there more danger with the small guns than from the big ones. The shell, none the worse for wear, is on exhibition in the wheelhouse of the* ***WELLS****. No charge is made for the show.*

New York Times - July 28, 1911

SAYS SHELL STRUCK VESSEL

Captain of Fishing Steamer Declares it Came from Fort Greble

NEWPORT, R.I., July 27. - Captain Frank Macomber of the fishing steamer ***W.S. WELLS****, of Providence has reported to the customs officials his ship was struck this afternoon by a small shell weighing ten pounds which he asserts came from a mortar at Fort Greble, where the One Hundred and Ninth and One Hundred and Tenth Coast Artillery Companies were having sub-calibre practice. While off Narragansett Pier the target the coast artillerymen were firing at was half a mile away from the steamer, which was struck, the Captain says, near the after part of the deckhouse, passing down through the deck to the bottom of the fresh water tank and into the keelson. The engineer, it is further alleged, came near being struck, the shot passing only a short distance from his body. Last August Harry Paine Whitney and Eugene S. Reynal, sailing to Narragansett Pier from this place aboard the yacht Atlantic, were nearly struck by a sub-calibre shell from one of the guns about the Narragansett Bay forts, the shell ripping through the mainsail and falling into the sea beyond.*

The fishing steamer **WILLIAM A. WELLS** last appears in the vessel registry for the year 1925.

Research Sources

1. Newport Daily News, July 28, 1911 P5
2. Newport Mercury, July 29, 1911 P1
3. New York Times, July 28, 1911
4. Merchant Vessels of the United States—1911
5. Newport Custom House records

USS NEW HAMPSHIRE (BB-25)

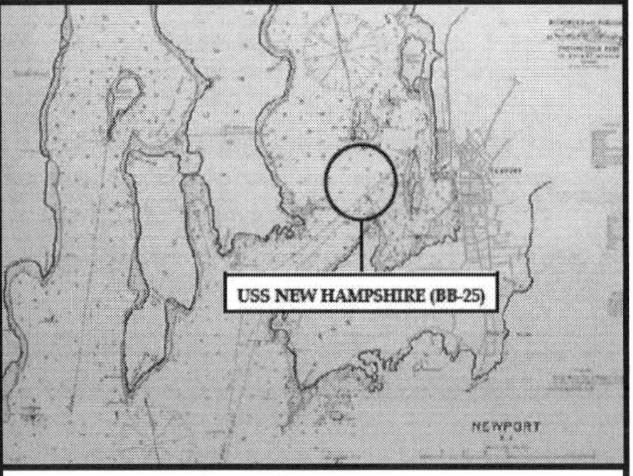

The Vessel

Type: Steamship
Construction: Steel
Use: Warship
Dimensions: 450′ x 76′ x 23′
Tonnage: 16,000
Launched: Camden, NJ in 1906
Nationality: American
Home Port: Newport, RI

The Event

Owner: US Navy
Master: James H. Oliver
Cargo: N/A
Date of Incident: July 7, 1912
Disaster Type: Damaged
Cause: Collision in fog
Status: Repaired
Location: At anchor in Newport Harbor

Narrative

New York Times - July 18, 1912 P2

WILL INVESTIGATE ACCIDENT

Board of Inquiry Ordered to Fix Responsibility for Collision

Washington, July 7. News of the accident to the battleship ***NEW HAMPSHIRE*** *reached the Navy Department today in an official report from Rear Admiral Aaron Ward, commanding the division of the Atlantic Fleet to which the battleship belongs. Department officials inferred from the description of the collision that the liner must have crashed head on into the* ***NEW HAMPSHIRE****'s stern. Admiral Ward's report follows:* ***NEW HAMPSHIRE****, at anchor at Newport, run into by steamer COMMONWEALTH this morning. Dense fog. Stern of the* ***NEW HAMPSHIRE*** *much crushed to the water's edge. Vessel needs extensive repairs and some temporary work before going to dock. Have requested the commandant of the navy yard at Boston to send a naval constructor to examine damage, and to recommend work needed now. Nobody hurt. Board of investigation has been ordered. Ship cannot go to sea without some repairs. The* ***NEW HAMPSHIRE*** *is one of the finest vessels of the new navy. She was completed in 1905, her sister ship being the first-class battleship CONNECTICUT, the flagship of the fleet. With a displacement of 16,000 tons and a speed of 18.16 knots, the* ***NEW HAMPSHIRE*** *mounts four twelve- inch, eight eight-inch, and twelve seven-inch guns, and two torpedo tubes. She is commanded by Capt. James H. Oliver. Officials of the department declined to venture an opinion as to which vessel was to blame for the accident. The navy regulations are very strict concerning the display of warning lights when vessels are at anchor in peaceful waters. No action will be taken by the department until after the investigating board has fixed the responsibility.*

USS NEW HAMPSHIRE (BB-25)

Research Sources

1. New York Times, July 8, 1912 P2
2. Merchant Vessels of the United States—1912
3. Dictionary of American Naval Fighting Ships
4. Photo courtesy of US Naval Historical Center

STILETTO

The torpedo boat STILETTO (pictured) when still in service for the navy.

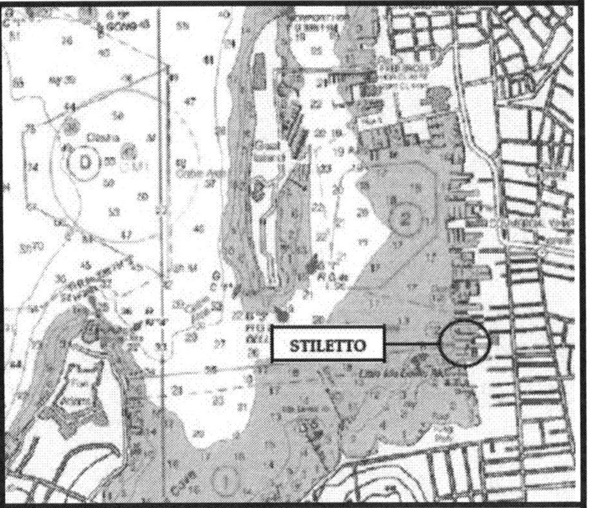

The Vessel

Type: Steamship
Construction: Wood
Use: Torpedo Boat
Dimensions: 94′ x 11′ x 5′
Tonnage: 31
Owner: James F. Nolan
Launched: Bristol, RI in 1885
Nationality: American
Official No.: 116040

The Event

Master: N/A
Home Port: Newport, RI
Date of Incident: October 23, 1912
Disaster Type: Sunk
Cause: Accident
Status: Raised
Location: At her dock at the Newport Foundry & Machine Works

Narrative

Newport Daily News - October 23, 1912 P5

SUNK AT HER DOCK

Old Torpedo Boat Stiletto Shipwrecked in Sight of the Shipyard

The old torpedo boat ***STILETTO*** *is sunk at her dock at the Newport Foundry & Machine Works—shipwrecked in sight of the shipyard is what they say. The owner has about completed arrangements to have her taken to Boston, and she went and sunk. He is here today making arrangements to float her. The trouble is that she was left without being pumped, until the ash chute was level with the water when things happened fast. There was a time when the* ***STILETTO*** *was the speediest torpedo boat in the navy, but she has been out of the navy for two years, having been sold to a Boston man who has not yet taken her away. While the* ***STILETTO*** *is the most celebrated wreck along the harbor front she is not exclusive...*

Research Sources

1. Newport Daily News, October 23, 1912 P5
2. American Yacht List (1885)
3. Merchant Vessels of the United States—1911
4. John Palmieri, Curator, Herreshoff Marine Museum
5. Norene Rickson, Librarian/Archivist, Herreshoff Marine Museum

USS VESUVIUS

The **USS VESUVIUS** (pictured) was originally built as a dynamite launching vessel but served for a number of years as a torpedo training boat in Newport.

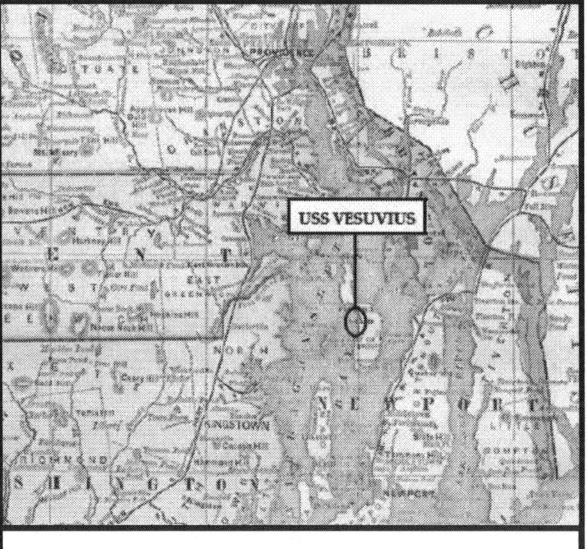

The Vessel

Type: Steamship
Construction: Wood
Use: Torpedo Boat
Dimensions: 252′ x 26′ x 11′
Tonnage: 930
Launched: Philadelphia, PA in 1888
Owner: US Navy
Nationality: American
Official No.: N/A
Home Port: Newport, RI

The Event

Port of Departure: Newport, RI
Port of Destination: Torpedo Practice Area
Master: Chief Gunner Thomas Smith
Cargo: N/A
Date of Incident: May 19, 1913
Disaster Type: Stranding
Cause: Torpedoed
Status: Towed in
Location: About 1 mile east southeast from Pine Hill Point, on west side of Prudence Island

Narrative

Newport Daily News - May 20, 1913 P5

VESUVIUS TORPEDOES HERSELF

Beached on Prudence Island, and Wrecking Party Summoned by Wireless

*Torpedo experimental ship **VESUVIUS**, formerly the dynamite cruiser which bombarded Santiago and scared the wits out of the Spaniards, torpedoed herself on the practice grounds off the west side of Prudence shortly before 4 o'clock Monday afternoon. She had to be beached to save her from sinking in deep water. The accident was probably due to one of the propeller of the torpedoes turning faster than the other, and thus causing it to describe a circle rather than run a straight course as intended. A similar thing had happened off the Torpedo Station in trying out another torpedo in the morning. These erratic feats of torpedoes are not unusual, and many more occur than ever reach the ears of the public. Two years ago battleship CONNECTICUT had a similar occurrence while off Provincetown, when a torpedo fired from one side came round and hit the ship at the end of its run on the other. Awhile ago a torpedo boat was hit after the same fashion by a boomerang torpedo in Coddington Cove, and at this point a most spectacular thing happened with another torpedo. It was fired at a net for a target and made a perfect run, hitting the target in the center and going through. Then it circled, coming back and hitting the target from the same side again. It was approximately 3:45 o'clock when a wireless message took the air announcing that the **VESUVIUS** had been hit by a torpedo and was sinking. The radio station at the Torpedo Station was not*

USS VESUVIUS

slow in telephoning the word to Commander Williams, Inspector in charge at the station and he in turn became active in giving orders to people on various parts of the island for the organization of a wrecking party. In 12 minutes the inspector and a small party, with some hastily gathered gear on torpedo boat MORRIS, was underway for the scene up the bay. The BLAKELY and GUINN cleared soon after, with more men, divers and gear. Six hours later the **VESUVIUS** *was at the station, having been towed down the bay by the tug SONOMA of the Atlantic fleet, until off the War College, and then she came under her own steam. The* **VESUVIUS** *was under way when she was hit, so, with no loss of time, Chief Gunner Thomas Smith, who is in charge of the ship, headed her toward the beach as soon as he found that she was making water in a dangerous quantity. The hull of the ship is comparatively thin, so when the torpedo hit her, though it had nearly run out its power, it was only to be expected that the hull would be punctured. The puncture was well aft on the port side, and when the wreckers arrived the after-compartment was flooded, but the bulkheads saved the engine room from meeting the same fate. When it was realized just what sort of work lay before the wrecking party one of the relief boats was sent back to the station for food for the workers and for additional supplies, and it was a tired crowd that came down the bay last evening. Luck favored the tide being well down at the time of the accident, and the wreckers were able to make temporary repairs before the coming of high water, when the* **VESUVIUS** *was pulled off so little damaged that Captain W.L. Rodgers, acting commandant of the Naval Station, Narragansett Bay, thought she might be able to return to duty by Wednesday. Today a concrete patch is being put into the craft, and this will serve for all needed repairs until the regular repair period, which will not come for some time. The officer's quarters, too, are receiving attention, for it is this part of the ship which was flooded, and the day is excellent for drying out. The place where the ship was beached was on the sandy shore above Prudence Park landing and at a point about one mile east southeast of Pine Hill Point. She was making use of the sandy-bottomed cove south of Pine Hill, as a practice ground, as this place has a favorable bottom for finding lost torpedoes and is out of the way of navigation and well removed from inquisitive observers. Torpedo practice ship MONTGOMERY is on the other side of the island, off Sand Point, and hence learned of the accident only by wireless, but as the call for assistance was sent out only to the Torpedo Station she, like other available craft - tugs ONTARIO and SONOMA, the PANTHER, LEBANON and YANKTON - did not respond, and the SONOMA went to the scene only when especially ordered. Torpedo practice is Almost always carried on with practice heads and there is not the danger to crews from these erratic runs which some persons may imagine. On very special occasions torpedoes have been fired with war heads attached, and of course have thereby been expended, for they are blown to pieces together with the object they strike. Comparatively few persons have had the experience of being present during the firing of a war-headed torpedo, and those who have remember the events well. Such an occasion took place up the bay, a little below where Monday's accident occurred, nearly twenty years ago. The torpedo was directed toward the rocks at the south end of Prudence, and when it struck there was a mighty concussion, but it is needless to say every person on board the firing vessel was deeply interested in the course the missile was taking. The torpedoes have been performing strange stunts always, and probably will continue to do so.*

Research Sources

1. Newport Daily News, May 20, 1913 P5
2. New York Times, May 20, 1913
3. Merchant Vessels of the United States—1913
4. Dictionary of American Fighting Ships

Section III - WWI, WWII and Postwar

Beginning with the earliest years of United States military involvement in the First World War, the nature of military vessels and maritime disasters associated with them in Narragansett Bay changed. Technology continued to be the ruling element and with change came unexpected consequences. Of particular interest during this period is the number of incidents where vessels have been accidentally torpedoed during normal testing. Initially thought to be a rarity, it has been found that this act has occurred a number of times, luckily without fatality, but certainly with a large degree of surprise to the testers and the "victims". And with Narragansett Bay being a major training area for naval personnel, the number and variety of ships present increased greatly. However, as was the case during the period that followed the colonial period, technology in the area of navigational safety greatly reduced, though could not eliminate, the number of maritime disasters which took place. During the Second World War, Rhode Island was relatively untouched, in a direct sense, by the presence of enemy ships with the exception of the incident that resulted in the loss of the coal collier BLACK POINT, which was torpedoed by the German U-853, and the destruction of her attacker by United States naval forces in the area. In the much more recent past which can be referred to as the postwar years, the number of maritime disasters to military vessels in state waters has diminished to a level where their occurrence now becomes an event of some notoriety. It is abundantly clear that the reduction in number of maritime disasters to military vessels is directly proportional to two factors, the sophistication in technology and the reduction of U.S. naval operations in Rhode Island. By 1973 active naval operations in Narragansett Bay had ceased and the majority of the fleet was relocated elsewhere.

LT. WILLIAM H. SMITH

Pictured above is the USN FERRY LAUNCH NO. 132 which was built in the same year and is of the same dimensions as the LT. WILLIAM H. SMITH

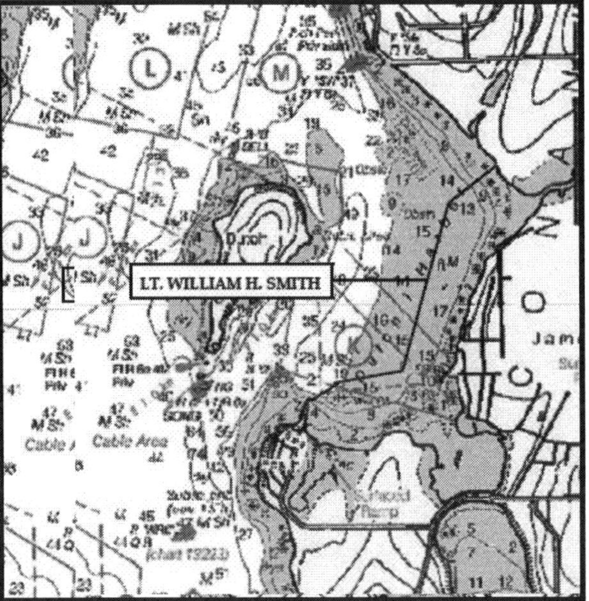

The Vessel

Type: Steamship
Construction: Wood
Use: Launch
Dimensions: 65′ x 13′ x 7′
Tonnage: 38
Launched: Muskegon, MI in 1909
Owner: U.S. Army
Nationality: American
Home Port: Newport, RI

Final Voyage

Port of Departure: N/A
Port of Destination: N/A
Cargo: N/A
Date of Loss: December 14, 1917
Disaster Type: Stranding
Cause: Storm
Final Status: Pulled Off
Location: Drifted from Fort Greble to the Conanicut shore above Hull's Swamp

Excerpt from Annual Report of the Secretary of War for 1909

HARBOR-BOAT SERVICE

Plans and specifications have been prepared and contracts awarded during the fiscal year for the construction of the following vessels required to provide additional water transportation where needed:

One steel harbor steamer, length 120 feet, cost $78,833.33.
One steel double-ended ferryboat, length 114 feet, cost $88,846.
Six wooden steamers, length 65 feet, cost $114,575.
One gasoline launch, length 26 feet, cost $1,994, for cable steamer JOSEPH HENRY.

The wooden steamers were completed during the year and named LIEUTENANT E.F. KOEHLER, ***LEIUTENANT WM. H. SMITH****, LIEUTENANT WM. F. SCHENCK, LIEUTENANT W.L. MURPHY, LEIUTENANT J.A. GURNEY, and CAPTAIN ANTON SPRINGER... These tugs are for service in the transportation of passengers and package freight, mail, commissary supplies, etc. at posts or to subposts where larger vessels are not required. They are single screw steamers with trunk cabin and freight space on main deck forward and under pilot house. The principal dimensions are: Length, 65 feet; beam, 13 feet; draft, 5 feet, with a speed of 10 miles per hour.*

LT. WILLIAM H. SMITH

Narrative

Newport Journal and Weekly News - December 21, 1917 P1

IN THE STORM AT GREBLE

Many Boats Damaged, the Lieutenant Smith on the Conanicut Shore

The wharf at Fort Greble proved a trap for boats tied up there and nothing survived without damage in Friday morning's storm. Some of the smaller craft were broken to splinters. The most novel experience was that of steamer ***LIEUTENANT SMITH****, which broke her lines and with a deckhand sound asleep below drifted across to the Conanicut shore above Hull's swamp, where she went bow on, as if she had been deliberately navigated there. On the high tide she was thrown far on the shore between two rocks and when she ceased to toss and pitch the deckhand awoke, got up steam and tooted for assistance. She is so far out of the water that Saturday when steamer GENERAL ARNOLD tried to haul her off a six-inch hawser was snapped, and the* ***SMITH*** *did not budge. It is probable that she will be cradled and then hauled off, for it apparent that power enough to pull her off would cause the tearing of her bottom to pieces. It is believed that she is practically uninjured.*

Newport Journal and Weekly News - December 21, 1917 P6

... The effect of the storm on Dutch Island, where Fort Greble is located, was marked. Not only individual owners suffered, but also the government. Launch ***LIEUTENANT SMITH*** *broke from her moorings early in the gale and was beached on the shore of Conanicut Island when the wind shifted. So far as can be ascertained no damage has been done although it will be impossible to remove the boat before the next high tide.*

Newport Journal and Weekly News - March 8, 1918 P7

Local Briefs

The Fort Greble launch, which went ashore on Conanicut Island weeks ago, after having been torn away from her dock at the fort during a heavy storm, has been floated and returned to duty. It was not felt that she could be spared for an overhaul, and her record is now one of continual trouble.

Research Sources

1. Newport Journal & Weekly News, December 21, 1917 P1
2. Newport Journal & Weekly News, December 21, 1917 P6
3. Newport Journal & Weekly News, March 8, 1918 P7
4. Merchant Vessels of the United States—1916
5. Merchant Vessels of the United States—1918
6. Annual Report of the Secretary of War for 1909, Vol. 2
7. U.S. Naval Historical Center

USS SCOUT (SP-907)

Section Patrol boats came in a variety of shapes and sizes. The one pictured is the first of two named USS SCOUT. This one was SP-114; later came the SP-907.

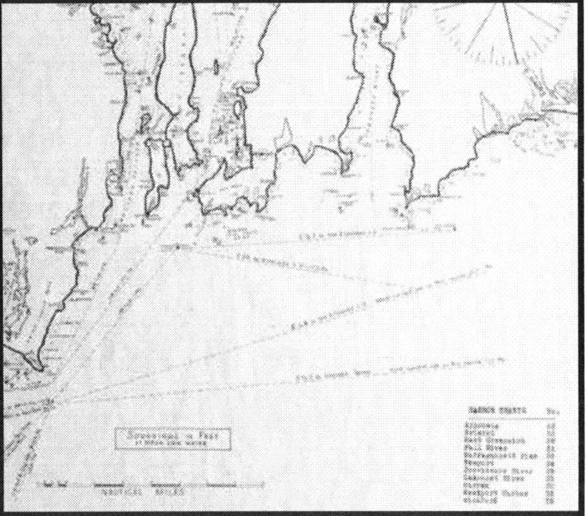

The Vessel

Type: Motorboat
Construction: Wood
Use: Patrol Boat
Owner: US Navy
Nationality: American
Home Port: Newport, RI

Final Voyage

Date of Loss: September 18, 1918
Disaster Type: Burned & sunk
Cause: Fire
Final Status: Total loss
Location: At an unspecified location at the entrance to Narragansett Bay

World War I Era Patrol Vessels and Other Acquired Ships and Craft

The **SP-907**, lost at the entrance to Narragansett Bay in the middle of September, 1918, belonged to a group of vessels which were privately owned prior to the war, acquired by the Navy for use in performing coastal patrols and other support type duties, and, when possible, were returned to their original owners at the end of hostilities. In all there were more than 1,900 vessels which carried the designation "SP". This diverse group of vessels came in a variety of sizes and rigs. The vessels ranged in size from just over 30 feet to more than 400 feet in length. They were usually powered but not necessarily and could be wind powered, though more were engine driven vessels ranging between 50 feet and 100 feet in length. There is not a lot of detail about many of these, including **SP-907** (sometimes referred to as YARD NO. 210) as their length of service was not long. They did, however, fill a void during a period when the number of naval vessels was small yet the need was significant.

Research Sources

1. "US Naval Ships Sunk or Damaged from Various Causes During World War I" (Internet)
2. "SP #s and ID #s—World War I Era Patrol Vessels and other Acquired Ships and Craft" - from the US Naval Historical Center

USS CERO (SP-1189)

The motorboat **CERO** (pictured) was one of numerous private craft which were selected for use by the US Navy during World War I as patrol craft.

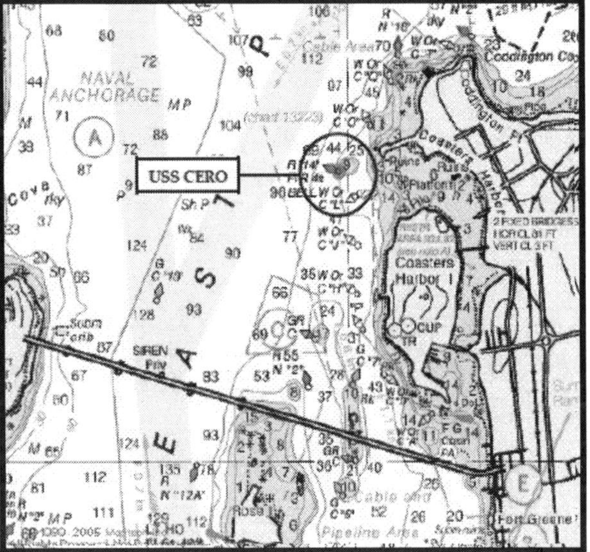

The Vessel

Type: Motorboat
Construction: Wood
Use: Patrol Craft
Dimensions: 40′ x 9′ x 6′
Launched: Stamford, CT in 1915
Nationality: American
Home Port: Newport, RI

Final Voyage

Owner: U.S. Navy
Date of Loss: October 21, 1918
Disaster Type: Burned & sunk
Final Status: Total loss
Location: 50 feet west of Bishop's Rock and about 500 yards west of Coasters Harbor Island

Narrative

The loss of the patrol craft **USS CERO (SP-1189)** is a bit of a mystery. This vessel appears on several lists as being lost on this date and at this location but no details concerning the disaster have been located probably because she was a small vessel and the focus of the news was the end of World War I.

Research Sources

1. US Navy Ships Sunk or Seriously Damaged by Fire or Explosion
2. Dictionary of American Naval Fighting Ships
3. Connecticut Ship Database
4. Photo courtesy of the US Naval Historical Center

NO NAME

Pictured is a 36′ Navy motor launch that would be identical to the launch lost.

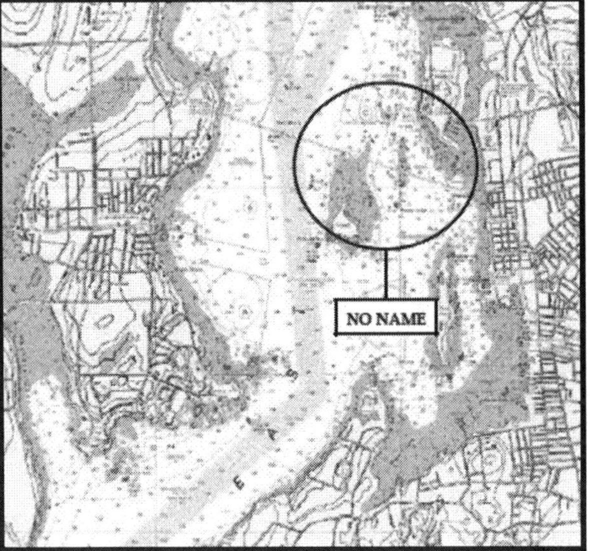

The Vessel

Type: Gas screw
Construction: Wood
Use: Launch
Dimensions: 36′ x 9′ x 2′
Tonnage: 11
Owner: U.S. Navy
Nationality: American
Home Port: Newport, RI

Final Voyage

Port of Departure: A wharf at Newport
Port of Destination: Destroyer anchorage
Cargo: supplies
Date of Loss: November 6, 1919
Disaster Type: Sunk
Cause: Storm
Location: About one mile from Gull Rock Light, Newport

Narrative

Boston Globe - November 7, 1919 P10

FOUR SAILORS LOST FROM NAVY LAUNCH

Craft with Nine Capsizes in Narragansett Bay

Five Rescued After Hard Struggle by Newport and Naval Boats

NEWPORT, R.I., Nov. 6 - Four sailors were probably drowned today when a Naval launch containing nine men from the destroyer LONG capsized during a gale in Narragansett Bay. Seaman Arthur H. Shannon was rescued at the point of exhaustion from a rock over which great seas were breaking. Four others were taken from the water after a half hour's battle with the waves. Search for the missing was continued tonight. The launch, a 35-footer, was headed out of the harbor with supplies when a big sea turned it completely over. A mile away, the keeper of Gull Light saw the men thrown into the water and notified the Naval Station, but could not himself launch a boat against the heavy sea. It was a half-hour before Harry Champion, a local boatman, and three steam launches from the Naval Station and the Naval tug OLIDA reached the scene and effected the rescues. The survivors, in addition to Shannon, all seamen, were: Fred H. Siegner, Clarence B. Rausch, L. Eistasio and M. Morgan. The names of the missing men were announced tonight as Electrician Francis D. Dillard, Fireman William H. Hager and Seamen Albert P. Patrick and Harry W. Student.

Research Sources

1. Boston Globe, November 7, 1919 P10
2. Photo courtesy of the U.S. Naval Historical Center

USS G-1

Pictured is the **USS SEAL**, the first submarine of the "G" series and which carried the number G-1. In order of construction she fell between the 19th and 20th subs built, hence she carried the unusual designation of SS 19½.

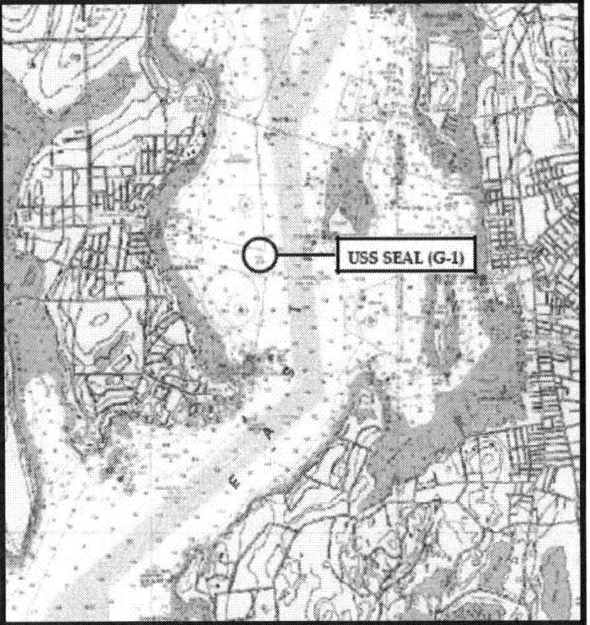

The Vessel

Type: Submarine
Construction: Steel
Use: Warship
Dimensions: 161′ x 13′ x 12′
Tonnage: 516
Launched: Newport News, VA in 1911
Owner: U.S. Navy
Nationality: American
Official No.: SS 19½
Home Port: New London, CT

Final Voyage

Port of Departure: N/A
Port of Destination: N/A
Master: N/A
Cargo: N/A
Date of Loss: June 21, 1921
Disaster Type: Sunk
Cause: Intentional (depth charge target)
Final Status: Total loss
Location: 41-29-30.92N 71-21-00.78W, off Taylor's Point, Jamestown

Simon Lake and the USS SEAL (G-1)

In any discussion of submarines, the name Simon Lake can be found prominently, particularly in matters of design and modification. The Lake Submarine Company of New Jersey was formed in 1895 and in short order the first Lake submarine, THE ARGONAUT, was launched. The next few years were spent in testing the vessel which in 1898 resulted in her becoming the first submarine ever to make a successful voyage in the open sea. You would think that this would be enough to interest the government in making him a prime contractor but when Lake launched his next submarine, THE PROTECTOR, in 1901, it was rejected by the US Navy who contracted with John Holland to make the HOLLAND VI the first official submarine in the United States. Undaunted, Lake found a buyer, the Russian Navy, who was at war with Japan at the time. For some reason either the US Navy was not completely satisfied with the Holland sub or they decided to have more than a single contractor available and contacted Lake in 1908 with a request to design and build a new submarine, possibly for a different specific use. This submarine was to become the USS SEAL aka G-1.

USS G-1

The keel for the **USS SEAL** was laid down in early 1909 at the Newport News Shipbuilding and Drydock Company in Virginia. Two years later, almost to the day, the sub was launched and nine months later she was renamed G-1. The early service years of this vessel are somewhat obscure but it is a good bet that she was kept busy acting as a training vessel for members of the fledgling submarine service. In 1913 the **G-1** established a record with a deep dive in Long Island Sound to a depth of 256 feet as part of her final acceptance trials for the navy. This event was followed by a cruise to Chesapeake Bay where she was overhauled and then assigned to Newport, R.I. where she played a triple role as training ship, harbor defense vessel and torpedo testing vessel. In her role as a school ship and in the performance of experimental testing she was kept busy over the next several years. After the end of the First World War, the USS G-1 failed to pass a routine inspection by the Board of Inspection and Survey and from that point on her days were numbered. She was laid up in New London in preparation for final disposal. In early 1920 she was stripped of all useful equipment and decommissioned. A few months later she was designated as a target for depth charge experiments under the direction of the U.S. Bureau of Ordnance. For her final trip she was under tow from the USS GREBE to Narragansett Bay and subjected to eight depth charge attacks as she lay off Taylor's Point in Jamestown. She was damaged and flooded but sinking was apparently not part of the plan. She ended up on the bottom of the bay in 90 feet of water and after sever unsuccessful attempts were made to raise her she was abandoned at that location. Her remains today are reported as few, perhaps the result of further action to see that no one else would attempt to raise her.

Research Sources

1. Automated Wreck and Obstruction Information System (AWOIS) - Record #7347
2. Merchant Vessels of the United States - 1903
3. Department of the Navy - Naval Historical Center (photo and data)
4. "Through the Looking Glass", The G-Boats
5. http://www.subnet.com

USS WILLIAMSON (DD-244)

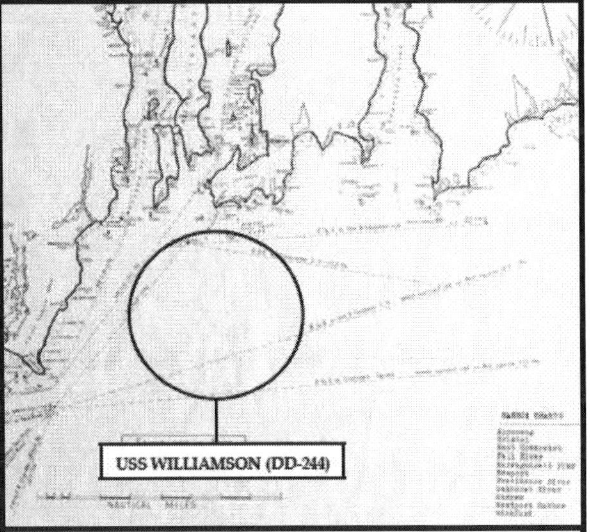

During three decades of service and one world war, the destroyer pictured above, the **USS WILLIAMSON (DD-244)**, was one of the four-stackers which served her country well. This fatal incident off Newport occurred very early in her career when she was only four years old.

The Vessel

Type: Steamship
Construction: Steel
Use: Destroyer
Dimensions: 314′ x 30′ x 9′
Tonnage: 1,190
Launched: Camden, NJ in 1919
Owner: US Navy
Nationality: American
Home Port: Newport, RI

The Event

Port of Departure: Newport, RI
Port of Destination: Outer Torpedo Range, off Newport
Master: H.E. Knauss
Date of Incident: June 30, 1923
Disaster Type: Damaged
Cause: Engine room incident
Status: Repaired
Location: Off the Brenton Reef Lightship

Narrative

New York Times - July 1, 1923 P1

5 KILLED, 3 INJURED BY DESTROYER STEAM

Hot Water Floods the Fireroom of the Williamson at Practice Near Newport

*NEWPORT, R.I., June 30. – Five men lost their lives from steam, boiling water and a flareback from the oil furnace in Fireroom No. 2 of the destroyer **WILLIAMSON**, off this port this morning. Three others are in the naval hospital here severely scalded, burned and otherwise injured. How any member of the crew of this fireroom came out alive is a mystery. Four of them did and one was able to walk to the naval hospital. The primary cause of the accident was the sudden closing of the cover to the ventilator that fed the forced draft blower in the fireroom. The cover was supposed to be securely fastened, and what caused it to close is being investigated by the board of inquiry headed by Commander F.H. Sadler, executive officer of the Naval Torpedo Station. … The **WILLIAMSON**, which is attached to the torpedo station for torpedo work, started early in the morning for what is known as the outside torpedo range, off Brenton's Reef Lightship to test torpedoes. She was steaming along at a rapid rate and one of the deck torpedo tubes had just been trained preparatory to the firing of the first torpedo when the accident occurred.*

Immediately Lieutenant Commander H.E. Knauss, in command, headed back to this city. Radio notice was sent to shore of the accident and everything was in readiness at the hospital when the destroyer with her engines crippled arrived. Commander Sadler was waiting to board the destroyer as soon as she came into

USS WILLIAMSON (DD-244)

the bay and launches from the naval station were in waiting to transfer the injured to the hospital. The shutting off of the air supply to the blower caused it to race and the governor on it, which is intended to slow down the fan, in such an emergency, failed to function. Before the racing fan could be shut off the great strain caused it to break and the flying pieces cut through the steam and hot water pipes, permitting great streams of both to pour into the fireroom. Before long there was a flareback from the oil burning furnaces which added more horror to the scene. There was no chance for the eight men in the fireroom to escape. Four were scalded to death almost immediately and the others fell to the floor unable to move. … At the risk of their lives Commander Knauss and other officers and members of the crew entered the steam filled compartment and rescued the four living men. Because of the steam which was escaping and the heated condition of the fireroom, it was some time before the bodies of the dead could be taken out.

The USS Williamson (DD-244)

The following data is derived from the Dictionary of American Fighting Ships (DANFS) with regards to the history of this vessel. The **WILLIAMSON** (Destroyer No. 244) was laid down on March 27th, 1919 at Camden, NJ by the New York Shipbuilding Company and was launched on October 16th of that year. Her fitting-out began in Philadelphia after which she went to Newport to received her torpedo equipment at the Naval Torpedo Station and then completed her fitting-out at the New York Navy Yard. She left for Europe in early 1921, arriving in France in February before proceeding to her assigned station, at Turkey and, for awhile, at Odessa, Russia. She returned to the United States in 1922 and served on the east coast and in the Caribbean for the next five years. In the Spring of 1928 she was overhauled and then carried out training cruises for naval reservists until mid 1931. She was reassigned briefly to the west coast of the United States in 1932 but then returned to the east coast to act in reserve. She apparently moved back and forth between the east and west coast for a number of years often serving as part of the protective screen of vessels that accompanied aircraft carriers. In 1938, along with the destroyer CHILDS (DD-241) she was converted to a light seaplane tender (AVP) for which she had to give up several of her guns and her torpedo launching equipment. In this capacity she served on the west coast and in Alaska until the war broke out in Europe in 1939. Her service prior to the attack on Pearl Harbor in late 1941 included some surveying work between Acapulco, Mexico and the Aleutian Islands. She remained in Alaskan waters even after the Japanese invaded the Aleutian Islands in 1942. Later that year she was converted again and reclassified as an AVD (Escort) and returned to her former role of escorting aircraft carriers. The **WILLIAMSON** supported the invasion of the occupied Alaskan islands in 1943 and was attacked by an enemy submarine but avoided destruction. In late 1943 she was reclassified again, this time back to her identity as DD-244. She then headed for the Pacific Theater where she spent the remaining years before the end of the war in escorting, refueling and rescue duty and was part of the invading force at Okinawa. She was decommisioned in late 1945, sold in October of 1946 and later scrapped. For her war service she received four battle stars.

Research Sources

1. The New York Times, July 1, 1923 P1
2. Dictionary of American Naval Fighting Ships (DANFS)
3. Photo courtesy of Navsource.org

USS S-51 (SS 162)

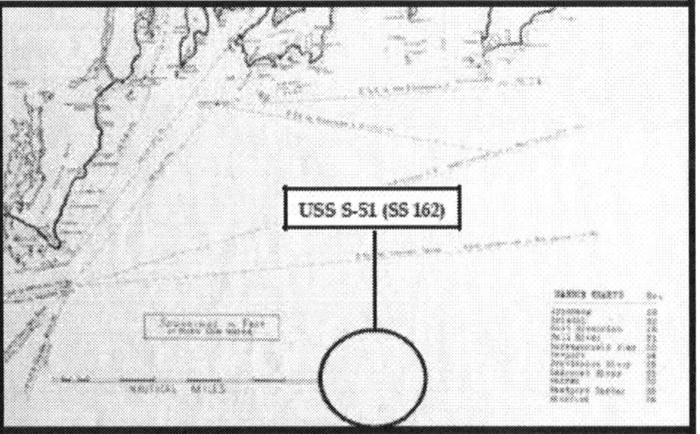

The Vessel

Type: Submarine
Construction: Steel
Use: Warship
Dimensions: 240′ x 21′ x 13′
Tonnage: 993
Launched: Bridgeport, CT in 1922
Owner: US Navy
Nationality: American
Home Port: New London, CT

Final Voyage

Port of Departure: New London, CT
Port of Destination: training cruise
Master: Rodney H. Dobson
Date of Loss: September 25, 1925
Disaster Type: Sunk
Cause: Collision
Final Status: Raised and scrapped
Location: 41-14-30N 71-16-16W; east of Block Island in Rhode Island Sound

Narrative

On a cold night in September, the **S-51** departed New London for routine exercises at sea. While cruising on the surface off Block Island with her navigational lights fully visible, her commander spotted a coastal freighter, the CITY OF ROME, in the distance. Apparently both captains saw each other's vessel, and were aware that the sub had the right of way, but no course adjustment was made by either until it was too late. The freighter sliced into the sub's hull and sent her to the bottom in minutes. The following newspaper article, the first to hit the press, contained errors including the subs size but, of most interest, stated that she was submerged when the accident occurred. Years later a court ruling found both vessels to be at fault for the collision.

New York Times - September 26, 1925 P1

US SUBMARINE S-51 SUNK, 37 LIVES LOST

Hit By Steamship off Block Island While Submerged on a Practice Cruise

Washington, Sept. 26 - The Navy Department early today has received no official confirmation of the reported sinking of the submarine ***S-51*** *off Block Island. The ship left New London Sept. 20 on what was understood to be a practice cruise. The submarine* ***S-51*** *was one of four submarines of that type built by the Lake Torpedo Boat Company in 1921. It was built to carry a crew of 38 men and 14 torpedoes. The* ***S-51*** *was 240 feet long. It had a beam of 21 feet. She was propelled by two sets of 750 horse-power engines. The S-51 was of 1,500 tons burden, when submerged, and of 1,200 tons burden when cruising on the surface. Lieutenant R.H. Dobson was the commanding officer of the submarine. The roster sent out in July mentioned the other officers as Lieutenant G. Bannerman and Lieutenant (Junior Grade) H.M. Pino. The CITY OF ROME is a 3,000-ton steel steamship, which has been engaged in coastwise and West Indian trade from Savannah, Ga. It is owned by the Ocean Steamship Company and was built in Camden, N.J. by the New York Shipbuilding Company, being launched in March, 1911. ...*

USS S-51 (SS 162)

Plans were initiated immediately for raising the submarine but the task would not be easy. Winter came and went and more plans were prepared and more equipment gathered for the continuing project. In May, the following article was found in the local news.

Newport Mercury - May 1, 1926 P1

TO RAISE SUBMARINE

Work has begun in earnest on the great task of raising the sunken submarine ***S-51****, which lies on the ocean bottom off Block Island as the result of a collision with a merchant ship last summer. A large fleet of vessels, with every known equipment for the work has been assembled at the spot, and if the weather is favorable, it is expected that the vessel can be raised and towed to New York within a comparatively short time. Upon arrival at the Navy Yard there, the submarine will be opened and the bodies of the officers and crew will be removed for proper internment. When the fleet of wrecking vessels arrived at the marking buoy which had been placed to indicate the location of the wreck when work was abandoned last December, it was found that the heavy storms had shifted the marker and that the exact spot was unknown. Trawls were at once put overside and a persistent effort was made to find the wreck. In a few hours success crowned their efforts and divers were sent down to examine the condition of the vessel. It was found that mud had settled over it during the winter and this will have to be cleared away. After the preliminary work has been completed, chains will be attached around the hull, and pontoons will then be placed in position. After the water is pumped out and air injected, it is believed that the great pontoons will be sufficient to bring the wreck from the bottom.* Two months later the salvagers were still at it and the following article appeared.

New York Times - June 24, 1926 P23

S-51 WORK HALTED AS RAIN SWEEPS SEA

Crew Gets Leave Before Starting Again to Lift Sunken Submarine

New London, Conn., June 23 - The salvage crews that for the last two months have been working night and day on the wreck of the ***S-51*** *made no attempt today to resume operations. A rainstorm swept in by high winds from the northeast kept the salvage fleet at Point Judith where they went last night after the submarine had slipped back to the ocean floor. ... Naval officers said today that the seas kicked up by the northeast wind might not subside for many days, even after the storm had passed. This would cause additional delays, but the time will be utilized in rigging tackle, repairing the two pontoons that tore loose from the stern of the wreck yesterday and getting ready for the next lift. ... "This morning's disappointment," Lieutenant Commander Ellsberg said, "was just one more and that is all it means to us. This job from the beginning has been a continuous series of mishaps, delays and disappointments, so that we have come to consider such things as part of the day's work, but not once has there been any thought of giving up and this experience today is cheering rather than depressing for now we know she will come up and that we cannot fail".*

Two weeks later the salvage effort was rewarded and the **S-51** was finally raised. She was towed to New York where her crew were removed. The sub was sold for scrap in 1930.

Research Sources

1. New York Times, September 26, 1925 P1 (3 articles)
2. Newport Mercury, May 1, 1926 P1
3. Merchant Vessels of the United States—1925
4. Dictionary of American Naval Fighting Ships
5. Photo courtesy of the National Archives and Records Administration

USS L-8 (SS 48)

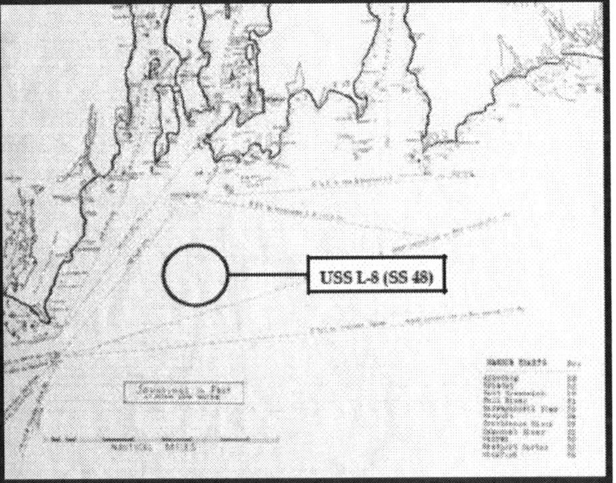

The Vessel

Type: Submarine
Construction: Steel
Use: Warship
Dimensions: 165′ x 15′ x 13′
Tonnage: 456
Launched: Portsmouth, NH in 1917
Nationality: American
Home Port: New London, CT

Final Voyage

Owner: US Navy
Date of Loss: May 25, 1926
Disaster Type: Sunk
Cause: Intentional as a test target for magnetic exploders
Final Status: Total loss
Location: North of Block Island at 41-23.196N 71-22.501W

Narrative

Laid down in late February, 1915, the **USS L-8** was launched two years later. After shakedown, the sub headed to the Azores with SubDiv6 whose goal was to intercept and destroy enemy surface raiders or submarines in the eastern Atlantic. Two days before she reached Bermuda for a scheduled fuel stop, the Armistice to end hostilities was signed, effectively bringing the patrol to an end. Returning to the United States, the **L-8** was deployed to the west coast. She sailed via the Caribbean and Central America and finally arrived at San Pedro, CA in 1919. The sub remained on active duty on the west coast until 1922, assigned to a group experimenting with new torpedo technology and the refinement of underwater detection equipment. The **L-8** departed California in early 1922, arriving at Hampton Roads in the fall for decommissioning which took place in November. Although she was sold for scrapping on December 21, 1925, she was sunk in testing just five months later.

L-Class Submarines

The production of L-Class submarines began with the keel laying of the L-1 on April 13, 1914. She was the 40th official US submarine built. The differences between the "K" and "L" class boats were subtle. About 12 feet of additional length, the addition of a 3" deck gun, and, most importantly, improvements in stronger internal bulkheads and the introduction of air purification systems to the submarine fleet. Eleven L-Class submarines were built, the last of the class being decommissioned in 1930. All survived to meet the fate of scrapping or to be intentionally sunk for testing purposes.

USS L-8 (SS 48)

Research Sources

1. Dictionary of American Naval Fighting Ships
2. Merchant Vessels of the United States—1924
3. www.subnet.com
4. Shipwrecks of New England (www.techdiving.us)
5. "Located Sunken Submarines" (Internet site)

NO NAME

RANGE BOAT 132 was apparently not "watching the road" when it came in collision with and sank an unnamed lobster boat (not the boat in the photo).

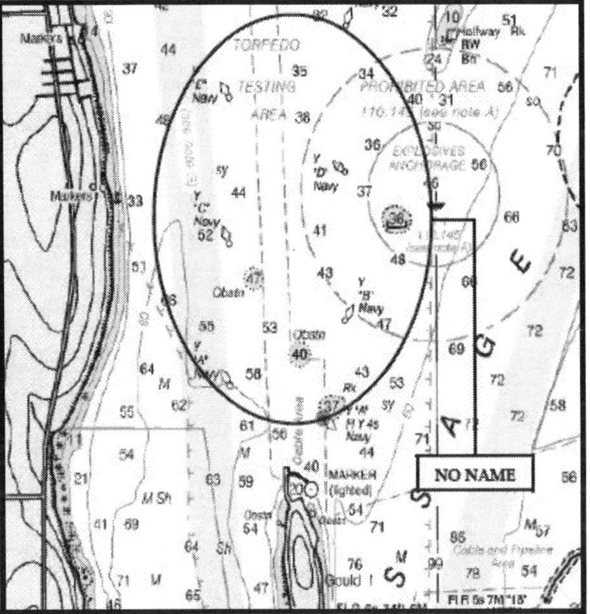

The Vessel

Type: Gas Screw
Construction: Wood
Use: Fishing
Owner: Jesse B. Crowell
Nationality: American
Home Port: Newport, RI
Master: Jesse B. Crowell

The Event

Port of Departure: Newport, RI
Port of Destination: Fishing
Date of Incident: June 26, 1930
Disaster Type: Damaged
Cause: Collision
Status: Towed in
Location: Off Gould Island

Narrative

Newport Mercury & Weekly News - June 27, 1930 P7

BOAT SUNK; LIVES OF OWNERS ENDANGERED

Lobster Craft of Jesse B. Crowell and His Son Run Down by Range Boat

The lobster boat of Jesse B. Crowell and his son, Harry B. Crowell, of 17 Pope Street, was sunk and the lives of the owners endangered, Friday of Gould Island, when the craft, which was being used in hauling lobster pots, was struck by RANGE BOAT 132 from the Torpedo Station. The men were taken on board the range boat and brought to Lee's Wharf, where it was found that the younger man had sustained a bruise on his leg. Later the damaged lobster boat was towed to a repair dock, and the men conferred with Captain Joseph R. Defrees, inspector of ordnance in charge of the Torpedo Station, who assured them that everything possible would be done regarding reparation for the loss. At the time of the crash, Mr. Crowell and his son were hauling pots and moving slowly, when the range craft approached on its way to the WRIGHT, going at a fast speed, according to the men, and ran them down. The lobster boat immediately sank to the gunwales and the men were taken on board the range boat. It is thought that the high prow of the naval craft caused difficulty for the coxswain to see clearly.

Research Sources

1. Newport Mercury & Weekly News, June 27, 1930 P7

RANGE BOAT NO. 31

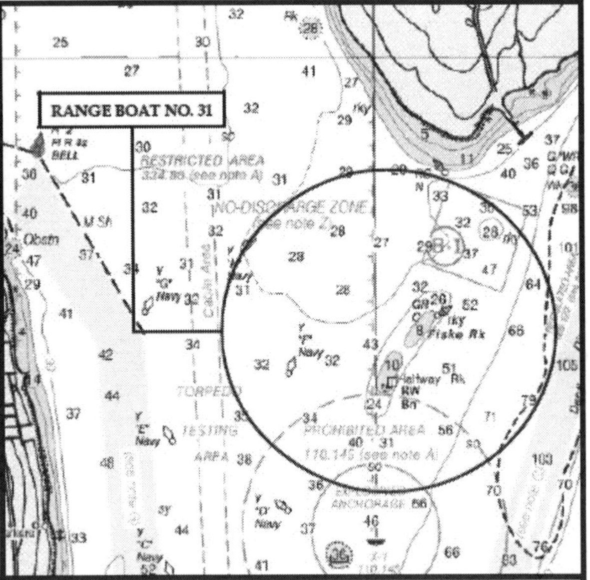

Although RANGE BOAT NO. 6 (photo above) was from the torpedo testing area in Washington state, it was probably similar to **RANGE BOAT NO. 31** which was accidentally torpedoed off the south end of Prudence Island.

The Vessel

Type: Gas Screw
Construction: Wood
Use: Torpedo Range Boat
Owner: US Navy
Nationality: American
Home Port: Newport, RI

The Event

Date of Incident: October 13, 1930
Disaster Type: Damaged
Cause: Torpedoed by accident
Status: Towed in
Location: Off the south end of Prudence Island, Narragansett Bay

Narrative

Newport Mercury & Weekly News - October 17, 1930 P3

HOLE PUNCTURED IN SIDE OF RANGE BOAT

Torpedo Fired by V-5 During Target Practice Hits Craft; Men Rescued

A torpedo fired by the V-5, latest and also largest of the submarines, during testing practice Monday afternoon in Narragansett Bay, struck ***RANGE BOAT NO. 31****, off the southern end of Prudence Island, and punctured a hole in the side of the craft. Two men who were in charge of the range boat escaped injury, and were later rescued from the boat, which commenced to fill rapidly with water. The torpedo was fired at a range of about 6,000 yards and contained no explosive. As it approached the range boat, the missile veered sharply and crashed into the smaller vessel. The torpedo was retrieved, while the range boat with the aid of a lighter was brought to the Torpedo Station.*

Research Sources

1. Newport Mercury & Weekly News, October 17, 1930 P3
2. Photo courtesy of the Historic Naval Ships Association

UNIDENTIFIED

The three men lost while off for a short row around the bay were attached to the **TORPEDO TESTING BARGE #4** in the photo above in the process of launching a practice torpedo.

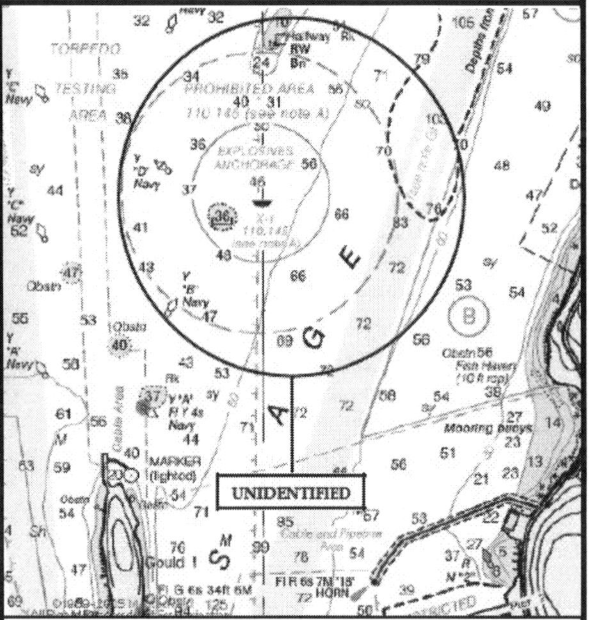

The Vessel

Type: Boat
Construction: Wood
Owner: U.S. Navy
Nationality: American
Home Port: Attached to torpedo station

The Event

Date of Incident: May 16, 1931
Disaster Type: Capsized
Cause: Unknown
Status: Towed In
Location: Between Gould Isl. & Prudence Isl.

Narrative

Newport Mercury and Weekly News - May 22, 1931 P1

ENLISTED MEN BELIEVED DROWNED

Hope for Safety of the Three Whose Boat Capsized Now Practically Abandoned

That the three enlisted men attached to the TESTING BARGE NO. 4 at the Torpedo Station were drowned, when the small boat in which they went for a trip last Saturday capsized, was regarded as almost a certainty Wednesday when the prolonged search for the men, under the direction of Commander David A. Stuart, executive officer at the Station failed to reveal any trace of them. The sailors – Michael Hrapek, George Frederick Wilson and Edward Anthony Norton – left the barge, off Gould Island, Saturday morning and when they failed to return the same day, a search was instituted, with the result that the boat was found overturned in the water near Prudence Island. With the aid of a seaplane, in charge of Lieutenant Paul Roswell, in command of the naval air detail at Gould Island, and range boats from the station, the waters in this vicinity and also the island were searched without avail, and hope that the men in some manner escaped death by drowning had been practically abandoned.

Newport Mercury and Weekly News - May 22, 1931 P2

NO CLEW TO FATE OF ENLISTED MEN

Set Out in Small Boat and Probably Drowned

Although a search covering a steadily increasing area is still in progress, absolutely no clew as to the fate of the three enlisted men, attached to TESTING BARGE NO. 4 of the Torpedo Station, who set out in a small boat last Saturday morning, had been revealed at 2 o'clock Tuesday afternoon, the conviction has grown

UNIDENTIFIED

that the men were drowned when the tiny craft overturned during the wind and rainstorm Saturday afternoon. The missing sailors are Michael John Hrapek, 22, of Springfield, Mass., fireman, first class; George Frederick Wilson, 21, ship's cook, and Edward Anthony Norton, 32, coxswain, both of Washington. In addition to the power boats from the Torpedo Station, which have been conducting the search in charge of Commander David H. Stuart, executive officer, Lieutenant Paul F. Roswell, commanding the naval air detail at Gould Island, with a mechanic, flew over the long stretch of water between the Station and Prudence Island, where the craft used by the three men was found overturned near the shore, Monday, with the oars floating nearby. At the time the missing sailors left on the trip, the barge was stationed off Gould Island and while the weather was clear, there was a storm later in the day, but this was not considered as sufficiently severe to cause the boat to capsize. Hope was at first held out that the men had gained the shore at Prudence Island and were awaiting rescue, but when Lieutenant Roswell and a searching party scoured the island Monday afternoon, there was no trace of the sailors and resident's there had failed to sight them according to the report. There is no communication between Prudence and the mainland, as a boat touches there but once each week.

Newport Mercury and Weekly News - June 12, 1931 P7

BODY OF SECOND OF ENLISTED MEN FOUND

Discovered Floating Near Shore at Lawton's Valley About Mile Below Melville

The body of Michael John Hrapek, of Springfield, Mass., the second of the three enlisted men from TESTING BARGE NO. 4, anchored off Gould Island, who lost their lives by drowning May 16th last, was found Saturday, shortly before 8 o'clock, floating near the shore at Lawton's Valley, about a mile below the Melville Fuel Station. The remains were discerned by a group of workmen proceeding to the Station by train, and later recovered by Foreman Joseph Brown and Augustus Brown who were summoned from the depot. Chief of Police William J. Deegan of Portsmouth and Sergeant Mitchell of the state police were notified and visited the scene, and permission for removal of the body to the Naval Hospital on a range boat from the Torpedo Station was given by Dr. Bertram Storrs, medical examiner of Portsmouth. When found in the water the body was clothed in dungarees and a shirt, the shoes being missing according to report. Upon arrival at the hospital a board of inquest was immediately held and the identity of the missing man established. The place where the body was found is a considerable distance from the waters off the Maxmillian Agassiz estate, Castle Hill, at which point the remains of Edward Anthony Norton of Washington were found last Tuesday. The three men started on a trip up the bay from the testing barge in a small boat, and when they did not return the same night a search was instituted. Two days later their boat was found overturned near Prudence Island, and the search by range boat and airplane was intensified under the direction of Commander David A. Stuart, executive officer at the Torpedo Station.

The body of the third man was recovered at Prudence Island on Tuesday afternoon in the second week on June and sent to the naval hospital where a board of inquest was convened and the remains were identified as those of George Frederick Wilson, of Washington.

Research Sources

1. Newport Mercury & Weekly News, May 22, 1931 P1
2. Newport Mercury & Weekly News, May 22, 1931 P2
3. Newport Mercury & Weekly News, June 12, 1931 P2
4. Newport Mercury & Weekly News, June 12, 1931 P7
5. Newport Mercury & Weekly News, June 8, 1951 P4

NICHOLAS

The unidentified modern lobster boat pictured above has changed little in both size and design over the years. The sunken **NICHOLAS** was quite similar.

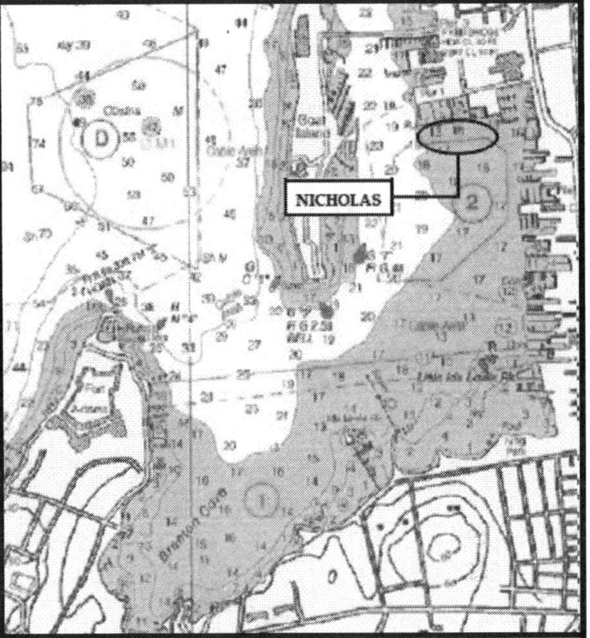

The Vessel

Type: Gas Screw
Construction: Wood
Use: Fishing
Owner: Peter N. Batlis
Nationality: American
Home Port: Newport, RI
Port of Departure: Newport, RI
Port of Destination: Fishing Trip

The Event

Master: Peter N. Batlis
Date of Incident: May 15, 1935
Disaster Type: Sunk
Cause: Collision
Status: Raised
Location: 100-150 feet south of City Wharf, Newport

Narrative

Newport Mercury & Weekly News - May 17, 1935 P2

NOTED DIVER TO TRY TO RAISE LOBSTER BOAT

Eadie to Work on Craft Sunk by Range Boat

Torpedo Station Holds Inquiry Into Harbor Crash and Rescue of Peter N. Batlis

Thursday afternoon Thomas Eadie, noted diver, began operations to raise the lobster fishing boat of Peter N. Batlis of 127 Long Wharf, which was sunk by a range boat from the Torpedo Station off the City Wharf last Thursday morning. The fishing boat was rammed on its starboard side by the range boat, which was on its way from the Torpedo Station to the Government Landing. It sank shortly afterwards., Batlis saving himself by clinging to the government craft. Since the sinking a court of inquiry has been held at the Torpedo Station, the findings of which have been sent to the Navy Department in Washington. Batlis was represented at the hearings last Monday by Edward J. Corcoran, of Burdick, Corcoran & Peckham. The naval officers appointed by Captain Harvey Delano, inspector of ordnance in charge, gave the fullest possible latitude to the hearings in order to ascertain all the facts. An attempt was made by Batlis, through his attorney and other interested parties, to have the navy use its own divers and equipment to raise the fishing boat, which lies at a point between 100 and 150 feet directly south of the City wharf. The navy was

NICHOLAS

forced to decline the request, in view of the circumstances as it found them. Then Eadie's aid was requested and secured. Eadie, winner of the Congressional Medal of Honor for his feats in diving for sunken submarines, retired from the navy several years ago, and in employed in a civilian capacity at the Torpedo Station. Diving equipment is loaned him for this afternoon's work. It is not anticipated that the work of raising the small fishing craft will be particularly difficult. It comprises temporary patching of the side and pumping out the craft, after which permanent repairs can be made. Conflicting stories of responsibility were given the court of inquiry, it is understood. The coxswain of the range boat, contended he had the right of way, and offered as evidence the fact that the fishing boat was rammed on the starboard side. Batlis thought the government craft could have avoided the crash, as he was in the clear, some distance from the dock, when the collision occurred. Batlis told the court that he had turned to adjust his engine, which had been skipping, and when he turned back, he looked, in several directions, but not that in which the range boat was coming.

Newport Mercury & Weekly News - May 24, 1935 P7

NAVAL COURT COMPLETES HEARING ON SUNKEN BOAT

Report of Testimony Will Be Forwarded to Navy Department

The Naval Court of Inquiry, appointed to investigate the sinking of Peter N. Batlis's fishing boat ***NICHOLAS*** *by a Torpedo Station range boat in the harbor last Saturday morning, held its final hearing Saturday at the Torpedo Station. The court, of which Lieutenant Commander William C. Vose is chairman, had a view of the rammed craft Friday afternoon, during which measurements were taken. Edward J. Corcoran, to whom a transcript of the testimony was given Friday afternoon, represented Batlis at today's hearing and made the argument in his behalf. Lieutenant William G. Dow was counsel in behalf of the naval coxswain who commanded the range boat. After completion of its study of the testimony, the naval court will file its report with Captain Harvey Delano, inspector of ordnance in charge, who will forward it to the Navy Department. About $200 damage was done to the* ***NICHOLAS****, which was sunk in the collision. The court will determine the responsibility.*

Research Sources

1. Newport Mercury & Weekly News, May 17, 1935 P2
2. Newport Mercury & Weekly News, May 24, 1935 P7

FOLLOW THE LEADER

Vessels Involved

TUNA - American torpedo range boat - 30′ in length—used as a diving support craft during testing.

RANGE BOAT NO. 28 - American torpedo range boat - 30′ in length—exact use not specified.

These boats had been in use during a testing session at the outer torpedo range on the day of the incident and were on their way back to the Torpedo Station. It was early evening and the boats were traveling in line when the first and then the second ran aground on the rocks at Brenton Reef, off Newport's Ocean Drive.

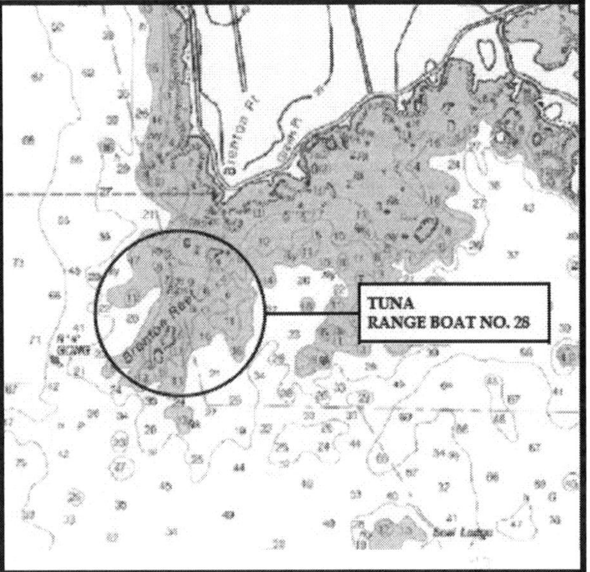

Narrative

Newport Mercury and Weekly News - January 17, 1936 P1

SEVEN NAVY MEN ARE SAVED WHEN TWO RANGE BOATS SINK

Lieutenant Porter Takes Prominent Part in Rescue Effort At Brenton's Reef

Seven naval men attached to the Torpedo Station were rescued as two range boats piled up on Brenton's Reef while returning from the outer range early Tuesday evening, sank. The rescue was effected by the navy, assisted by the life saving boat from the Price's Neck Coast Guard station. In it the efforts of Lieutenant (junior grade) George E. Porter, Jr., of the destroyer HAMILTON, which was among the craft responding to aid the stranded boats, was outstanding. Lieutenant Porter was twice in the water as two boats sank under him during the rescue operations. Those saved were the following:

Chief Gunner M.V. Evans
Boatswain's Mate, First Class J. Levesque
Machinist's Mate, First Class, A.J. Schwartz
Pharmacist's Mate, Second Class, W.R.. Barnet
Seaman First Class, S.H. Wood
Machinist's Mate, First Class, H.B. Melleski
Seaman, First Class, G. Carlson

All but Melleski and Carlson, who were on ***RANGE BOAT NO. 28****, were on the* ***TUNA*** *which is used for diving purposes. Captain Isaac C. Johnson, inspector of ordnance in charge at the Torpedo Station Wednesday ordered work to proceed in raising the sunken boats, which are about 30 feet long each. He said that the facilities at the Station were ample for this without outside assistance. As is customary in such matters, Captain Johnson said he would appoint a board of investigation. The* ***TUNA*** *and* ***NO. 28****, which had been on duty at the outer range, were returning after dark, and were closely following one another when they both piled into the rocks at Brenton's Reef. While the men were not in immediate danger from the pounding surf, their plight was considered one which demanded quick action. One of the craft nearby had a radio, which it used to signal, both the Torpedo Station and the Coast Guard being informed. Authorities hastened vessels to the rescue. The destroyer HAMILTON, Lieutenant Commander Lester M. Harvey in charge, the YP-36, and a range boat went from the Torpedo Station, the Coast Guard Cutter ARGO from its base, and the motor dory from Price's Neck, Chief Boatswain's Mate George Lewis, responded promptly. Lieutenant Porter, from the HAMILTON, went into a small skiff from the YP-36, taking an enlisted man with him. He attempted to row the skiff into the stranded boats, but the breakers*

FOLLOW THE LEADER

*capsized it as he approached and he was thrown into the water. With the enlisted man he made his way to the **TUNA**, where he directed the rescue work. Two naval rafts of the kind used on destroyers were launched, and they were maneuvered into a position near the stranded craft. The two men from the **NO. 28** had joined their shipmates on the **TUNA**, and when the first raft arrived, five transferred to it, and were being towed to the HAMILTON when the raft broke away. It was there that the Coast Guard from Price's Neck gave valuable aid in securing it and bringing the men to the HAMILTON. By that time the tide had risen sufficiently to cause the **TUNA** to slip off the rocks. As it did so, it sank, tossing Lieutenant Porter and two enlisted men into the waves. The second of the rafts was nearby, having been rowed in by enlisted men. Those struggling in the water made their way to it, after which a range boat took it back to the HAMILTON. All were then brought to the Torpedo Station. There was no official explanation forthcoming today as to how the range boats happened to be so close to the reef. They piled up about a quarter of a mile from the shore, it was said, and it required some intensive efforts to bring all concerned back safely.*

The final fate of the diving tender **TUNA** is not certain and she may have ended her days with the countless number of other vessels whose voyages ended here. **RANGE BOAT NO. 28**, however, did survive this incident to be lost when thrown ashore in a storm in Newport eight years later on December 7, 1944 (see separate data sheet).

Research Sources

1. Newport Mercury & Weekly News, January 17, 1936 P1
2. Newport Mercury & Weekly News, December 8, 1944 P6

YP-15

This photo is described as one of the old wooden 75 footers and is dated 1928. It is possible it is very much like the patrol boat **YP-15** when she was CG-149.

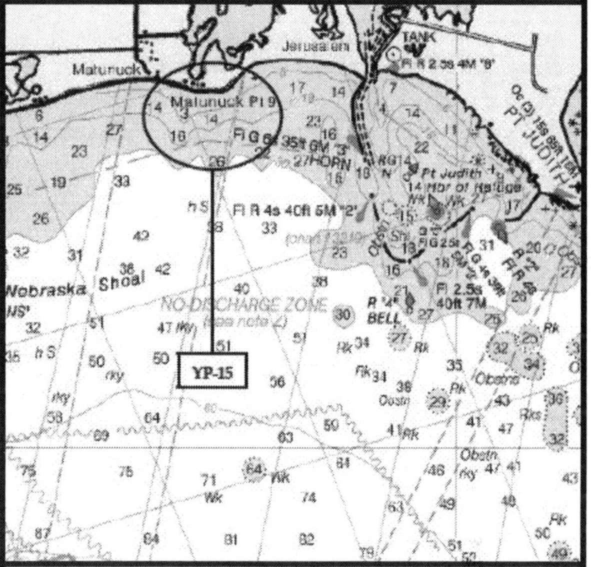

The Vessel

Type: Gas Screw
Construction: Wood
Use: Ferry
Dimensions: 75′ x 13′ x 3′
Tonnage: 37
Launched: Benton Harbor, MI in 1925
Owner: US Navy
Nationality: American
Home Port: Newport, RI

The Event

Port of Departure: Whitestone, NY
Port of Destination: Newport, RI
Master: Unknown
Date of Incident: July 25, 1937
Disaster Type: Stranding
Cause: Fog
Status: Got off
Location: Near Matunuck Point

Narrative

New York Times - July 27, 1937 P40

Grounded Navy Ship Refloated

Wakefield, R.I., July 26. - The 75-foot navy boat YP-15 was refloated by Watch Hill Coast Guards at high tide early today after being grounded more than five hours off Matunuck Point. An unidentified sailor swam ashore to summon Coast Guards after the navy boat grounded in the fog.

Newport Mercury & Weekly News - July 30, 1937 P8

EMERGENCY ALARM CALLS COAST GUARD FOR DUTY

Box 4321 Sounds as Navy Boat Grounds off Matunuck

Argo Officers and Crew Summoned This Morning: Point Judith Crew Frees YP-15, However

Box 4321, new emergency call for the Coast Guard was sounded for the first time Monday morning at 4:48 o'clock, calling officers and crew of cutter ARGO from their homes for immediate duty to aid a disabled ship at sea. It proved to be the ***YP-15****, a 75-foot navy craft bound from Whitestone, Long Island, to this city, which went ashore at Matunuck Point near Narragansett in a heavy fog at 1:20 this morning. Coast Guardsmen from the Point Judith station freed the navy ship later in the morning, just before the arrival of ARGO. The officers of the latter ship asked if any further aid was needed and*

YP-15

received information in the negative. The ***YP-15*** *was towed into harbor of refuge by the Point Judith Coast Guardsmen and was then able to proceed under her own power, apparently undamaged. Sounding of Box 4321 for the first time was puzzling to many, as the new signal, although recently announced, is not on the new fire alarm cards. Some people thought the first round sounded 431, but the fire department's records show that it struck 4321 clearly twice. The ARGO left here at 5:37 and made the run to Matunuck in about an hour and a half. An enlisted man from the* ***YP-15*** *swam ashore And walked some distance to a house from where he telephoned the Point Judith Coast Guard Station for aid. When she grounded on the sandy shore about 100 yards east of the summer home of Joseph W. Grimes, the craft still had considerable water around her, but an hour later the receding tide had left her nearly on the beach. A moderate surf was running at the time. Watch Hill Coast Guardsmen under command of skipper Alvin Newcomb pulled the craft off with their motor surfboat, at high tide five hours later. The* ***YP-15*** *is a former Coast Guard boat which was turned over to the navy some time ago. It was used chiefly for the ferrying of navy personnel.*

Research Sources

1. New York Times, July 27, 1937 P40
2. Newport Mercury & Weekly News—July 30, 1937 P8
3. Newport Daily News, July 25, 1957 P6
4. Merchant Vessels of the United States—1934
5. www.shipbuildinghistory.com
6. www.navsource.org

SPRAY

Although not the fishing boat **SPRAY**, the unidentified vessel (pictured above) is typical of the era and similar in size.

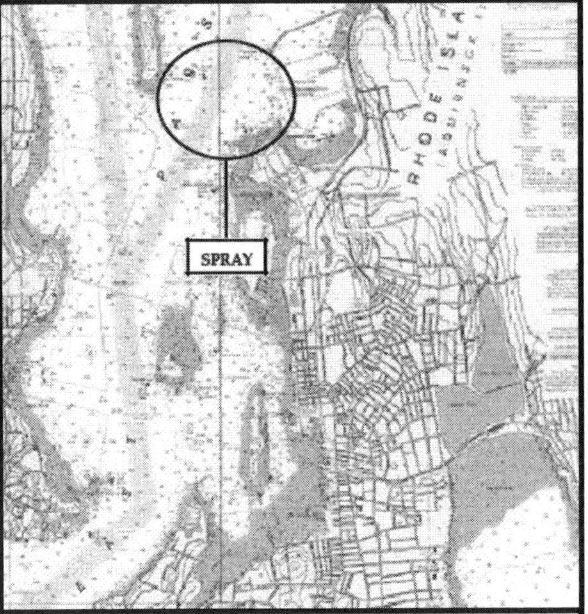

The Vessel

Type: Gas Screw
Construction: Wood
Use: Fishing
Dimensions: 46′ x 12′ x 4′
Tonnage: 15
Launched: Fall River, MA in 1902
Owner: Manuel Bonas
Nationality: American
Official No.: 117169
Home Port: Newport, RI

The Event

Port of Departure: Newport, RI
Port of Destination: Fishing trip
Master: Manuel Bonas
Date of Incident: August 30, 1937
Disaster Type: Sunk
Cause: Struck by a torpedo
Status: Raised
Location: Off Coddington Cove, in the vicinity of the torpedo range

Narrative

Newport Mercury and Weekly News - September 3, 1937 P1

PLANE'S TORPEDO SINKS FISHING BOAT IN BAY

Range Boats Rescue Crew of Bonas Craft

Attempt To Beach Vessel Unsuccessful; Captain Johnson Orders Investigation

A torpedo fired from a naval airplane into the range off Coddington Point at 10 o'clock Monday hooked off its course, struck and sunk a fishing boat belonging to Manual Bonas, of this city. Bonas and two of his crew were taken off the craft by government range boats before she sank. An attempt was made to beach the leaking craft, but the boats could not reach the shore in time. Striking the fishing boat in the side and drilling a gaping hole in her hull, the torpedo continued to churn water, while the fishermen sought safety and range boats from Barge No. 4 hastened to the scene. Fastening a line to the stricken fishing boat, the range boats started for shore, but went only a short way when she sank. Tuesday morning, Lighter No. 49 will go from the Torpedo Station with divers and equipment to inspect both the wreck and the torpedo. If possible the lighter will drop lines over and haul the torpedo to her deck and the boat to the surface for

SPRAY

towing to the harbor where a detailed inspection may be made by Captain Isaac C. Johnson, inspector of ordinance-in-charge of the Torpedo Station and a board of officers. Mr. Bonas has been fishing regularly off the torpedo range. Monday morning he had dropped his nets but had not managed to maneuver the boat entirely clear of the field when the fast traveling projectile struck his craft. Observers saw the hit and ordered range boats rushed to his rescue. Naval divers Tuesday got one strap around the 40-foot fishing boat ***SPRAY****. The diving operations to raise the sunken craft continued Tuesday afternoon. It was said that two straps will have to be placed around the craft and joined together for the raising operation by the No. 49, a derrick tug owned by the navy. It has equipment designed to raise sunken craft, and no undue difficulty is expected in bringing the* ***SPRAY*** *to the surface, it was indicated by naval officials. Captain Isaac C. Johnson, inspector of ordnance in charge of the Torpedo Station said Tuesday that the torpedo that struck the fishing boat had been recovered. Investigation showed that it had escaped damage in the collision, unlike the errant torpedo that charged through the lower bay August 13 and smashed itself on the ledge off "Pen Craig", the Hamilton Fish Webster estate. The usual procedure in determining responsibility and making reparations for damage done will be followed, Captain Johnson said. The* ***SPRAY*** *will be inspected to determine whether she can be repaired. Enos Bonas of this city, brother of the owner, said that it might cost between $5,000 and $6,000 for a new boat to replace the* ***SPRAY****, although the latter has been in use for some years.*

Newport Mercury and Weekly News - September 10, 1937 P7

DECISION TO REPAIR FISHING BOAT AWAITED

Owner of Craft Damaged by Torpedo Files Claim Through Attorney

What will be done by Manual Bonas of Fall River, owner of the fishing boat ***SPRAY****, which was sunk in Narragansett Bay Monday by an errant torpedo fired from a naval airplane was not fully decided. The boat, which rested at the bottom of 100 feet of water near Coddington Cove, is now at the Torpedo Station, where inspection by a naval board, headed by Commander John R. Palmer indicated that it would be "uneconomical" to repair her. Under naval regulations, the Secretary of the Navy is allowed a maximum expenditure of $500 for damage done by airplanes. He can pay this sum without further action of the department but, if an amount in excess of this sum is demanded, Congressional action would be required. This would mean the submission of a special bill to be passed by both branches of Congress and signed by the President, it was explained. It is possible to make repairs to the* ***SPRAY*** *but the cost might be excessive, it was indicated. Bonas has been in touch with naval officials and he has also been consulting an attorney, who has filed a claim for damages.*

Over the years, a number of vessels have been struck and sunk by runaway torpedoes in the confines of Narragansett Bay. The sinking of the fishing boat **SPRAY**, however, is unique in that it probably represents the only one fishing boat known to have been sunk by an airplane.

Research Sources

1. Newport Mercury and Weekly News, September 3, 1937 P1
2. Newport Mercury and Weekly News, September 10, 1937 P7
3. Merchant Vessels of the United States—1936
4. Merchant Vessels of the United States—1938 (Loss List)
5. Newport Custom House records

UNIDENTIFIED

Torpedo range boats were classified as YTT (Torpedo Trials Craft) or YFRT (Range Tender) at various times. It is not certain which, if either, designator **RANGE BOAT No. 6** (pictured) carried.

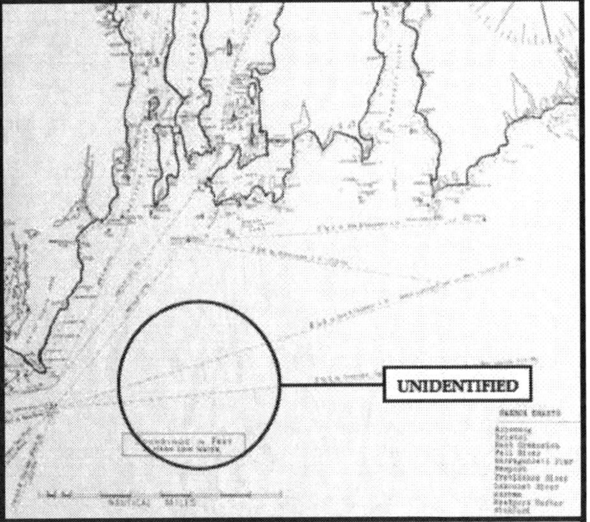

The Vessel

Type: Gas Screw
Construction: Wood
Use: Torpedo Range Boat
Tonnage: Unknown
Owner: US Navy
Nationality: American
Official No.: Unknown
Home Port: Newport, RI

The Event

Port of Departure: Newport, RI
Port of Destination: Outer Torpedo Range
Date of Incident: November 11, 1937
Disaster Type: Sunk
Cause: Collision
Status: Raised
Location: Near the outer torpedo testing range, off Brenton Reef Lightship

Narrative

Newport Journal and Weekly News - November 12, 1937 P1

NAVY DIVERS RAISE SUNKEN RANGE BOAT

Board Investigates Collision of Two Craft on Outer Torpedo Range

Divers from the Torpedo Station have completed the task of raising the sunken range boat on the outer torpedo range off Brenton Reef Lightship. The craft was taken to the Torpedo Station for investigation and repairs as soon as the weather is favorable. According to details, the range boat was sunk last Thursday in a collision with one of the 75-foot YP boats from the Torpedo Station. A fishing boat was on the range, and the target boat proceeded to order it out of danger's way. The smaller range boat was on the other side of the fishing boat, concealed from the YP craft. In some manner they came together, and the damage to the smaller craft resulted in her sinking. Two sailors were taken off before she went down. Commander John R. Palmer has been named head of the investigating board by Captain Johnson.

Research Sources

1. Newport Mercury & Weekly News, November 12, 1937 P1
2. Photo courtesy of the Historic Naval Ships Association

YP-5

The **YP-5** (pictured above) started out as a Coast Guard patrol boat (CG-102) in 1924 but was transferred for use by the Naval Torpedo Station as a support craft for diving operations.

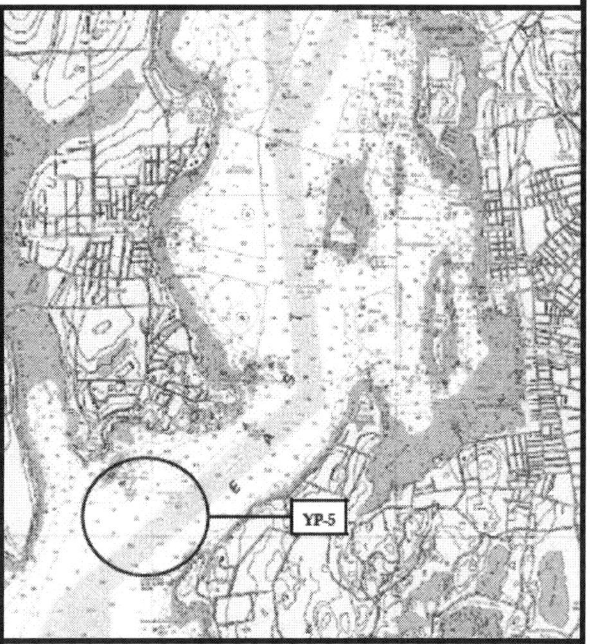

The Vessel

Type: Gas Screw
Construction: Wood
Use: Diving Tender
Dimensions: 74′ x 13′ x 3′
Tonnage: 37
Launched: Camden, NJ in 1924
Nationality: American
Home Port: Newport, RI

The Event

Owner: US Navy
Cargo: Diving equipment and pumps
Date of Incident: August 19, 1938
Disaster Type: Sunk
Cause: Torpedoed by accident
Status: Raised
Location: In 140′ of water in the East Passage of Narragansett Bay

Narrative

New York Times - August 20, 1938 P19

SPENT TORPEDO SINKS BOAT

Projectile 'Hooks' Into Bow on Narragansett Bay Range

*NEWPORT, R.I., August 19.– The **YP-5**, a 75-foot converted rum runner now used by the naval torpedo station here as a diving boat, lay 80 feet underwater in the East Passage into Narragansett Bay tonight as the result of being struck by a 21-inch practice torpedo on the outer range this morning. Capt. Isaac C. Johnson, U.S.N., commanding the torpedo station, said the boat and several thousand dollars worth of diving equipment, including tanks and pumps, could be salvaged. He described the accident as "just one of those things" which happen every once and awhile due to the eccentricities of spent torpedoes as they come to the surface. The torpedo had finished its normal course of about 5,000 yards and had come to the surface apparently spent, he said. The **YP-5** approached it to pick it up, as usual, when it suddenly circled, or "hooked," and struck the **YP-5** on the port bow and went through the double engine room bulkhead.*

YP-5

Newport Mercury and Weekly News - August 26, 1938 P2

SUNKEN NAVY BOAT BROUGHT TO HARBOR YP-5

Raided and Towed to Torpedo Station

Will Undergo Temporary Repairs Before Going on Marine Railway at Training Station

The navy diving boat ***YP-5****, sunk Friday noon after it had been rammed by an errant torpedo, was raised from 140 feet of water off Castle Hill Tuesday afternoon and brought into shallow water near the torpedo station for temporary repairs before being taken to the marine railway at the training station for permanent repairs. The raising climaxed four days of almost continuous effort by forces from the Torpedo Station. The craft was towed in by the FALCON. Fighting the tides and working in mud, sand and rocks under 140 feet of water, divers from the Torpedo Station succeeded in putting the forward strap around the sunken diving boat Monday afternoon. The strap aft had been placed about the* ***YP-5*** *last Saturday. With two straps forming a sling, Captain Isaac C. Johnson, inspector of ordnance in charge of the Torpedo Station sent a derrick to the scene Tuesday to aid the salvage operations. Commander J.R. Palmer, executive officer has been in charge. The navy was desirous of raising the boat because, it is believed, repairs can be made and the craft put into use again. The* ***YP-5*** *is a 75-foot former rum runner, with valuable diving equipment on board. When the* ***YP-5*** *first sank while being towed in from the outer range, where she had been hit, she rested in 80 feet of water. Shifting tides caused her to slip, bow first, into 140 feet of water, adding to the difficulties of raising her.*

The diving tender was apparently returned to service and was struck from the Naval Register in 1945. At an unknown date she was rebuilt and documented as the merchant barge AMVET and owned out of Gloucester, MA. She disappeared from the Merchant Vessels list after 1956.

Research Sources

1. New York Times, August 20, 1938 P19
2. Newport Mercury & Weekly News, August 26, 1938 P2
3. Photo courtesy of NavSource online

UNIDENTIFIED

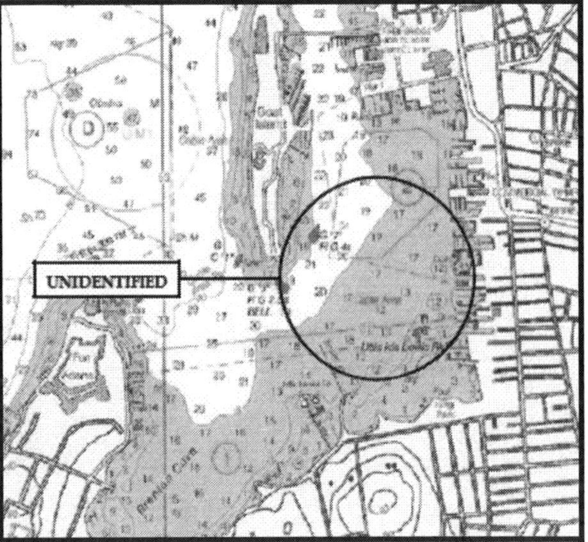

Although range boats were probably not standardized, RANGE BOAT NO. 6 (in the photo above from Keyport, WA) was probably similar to the **UNIDENTIFIED** range boat burned in Newport Harbor.

The Vessel

Type: Gas Screw
Construction: Wood
Use: Torpedo Range Boat
Owner: US Navy
Nationality: American
Home Port: Newport, RI

The Event

Master: T.I. Gregory
Date of Incident: September 29, 1939
Disaster Type: Burned
Cause: Explosion
Status: Towed in
Location: Newport Harbor

Narrative

Newport Mercury & Weekly News - October 6, 1939 P6

RANGE BOAT SURVIVORS ARE PAINFULLY INJURED

Three Who Escaped Blaze Friday Suffer Bad Burns, Shock

The three enlisted men who jumped from a blazing range boat into the harbor last Friday and swam ashore will be under treatment for first and second degree burns at the Naval Hospital for a considerable time, it was said Saturday. All three suffered shock incident to their painful injuries to their hands and faces. Quartermaster W.A. Sargent, Jr., of ferryboat GOVERNOR CARR saw the craft burst into flames and notified Captain Fillmore who immediately sent the Jamestown craft to the scene. Moving close to the burning craft the ferry turned one of its water streams on the flames and speedily drowned them out. Meanwhile other navy craft had rushed to the rescue and were standing by waiting to get close to the craft. With the fire extinguished, one of these put a line aboard and took the blackened hull in tow to the Torpedo Station. The entire superstructure of the craft was demolished and considerable damage done the interior of the hull. The crew of the damaged craft who are in the hospital are T.I. Gregory, O.M. Sumner and W.E. Boyle.

Research Sources

1. Newport Mercury & Weekly News, October 6, 1939 P6
2. Photo courtesy of the Historic Naval Ships Association

YW-5

A local photographer snapped this view of the sunken water barge YW-5 after she had settled to the bottom between "The Point" section of Newport and the light on the northern end of Goat Island (then known as the breakwater light at the northern entrance to the harbor)

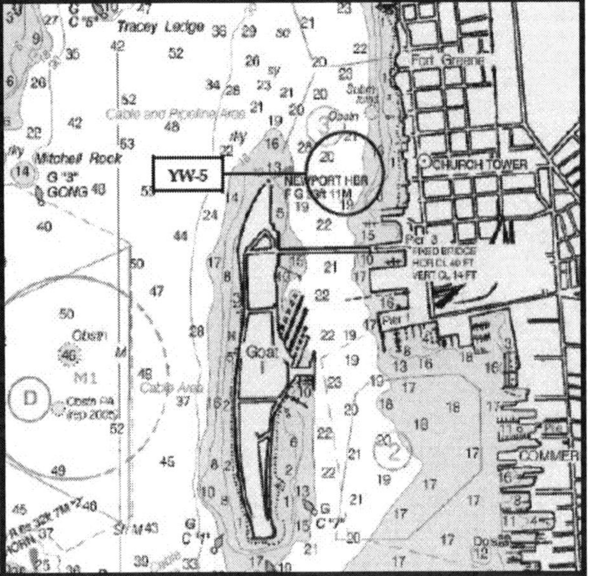

The Vessel

Type: Barge
Construction: Wood
Use: Water Carrier
Dimensions: 110′ long
Owner: US Navy
Nationality: American
Official No.: N/A
Home Port: Newport, RI
Port of Departure: Torpedo Station, Newport

The Event

Port of Destination: Gould Island, Narragansett Bay
Cargo: water
Date of Incident: January 24, 1940
Disaster Type: Sunk
Cause: Leak
Status: Raised
Location: About 200 yards east of the Breakwater Light, Newport Harbor

Narrative

The old water carrier YW-5 was said to be a half-century old at the time of this incident and the leak was perhaps just an issue of her age. That said, she sank in a most unfavorable location and had to be removed lest she cause trouble for other traffic bound in and out of Newport.

Newport Mercury & Weekly News - January 26, 1940 P1

NAVY WATER BARGE SINKS IN HARBOR

Stern Settles Quickly Leaving Bow Above Surface

Mysterious Accident Takes Place East of Breakwater Light; Two Men Escape to Tug

A navy water barge, 110 feet long, sank mysteriously in about two minutes Wednesday while being towed from the Naval Torpedo Station with a supply of water for Gould Island. Two men on board escaped by stepping onto the towing tug IWANA. The sunken craft rests in the harbor channel about 200 yards east of the breakwater light, with various authorities warned. Because of the weather the task of raising the craft, which the navy will undertake, was delayed today, Commander John R. Palmer, executive officer at the station said. The work will be started as soon as possible he announced, adding that a board of inquiry headed by Commander Samuel B. Brewer had already started its duties. Among those who witnessed the

YW-5

barge sink about 8:30 was Patrolman Charles Wilcox, who was on the Point shore. She went down so rapidly that he could scarcely believe his eyes, he said, as he reported the happening to Lieutenant Alexander Boss at the police station. It was said Wednesday that the water barge was an old craft. She had been used at the Torpedo Station about 25 years, and was estimated to be 50 years old. She is used to bring water supplies to Gould Island, where the navy has a seaplane base. The barge, in sinking from the stern, left the bow still protruding from the water. Authorities said they have not been able to check a report that a seam may have opened. The fact that the barge was loaded with water is believed to be a factor in her quick sinking.

Newport Mercury & Weekly News - February 23, 1940 P2

PUMPING OPERATIONS FAIL TO RAISE CRAFT

Navy May Use Pontoons on Sunken Water Barge in Inner Harbor

Due to openings that have developed in the 50-year old craft since she sank unexpectedly several weeks ago while being towed to Gould Island, naval forces from the Torpedo Station have found it difficult to raise the 110-foot water barge by pumping from 23 feet of water in the inner harbor. Divers sealed the hatches, but pumping operations in the past have been in vain. The navy will raise the craft, which would be a menace to navigation at that point were it not for the fact that the Coast Guard has placed a warning buoy. It may be necessary to use pontoons in the raising effort, it was said.

No account of the actual raising of the barge has been found nor details of any subsequent service but it is most likely that if her condition was not good resulting in the sinking, that her career ended with this event.

Research Sources

1. Newport Mercury & Weekly News, January 26, 1940 P1
2. Newport Mercury & Weekly News, February 23, 1940 P2
3. "A Gould Island Chronology" by Captain Frank Snyder (USN Retired)

USS CAPELLA (AK-13)

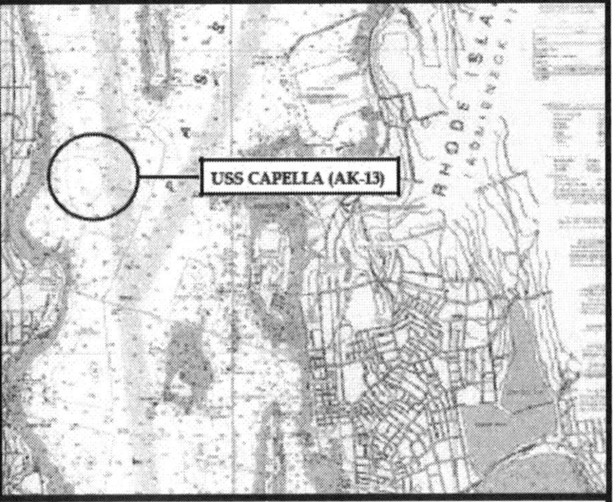

The Vessel

Type: Steamship
Construction: Steel
Use: Freighter
Dimensions: 401′ x 54′ x 24′
Tonnage: 4037
Launched: Hog Island, PA in 1920
Owner: U.S. Navy
Nationality: American

Final Voyage

Port of Departure: N/A
Port of Destination: N/A
Date of Loss: April 9, 1942
Disaster Type: Damaged
Cause: Accidentally torpedoed
Final Status: Repaired
Location: Anchored 3/4 miles southwest of Gould Island

Narrative

Newport Mercury and Weekly News - April 17, 1942 P1

SHIP ACCIDENTALLY TORPEDOED IN BAY

Eight Enlisted Men Injured, Taken to Hospital

Projectile Believed To Have Been Discharged By Defective Firing Circuit

*The **U.S.S. CAPELLA**, a 4,070 ton naval cargo vessel is lying at anchor in shoal water at Potter's Cove, Jamestown, after having been accidentally torpedoed by a motor torpedo boat in Narragansett Bay early last Thursday evening. A Navy release from Washington last Friday said that the craft "is in no immediate danger." This report through the Associated Press said the torpedo was discharged because of a defective firing circuit in the PT boat and traveled a total distance of 10,000 yards through the bay before striking the vessel. Eight enlisted men are at the Naval Hospital with injuries suffered in the accident and, as far as it could be learned, none is in serious condition. They were hurried ashore in speedy boats, probably of the same type that the torpedo came from, to the Government Landing, and taken to the hospital in ambulances. Rear Admiral Edward C. Kalbfus, commanding the Naval Operating Base, said today that all should be returned to duty in due time. ... While the navy did not say whether the torpedo exploded, reports from Jamestown said a smaller explosion and then a larger one were heard at around 6:30 P.M. Observers said they saw the **CAPELLA** settling at the stern, and it appeared that efforts were being made to beach her. Houses on the northern end of Jamestown were shaken by the second explosion, reports from the island said. There was immediate activity as numerous naval boats rushed to the scene with tugs pushing the cargo vessel towards the shore. There was no sign of fire from the shore, it was reported. At the time of the mishap, the craft was lying about three-quarters of a mile southwest of Gould Island, reports said. The accident happened in broad daylight. Attention was attracted in Newport, when Naval Hospital ambulances dashed along Thames street with sirens sounding and took off the injured men at the landing.*

USS CAPELLA (AK-13)

The ***CAPELLA****, it is believed, was the only large naval vessel in the bay at the time. It is not the first time that torpedoes have run wild. Several years ago one darted between two large private yachts and finally landed against a breakwater at the southern end of the harbor. This occurred during practice, with the torpedo having a dummy head. An aerial torpedo sank a fishing craft in another mishap two years ago.*

The Other Side of the Story

On April 9, 1942, Lt. Charles A. Mills, Jr. ordered the lines cast off and PT-59, under his command, set out from Melville. Guiding his motor torpedo boat toward the Portsmouth shore, he passed Dyer Island before turning southward toward the designated torpedo practice area, or range, in Rhode Island Sound. The process for launching a torpedo was fairly simple. The firing switch was key operated and the launcher needed only to be cranked into the correct position and the key fully turned for the torpedo to be released. The experienced commander set the switch with his key and went below to check on his navigational charts of the bay to set his course for the range. While below, one of his trainees accidentally turned the key to the firing position and the torpedo was suddenly launched. Although alarmed at this accidental firing, Mills was aware that the Mark 8 torpedo was prone to problems, often rolling erratically, nose diving for the bottom or veering off course. As he sped after the torpedo in the PT boat, Mills was reasonably confident that the odds of failure were in his favor. Such was not to be the case on this occasion and the weapon continued to run "hot, straight and true" down the bay. One can only imagine the thoughts running through his mind as he realized that the runaway torpedo was going to strike the large freighter sitting idly at anchor off the Jamestown shore. Mills could only watch as the **CAPELLA** was struck and his naval career disappeared. He did, however, do exactly the right thing given the circumstances at hand. He brought his small PT boat up alongside the damaged freighter, tied off to her, and immediately began pushing her into the shallows so that if and when she sank, it would not be in the deep water where she had been anchored. Reality was not quite the defective firing circuit reported in the newspapers.

Research Sources

1. Newport Mercury & Weekly News, April 17, 1942 P1
2. Naval Historical Center Library

UNIDENTIFIED

Pictured is a US Navy motor whaleboat of WW2 vintage, sometimes referred to as a motor launch or liberty boat. On December 2, 1942 a launch of this type was involved in one of the worst disasters in RI history.

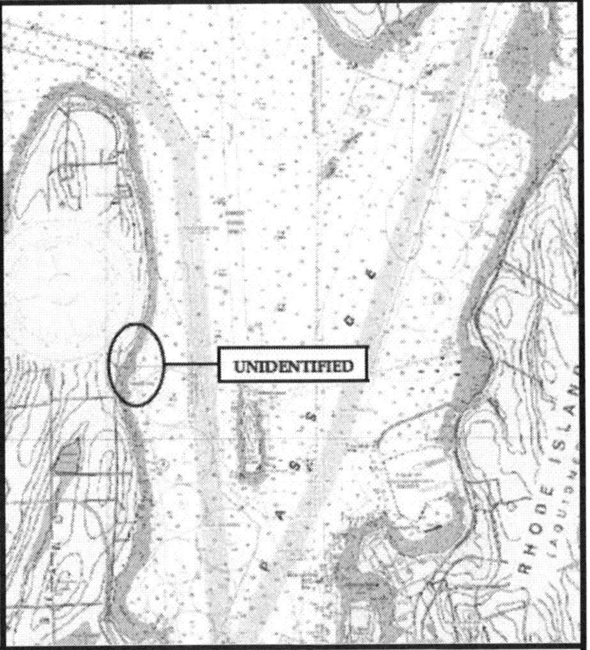

The Vessel

Type: Gas Screw boat
Construction: Wood
Use: transport
Dimensions: 26′ x 7′ x 2′
Owner: US Navy
Nationality: American
Home Port: Newport, RI

Final Voyage

Port of Departure: Newport, RI
Date of Loss: December 2, 1942
Disaster Type: Stranding
Cause: Storm
Final Status: Remains probably removed
Location: About 3½ miles north of the ferry landing on the east side of Conanicut Island

Narrative

New York Times - December 3, 1942 P1

15 Sailors Drown as Wind Upsets Boat off Rhode Island Coast

NEWPORT, R.I., Dec. 2. – Fifteen sailors out of a party of seventeen in a twenty-eight foot boat lost their lives early today when the craft was capsized in a storm. Five bodies had been recovered tonight, and virtually no hope was held for the ten missing men for whom the search continued. The two survivors are L.J. Hinsen, who is at the Newport Naval Hospital, well on the way to recovery, and J.B. Kelly, who has returned to duty. Both are seamen, second class. The Navy withheld the names of the five men whose bodies were recovered until their next of kin had been notified. The high wind which swamped the boat gave Rhode Islanders their worst storm scare since the hurricane of 1938. ... Navy officers offered two possible versions of the loss of life. The boat might have hit an obstruction in the water, reversed her engines to back away and capsized in doing so, they say, or a large wave may have overturned her. The capsized craft was one of two liberty boats which left the government landing in Newport loaded with sailors. The other boat reached her destination safely. The wrecked craft was found wedged between rocks on Conanicut Island, about three and a half miles north of Jamestown ferry landing. The body of one sailor was found 500 yards south of the boat.

UNIDENTIFIED

Newport Mercury & Weekly News, December 4, 1942 P2

SEARCH CONTINUES FOR MISSING SAILORS

Bodies of Five Have Been Recovered in Bay

10 More Believed Drowned When Craft Capsized in Storm; Two Survived

Search was being continued Thursday along the Jamestown shore for bodies of 10 additional sailors believed drowned Wednesday night when the motor whaleboat, on which they were returning from liberty, capsized in the harbor. The bodies of five others were recovered Wednesday after the disaster, believed to be the worst of its kind here. Two men were saved. The liberty boat was one of two that left the Government Landing to return to the ship off the Jamestown shore. One left at midnight and the other five minutes later, it was announced by navy officials. One arrived safely. Details concerning the tragedy became known during the morning and early afternoon, but official naval circles requested no announcement be made until families of those known to have perished were notified. The Daily News complied with the request. It was not until 4:30 Wednesday afternoon that authorization was given to publish the story. Rough water, with the possibility that it hit an obstruction, caused the 28-foot boat to capsize. It eventually drifted up on the Jamestown shore at Carrs lane. J.B. Kelly and L.J. Hinsen, both seamen, second class, were the ones saved. They owed their rescue to their ability to cling on to the overturned boat until it reached shore. ... Early reports said there were as many as 23 on the overturned craft, but a close check of the roster showed the actual number to be 17. Pending notification of next of kin, names of victims were withheld Wednesday and today. First intimation of the tragedy came when Manuel L. Machado, a Jamestown farmer, who was awakened before dawn by the shouts of a survivor, who proved to be Hinsen. He told the farmer that the accident happened off Rose Island, and that it seemed that the liberty-boat had struck something, possibly a buoy. The sailor said the motor stopped, water came into the craft, and it capsized. Hinsen said he managed to cling to the overturned boat, and hung on for what seemed to him a long time before the boat went crashing into the shore with such force that two holes were stove into the craft. The boat's gasoline tank was thrown clear, and debris of the craft was along the shore, with the rudder missing. Kelly, the other survivor, made his way to a haystack, where he passed the night. ... Kelly was seen walking along the East Shore road, Jamestown, his clothing covered with hay. Norman Caswell, passing in an automobile took him to a restaurant and later Lieutenant Commander Constantine Clay brought him to the Naval Hospital.

Newport Mercury & Weekly News, December 11, 1942 P3

BODY OF ANOTHER MISSING SAILOR FOUND

Search Continues for Nine Others Believed Drowned When Boat Capsized

The sixth body of the 15 enlisted men believed lost in the harbor when a Navy liberty boat capsized Wednesday night, has been found, the Nay announced Monday. It is that of Wilbur Edgar Martin, fireman, first class, whose address is Box 963, Cody, Wyo. It has been taken to the Naval Hospital, while relatives have been notified. A fishing dragger located the body at the southeasterly end of Gould Island, the navy said. It was turned over to the Coast Guard and then taken to the hospital. Coast Guard and Navy patrols are continuing along the shore in this vicinity as the attempt to recover the men still missing is being continued.

Research Sources

1. New York Times, December 3, 1942 P1
2. Newport Mercury & Weekly News, December 4, 1942 P2
3. Newport Mercury & Weekly News, December 11, 1942 P3

UNIDENTIFIED

The **UNIDENTIFIED** range boat that sank in a storm in Newport Harbor was similar to the RANGE BOAT NO. 6 (pictured above) which was used at the west coast torpedo testing facility.

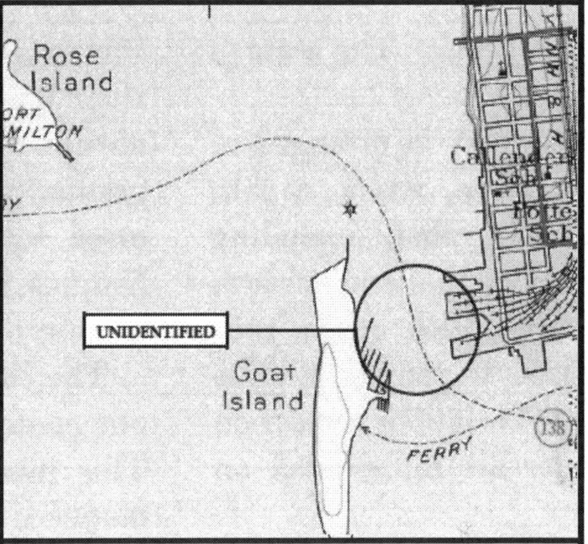

The Vessel

Type: Gas Screw
Construction: Wood
Use: Torpedo Range Boat
Owner: US Navy
Nationality: American
Home Port: Newport, RI

The Event

Date of Incident: December 13, 1943
Disaster Type: Sunk
Cause: Storm
Status: Raised
Location: Off Newport Shipyard, Newport Harbor

Narrative

Newport Mercury & Weekly News - December 17, 1943 P5

RANGE BOAT SINKS

A small range boat that sank in rough water off the Newport Shipyard Monday was found by divers from the Naval Torpedo station. The craft was raised and taken to the station where repairs were made and the boat made serviceable for operation Tuesday.

Support for Torpedo Testing in Rhode Island

The science of self-propelled torpedoes began in the years following the Civil War and it was found that Narragansett Bay was most suitable for testing each new design developed. For more than eighty years the technological improvements brought a need for constant testing. To support the testing required not only countless technicians and inspectors at the manufacturing stage but numerous watercraft of various designs at the testing stage. In a paper entitled, "A Gould Island Chronology", retired navy captain Frank Snyder brought many interesting facts to light in a discussion of just one of several islands in Narragansett Bay where the business of torpedoes was the only business. Before modern day sensing equipment was available, testing was more often than not performed from the deck of vessels "on the range" as torpedoes were fired and there was so much activity that at one time, *over 50 range boats, including 35 torpedo retriever boats, were moored on the northeast side of Gould Island in an area protected to its north by a breakwater.* One can only imagine the coordination necessary to keep this fleet in order.

UNIDENTIFIED

Research Sources

1. Newport Mercury & Weekly News, December 17, 1943 P5
2. "A Gould Island Chronology" by Captain Frank Snyder (USN Ret)

RANGE BOAT NO. 28

Pictured is RANGE BOAT NO. 6 from the Washington State torpedo testing base. **RANGE BOAT NO. 28,** assigned to the Newport Torpedo Station, was of similar size and design.

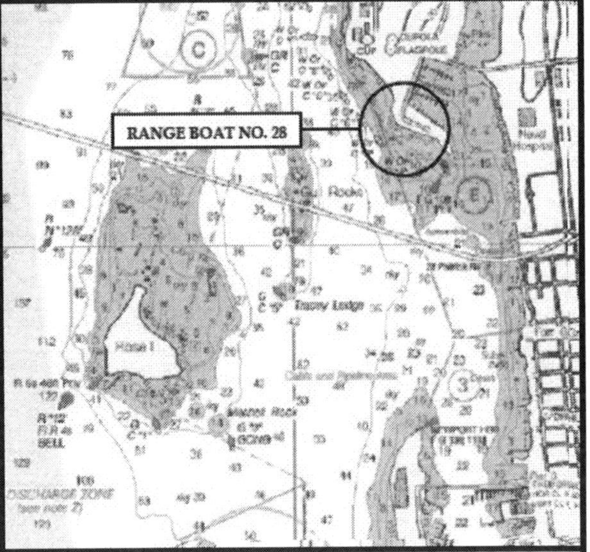

The Vessel

Type: Gas Screw
Construction: Wood
Use: Torpedo Range Boat
Owner: US Navy
Nationality: American
Home Port: Newport, RI

Final Voyage

Date of Loss: December 7, 1944
Disaster Type: Stranding
Cause: Hurricane
Final Status: Went to pieces
Location: On the beach, inside Gull Rock, near the Navy Training Station

Narrative

Newport Mercury and Weekly News - December 7, 1944 P6

HEAVY STORM RAISES RAINFALL TO RECORD

Newporters Rescue Navy Men From Range Boat

The southeast storm that swept the city last Thursday, coming on heel of several others in the last few weeks, brought the rainfall for November to a record for that month for almost the last 60 years. ... Most of the damage from the coastal storm that hit Newport with driving winds and rain was counted in the vicinity of the Newport Yacht Club where three boats were battered and sunk and small craft were capsized, as the fury of the storm seemed to concentrate in the harbor's northeast corner. Two Newporters were praised for heroic action in rescuing navy enlisted men from a small motor launch off the Training Station. Skiffs, buoys and floats along the Newport shore were blown adrift, the shore was littered with debris under a wind that reached a 54-mile-hour velocity between 2 and 3 o'clock in the afternoon, according to a Training Station check. Fears were expressed for conditions at night as the wind failed to die down, but with a shift in its direction eliminated danger of the incoming full moon tide causing greater damage. ... Many sightseers visited the harbor front and the ocean side of the city to watch the sea and surf. ... On the whole, Newport emerged without any great damage outside of that to the boats. ... The Jamestown and Newport ferry tied up between 2:30 and 4 o'clock at this end, and then resumed its regular trips. The ferry between the North dock at the Torpedo Station and Washington Street had a tug standing by to assist her at the peak of the gale. The regular ferry from the Torpedo Station to the Government Landing missed only one trip. ... William Sweet, of 41 Mary Street and Frank Marshall, of Fenner

RANGE BOAT NO. 28

Avenue, Naval Training Station employees, plunged into the cold waters off the Training Station to rescue injured members of ***RANGE BOAT NO. 28*** *when it went aground. The craft was headed toward the Torpedo Station at the height of the storm with two others when it developed engine trouble off Gull Rock. Rough seas carried it to the beach. The Newporters dashed into the water just as the wave threw the launch onto a rock off shore, spilling out two crewmen. They dragged the men to shore as the boat broke up. One of the sailors was bleeding profusely, it was reported, the other was shaken up.*

Research Sources

1. Newport Mercury & Weekly News, December 7, 1944 P6

USS BASS (SS 164)

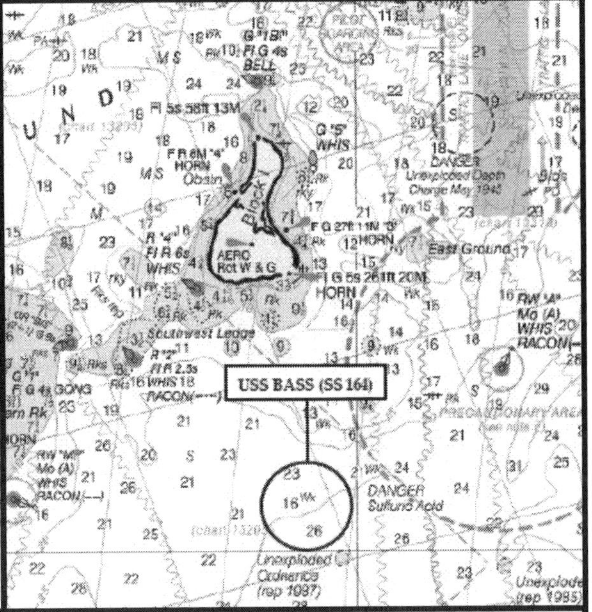

The **USS BASS (SS 164)** was launched as the V-2, the second of three fleet boats in the Barracuda Class. After more than two decades of service, her final role was as a target for other naval vessels.

The Vessel

Type: Submarine
Construction: Steel
Use: Warship
Dimensions: 341′ x 27′ x 16′
Tonnage: 2,600
Launched: Portsmouth, NH in 1924
Owner: US Navy
Nationality: American
Home Port: Groton, CT

Final Voyage

Port of Departure: N/A
Port of Destination: N/A
Date of Loss: March 14, 1945
Disaster Type: Sunk
Cause: Intentional—SONAR testing
Final Status: Total loss
Location: About 7½ miles south from the Southeast Light, Block Island (41-01-09N 71-32-50W or 41-01-12N 71-33-00W)

Narrative

The **USS BASS (SS 164)** began her career as the Barracuda class submarine V-2. Assigned to SubDiv20, she spent two years cruising along the Atlantic coast and in Caribbean waters before heading for San Diego, CA. In 1931 she was renamed the **USS BASS** and joined SubDiv12. Two years later she was moved to the Rotating Reserve SubDiv15 and returned to San Diego, but after a short period was returned to active duty to cruise the west coast, off the Canal Zone and as far west as Hawaii. In 1937 she was ordered to return to the east coast to be decommissioned in June. Three years later, in 1940, the **BASS** was recommissioned and assigned to SubDiv9. During this assignment she cruised the Atlantic coast and also made a couple of short trips to Bermuda. On November 24, 1941 she was placed on duty at Coco Solo (Panama Canal Zone) and was there when the Japanese attacked Pearl Harbor. In 1942 she made four war patrols in the Pacific Ocean. In late 1942, the sub was sent to the Philadelphia Navy Yard for repairs after an accidental fire after which she proceeded to New London, CT and was assigned to perform secret experiments off Block Island. A few months later she again put in at Philadelphia for repairs and was then returned to patrol the waters off Long Island and Block Island. She was decommissioned in early March, 1945 and destroyed off Block Island less than two weeks later.

USS BASS (SS 164)

Barracuda-Class Submarines

The first three V-Class boats were requested in 1919 and would be built in the Portsmouth Navy Yard. They were commissioned between 1924 and 1926 and became the only members of the Barracuda Class to achieve the navy's original "fleet boat" requirement for high speed while running on the surface. These boats were large and had powerful engines with an unusual arrangement of having two separate engine rooms—one on either side of the control room. The forward engine room had two independent 1,000 horsepower diesel generators used primarily for charging batteries while the after engine room had two 2,250 horsepower main propulsion diesel engines. Armed with six torpedo tubes (four forward and two aft) and specially fitted buoyancy tanks for better surface trim, they were to be capable of 21 knots on the surface and 9 knots submerged, but their operational records indicated that they fell short of those goals. In late 1942 and early 1943 all three were modified to become "cargo submarines" with removal of their main propulsion diesels to provide more room for cargo. As it worked out, using the forward engine room facilities only did not provide adequate power and were never used in an operational capacity for that intended use and were relegated to use as training subs for the remainder of their careers. The V-1 (renamed BARRACUDA) and V-3 (renamed BONITA) were scrapped while the **USS BASS** ended her days scuttled as a SONAR target off Block Island.

Research Sources

1. Merchant Vessels of the United States—1934
2. "The Vanishing Fleet" by Brad Luther
3. "Encyclopedia of American Shipwrecks" by Bruce Bermen
4. Dictionary of American Naval Fighting Ships
5. Automated Wreck and Obstruction Information System (AWOIS) - Record #1767
6. www.subnet.com
7. www.navalships.org
8. www.TechDiving.com
9. www2.scubadiving.com

BLACK POINT

The BLACK POINT was also known as the NEBRASKAN during a career which spanned more than a quarter century but was launched as the FAIRMONT (pictured)

The Vessel

Type: Steamship
Construction: Steel
Use: Freighter
Dimensions: 396′ x 55′ x 30′
Tonnage: 5,353
Launched: Camden, NJ in 1918
Owner: C.H. Sprague & Son
Nationality: American
Official No.: 215957
Home Port: Boston, MA

Final Voyage

Port of Departure: New York City, NY
Port of Destination: Boston, MA
Master: Charles Prior
Cargo: 7,595 tons of coal
Date of Loss: May 5, 1945
Disaster Type: Sunk
Cause: Torpedoed by U-853
Final Status: Total loss
Location: 3.75 miles southeast from Point Judith in two pieces

The Black Point and the U-853

The story of the sinking of the collier **BLACK POINT** by the German submarine U-853 is well known to most Rhode Island residents. The meeting took place near the end of World War II and one question that has always remained unanswered is whether or not the captain of the submarine knew the war was soon to be over or was operating under a condition of radio silence at the time. In any case, the two vessels met just once and the outcome proved to be fatal for both. The submarine had been patrolling off New England for weeks prior to the sinking and history has shown her to be responsible for at least one other vessel lost. The collier was northbound and hugging the shore, a common practice during the war. The crew of the steamship were aware that the war was drawing to a close and were likely in a jubilant mood that they had survived when many of their comrades had not. A single torpedo was fired by the U-boat in the early evening hours, tearing away forty feet of the stern of her victim. Within a half hour the steamship was on the bottom with a loss of thirteen men. The U-853 dived and evaded detection for some time but before long became a victim herself to US Navy forces.

BLACK POINT

Narrative

New York Times - May 10, 1945

14 Dead in 2 U-boat Sinkings Off East Coast as V-E Neared

Special Dispatch to the New-York Times

BOSTON, May 9 - Twenty-seven hours before Germany surrendered a Nazi U-boat torpedoed an American collier in a daylight attack within sight of Block Island and Point Judith, with a loss of thirteen lives.

The collier, the ***BLACK POINT****, was presumably the last victim of undersea warfare in New England waters and perhaps the last off the United States coast. The loss of life put at sixty-two the number killed or missing in waters of the area within three weeks.*

...

Thirty merchant seamen and four members of a Navy armed guard escaped to life rafts and boats from the BLACK POINT before the vessel turned over and went down within twenty-five minutes after being hit at 5:40 P.M. Saturday, less than five miles off Point Judith. The survivors were picked up within an hour by other merchant vessels. The submarine which torpedoed the BLACK POINT dove to the bottom, but was caught there 130 feet down by depth charges from Navy attack vessels.

Tanker Had Left Convoy

The collier, a 5.353-ton bulk cargo carrier owned by the C.H. Sprague & Son Company of Boston from Norfolk and had left a convoy off New York. The torpedo tore away forty feet of the stern section

...

The gun crew had no chance to fire a shot, according to the survivors. Captain Charles E. Prior of Belfast, Me., reported that none on the vessel saw a torpedo or a trace of the submarine. Captain Prior said that none of the thirteen men lost were seen by the other crew members after the torpedoing. Those lost were in the stern of the vessel and undoubtedly were killed by the blast. The survivors got off in lifeboats and a life raft. They were mostly from New England...

Research Sources

1. New York Times, May 10, 1945 P1
2. Merchant Vessels of the United States—1946
3. US Merchant Ship Losses During the Second World War - May, 1945
4. "Last Chapter for U-853", US Naval Institute Proceedings, Dec., 1960
5. "The Vanishing Fleet" by Brad Luther
6. "Encyclopedia of American Shipwrecks" by Bruce Bermen
7. "Axis Submarine Successes" by Jurgen Rohwer
8. "A Guide to Sunken Ships in American Waters" by Lonsdale and Kaplan
9. Alphabetical List of all US Merchant Ships Sunk or Damaged in WW2
10. The Battle of Point Judith
11. Battle of the Atlantic
12. Automated Wreck and Obstruction Information System (AWOIS) - Records #1874 & #2712

U-853

The U-853 (pictured) has the dubious distinction of being the last German sub sunk by military forces in World War II.

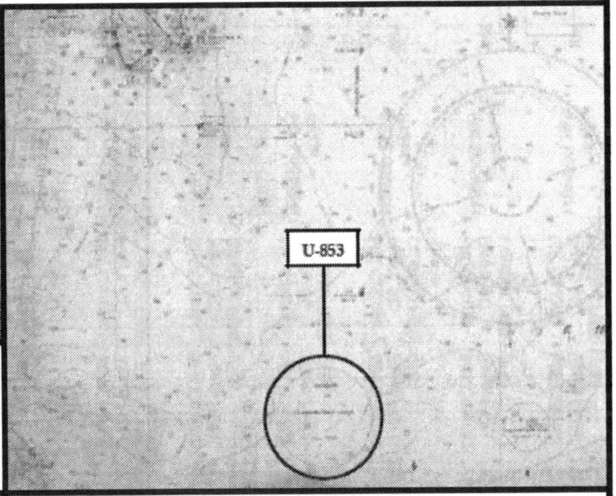

The Vessel

Type: Submarine
Construction: Steel
Use: Warship
Dimensions: 251′ x 22′ x 15′
Tonnage: 1,545
Launched: Bremen, Germany in 1943
Owner: German Navy
Nationality: Germany
Home Port: Bremen, Germany

Final Voyage

Port of Departure: Stavenger, Norway
Port of Destination: Patrol off US east coast
Master: Oblt. Helmut Fromsdorf
Date of Loss: May 5, 1945
Disaster Type: Sunk
Cause: War loss (attack)
Final Status: Total loss
Location: 6¼ to 7 miles east of Block Island on "East Ground" near 41-13-00N 71-25-00W

The U-853 and the Black Point

The story of the **U-853** and the collier BLACK POINT (see separate data sheet) is, arguably, one the most well known of Rhode Island maritime history. The **U-853** was one of 87 Type IXC/40 submarines built in Bremen, Germany in the latter part of the war. A member of the Gruppe Seawolf, the **U-853** was on her third mission when lost. Ironically, her loss was not necessary. On May 4th, a radio message was sent from Admiral Karl Donitz to all U-boats to cease hostilities starting at 0800 on the morning of May 5. For whatever reason, the **U-853** did not receive the message and at 1740 hours on the 5th, attacked the BLACK POINT which capsized and settled to the bottom of Rhode Island Sound, off Point Judith. Before sinking, the collier sent a distress signal which was first received by the radio operator on board the USS MOBERLY, a patrol frigate which was about 30 miles south of the area. With the MOBERLY were the destroyer escorts AMICK and ATHERTON, enroute to New York. In the other direction from where the freighter sank, the destroyer ERICCSON was alerted to the attack but being in a less convenient position to quickly change course, her commander (who had overall command of the attack) assigned tactical command to the captain of the MOBERLY. At about 1930 the MOBERLY, ATHERTON and AMICK reached the site of the sinking and set up a sweep line heading south in search of the attacking vessel. With detailed knowledge of local waters, it was deduced that the sub might try to hide near a steep shoal in the "East Ground", off Block Island. Less than forty-five minutes after starting their sweep a signal was picked up which was deemed to likely be that of a sub. At 2029, thirteen depth charges were dropped from the ATHERTON in

U-853

the area of the signal. A little while later she performed an attack with hedgehogs followed by a second hedgehog attack shortly after. Despite sighting some debris, confirmation of a "kill" could not be made at this point so the attack continued. Upon arrival of the ERICCSON, the American vessels returned to their scanning duties, proceeding several miles in either direction of the area bombed. As they returned toward that spot, and when about 4,000 yards away, they made contact again and ATHERTON was ordered to make another hedgehog attack at 2343 with more floating wreckage the result. Forty-five minutes later, another hedgehog attack was ordered followed by more depth charging, the latter attack causing some damage to the ATHERTON due to the proximity of the explosions to the stern of that ship. The MOBERLY took the place of the ATHERTON and attacked the contact at 0200 and then at 0530. By this time the American commanders were convinced that the sub had been discovered and neutralized but it was decided to continue the attack until a greater degree of confirmation of the "kill" could be achieved. Attacks were discontinued at 1224 on the 6th of May. Later that afternoon, divers from the USS PENGUIN made a descent to the bottom at the contact site and determined that the U-853 had been effectively destroyed.

German Type IX Submarines

The following information comes from an internet site which specializes in the history of German submarines, or U-boats, and offers some details on the Type IX class of boats built:

The Type IX was designed with two objectives in mind – to be the long range counterpart to the medium-range Type VII, and to serve as a tactical command boat for the leader of a wolf pack. ... The Type IXs were excellent sea boats, which had sufficient range to operate in distant waters in the South Atlantic, Indian and even the Pacific oceans. ... It was designed to travel fast to and from distant operational zones, while carrying an adequate supply of torpedoes and stores for sustained solo patrols. It carried more torpedoes than the type VII but was handicapped with a slow diving time and was more vulnerable to attack - mainly due to its comparatively large size.

There were nearly two hundred Type IX U-boats built, starting as early as 1938. Generally the difference between them was the size of the fuel tanks for greater distance capability but some of the very last version, the Type IX-D2, were also given more power for greater speed.

The influence of submarines, particularly on the part of the Germans, cannot be overestimated. During the earliest years of WW II, these denizens of the deep were able to hunt merchant vessels as well as warships almost at will until technological advances by the Allies turned the tables on them. Their place in the history of maritime events in Rhode Island is secure.

Research Sources

1. "Last Chapter for U-853" by Ensign D.M. Tollaksen (Naval Institute Proceedings, Dec. 1960)
2. "The Vanishing Fleet" by Brad Luther
3. "Encyclopedia of American Shipwrecks" by Bruce Bermen
4. "A Guide to Sunken Ships in American Waters", by Lonsdale and Kaplan
5. Automated Wreck and Obstruction Information System (AWOIS) - Record #1833
6. U.S. Naval Chronology of WWII (1945)
7. www.uboat.net
8. www.uscg.mil
9. Providence Daily Journal, May 31, 2010 ("Nazi Sub Sunk off R.I. Coast")

PT-95

The **PT-95** (pictured) was the lead boat in what was known as the PT-95 class of motor torpedo boats. Eight were built and the first three served at the Motor Torpedo Boat Training Center in Melville as part of PT Squadron 4.

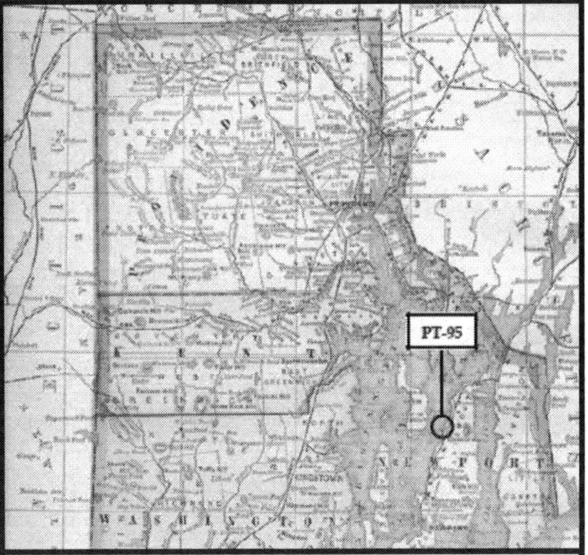

The Vessel

Type: Diesel Screw
Construction: Wood
Use: Warship
Dimensions: 78′ x 19′ x 5′
Tonnage: 48
Launched: Jacksonville, FL in 1942
Owner: US Navy
Nationality: American
Official No.: N/A
Home Port: Melville, RI

Final Voyage

Port of Departure: N/A
Port of Destination: N/A
Master: N/A
Cargo:
Date of Loss: September 26, 1945
Disaster Type: Destroyed (burned?)
Cause: Intentional (surplus?)
Final Status: Total loss
Location: At the training station at Melville (one source says at Davisville, near Quonset)

The Huckins PT Boats

There were four builders of motor torpedo boats during WWII. These were Elco (Electric Launch Company), Higgins (Higgins Industries), Huckins (Huckins Yacht Company) and the Canadian Power Boat Company. One of the early concerns about the different builders was the lack of a standard design and size. Ultimately, Elco built the greatest number of these boats followed by Higgins , Huckins and the Canadian firm. The Huckins Yacht Company of Jacksonville, Florida went into the business of building custom yachts, one at a time, in 1928. A decade later they became involved with the building of PT boats. In the opening rounds of the competition to design the best boat, Huckins produced a prototype 72 foot long boat which was just a bit larger than the Elco 70 footer and shorter than the 81 foot long Higgins entry. After a few years of experimentation to determine the best size, power and layout of equipment, made a bit more difficult by the improved designs and sizes of torpedoes and torpedo launching equipment, two rather standard sizes emerged as the top choice, the 77-foot Elco and the 80-foot Elco designs. All together Huckins built just 18 torpedo boats. The first set was numbers 95 through 102 (the first three for the Training Center at Melville and the other five became Squadron 14). The second set was numbers 255 through 264 which made up Squadron 26 and was assigned to the Hawaiian Islands though none of these vessels saw combat.

PT-95

Narrative

Although it was never used in battle **PT-95** served an integral role in the war. The Motor Torpedo Boat Squadrons Training Center at Melville, RI was the principal training center in the United States. We can only imagine the number of "near miss" accidents the boat suffered being continually in the hand of trainees but it is certain that the vessel had some interesting stories to tell. After twenty-six months of service (not long after the end of the war) **PT-95** was no longer of use to the now overstocked (with vessels) navy and was decommissioned on September 4, 1945. She and her sisters (PT-96 and PT-97) were destroyed later that month.

Research Sources

1. "At Close Quarters—PT Boats in the United States Navy" by Robert J. Bulkley, Jr. (1962)
2. "Ships of the US Navy 1940-1945"
3. NavSource Online (Internet)
4. www.ptboats.org
5. www.uboat.net

PT-96

The **PT-96** (pictured) probably on duty in Narragansett Bay. After a short career as a training vessel she was destroyed with other PT boats in Narragansett Bay.

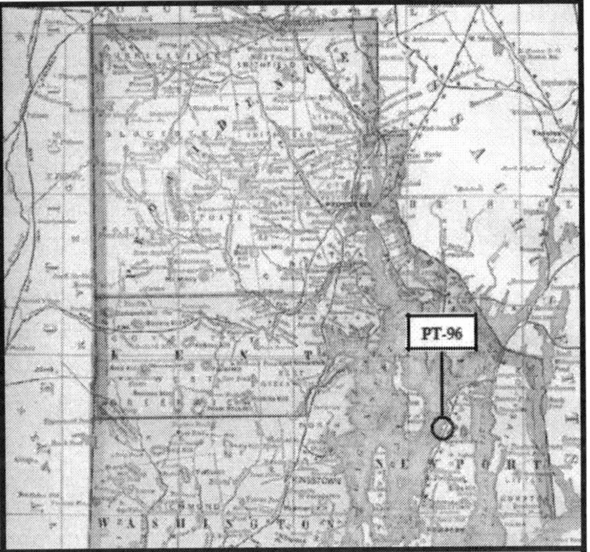

The Vessel

Type: Diesel Screw
Construction: Wood
Use: Warship
Dimensions: 78′ x 19′ x 5′
Tonnage: 48
Launched: Jacksonville, FL in 1942
Owner: US Navy
Nationality: American
Official No.: N/A
Home Port: Melville, RI

Final Voyage

Port of Departure: N/A
Port of Destination: N/A
Master: N/A
Cargo:
Date of Loss: September 13, 1945
Disaster Type: Destroyed (burned?)
Cause: Intentional (Ssurplus?)
Final Status: Total loss
Location: At the training station at Melville (one source says at Davisville, near Quonset)

The Motor Torpedo (PT) Boat

The history of the torpedo boat is directly related to the history of the torpedo. The term "torpedo" originally referred to a submersible device that would explode, hopefully destroying an enemy's warship. With few exceptions, these were originally stationary devices tactically placed where the warship could be expected to travel. After the Civil War, in the 1870's, the concept of a self propelled torpedo was developed with the terms "locomotive torpedo" or "fish" used to distinguish between them and traditional stationary torpedoes. But a locomotive torpedo needed a platform from which it could be launched, hence the idea of a torpedo boat. Although the earliest torpedo boats were developed and built as early as the 1880's, the "modern" torpedo boat was not developed until about 1905 in England by the British ship designer Alfred Yarrow and his design was for a lightly armed and armored vessel designed with channel service and harbor defense in mind. Perhaps the most influential change in the design and use of a torpedo boat came with the development of the internal combustion engine which allowed these boats to be much faster than their earlier steam counterparts. At this point, and after limited offensive use in the Spanish-American War, it was decided that the torpedo boat needed to fulfill three requirements to be effective: high speed, economy, and small size (to present the smallest possible target for the enemy to hit). Yarrow's experimental torpedo boat was just 15′ long,

PT-96

cruised at 25 knots and carried two torpedoes. The idea quickly caught on and in short order a number of countries including Italy, France and the United States were working on their own designs of a motor torpedo boat of various sizes and designs. During WWI the British and Italian navies improved on the design and it was determined that the optimum size of a torpedo boat would be no less than 40′ in length but no more than 100′ in length. Interestingly, although the British were leading in the design work, an American firm, the Electric Launch Company (better known as Elco) was the primary manufacturer. It appears that no one considered standardizing these craft, perhaps since the weaponry also continued to evolve and change in size, and two decades after the end of WWI there were still many different versions to choose from. The idea of standardization was not lost on those in power in the U.S. Navy and it was decided that a competition among designers would result in the best product for what was shaping up to be another world war. Thirty-seven designers presented plans for two classes of torpedo boats. The smaller class were to be no less than 50′ and no greater than 60′ in length; the larger, no less than 70′ and no greater than 80′ in length. Ultimately there were two specific designs, both in the range of the larger class, that proved to be most acceptable - a 78-foot long Higgins design and an 80-foot long Elco design. Both designs were utilized and provided the bulk of nearly 600 boats built for use in WWII. There were four builders of these boats, Elco (who with their earlier experience in building motor torpedo boats received the greatest number of contracts and produced 357 craft), Higgins Industries (who provided the second most favorable design used and were contracted for and produced 210 craft), Huckins (who built a 78-foot craft similar to the Higgins and produced 18 craft), and the Canadian Power Boat Company (who built just 4 smaller vessels for this purpose). The concept of the motor torpedo boat proved its worth during the war years in theaters of operation around the world. Many, like the **PT-96**, survived the war only to be destroyed as unneeded surplus equipment.

Narrative

Although it was never used in battle **PT-96** served an integral role in the war. After twenty-six months of service (not long after the end of the war) **PT-96** was no longer of use to the now overstocked (with vessels) navy and was decommissioned on September 4, 1945. She and her sisters (PT-95 and PT-97) were destroyed later that month.

The Trials and Tribulations of Training

Training torpedo boat crews involved both classroom and hands-on experience. Usually things went well and the trainees spent eight to twelve weeks at the training center in Melville. On at least one occasion, however, things did not go exactly as planned with the result that a 4,000 ton freighter, the USS CAPELLA, was struck by an accidentally launched torpedo while at anchor off Conanicut Island. Although not a deadly disaster, it certainly was a "wake-up call" to her crew (see separate data sheet for this incident).

Research Sources

1. "At Close Quarters—PT Boats in the United States Navy" by Robert J. Bulkley, Jr. (1962)
2. "Ships of the US Navy 1940-1945"
3. NavSource Online (Internet)
4. www.ptboats.org

PT-97

Although not specifically identified as **PT-97**, the vessel pictured above belongs to the PT-95 class to which she belonged.

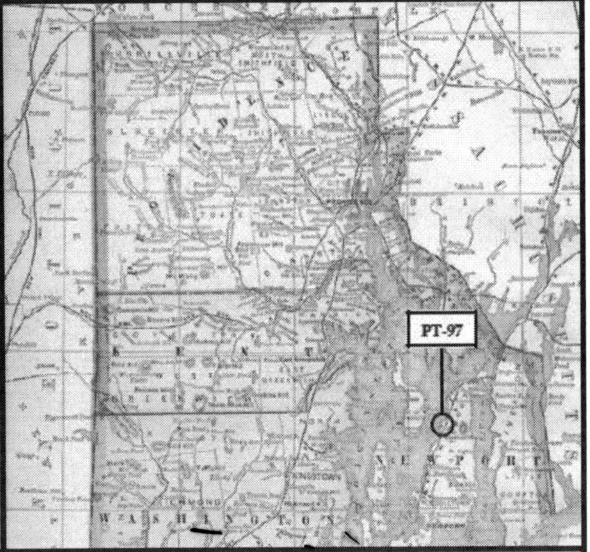

The Vessel

Type: Diesel Screw
Construction: Wood
Use: Warship
Dimensions: 78′ x 19′ x 5′
Tonnage: 48
Launched: Jacksonville, FL in 1942
Owner: US Navy
Nationality: American
Official No.: N/A
Home Port: Melville, RI

Final Voyage

Port of Departure: N/A
Port of Destination: N/A
Master: N/A
Cargo:
Date of Loss: September 13, 1945
Disaster Type: Destroyed (burned?)
Cause: Intentional (surplus?)
Final Status: Total loss
Location: At the training station at Melville (one source says at Davisville, near Quonset)

The Motor Torpedo Boat Squadrons Training Center

According to research by Captain Robert J. Bulkley Jr. in his book, "At Close Quarters, PT Boats in the United States Navy," Melville, Rhode Island was selected as the main training center for torpedo boat squadron members during the war. He provided the following background. "... *After the designation of Squadron 4 as the training squadron, the Secretary of the Navy on February 17, 1942, directed the establishment of the Motor Torpedo Boat Squadrons Training Center at Melville, RI on Narragansett Bay just north of Newport. William C. Specht, who had been promoted to lieutenant commander, was relieved of command of Squadron 1 at Pearl Harbor in order to organize the training center, which inevitably came to be known as "Specht Tech". It began operations in the middle of March, 1942. From the beginning it was the policy of the training center to use combat veterans as instructors. ... By the first week in April, 51 officers and 177 enlisted men were under instruction; the boats of Squadron 4 were available for training; 47 Quonset huts were in various stages of completion, and a request had been made for the construction of 44 additional huts. Eventually the Training Center acquired 13 structures devoted to office space, 34 classrooms, 42 maintenance buildings, and 197 huts for living quarters. It was equipped to handle a normal load of 860 enlisted students and 90 student officers. Squadron 4 was gradually enlarged until the end of 1944 it comprised 28 boats of 4 distinct types. ... In time, the Training Center acquired a vast array of training devices. Well-equipped shops made possible not only the training*

PT-97

of personnel but a large-scale experimental program. Development of a lightweight torpedo rack to replace the old tube is an outstanding example of the work accomplished under this program. The period of training originally was 2 months. In 1943 a third month was added to the training period for officers and certain specialized enlisted rates. ... The Training Center became the personnel clearinghouse for the enlisted PT service. Officers and men returning from combat areas were ordered there for temporary duty... The Repair Training Unit was established at the Training Center in March 1944 to give specialized instruction to personnel for PT bases and tenders. In November 1944, a special command course was established for prospective squadron commanders and executive officers. By the time of its third anniversary, March 16, 1945, the Training Center had trained 1,797 officers and 11,668 enlisted men.

Less than two months after that anniversary, in early May, the European Theater of War ceased its activities with the surrender of Germany; it was several months later, in mid August, when Japanese forces agreed to surrender. Just over a month later, the following article appeared.

Newport Mercury & Weekly News - September 21, 1945 P5

MELVILLE BASE SALE PROPOSED IN CONGRESS

Senator Green Acts in Effort to Draw Private Enterprises to This Area

Legislation authorizing the navy department to dispose at private sale of the Motor Torpedo Boat Squadron Training Center at Melville was introduced in Congress by Senator Theodore Francis Green. This followed notification from the navy that the base will not be used as a permanent installation, according to B.F. Linz, Washington correspondent to the Daily News. ...

And so it seems that as quickly as the training center was brought into existence in 1941, so was it brought to closure just four years later. There can be no doubt that for the short period of its existence, the training center provided an important service to the country and aided greatly in making our naval forces successful. The Training Center was formally decommissioned in early 1946, but by that time all the boats that had been assigned there were placed "out of service".

Narrative

Although it was never used in battle **PT-97** served an important role in the war. The Motor Torpedo Boat Squadrons Training Center at Melville, RI was the principal training center in the United States. After twenty-six months of service (not long after the end of the war) **PT-97** was no longer of use to the now overstocked (with vessels) navy and was decommissioned on September 4, 1945. She and her sisters (PT-95 and PT-96) were destroyed later that month.

Research Sources

1. Newport Mercury & Weekly News, September 21, 1945 P5
2. "At Close Quarters—PT Boats in the United States Navy" by Robert J. Bulkley, Jr. (1962)
3. "Ships of the US Navy 1940-1945"
4. NavSource Online (Internet)
5. www.ptboats.org
6. www.uboat.net

USS LONE WOLF (YTB-179)

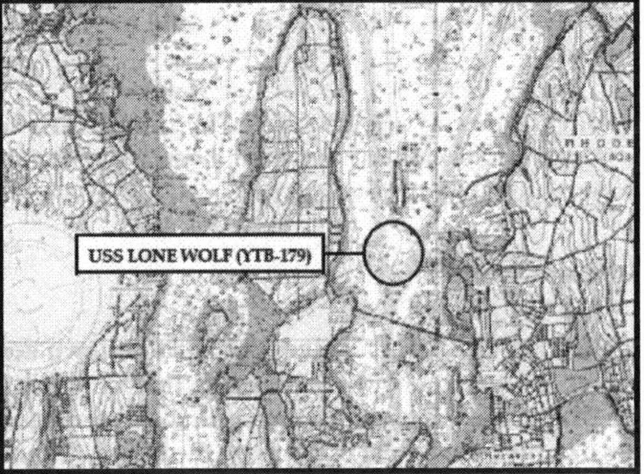

The Vessel

Type: Diesel Screw
Construction: Steel
Use: Tug
Dimensions: 100′ x 25′ x 10′
Tonnage: 218
Launched: Jacksonville, FL in 1942
Owner: US Navy
Nationality: American
Home Port: Newport, RI

The Event

Port of Departure: US Navy Base
Master: Unidentified Chief Boatswains Mate
Date of Incident: December 10, 1946
Disaster Type: Sunk
Cause: Collision
Status: Raised
Location: About 1,800 yards off the Jamestown shore

Narrative

Newport Mercury and Weekly News - December 13, 1946 P1

SAILOR DROWNED AS TUG SINKS OFF JAMESTOWN

One sailor was drowned and seven other crew members of the navy tug **LONE WOLF** *leaped to safety as their vessel sank quickly in 126 feet of water off the Jamestown shore Tuesday afternoon, her hull ripped open by the propeller of a large tanker that she was moving. Divers attached to the Naval Base here are still trying to raise the body of Joseph Peter Santoro, 18, seaman first class, of Center Street, Wallingford, Conn., this morning without success, while an Investigation board appointed by Commodore Paul S. Theiss, commanding officer of the Naval Base, Newport, began inquiries into the cause of the sinking and the man's death. The* **LONE WOLF**, *with a chief boatswain's mate in charge, and a crew of seven, was engaged in warping the tanker CALOOSAHATCHEE alongside navy relief ship VULCAN at 12:30 PM Tuesday when the tanker started her starboard engine to aid in the movement. The tug, swinging in under the stern of the larger vessel received the impact from the CALOOSAHATCHEE's propeller that spelled her doom. As water poured into the hole in the* **LONE WOLF**'s *hull, crew members jumped aboard smaller boats which had come alongside to the rescue. Later, several crew members, including Santoro, climbed back aboard the tug supposedly to recover personal belongings. Santoro is believed to have been trapped below decks, a navy spokesman said, as the* **LONE WOLF** *sank quickly, while the others who had returned to the vessel leaped clear again. A launch from the VULCAN which was assisting in the rescue operation, capsized as the* **LONE WOLF** *sank but remained afloat and was lifted back aboard the VULCAN without injury to its crew. Loss of the* **LONE WOLF**, *which was attached to the Naval Base for local work, leaves the base without a navy fire-boat it having been the only one equipped for fire-fighting operations, it was said at the Naval Base this morning.*

USS LONE WOLF (YTB-179)

Newport Mercury and Weekly News - December 13, 1946 P2

DIVERS FAIL TO LOCATE VICTIM OF TUG CRASH

Divers attached to the Naval Torpedo Station here were unsuccessful Thursday in attempts to reach the navy tug **LONE WOLF** *and recover the body of the seaman who was drowned when the vessel sank. Meanwhile, a navy board of investigators pushed twin inquiries into the cause of the freak collision between the* **LONE WOLF** *and the navy tanker CALOOSAHATCHEE off Jamestown on Tuesday. Results of the investigation will not be revealed, it was said today, until it is complete. High winds at the scene of the mishap prevented the undersea workers from diving, a navy spokesman said. Depth of the water at the scene was reported at 126 feet. Exact location of the spot is still not determined, it was learned late this afternoon. Electrical sound apparatus of the type used in locating torpedoes has been used and what is thought to be the spot has been found. However, when attempts to hook onto the tug with grappling irons were made, a running tide estimated at four knots an hour prevented the line from touching bottom. Navy spokesmen were not optimistic about chances to proceed with the work as weather forecasts indicated high winds and rough accompanying seas.*

Newport Mercury and Weekly News - July 4, 1947 P4

SUNKEN NAVY TUG SOUGHT

Two navy salvage ships, the WINDLASS and SALVAGER, were attempting today to locate the sunken navy tug **LONE WOLF** *which went down with one sailor aboard off the Jamestown shore last December 10 after a tanker she was moving tore a hole in her hull. Salvage operations from the two newly equipped vessels are expected to last about 10 days, a navy spokesman said today. The two boats, in command of Captain John Zabilsky, U.S.N., made a preliminary survey Tuesday of the area where the* **LONE WOLF** *sank, but divers were unable to locate her.*

Newport Mercury and Weekly News - July 25, 1947 P2

NAVY TUG LONE WOLF BROUGHT TO SURFACE

Navy tug **LONE WOLF** *was above water Thursday at deck level for the first time since she sunk in 150-foot depth off the Jamestown shore more than eight months ago. Salvage crews who raised her from the bottom prepared to patch the ragged hole in her hull torn by propeller of tanker CALOOSAHATCHEE, which the* **LONE WOLF** *was moving when she met with tragedy. So far, a navy public information spokesman said, no trace has been discovered of the remains of the young seaman – one of the crew of eight aboard – who went down with her last December 10. A navy board of investigation, it was learned today, has absolved anyone of negligence in connection with the disaster and said the death of Joseph P. Santoro, 18, was "in the line of duty". Though heavily encrusted with a variety of marine life, mud and rust, accumulated during her long stay on the bottom, the* **LONE WOLF** *appears to be structurally sound. Pumping apparatus was put aboard her while she was still suspended from the cables of the salvage vessels, commanded by Capt. John Zabilski, naval salvage expert. Plans call for the tug to be beached on Jamestown shore, if necessary, near where she has been towed by slow stages.*

Whether or not the tug was returned to service after the successful salvage effort is not known.

Research Sources

1. Newport Mercury and Weekly News, December 13, 1946 P1 & P2
2. Newport Mercury and Weekly News, December 27, 1946 P1
3. Newport Mercury and Weekly News, July 4, 1947 P4
4. Newport Mercury and Weekly News, July 11, 1947 P1
5. Newport Mercury and Weekly News, July 25, 1947 P2

ON TIME

The fishing vessel ON TIME was similar in design and size to the unidentified vessel pictured above.

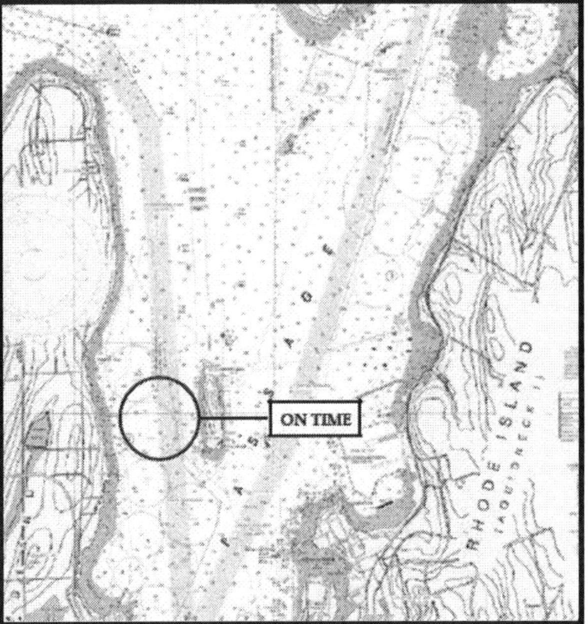

The Vessel

Type: Boat
Construction: Wood
Use: Fishing
Dimensions: 30′ x 10′ x 4′
Tonnage: 8
Launched: Westerly, RI in 1913
Owner: Edward Grimes
Nationality: American
Official No.: 211645
Home Port: Newport, RI

The Event

Port of Departure: Unknown
Port of Destination: Unknown
Master: Edward Grimes
Cargo: Unknown
Date of Incident: May 22, 1951
Disaster Type: Sunk
Cause: Struck by a torpedo
Status: Raised
Location: Between Gould Island and Jamestown

Narrative

Newport Daily News - May 23, 1951 P1

NAVY SALVAGING FISH BOAT SUNK BY STRAY TORPEDO

The navy this afternoon started salvage operations on the 30-foot fishing boat ON TIME owned by Edward Grimes of 11 Cannon street sunk Tuesday by a stray torpedo between Gould Island and Jamestown. At the same time it initiated action for an investigation of the mishap, which caused a torpedo with a dummy head, officially described as "erratic" to crash into the boat's hull and send it to the bottom. Grimes, the only person aboard at the time, was picked up from the water a few minutes later by a range boat from the Torpedo Station. He was treated at a navy dispensary for a slight scratch on the leg. The navy said the ON TIME was not close to the prohibited area of the test torpedo firing range. Grimes saw the torpedo headed toward his craft and tried to dodge it by swinging the boat around, but the missile crashed amidships, making a large hole in the hull. The Torpedo Station has already recovered the torpedo from the bottom approximately 60 feet down. The case is already in the hands of the First Naval District Headquarters in Boston, the navy said.

ON TIME

Research Sources

1. Newport Daily News, May 23, 1951 P1
2. Newport Mercury and Weekly News, May 25, 1951 P1
3. Merchant Vessels of the United States—1950
4. Newport Custom House records

UNIDENTIFIED

The ill-fated and overloaded launch that capsized in heavy seas on the morning on May 24th was later retrieved by the crew of USS YELLOWSTONE (AD-27). The final fate of the launch is unknown.

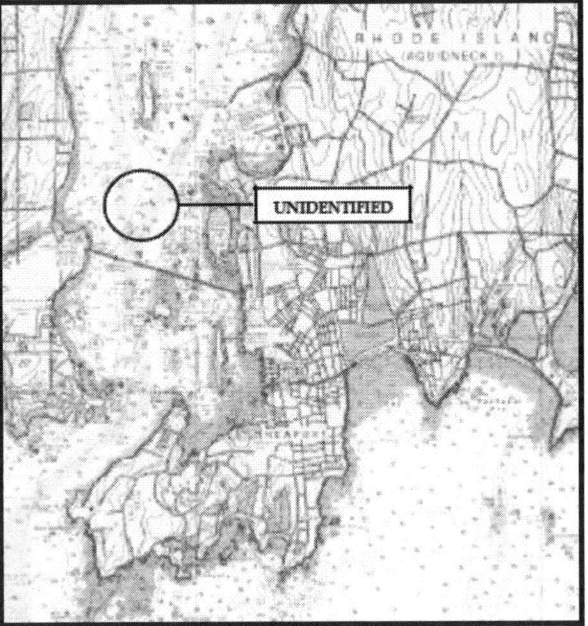

The Vessel

Type: Gas Screw
Construction: Wood
Use: Liberty Boat
Dimensions: 50′ x 14′ x 3′
Tonnage: 9
Launched: 1943
Owner: US Navy
Nationality: American
Home Port: Newport, RI

The Event

Port of Departure: Long Wharf, Newport
Port of Destination: Navy Anchorage, north of Rose Island
Master: James D. Egler, Acting Coxswain
Date of Incident: May 24, 1951
Disaster Type: Sunk
Cause: Capsized
Status: Retrieved
Location: About 1 mile north from Rose Island

Narrative

Newport Mercury and Weekly News - May 24, 1951 P1

NAVY LAUNCH SINKS; 2 DIE; 24 HURT

About 90 Pulled Out of Harbor; Two From County

Tanker, Navy Craft Aid in "Rescue By Grace of God" During Storm

At least two sailors were drowned and about 90 rescued when the 50-foot liberty boat in which they were returning to their ships capsized in the rough water of the outer harbor at 7:45 o'clock this morning. Twenty-four sailors were under treatment in the Naval Hospital. Fifteen of them were stretcher cases. The sinking occurred in an "edge of the hurricane" storm with winds up to 30 miles an hour whipping up the waters. The liberty boat took so much water over her bow that she soon sunk. Names of the dead were withheld by the navy pending notification of next of kin. The capsized launch carried personnel from destroyers POWER, GLENNON, PERRY and BAILEY and destroyer tender YELLOWSTONE. It left the fleet landing on Long Wharf a few minutes previously. Navy officials did not know the exact number of men in the liberty boat. Had it not been for the fortunate circumstances of a number of navy and other boats being nearby at the time, it is believed that the casualty list would have been much greater. As it was

UNIDENTIFIED

heroic rescue operations were conducted. Sailors threw themselves from other liberty boats into the stormy water to save shipmates. This aided in keeping down the losses. The sinking occurred in midstream at a point a mile north of Rose Island. Rear Admiral Frank G. Fahrion, commanding destroyers, Atlantic Fleet, immediately appointed a court of inquiry headed by Captain George W. Stott. This convened this afternoon. M.S.T.S. NODOWAY, a 325-foot gasoline tanker on her way to Tiverton at the time of the capsizing, threw out life rafts and life preservers to the men struggling in the water between Rose Island and the West Breakwater. The NODOWAY acted as a rescue point for boats in the harbor and from shore which took part in the rescue operation. The tanker had 48 survivors on board when rescue operations ended. In addition five Coast Guard boats and a Coast Guard helicopter joined in the search. "It was a rescue by the Grace of God," said Capt. Thomas H. Templeton, Naval Base Chief of Staff, "It was only by that grace that the harbor was so full of boats going back to other ships. Our boys did a wonderful job. And that storm was the edge of a hurricane." In all, more than 130 sailors were recovering from emersion in the cold waters. They included the crewmen who had jumped from other boats to rescue the men in the liberty boats. They were in the Naval Hospital and two Training Station dispensaries. Gabriel M. Fattel, 35, of Aquidneck Avenue, Middletown and George R. Nolmgren, 24, of 34 Mt. Vernon street, were among those who escaped with only a cold ducking. Each of the two men was in the water 30 minutes before being picked up by a small boat. They were able to grab lifejackets as the launch tipped over. They described the scene as orderly and said the sailors were cool and collected about the incident. "Everything was calm but the waves," said a third survivor, who clung to the keel of the liberty boat until picked up. If it had been at night probably all would have drowned, another said. Commander George F. Dalton, commanding officer of the Destroyer GLENNON, who was in a boat just north of the capsized craft and went to the rescue of the sailor, praised the officers and crew of the merchant tanker. Headquarters of the Destroyer Force, Atlantic Fleet, said that at the time of the capsizing a stop boating message was issued to harbor craft but that the message was independent of the 7:45 incident. That meant that if the boat had delayed leaving the Fleet Landing, it would not have left at all. DESLANTS said the boat had an approximate capacity of 190, and it was estimated to be half full. The master of NODOWAY, operated by the military sea transportation service is William Cowan. Its pilot is Leonard Hemmalin of Providence. The navy said the liberty boat was observed to take water over the bow and then capsize. The boat following immediately started rescue operations. The commanding officer of the BAILEY was aboard the second craft. The 48 sailors aboard the NODOWAY were transferred to a navy tug and thence to waiting ambulances at the naval base. No count of persons rescued by numerous other small craft was immediately available. A naval investigation was convened to determine the cause of this disaster which cost 18 lives. It was determined that the liberty boat was rated for a maximum of 135 passengers with a heavy weather capacity of no more than 80. At the time of the incident, she was loaded with 145 men. It was also noted that the seaman in charge of the boat, acting coxswain James D. Egler, was an inexperienced operator, but no charges of negligence were ever raised. Overall, it seems that there was an error in judgment to run the overloaded launch in the severe weather but this was somewhat offset by the good fortune of the time of day and the presence of other boats in the vicinity of the capsizing. If the accident had happened at night, all might have been lost.

Research Sources

1. Newport Mercury & Weekly News, May 24, 1951 P1
2. Newport Mercury & Weekly News, May 25, 1951 P2
3. Newport Mercury & Weekly News, June 1, 1951 P1
4. Newport Mercury & Weekly News, June 1, 1951 P2
5. Newport Mercury & Weekly News, June 22, 1951 P8

USS DEUEL (APA-160)

USS DEUEL (APA-160) was a Haskell Class Attack Transport Ship built by the US Navy during World War II. She was a Victory Ship design VC2-S-AP5 vessel.

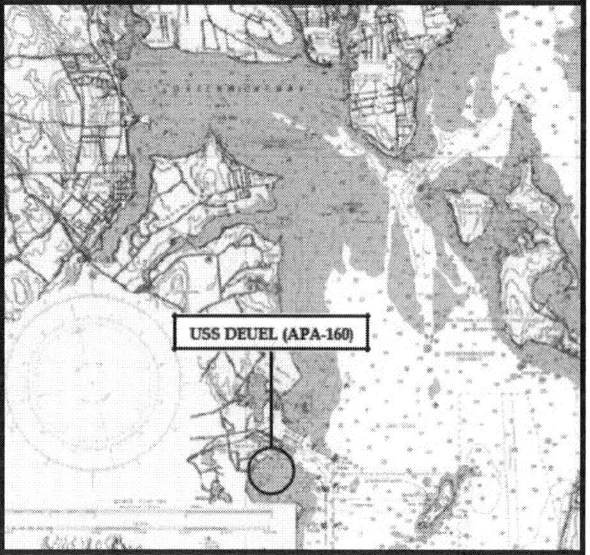

The Vessel

Type: Diesel Powered, Screw Driven
Construction: Steel
Use: Attack Transport Ship
Dimensions: 455′ x 62′ x 24′
Tonnage: 6,873
Launched: Portland, OR in 1944
Owner: US Navy
Nationality: American

Final Voyage

Port of Departure: Caribbean port
Port of Destination: Quonset Point, RI
Date of Loss: August 31, 1954
Disaster Type: Stranding
Cause: Hurricane Carol
Final Status: Got off
Location: On the flats off the pier at Davisville

Narrative

Newport Daily News - September 3, 1954 P13

Navy Continues Efforts to Refloat Beached Vessel

DAVISVILLE, R.I. - The Navy said today dredging operations will continue today to refloat the attack-transport ***DEUEL****, which was beached off Narragansett Bay during Tuesday's hurricane. No injuries were reported and damage to the vessel was described as "Negligible". The Navy said refloating operations may take several days since test borings disclosed that the amphibious ship is grounded in deep silt about 30 feet from the shore line.*

Newport Daily News - September 7, 1954 P10

Navy Estimates Loss at $4 Million

The Navy today estimated its hurricane loss on both sides of Narragansett Bay as $4,000,000. Work at repairing the storm damage is preceding here and across the bay. But at Davisville, an attempt to refloat the grounded transport ***USS DEUEL*** *was abandoned for today because of weather conditions. Dredges worked over the weekend to dig a channel alongside the transport. A tug using water pressure has been trying to scour the mud out from around the ship, and cumbersome "beaching gear" has been used to try and refloat the vessel. A salvage ship, the OPPORTUNE, has been aiding in the work.*

USS DEUEL (APA-160)

Research Sources

1. Newport Daily News, September 3, 1954 P13
2. Newport Daily News, September 7, 1954 P10
3. www.usnavyships.com
4. www.navsource.org

USN TORPEDO RETRIEVER

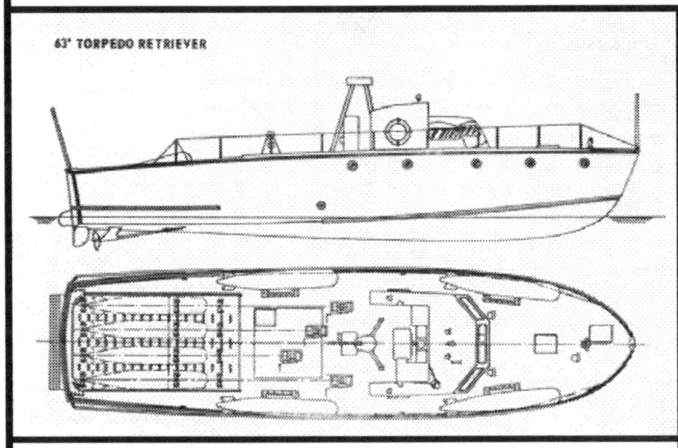

The standard 63 foot torpedo retriever as documented in the US Navy Catalog - NAVSHIPS 250-242.

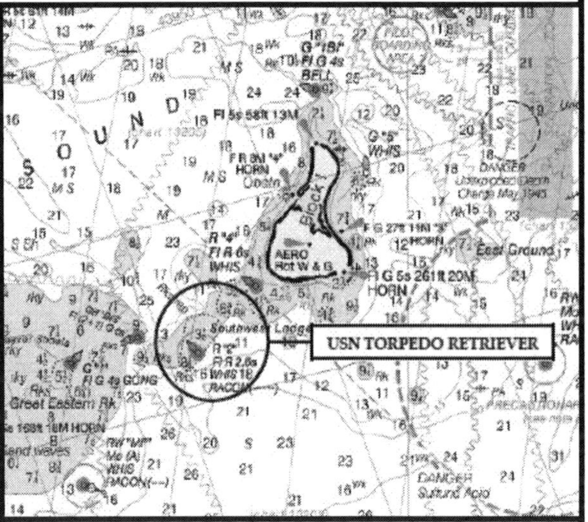

The Vessel

Type: Diesel Screw
Construction: Steel
Use: Torpedo Retrieval Vessel
Dimensions: 63′ x 15′
Owner: US Navy
Nationality: America

Final Voyage

Home Port: Unknown
Date of Loss: 1957
Disaster Type: Sunk?
Cause: Unknown
Final Status: Probably a total loss
Location: Southwest Ledge, off Block Island

Narrative

Sometime during 1957 an accident claimed an unidentified US Navy torpedo retriever but the details have, as yet, proven to be elusive. Perhaps the most interesting question involves how a torpedo retriever would end up in this location at all. But there are a number of possibilities. Although the torpedo testing range in Rhode Island is located well inside Narragansett Bay between Conanicut, Gould and Prudence Islands, there is one located in Fort Pond Bay, on the northern side of Long Island, near Montauk Point. The latter range is more than a dozen miles from Southwest Ledge. So it would seem that the torpedo retriever was not retrieving a torpedo at the time of her loss. That prompts another question...was the vessel even being used in the capacity of a testing vessel at the time? Since we do not yet know the exact time of year of the disaster, that is hard to prove or disprove. There is one more, less likely, possibility which is that though the vessel was described as a navy torpedo retriever, she may have been sold to a private party to be used for fishing. Although that is probably the least likely possibility, it should, nonetheless, be left on the list of choices.

Research Sources

1. "Encyclopedia of American Shipwrecks" by Bruce Bermen
2. NavShips 250-242 published by the Bureau of Shipping
3. Historic Naval Ships Association (1967)
4. The Code of Federal Regulations of the United States Government (1943 & 1967 editions) for information on the location of torpedo testing ranges

UNIDENTIFIED

Some WWI ammunition lighters were like the YE-27 (pictured). Although the specifics of the barge which stranded in 1960 are not known, she was probably considerably larger than this 86′ vessel.

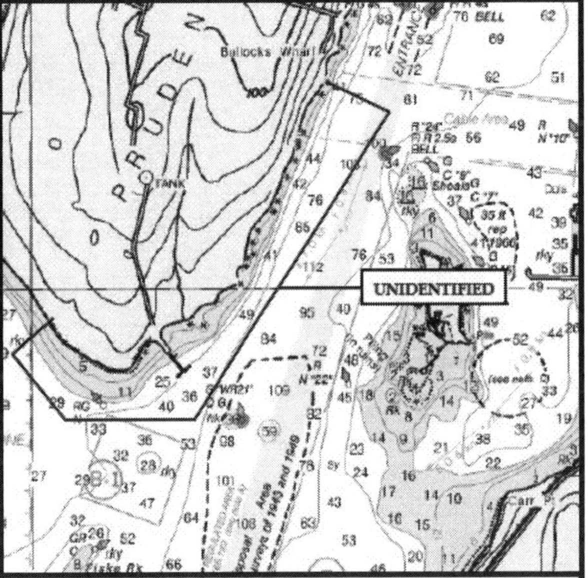

The Vessel

Type: Barge
Construction: Unknown
Use: Transportation of ammunition
Owner: US Navy
Nationality: American
Home Port: Newport, RI

The Event

Cargo: None
Date of Incident: September 12, 1960
Disaster Type: Stranding
Cause: Hurricane Donna
Status: Probably pulled off
Location: On the south end of Prudence Island

Narrative

Although there is not a lot known about the specifics and aftermath of this stranding, there is information on the storm which makes note of the stranding.

Newport Daily News - September 14, 1960 P4

City Presses Its Mopup After Donna

Newport was making good strides today in recovering from Hurricane Donna's assault on Monday, but numerous trouble spots remained to be cleared up. ... A gentle rain fell last night, scarcely enough to do much washing. Oil is a problem in many areas. On Carroll Avenue, nearly a mile from the ocean, one home owner showed a brownish stain on new aluminum siding he had just had installed. At the naval base, all shorefront buildings are stained with oil that blew from the harbor, where it had lain since the grounding of the commercial tanker P.W. THIRTLE off Jamestown on September 1 [see separate data sheet for the story of that stranding]. *Fresh blankets of oil were reported lying in wharves and slips along the waterfront. ... The Naval Base reported today that its yard tug, YTB 175 was still hard aground on the southern end of Prudence Island and that an attempt to pull her free at high tide early today failed* [see separate data sheet for the story of that stranding]. *The tug is in four feet of water and normally draws 10 feet, so is quite high and dry. All equipment and fuel is being taken off the tug which has no apparent hull damage. It was disclosed today that another craft, an* ***unloaded ammunition barge****, had also run ashore during the storm at Prudence island. No attempt has been made to refloat her yet, as the Navy's prime need is for the services of the tug, one of nine used here.*

UNIDENTIFIED

Research Sources

1. Newport Daily News, September 12, 1960 P4
2. www.navsource.org

YTB 175

The YTB 174 (pictured) was identical in size to the **YTB 175** (which was launched as the CHEKILLI) in 1941. The **YTB 175** survived and was later sold by the navy.

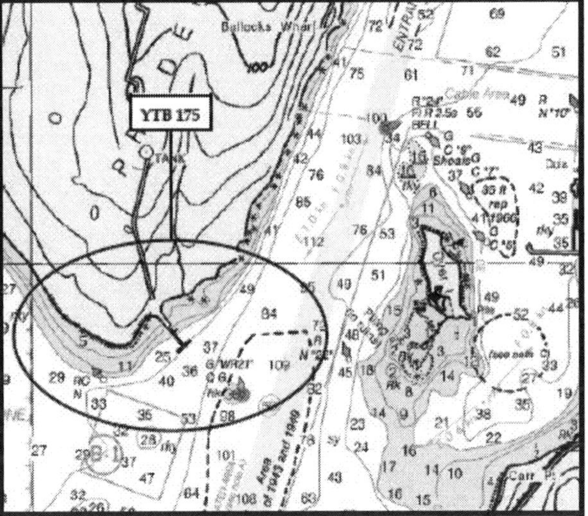

The Vessel

Type: Diesel Screw
Construction: Steel
Use: Tug
Dimensions: 102′ x 24′ x 10′
Tonnage: 206
Launched: Port Arthur, TX in 1941
Nationality: American

The Event

Owner: US Navy
Home Port: Newport, RI
Date of Incident: September 12, 1960
Disaster Type: Stranding
Cause: Hurricane Donna
Status: Got Off
Location: On the south end of Prudence Island

Narrative

Newport Daily News - September 14 1960 P4

CITY PRESSES ITS MOPUP AFTER DONNA

Newport was making good strides today in recovering from Hurricane Donna's assault on Monday… A gentle rain fell last night, enough to do much washing. Oil is a problem in many areas. At the naval base, all shorefront buildings are stained with oil that blew from the harbor where it had lain since the grounding of the commercial tanker P.W. THIRTLE [see separate data sheet] *off Jamestown on September 1. … The Naval Base reported today that its yard tug,* ***YTB 175****, was still hard aground on the southern end of Prudence Island and that an attempt to pull her free at high tide early today failed. The tug is in four feet of water and normally draws 10 feet, so is quite high and dry. All equipment and fuel is being taken off the tug which has no apparent hull damage.*

Though details of the recovery have not come to light, it is known that she was saved as she was sold by the navy in 1974.

Research Sources

1. Newport Daily News, September 14, 1960 P4
2. NavSourceOnline
3. www.navytugs.com

USS SEVERN (A0-61)

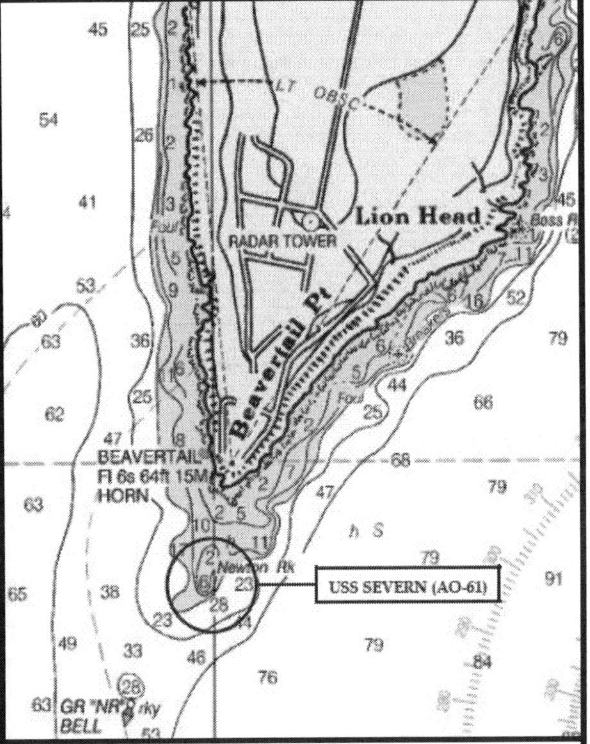

The Vessel

Type: Steamship
Construction: Steel
Use: Tanker
Dimensions: 553′ x 75′ x 32′
Tonnage: 25,440
Launched: Sparrows Point, MD in 1944
Nationality: American

Final Voyage

Owner: US Navy
Home Port: Newport, RI
Date of Loss: February 9, 1968
Disaster Type: Stranding
Final Status: Pulled off
Location: Struck on Newton Rock, off the tip of Beavertail Point

"Sometimes You Just Get Lucky"

What could be considered a very lucky incident could have been a disaster when the US Navy's fleet oiler USS SEVERN (AO-61) ran aground on Newton Rock in the late afternoon on February 9, 1968. The stranding of a sophisticated warship in modern times is a rarity but does take place on occasion. So how was this incident lucky? First, the oiler was carrying no cargo at the time; second, the weather was calm resulting in a very quick rescue effort in which the 500 footer came off with comparative ease before a day had passed. Not many vessels which have landed on Newton Rock have been so lucky.

Research Sources

1. Beavertail Lighthouse Museum Association
2. Photo courtesy of the Beavertail Lighthouse Museum Association

USS ALEXANDER J. LUKE (DE-577)

USS ALEXANDER J. LUKE (DE-577) was one of more than 150 Buckley class destroyer escorts built during WWII. This was the second of six classes of escorts and improved upon the Evarts class, by its length and increased range.

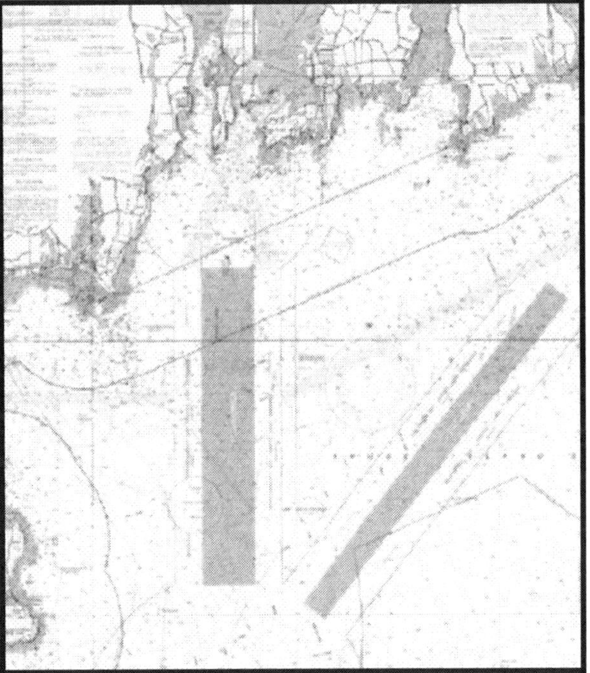

The Vessel

Type: Steamship
Construction: Steel
Use: Destroyer Escort
Dimensions: 306′ x 37′ x 13′
Tonnage: 1,740
Launched: Hingham, MA in 1943
Owner: US Navy
Nationality: American
Home Port: Charleston, SC

Final Voyage

Port of Departure: Charleston, SC
Port of Destination: Disposal Site
Date of Loss: October 22, 1970
Disaster Type: Sunk
Cause: Intentional—as a target
Final Status: Total loss
Location: No specific location other than off Newport, RI

The USS ALEXANDER J. LUKE (DE-577)

The **USS ALEXANDER J. LUKE (DE-577)** was laid down in November, 1943 and hit the water just 8 weeks later. In February of 1944 she was commissioned and headed out for a shakedown cruise but met with an accident in March when she ran aground receiving minor damage. One month later she returned to service to complete her shakedown and in June reported to duty at Norfolk, VA to conduct exercises as a training ship. Following two trips to the Mediterranean as an escort she sailed to Boston and joined in a series of antisubmarine warfare exercises until the spring of 1945. She made one more trip with a convoy and on her return was sent to Texas for conversion to a radar picket escort ship, coming out of the yard with the designator DER-577. The next six months were spent in the Caribbean before the **LUKE** headed northward again to New England waters. In late 1947, when just four years old, she was placed out of commission for the remainder of her career. In August of 1954 she was redesignated **DE-577** but was never modernized and an inspection found her unfit for further service. She apparently resided with the mothball fleet until May 1, 1970 when she was struck from the Navy list.

USS ALEXANDER J. LUKE (DE-577)

Buckley Class Destroyer Escorts

A website about destroyers and escorts offers the following detailed information about this class of warships. *The Buckley class was a product of the January 1942 expansion of the DE program from 50 ships to 300 ships. Availability of diesel engines was limited, however, by the higher priority submarine and landing craft construction. Accordingly, the Navy asked General Electric too develop a steam-powered turbo electric design, called the TE type – that would develop the 12,000 ship horse power (shp) and 24 knots of the original DE concept. The resulting design consumed more space than the original geared turbine plant, so the Evarts class hull was lengthened by six feet to accommodate it. Thereafter, the Buckley's 306 ft. "long hull" became the standard hull for all follow-on DE classes. After World War II, the TEs were favored over the other DE types. The general statistics for the class were as follows:*

Displacement: 1,400 long tons standard; 1,740 full load
Dimensions: 300′ at waterline; 306′ overall length; 37′ beam; 13′ 6″ draft
Power: Steam-powered turbo electric, total 12,000 horsepower, 23.5 knots, twin screws
Armament:

- *3 x 3″ guns*
- *1 x twin 40 mm Bofors*
- *9 x single 20 mm Oerlikon*
- *2 x depth charge tracks*
- *8 x depth charge projectors*
- *1 x hedgehog*
- *Crew – 213*

Research Sources

1. Dictionary of American Naval Fighting Ships (DANFS)
2. Buckley Class destroyer escorts in World War II
3. Destroyer Escort Historical Museum website
4. NavSource Online

APPENDIX—Disasters by Location

Maritime disasters can occur anywhere and at any time. For those of you with a particular interest in a specific area, the following lists of where these events took place are presented. The name of the vessel and date of disaster are provided. The page number is noted in brackets ( ) for easy reference.

Area 01 - Eastern Rhode Island - This area covers the shoreline from the state line between Rhode Island and Massachusetts, travels southward to Sakonnet Point and then northward for the entire length of the Sakonnet River. There have been eight incidents in this area.

ALARM - 7/30/1778 (81, 87)
HAMPDEN - 8/27/1777 (53)
HMS CERBERUS - 1/10/1877 (41)
HMS KINGFISHER - 7/30/1778 (83, 87)
OLIVER CROMWELL - 8/27/1777 (55)
PIGOT - 10/29/1778 (115)
SPITFIRE - 7/30/1778 (85, 87)
UNIDENTIFIED - 12/1748 (25)

Area 02 - Narragansett Bay - This area includes the waters from the northern end of the Sakonnet River at Mount Hope Bay northwestward to the head of the bay at Providence. There have been twenty-one incidents recorded in this area.

GASPEE - 6/9/1772 (33)
HMS CERBERUS - 8/4/1778 (89, 95)
HMS DIAMOND - 1/2/1777 (39)
HMS GLASGOW - 10/7/1775 (37)
HMS LARK - 8/4/1778 (91, 95)
HMS ORPHEUS - 8/4/1778 (93, 95)
JULIA - 12/15/1870 (137)
NO NAME - 6/26/1930 (213)
PT-95 - 9/26/1945 (249)
PT-96- 9/13/1945 (251)
PT-97 - 9/13/1945 (253)
RANGE BOAT NO. 31 - 10/13/1930 (215)
RENOWN - 1778 (117)
SPITFIRE - 3/13/1777 (49)
TRYALL - 2/14/1777 (47)
UNIDENTIFIED (Various) - 5/26/1778 (77)
UNIDENTIFIED - 5/31/1778 (79)
UNIDENTIFIED - 9/12/1960 (265)
VESUVIUS - 5/19/1913 (193)
WASHINGTON - 4/2/1777 (51)
YTB-175 - 9/12/1960 (267)

Area 03 - West Passage - This area includes the shoreline from the head of Greenwich Bay southward to the town of Narragansett. There have been three incidents recorded in this area.

USS DEUEL (APA-160) - 8/31/1954 (261)
WHAMPOA - 4/28/1813 (129)
WILLIAM A. WELLS - 7/28/1911 (187)

Area 04 - Conanicut Island - Situated south from Prudence Island and prominent in the center of the entrance to Narragansett Bay is Conanicut Island. There have been nine incidents recorded in this area.

BRENTON REEF (LV-11) - 12/3/1873 (139)
DIANA - 6/15/1775 (35)
LT. WILLIAM H. SMITH - 12/14/1917 (197)
NO NAME - 11/6/1919 (203)
UNIDENTIFIED - 12/2/1942 (237)
US GUBOAT NO. 46 - 9/29/1812 (127)
USS CAPELLA (AK-13) - 4/9/1942 (235)
USS G-1 - 6/21/1921 (205)
USS SEVERN (AO-61) - 2/9/1968 (269)

Area 05 - Newport - This area includes the shoreline from Third Beach, at the mouth of the Sakonnet River westward across the ocean side of Aquidneck Island and northward to the Newport Naval Base and includes the waters of the East Passage. There have been fifty-eight incidents recorded in this area.

A.D. BACHE - 4/20/1905 (175)
BETTY - 8/6/1778 (105)
BRENTON REEF (LV-11) - 10/19/1865 (135)
BRENTON REEF (LV-11) - 11/26/1890 (153)
BRITANNIA - 8/6/1778 (105)
CUSHING (TB-1) - 9/9/1896 (159)
EARL OF OXFORD - 8/6/1778 (105)
ESSEX - 12/24/1811 (125)
GEN. MONROE - 1/6/1891 (155)
GEN. MONROE - 9/7/1895 (157)
GENERAL JESSUP - 12/29/1876 (143)
GOOD INTENT - 8/6/1778 (105)
GRAND DUKE OF RUSSIA - 8/6/1778 (105)
GRAND TURK - 8/8/1778 (107)
HERMIONE - 4/13/1781 (119)
HMS FALCON - 8/5/1778 (101)
HMS FLORA - 8/8/1778 (109)
HMS JUNO - 8/4/1778 (97)
IDA LEWIS - 11/30/1909 (185)
JOSEPH HENRY - 9/24/1875 (141)
JOSEPH HENRY - 8/24/1884 (149)
LIBERTY - 7/19/1769 (31)
LORD SANDWICH - 8/6/1778 (103, 105)
MAIDSTONE - 6/4/1765 (29)
MALAGA - 8/6/1778 (105)
NERO - 7/1/1909 (183)
NICHOLAS - 5/15/1935 (219)
ON TIME - 5/22/1951 (257)
PIGOT - 8/4/1778 (99)
RACHAEL AND MARY - 8/6/1778 (105)
RANGE BOAT NO. 28 - 1/14/1936 (221)
RANGE BOAT NO. 28 - 12/7/1944 (241)
SCORPION - 7/23/1902 (171)
SPRAY - 8/30/1937 (225)
ST. JOHN - 7/9/1764 (27)
STILETTO - 9/9/1896 (161)
STILETTO - 10/9/1897 (165)
STILETTO - 9/24/1900 (169)
STILETTO - 5/18/1908 (181)
STILETTO - 10/23/1912 (191)
SUSANNA - 8/6/1778 (105)
TUNA - 1/14/1936 (221)
UNIDENTIFIED - 1/17/1778 (71)
UNIDENTIFIED - 4/30/1778 (75)
UNIDENTIFIED - 11/23/1883 (145)
UNIDENTIFIED - 5/16/1931 (217)
UNIDENTIFIED - 9/29/1939 (231)
UNIDENTIFIED - 12/13/1943 (239)
UNIDENTIFIED - 5/24/1951 (259)
UNION - 8/6/1778 (105)
USRC VIGILANT - 9/23/1815 (133)
USS BOSTON - 8/3/1889 (151)
USS CERO (SP-1189) - 10/21/1918 (201)
USS LONE WOLF (YTB-179) - 12/10/1946 (255)
USS NEW HAMPSHIRE - 7/8/1912 (189)
USS TEXAS - 9/16/1896 (163)
YP-5 - 8/19/1938 (229)
YW-5 - 1/24/1940 (233)

Area 06 - Rhode Island Sound - This area encompasses the waters of Rhode Island Sound which is bordered on the east by Buzzard's Bay and the west by Block Island Sound and Block Island. There have been nine incidents recorded in this area.

ACQUILLON - 8/14/1778 (111)
BLACK POINT - 5/5/1945 (245)
BRENTON REEF (LV-39) - 8/24/1905 (177)
UNIDENTIFIED - 11/11/1937 (227)
USS ALABAMA - 7/30/1906 (179)
USS L-8 - 5/25/1926 (211)
USS S-51 - 9/25/1925 (209)
USS SCOUT (SP-907) - 9/18/1918 (199)
USS WILLIAMSON (DD-244) - 6/30/1923 (207)

Area 07 - Point Judith - This area includes the shoreline from the town of Narragansett southward to Point Judith and west for about a mile from the lighthouse. There have been seven incidents in this area.

COLUMBUS - 3/28/1778 (73)
HMS SYREN - 11/6/1777 (61)
HMS TRITON - 11/10/1777 (67)
LEWISTON - 9/5/1898 (167)
SISTERS - 11/6/1777 (63)
TWO MATES - 11/6/1777 (65)
UNIDENTIFIED - 1/26/1777 (43)

Area 08 - South Shore - This area includes the shoreline from Point Judith westward to the state line between Rhode Island and Connecticut. There have been eight incidents recorded in this area.

ADMIRAL PARKER - 9/22/1777 (59)
HOLKER - 5/11/1813 (131)
MINERVA - 10/21/1778 (113)
REVENGE - 1/9/1811 (123)
SALLY - 1/12/1778 (69)
TWO BROTHERS - 2/3/1777 (45)
WAVE - 8/19/1884 (147)
YP-15 - 7/15/1937 (223)

Area 09 - Block Island Sound - This area encompasses the waters of Block Island Sound which is bordered on the east by Rhode Island Sound, on the south by Block Island and the west by Long Island Sound. There are no incidents recorded in this area.

Area 10 - Block Island - This area includes the entire shoreline and the near-offshore waters of Block Island. There are three incidents recorded in this area.

UNIDENTIFIED - 9/1/1777 (57)
USN TORPEDO RETRIEVER - 1957 (263)
USS LEYDEN - 1/21/1903 (173)

Area 11 - Offshore - This area encompasses the offshore waters in the state of Rhode Island. There are five incidents recorded in this area.

U-853 - 5/5/1945 (247)
UNIDENTIFIED - 12/25/1745 (23)
UNIDENTIFIED - 12/25/1745 (23)
USS ALEXANDER J. LUKE - 10/22/1970 (271)
USS BASS (SS164) - 3/14/1945 (243)

BIBLIOGRAPHY

Books

Allen, Gardner – "A Naval History of the American Revolution" (1913)

Arnold, Samuel Greene – "History of the State of Rhode Island and Providence Plantations" (1860)

Baker, Virginia – "The History of Warren, Rhode Island In the War of the Revolution, 1776-1783" (1901)

Bartlett, John Russell – "A History of the Destruction of His Majesty's Schooner Gaspee" (1861)

Bartlett, John Russell - "Records of the State of Rhode Island and Providence Plantations, Vol. VIII" (1863)

Bayles, Richard M. - "History of Newport County, Rhode Island, 1638-1887" (1888)

Bermen, Bruce - "Encyclopedia of American Shipwrecks" (1972)

Bulkley, Jr., Robert J. - "At Close Quarters - PT Boats in the United States Navy" (1962)

Carroll, Charles - "Three Centuries of Democracy (1932)

Carter, Margaret - "Shipwrecks off the Shores of Westerly" (1973)

Denison, Frederic - "Westerly and Its Witnesses" (1878)

Dring, Tim - "Summary of Wooden Motor Lifeboat Types of the US Coast Guard" (2007)

Dudley, William S. - "The Naval War of 1812 - A Documentary History, Volume 1" (1985)

Field, Edward - "Esek Hopkins, Commander-In-Chief of the Continental Navy" (1898)

Field, Edward - "Revolutionary Defences in Rhode Island" (1896)

Jurgen, Rohwer – "Axis Submarine Successes" (1998)

Lippitt, Charles W. - "The Battle of Rhode Island" (1915)

Lonsdale (& Kaplan) - "A Guide to Sunken Ships in American Waters" (1964)

Luther, Brad - "The Vanishing Fleet" (1965)

Maclay, Edgar Stanton - "A History of American Privateers" (1899)

Mackenzie, Frederick – "Diary of Frederick Mackenzie giving a daily narrative of his military service as an officer of the regiment of Royal Welch fusiliers during the years 1775-1781 in Massachusetts, Rhode Island and New York" (1930)

Marx, Robert F. - "Shipwrecks in the Western Hemisphere" (1971)

Marx, Robert F. - "Shipwrecks in the Americas" (1987)

Miller, William David - "The Capture of His Majesty's Ship Syren" (1924)

Norton, Louis Arthur - "Captains Contentious" (2009)

Paullin, Charles Oscar - "The Navy of the American Revolution" (1906)

Peterson, Rev. Edward - "History of Rhode Island" (1853)

Phillips, Michael - "Sailing Ships of the Old Navy" (1995)

Ritchie, David - "Shipwrecks - An Encyclopedia of the World's Worst Disasters at Sea" (1999)

Schoenwolff, Thomas - "Lightships of the United States of America, Vol. I - Northeast" (2010)

Silverstone, Paul H. - "The Sailing Navy, 1775-1854" (2006)

Snow, Edward Rowe - "Storms and Shipwrecks of New England" (1943)

Stone, Edward Martin - "Our French Allies" (1884)

Taylor, Erich A.O.D. - "Campaign on Rhode Island"

Walden, Scott E. - "The Revenue Cutter Service: Nine Cutters and the War of 1812" (2008)

Winfield, Rif - "British Warships in the Age of Sail, 1714-1792 (2007)

Magazines & Periodicals

Harper's Weekly, September 13, 1884

Popular Science, January, 1900

Providence Institute of Savings - "Ships and Shipmasters of Old Providence" (1919)

Snyder, Capt. Frank - "A Gould Island Chronology"

The Historical Magazine and Notes and Queries Concerning the Antiquities, History and Biography of America (1860)

Reference Material

American Lloyd's Register of American and Foreign Shipping

American Yacht List

Connecticut Ship Database

Record of American and Foreign Shipping

Sailing Ships of the Old Navy

Sailing Ships of the Royal Navy

US Naval Chronology of WW II (1945)

Newspapers

The following is a list of newspapers which are used in the shipwreck data sheets. Individual WDS offer specific information on the date and page location of newspaper articles.

Boston Daily Advertiser
Boston Daily Globe
Boston Globe
Boston Independent Chronicle and Universal Advertiser
Columbian Phenix
Connecticut Courant
Connecticut Gazette
Hartford Courant
Massachusetts Spy
Naugatuck Daily News
New Haven Journal
New London Gazette
New York Columbian
New York Gazette and Weekly News
New York Gazette
New York Herald
New York Times
New York Tribune
Newport Daily News
Newport Journal & Weekly News
Newport Mercury & Weekly News
Newport Mercury
Niles Weekly Register
North Adams Evening Transcript
Providence Daily Journal
Providence Gazette & Country Journal
Providence Gazette
Rhode Island American & Daily Advertiser
Rhode Island American
Rhode Island Republican
Rivington's New York Gazetter

Government Sources

Annual Report of the Secretary of War

Automated Wreck and Obstruction Information System (AWOIS)

Dictionary of American Naval Fighting Ships (DANFS)

Index to the Executive Documents of the House of Representatives for the Second Session of the Forty-Fourth Congress

Merchant Vessels of the United States

Naval Documents of the American Revolution (11 volumes)

Naval History and Heritage Command

NavShips 250-242

Newport Custom House records

NOAA History – Coast and Geodetic Survey Ships

Providence Custom House records

Report of the Secretary of the Navy US Coast Guard Archives

US Life Saving Service

US Naval Historical Center

US Naval Institute Proceedings

Organizations

Australian National Maritime Museum

Beavertail Lighthouse Museum Association

Escort Historical Museum

Historic Naval Ships Association

Jamestown Historical Society

Massachusetts Historical Society

Newport Historical Society Destroyer

Providence Public Library

Redwood Library

WWII PT Boats Museum and Archives

Internet Articles & Sites

"A History of Goat Island"

"Alphabetical List of All US Merchant Ships Sunk or Damaged in WW2"

"American Privateer Ship Oliver Cromwell"

"American War of Independence at Sea"

"Battle of the Atlantic"

"British Soldiers, American Revolution"

"Buckley Class Destroyer Escorts in World War II"

"Conway's All the World's Fighting Ships"

"First American Revolution Navy Ships"

"French Frigate Hermione (1779)"

"Located Sunken Submarines"

"Our Young Navy"

"Rhode Island Lighthouse History"

"SP #s and ID #s – World War I Era Patrol Vessels and other Acquired Ships and Crafts"

"The Battle of Point Judith"

"Through the Looking Glass", The G-Boats

"US Merchant Ship Losses During the Second World War"
"US Naval Ships Sunk or Damaged by Various Causes During World War I"
"US Navy Ships Sunk or Seriously Damaged by Fire or Explosion"
"Who Was Commodore Whipple?"
www.awiatsea.com
www.history.navy.mil
www.navalships.org
www.navsource.org
www.navytugs.com
www.ptboats.org
www.Shipbuildinghistory.com
www.subnet.com
www.techdiving.us
www.threedecks.org
www.uboat.net
www.uscg.mil
www.USMM.org
www.usnavyships.com

24950324R00157

Made in the USA
San Bernardino, CA
12 October 2015